Fostering Cognitive Development of Students

A New Approach to Counseling and Program Planning

John C. Barrow

Fostering Cognitive Development of Students

Jossey-Bass Publishers

San Francisco • London • 1986

FOSTERING COGNITIVE DEVELOPMENT OF STUDENTS
A New Approach to Counseling and Program Planning
by John C. Barrow

Copyright © 1986 by: Jossey-Bass Inc., Publishers
433 California Street
San Francisco, California 94104
&
Jossey-Bass Limited
28 Banner Street
London EC1Y 8QE

Library of Congress Cataloging-in-Publication Data

Barrow, John C. (date)
    Fostering cognitive development of students.

    (The Jossey-Bass higher education series) (The
Jossey-Bass social and behavioral science series)
    Bibliography: p. 353
    Includes index.
    1. Personnel service in higher education. 2. College
students—Counseling of. 3. College student development
programs. 4. Cognitive styles. I. Title. II. Series.
III. Series: Jossey-Bass social and behavioral science
series.
LB2343.B326   1986   378'.194   85-46005
ISBN 0-87589-676-6

Manufactured in the United States of America

The paper in this book meets the guidelines for
permanence and durability of the Committee on
Production Guidelines for Book Longevity of the
Council on Library Resources.

JACKET DESIGN BY WILLI BAUM

FIRST EDITION

Code 8621

A joint publication in
The Jossey-Bass
Higher Education Series
and
The Jossey-Bass
Social and Behavioral Science Series

Consulting Editors
Student Services and Counseling Psychology

Ursula Delworth
University of Iowa

Gary R. Hanson
University of Texas at Austin

Preface

Cognitive theories—theories that emphasize the role of mental processing of information in human experience, including affective and behavioral responses—have great potential for helping student development professionals design effective programs. They can be useful whether the program goals are remedial (for example, assisting a student with acute depression), preventive (helping academically at risk students learn skills for managing test anxiety), or developmental (fostering independent decision making) and whether the intervention mode is individual counseling, group counseling, or outreach educational workshops. There is, however, a need to integrate some of these diverse perspectives and consolidate our understanding of how the cognitive dimension can be productively used. My main goal in writing this book is to explore ways of achieving that integration and consolidation.

Like many in the student development field, my initial thought and work was influenced by the ideas of Carl Rogers, Charles Truax, and Robert Carkhuff—most notably, the belief that an empathic, supportive relationship is "facilitative," whether in formal individual counseling, group counseling, or naturally occurring relationships. As I began working in university counseling settings, my interests gravitated toward cognitive-behavioral ideas, because the structure that these ideas provided seemed to enable students to cope better with maladaptive emotions, such as anxiety and depression. As my experiences in the field continued, I began to incorporate ideas from a wider pool of concepts regarding the influence of cognitions on behavioral and affective responses—concepts such as those offered by George Kelly, social psychologists, and cognitive development researchers. In my attempt to integrate these concepts, I developed the Cognitive Intervention Planning Model that is the main subject of this book. As time has passed, I have used this model as my primary source of guidance in a range of interventions: conducting individual counseling with many kinds of students with a variety of difficulties, designing and leading structured and theme-exploration groups, presenting workshops in the residence halls, and designing media psychoeducational programs. This book represents my best effort to communicate my current thoughts, which I expect will evolve further as continued analysis and new experiences provide new insights. In short, the book is a thinking person's guide to thinking persons.

The conception of the role of cognitive processes that I developed here is broader than the one normally associated with the terms "cognitive-behavioral approach" and "cognitive modification." An effective counselor can productively attend to cognitive variables without applying specific cognitive modification techniques. Mental life is something to be explored, understood, and admired, not always something to be "modified." Desired cognitive growth and change can come about in many ways—sometimes unexpectedly and not only via a structured kind of training. Thus, while this book does describe certain structured cognitive-behavioral approaches and while I am deeply indebted to the innovative theorists who developed these approaches, I have attempted to do more than describe cognitive modification techniques for use in student development. My intent has been to integrate some of these ideas with other cognitive perspectives, including concepts from cognitive development theory.

Is there a need for such a book? Unfortunately, I cannot claim to take an unbiased position on this question. Even so, I think there is ample reason to believe that a book integrating various cognitive ideas and outlining a flexible and usable cognitive model would be very valuable in student development work. Times of financial crisis have made it all the more important for sound theory and research to guide the efforts of student development professionals. Research support exists for a number of facets of cognitive theory and for the efficacy of applying cognitive techniques with a number of difficulties. Further, interventions based on cognitive variables are well suited to the university student population. As noted, these interventions can be used in programs that address a variety of goals—remedial, developmental, and preventive. They are also more consistent with a humanistic-educational model of human functioning than with a medical-illness model and are thus compatible with the overall philosophy of the student development profession. Cognitive concepts are also consistent with higher education goals of intellectual development and allow students to capitalize on their intellectual strengths. (The advantages of these approaches for student development interventions are spelled out in more detail in the final section of Chapter One.)

This book is written with an array of professionals in mind: those engaged in student development services in universities and community colleges; counselors in counseling and mental health centers, whether they specialize in individual counseling or conduct a range of interventions, including group counseling and psychoeducational programs; professionals in other student affairs offices who advise and counsel students and/or conduct programming, including those in residential life, student life, student activities, career planning and placement, and academic advising offices; students in graduate programs in counseling psychology, counselor education, and student personnel; and mental health and counseling professionals who work with clients in the adolescent and early adulthood stages in nonuniversity settings, such as high schools and community mental health centers.

Chapter One provides an overview of some of the ideas

about cognitions that have influenced my approach. Basic theories are reviewed, followed by discussions of implications for an understanding of human experience and cognitive change. Included are George Kelly's role construct theory, social psychological theories, Albert Ellis's rational-emotive theory, cognitive-behavioral theory, cognitive development theory, and representational theory.

In Chapter Two an effort is made to integrate some of the important ideas reviewed in Chapter One into a flexible model that can guide counselors in assessing a variety of problems and planning a number of interventions. The eight-phase Cognitive Intervention Planning Model should not be treated as a lock-step method but should be used flexibly, in that users may frequently recycle to previous phases. The phases, in order, are (1) identifying cognitive events, (2) identifying cognitive systems, (3) considering developmental levels of cognitive functioning, (4) consolidating data and constructing formulations (of the problem, the client, and the interaction process), (5) setting goals, and then (6) designing, (7) implementing, and (8) evaluating the intervention. The assessment phases of the model (Phases 1-3) are then described, followed by a discussion of assessment goals and methods.

Chapter Three is devoted to the pivotal steps of the model—Phases 4 and 5. Ways of consolidating information obtained in Phases 1-3 and developing formulations of problems, clients, and process are presented. Then Phase 5, determining outcome and process goals for the intervention, is discussed. Three general sets of goals are described for individual counseling: rapport building and developmental counseling, cognitive coping skills training, and experiential cognitive dissonance counseling.

Chapters Four through Eight focus on the implementation and evaluation phases of the model (Phases 6 through 8) with several kinds of interventions. In Chapter Four the use of the model is discussed in rapport building and developmental counseling, where the counselor is attempting to establish a supportive climate for the client to explore feelings and thoughts. The focus in Chapter Five is on cognitive coping skills training, where the counselor adopts a more structured approach with a clearly specified problem, such as test anxiety. In Chapter Six the use of the model in experiential cognitive dissonance counseling—where the counselor uses methods to counteract resistance and indirectly promote cognitive change—is discussed. Case descriptions and excerpts from counseling sessions with three student clients—Marie, with confusion and with difficulties concerning autonomy development; Susan, with test anxiety; and Harvey, whose resistance to direct interventions necessitated an indirect, experiential approach—illustrate the methods discussed in Chapters Four, Five, and Six.

Chapter Seven outlines the application of Phases 6 through 8 of the model in conducting group counseling. In Chapter Eight applications to structured groups and psychoeducational workshops are discussed, with a number of descriptions of groups and workshops (in such areas as stress management, assertiveness training, and career planning) presented in Part Three. The last chapter briefly discusses potential applications of the model to areas not developed in the book—areas such as consultation and supervision—and offers some "concluding cognitions."

Throughout the book case examples are provided to illustrate important ideas. While these descriptions are formed from "real" counseling experiences, students' identities are disguised and no individual exists exactly as portrayed. Most examples are composites of elements from several actual cases. The illustrations of counseling interactions are approximate reconstructions of counseling dialogue—again, with the details altered to protect clients' identities.

It is indeed gratifying to have concluded the long process of writing this book—long for me, perhaps longer for family and friends. I would like to express my appreciation to my wife, daughter, and son for tolerating my time spent on the project, occasional irritability, and decision to deplete our family funds by purchasing a computer. I also thank the computer, without whose help this project might never have been completed, and Ursula Delworth, consulting editor for Jossey-Bass, without whose help this book might have been completed but probably not in a publishable form. Thanks are also due colleagues of mine at Dalhousie, Illinois State, and Duke universities—both for being supportive and for being appropriately argumentative at times. Finally, I would like to thank the psychology interns I have been fortunate enough to supervise over the last several years. One of my most stimulating and enlightening experiences has been the opportunity to observe the struggles of young professionals as they attempt to understand the complexities of human interactions. I hope that the book does justice to the richness of the contributions these individuals have made.

Durham, North Carolina   John C. Barrow
March 1986

Contents

The Author

John C. Barrow is currently a counseling psychologist and assistant director of career development and outreach services with Counseling and Psychological Services at Duke University. He received his B.A. degree (1965) in psychology from Davidson College, Davidson, North Carolina. He then began graduate training at Teachers College, Columbia University, where he received both an M.Ed. degree in vocational and rehabilitation counseling and an Ed.D. degree in counseling psychology (1971).

Barrow has worked extensively in the university counseling field, having held positions in university counseling centers at four universities—Pennsylvania State (internship), Illinois State, Illinois Weslyan, and Dalhousie in Halifax, Nova Scotia—prior to joining the staff at Duke. He was made a diplomate in counseling psychology by the American Board of Professional Psychology in 1983 and currently serves on the editorial board of the *Journal of College Student Personnel*. Throughout his career, he has maintained a strong interest in cognitive counseling methods and has explored ways of using cognitive approaches in individual counseling and psychotherapy, group counseling, and outreach educational programs. He is the author of articles on cognitive interventions, counseling process variables, stress, shyness, evaluative anxiety, perfectionism, needs assessment, program evaluation, and paraprofessional training. These have appeared in journals such as the *Journal of College Student Personnel, Psychotherapy: Theory, Research and Practice,* the *Personnel and Guidance Journal* (now the *Journal of Counseling and Development*), the *Journal of American College Health,* and the *Journal of Consulting and Clinical Psychology.*

Fostering Cognitive Development of Students

A New Approach to Counseling and Program Planning

Part One

A Flexible Model
for Fostering
Cognitive Development

ONE

Understanding Cognitive Development and Change in Young Adults

"I think; therefore, I am." This of course is the famous statement offered by René Descartes as his basic assumption in founding his theory of knowledge. Many people who are unfamiliar with formal philosophical teachings have this particular statement etched in their memories. Why? Perhaps because it concisely captures something each of us experiences as a basic truth. We know that our waking moments—and many of our sleeping ones—are filled with a rich mental life. We think; we think a lot—more than anyone outside us can ever know. And we privately think about and imagine many things that we will not share with anyone else.

Our nature as human beings is to think, analyze, plan, decide, intuit, interpret, expect, imagine, and remember, among many other *cognitive* processes. Our minds are alive with these powerful mental activities that place us on the highest evolutionary plane and contribute to our greatest, most meaningful, and most human joys. But there is another side to this valued coin. We can also misinterpret, distort, make irrational demands of ourselves and others, selectively perceive only *negative* possibilities, make erroneous assumptions, and construct rigid expectations for the future. These mental processes too are powerful and contribute greatly to some of our most human failings, such

3

as mood disorders, neuroticism, low self-esteem, and conflicted relationships. Just as the Jedi warrior from *Star Wars* must learn to balance the light and dark sides of the force, we in our development must learn to balance the negative side of cognitive life with the realistic yet encouraging side that helps us solve problems and increase effectiveness.

Cognitive processes are ever present and are interwoven with our feelings, behavior, physiology, and biochemistry. Yet only during the last ten to fifteen years has an emphasis on these basically conscious processes and on cognitive events (such as beliefs, images, expectations, attributions, labels, and worries) significantly influenced the counseling profession. The three most influential traditions have emphasized other realms of experience. In the Freudian school, conscious thoughts or images were considered of most value as symbolic reflections of unconscious motivations. What a person can extract from present conscious awareness was viewed as much less important than the vast pool of strivings thought to lie beneath awareness. Conscious thought was often treated as a product of the client's defensive system.

The Rogerian or client-centered tradition (Rogers, 1951) was founded on a phenomenological framework capable of embracing cognitive processes. Indeed, the word "self-concept" implies a system of thought about oneself. However, the client-centered movement gravitated to the position that clients are most often deficient in their awareness and acceptance of *affective* processes. "Cognitive" came to be associated with the *content* of the client's message, and counselors were taught to give particular attention to feelings. Proponents of the existential-humanistic and Gestalt movements joined Rogerians in emphasizing affective over cognitive expression.

The behavioral tradition emphasized observable behavior and held that private cognitive events are too subjective to be used in the science of behavior (Skinner, 1953). Thoughts were viewed as by-products of behavioral changes rather than as mediating events capable of producing those changes (Wolpe and Lazarus, 1966).

The two approaches that emphasized cognition did not

influence the counseling profession as much as the Freudian, Rogerian, and behavioral traditions. Kelly's (1955) role construct theory presented an interesting cognitive point of view; however, many counselors looked on his significance as primarily historical. Ellis's (1962) rational-emotive approach was regarded by many as an unacceptable deviation from the warm, respectful attention to affect favored by Rogerians.

But a shift in thinking has occurred. In his survey of trends in counseling and psychotherapy, Smith (1982) concludes that the cognitive-behavioral tradition is "one of the strongest, if not the strongest," theoretical emphases among counseling and clinical psychologists and that its strength has increased from the level represented in similar surveys in previous years. Counselors operating from a Freudian base, partly in response to the need for short-term interventions, have recognized the limitations inherent in a primarily historical, symbolic emphasis and have looked increasingly to the ideas of ego psychologists such as Erikson (1968) and Horney (1939), who place greater emphasis than strict Freudians on conscious activities. Client-centered and existential-humanistic counselors, having learned that thinking and feeling do not represent a dichotomy but are highly interactive aspects of experience, have become more accepting of the notion that clients can be helped to develop new behavioral *and* cognitive skills. Likewise, the behavioral tradition has become more diversified, with many theorists formerly known as "behavior therapists" developing more flexible and comprehensive systems. Lazarus's (1976) multimodal therapy is a good example of this trend. Counselors operating from a social learning orientation to personality have been led by Bandura (1977b) and others toward an appreciation of the significant role played by carefully defined internal processes. A cognitive-behavioral tradition has emerged, in which the alteration of problematic cognitive patterns is viewed as a powerful method of effecting behavioral *and* affective changes. Likewise, the study of cognition has been accepted into the empirical tradition of clinical and counseling psychology.

Counselors working in the student development field have begun to draw heavily from this emerging tradition. During the past several years, an increasingly large number of articles dealing with cognitive approaches have appeared in journals important to our field. Commonly faced student problems, such as career decision making (Keller, Biggs, and Gyspers, 1982; Knefelkamp and Slepitza, 1976; Lewis and Gilhousen, 1981), test anxiety (Denny and Rupert, 1977; Holroyd, 1976; Meichenbaum, 1972), assertiveness (Lange and Jakubowski, 1976), and social development (Barrow and Hayashi, 1980; Barrow and Hetherington, 1981; Glass, Gottman, and Shmurak, 1976) have been addressed with cognitive methods. Students' stages of cognitive development have been described, analyzed, and measured (Perry, 1970) and related to important areas of student need, such as career development (Knefelkamp and Slepitza, 1976). Indeed, many of us have found that university students are particularly well suited to intervention in the cognitive domain. They are generally bright and capable of observing, describing, and analyzing their cognitive processes. The developmental tasks faced by students involve self-clarification, exploration, and emerging independence (Chickering, 1969). In this stage their cognitive systems are consequently permeable and amenable to change.

As the foregoing discussion suggests, a great many counselors, psychotherapists, researchers, and theorists have developed ideas that contribute to our understanding of cognitive processes. They have come from diverse fields, including social psychology, educational psychology, mental health, counseling, and organizational/industrial psychology, and have consequently provided different perspectives on cognition. It is impossible to cover all these formulations in this book. The theories discussed here are those that have been most influential in shaping the ideas represented in the model I have developed.

Kelly's Role Construct Theory

George Kelly's theory is one of the approaches that have emerged from the counseling and mental health fields. Consequently, it contains both a system for understanding human motivation and choices and one for intervening in therapy.

Kelly's ideas, which represent an interesting departure from most of the popular schools of the day, were no doubt influenced by the pragmatism and stern values characteristic of his rural Kansas background and his devoutly religious parents. Except for a year at Edinburgh, he studied and did his formative work in the Midwest. At Fort Hays Kansas State College, where he initiated a program of traveling psychological clinics, he found that the intricate and indirect explanations of psychoanalysis were out of step with the direct, practical mentality of rural midwesterners. Consequently, he was stimulated to explore conceptualizations better suited to his clientele. His thinking was also greatly influenced by his teaching and counseling experiences with young people, particularly of college age. In 1955, during his tenure as director of clinical training at Ohio State University, he completed *The Psychology of Personal Constructs,* his primary written contribution.

   Review of the Theory. Kelly's theory is phenomenological, in the sense that he believes choices of behavior depend on how one perceives or construes the world. He coined the expression "every man a scientist" to describe his view that people's theories about the nature of the world are *constructed* from their experiences. They use these theories or models in *construing* events and in deciding how to behave, and they continually subject these theories to the test of how well they predict. An interesting feature of Kelly's theory is his assertion of "constructive alternativism"—the position that alternative mental constructions of any event are possible and that an individual has an element of choice in adopting a particular construction.

   The elements of a person's model are called "constructs," which Kelly likens to "templates" that a person creates and then uses to construe events and make predictions. They can also be likened to "tools" for processing information and to "containers" for storing data (Liebert and Spiegler, 1978). The term "personal constructs" refers to Kelly's belief that each individual has a unique set of constructs, which enable the individual to determine whether events are similar or dissimilar on a particular characteristic. Thus, Kelly envisions constructs as bipolar switches. When the construct is activated, either one or the other pole is operative. For instance, an individual might have a construct "smart versus dumb." When an event is in the "range of convenience" of a construct and the construct is activated, the event is labeled either "smart" or "dumb." No intervening shades of gray are encompassed by a single construct; however, what we would normally think of as continua can occur when blends of a number of constructs are involved. People evolve *construct systems,* composed of a number of constructs, in order to increase the convenience with which predictions can be made. Constructs are organized hierarchically, so that some are subsets of others, and there is a preset order to the sequence in which they will be applied. For example, the smart-dumb construct might have a number of constructs subordinate to it, such as "articulate" versus "inarticulate" and "good-at-math" versus "bad-at-math."

Individuals differ not only in the specific constructs they might have but in the number of constructs, the organization of constructs, and the permeability of specific constructs. A greater number of constructs allows a person more complexity with which to make predictions. Permeable constructs allow application to new events; impermeable constructs are locked into a range of events to which they can be applied and are unable to assimilate new experiences.

Construct systems are not static but are continually evolving as a person construes events, makes predictions, and tests the predictions in the laboratory of future behavior. Since the prime motivation is to predict future events accurately, individual constructs or groups of constructs that aid in accurate prediction are retained, whereas those that lead to errors in prediction are reorganized and/or new constructs are added. In Kelly's view, most dissonant psychological processes, such as anxiety, arise when a person's construct system is threatened with an inability to make good predictions.

Kelly envisions therapy as a process of helping individuals evolve construct systems that provide more reliable and accurate prediction. In order to conduct therapy, the counselor or therapist must attempt to construe the client's constructs or to determine how the client's world is constructed. The therapist must exercise creativity in challenging maladaptive constructs by creating situations in which old responses are not appropriate. The client can be led to hypothesize or explicitly make predictions and to interpret or explicitly gauge how predictions have fared. Using an interesting technique called "biographical hypotheses," the therapist asks clients to elaborate the biographical conditions under which they would behave differently. They can then be asked to assume the presence of these conditions and experiment with different modes of behavior (and thus with different constructs). In this context Kelly developed an approach called "fixed-role therapy," in which the therapist might prepare a "role sketch" for a client—a prescription containing a new set of constructs that the therapist thinks would enhance the client's system. The client would then be asked to play this role for a period of time.

Contributions to Our Understanding of Human Experience. Kelly's view is that humans are *active* in creating their models of the world and that their psychological processes are guided by the way in which they *construe* events. The constructs are never fully accurate representations of reality, so that successively more complex systems are always being formed. People always have choices as they go about construing their experiences, and each individual has a construct system that is unique. Mental life is constantly changing, since it is in continuous interaction with experiences of the environment; yet it is also actively organized by the individual. Perhaps the most interesting idea of all is that humans are *predicting* animals. One of our most compelling characteristics is to anticipate events and make predictions regarding outcomes.

Contributions to Our Understanding of Cognitive Change. In Kelly's theory, change is assumed to be an ongoing aspect, in that construct systems are continually evolving. One kind of change to a construct system occurs when a new event is construable by one or more constructs and necessary predictions can be made. This could be considered to be first-order change, although Kelly does not use this term. The system is changed in that new information is absorbed, although the structure of the constructs remains as it was. Structural change may occur when events are not construable or when the feedback from a prediction suggests that the templates have been inadequate. The structure of the constructs must be changed to account for the new information. In light of his edict of constructive alternativism, individuals can consciously examine and evaluate their construct systems. More than any other theory, Kelly's emphasizes that cognitive change occurs as the person's predictions interact with actual experiences. The role of the change agent is to enable the client to have experiences that are not construable with self-defeating aspects of their construct systems. Rather than restricting these experiences to ones the counselor can provide in the consulting room, Kelly emphasizes ongoing experimentation with new roles, as evidenced in fixed-role therapy. Kelly also seems to suggest implicitly that cognitive change can come about more quickly or fully if one assumes different behavioral strategies—a position very like the one advocated by behavior therapists (Wolpe and Lazarus, 1966).

Social Psychology: Concepts of Cognitive Dissonance and Attribution

Some concepts from the field of social psychology have been influential in the understanding of cognitive processes. Since these ideas have emerged from research, they are neither comprehensive theories of personality nor concepts developed to guide counseling and psychotherapy. Nevertheless, they provide some useful insights for counselors and student development professionals interested in changing cognitive processes.

Cognitive Dissonance. The concepts of cognitive dissonance and cognitive consistency were developed by Festinger (1957), although others have contributed to researching the construct. Festinger's central thesis is that humans are driven to maintain cognitive consistency—consistency between their beliefs and their perceptions. When two beliefs conflict or an old belief is inconsistent with incoming data, a state of cognitive dissonance is produced. This state is uncomfortable, and the person holding it is motivated to reduce the dissonance by revising one of the conflicting beliefs or by distorting or negating the new data that conflict with an old belief. Aronson (1972), for example, found that students who were paid little for boring work were more likely to profess to enjoying the work than were those who received more pay. The implication is that the poorly paid students altered their concept of the work (from boring to enjoyable) so that their experience of doing this work would be consistent with their views of what they should allow themselves to do.

Cognitive dissonance theory makes some useful contributions to our understanding of human experience. Like Kelly's theory, it suggests that we are inclined to organize our cognitions. In order to be able to make quick decisions, we seek consistency and experience discomfort when our beliefs are inconsistent with one another. Like Kelly's person, we are active in the models we build of our experiences and can rearrange the constructions of events so that they are more consistent with long-standing beliefs.

The theory does not offer extensive thoughts on how change agents can help others achieve productive cognitive change; however, the concept can be helpful to counselors in a couple of ways. First of all, counselors must be aware of clients' distorting potential—their possible distortion of the counselor's suggestions and behavior or their distortion of events in order to maintain a belief that may warrant reevaluation. Second, counselors may at times be able to make the need for cognitive consistency work for the client's benefit by creating cognitive dissonance. The very act of listening empathically to disclosures that clients find embarrassing may create dissonance, which they may resolve by reconstruing the shameful secret as "not so bad" or "human." Kelly's method of prescribing a fixed role for clients could well engender cognitive dissonance.

Attribution Theory. This perspective comes from a body of social psychological research and, like cognitive dissonance, is not really a comprehensive theory. (A discussion by Liebert and Spiegler (1978) is helpful in understanding attribution and was used extensively in the organization of this review.) Like Kelly and Festinger, those studying attributions believe that humans are inclined to organize their cognitive experiences and that they actively contribute to their organizations. Whereas Kelly emphasizes the prediction of future behavior, attribution theorists view the understanding of past experiences as a major goal of human cognitive functioning. We are "why-asking" animals and are inherently motivated to seek explanations for events, particularly the actions of others and our own feelings. Like George Kelly, a psychologist named Harold Kelley believes that we use an unsophisticated version of the scientific method in making these inferences (Kelley, 1973).

Much of attribution research has focused on understanding the conditions that lead to certain kinds of attributions, such as whether a person's acts are seen as arising from dispositions (personality traits) or from external circumstances or accidental events. People are more likely to make dispositional attributions when actors are judged to have knowledge of the effects of their behavior and the ability to perform the act and when the behavior is "out of role" or deviates from expected practices (Jones and Davis, 1965). Thus, a boy is more likely to be termed "violent" if he persists in aggressive acts in spite of knowing that he is hurting another, particularly if his behavior differs widely from the norm at his school. Also, Kelley (1973) notes that dispositional characteristics are more likely to be inferred when the actor has endured notable costs or sacrifices in performing the behavior. The "violent" characterization is particularly likely if the boy's aggressiveness persists despite almost certain punishment.

Some of the attribution research likely to be of most interest to counselors is on self-attribution. Bem (1972) suggests that people seek and interpret information about themselves in much the same ways they do about others. For instance, their interpretation of their own internal physiological cues may depend on the context of the situation. The implication is that our internal sensations, including general arousal, provide ambiguous information and require reliance on external cues to be interpreted. For instance, Valins (1966) gave males false heart rate feedback while they were looking at erotic pictures. Subjects were more likely to rate as attractive the pictures shown with high levels of the false feedback.

Attribution researchers have also been interested in attribution errors, such as the overattribution to dispositions rather than situational causes in accounting for behavior (McArthur, 1972). Even in events such as accidents, natural disasters, and rape, there is a tendency to blame the victim's personality traits rather than external events (Smith, Keating, Hester, and Mitchell, 1976). Lerner (1965) ascribes this error to people's need to view themselves as living in a just world, in which they can control their destinies by regulating their behavior. According to Jones and Nisbett (1972), however, people tend to overattribute external influences, rather than dispositions, when interpreting their own behavior. Evidently, we regard ourselves as too complex and adaptable for our actions to be explained by dispositions. Another common attribution error is made when our preconceptions result in selective attention and shape our perceptions of events. Chapman and Chapman (1967) found, for instance, that both naive undergraduates and experienced clinicians have preconceptions about how certain kinds of people will respond to projective tests; they then perceive the expected relationships, even though these are not present in the actual test protocols.

Attribution theory presents us with some enlightening insights on the nature of human experience. Kelly emphasizes our predicting nature; attributionists emphasize our need to seek explanations and ask "why." We make attributions about others' actions, often overattributing these actions to dispositions rather than situational circumstances. We also make attributions about our own reactions, which are influenced by our understanding of the context of our responses. In this way, we can be fooled regarding the explanation of internal responses. We also tend to allow our preconceptions to flavor the way we perceive events.

Some have suggested specific ways in which attribution theory can be used in effecting cognitive changes. Certainly, much of the work of any pragmatic counselor can be viewed as helping clients examine and revise misattributions concerning other people and themselves. Storms (1973) found that providing subjects with videotape feedback can help them form more accurate attributions of their actions and understand how these actions can be construed by others. Another approach has been to induce subjects to make misattributions that lead to improved coping or self-image. Valins and Ray (1967) gave subjects false heart rate feedback and found that those who were "tricked" into believing that their heart rates had not changed when these subjects were exposed to snakes were more likely to handle snakes than were control subjects. While some have advocated more extensive application of this method, many counselors, including myself, have ethical objections to purposely misinforming clients.

It is also important for counselors to remember the lesson from attribution research that we err on the side of inferring dispositional causes for others' behavior. Therefore, counselors must make sure that they are sensitive to important situational factors, a position favored by social learning theorists (Mischel, 1968).

Ellis's Rational-Emotive Therapy Approach

Like most clinical psychologists trained when Albert Ellis was in school, he began as a psychoanalytically oriented psychotherapist. Also like others, he began to deviate from this method when he found that achievement of psychoanalytic insight did not always result in solution of the client's problems (Corsini, 1977). Partly because of the simple system he developed, which deviated substantially from psychoanalysis, and partly because of his strong, expressive personality, Ellis was initially viewed as a renegade, and his ideas were given little credence, particularly within the mainstream of counseling. Yet, his ideas have stood the test of time and examination and are now respectably subsumed within the empirically oriented cognitive-behavioral tradition.

Nonetheless, many within the counseling profession still have a negative bias toward Ellis. I suspect that one of the primary reasons is his highly confrontational therapeutic style, as presented in early tapes and films. Meichenbaum (1977) has jokingly speculated that rational-emotive therapy (RET) as conducted by Ellis would be successful only in New York, where

Ellis lives and works. As Meichenbaum notes, it is important to distinguish between the RET system and Ellis's personal style. While RET requires activity, directness, and some confrontation, these can be offered with empathy and warmth and need not be dispensed with the colorful language patterns for which Ellis is noted.

Review of the Theory. Ellis believes that affect, behavior, and cognition interact with one another in intricate ways; however, he accords cognition a particularly influential position in these interactions and considers it a more convenient point of intervention than the other processes. Like Kelly and the attribution theorists, he believes that dysfunctional psychological processes are caused not by external events themselves but by the individual's interpretation of these events. For instance, a student facing an examination might have good reason to believe that it will be difficult and therefore may experience a moderate degree of anxiety, which would not be dysfunctional. A debilitating degree of anxiety can arise only from an irrational belief about the exam—for instance, that one's self-worth depends on one's exam performance. The counselor's role is to help clients analyze their cognitive processes, identify irrational beliefs, learn to dispute these beliefs, and eventually substitute more rational positions.

Ellis (1977b) has stated that humans have innate dispositions toward certain kinds of irrational thinking and that other forms are acquired. Whether learned or innate, irrational patterns can be consciously identified and countered, and individuals can learn more rational positions. In order to provide therapist and client with a framework for addressing cognitions, he developed his simple yet effective A-B-C formulation (Ellis, 1962, 1977a; Ellis and Harper, 1975). An "activating event" at Point A is followed by an emotional or behavioral consequence at Point C. The degree to which this consequent reaction is dysfunctional depends on the interpretation of the event made at Point B. An irrational belief (iB) leads to an unproductive response, whereas a rational belief (rB) leads to desirable emotions and actions.

Ellis has produced several formulations of the irrational

beliefs that most often lie at the core of human psychological problems and has sensitized clients to the roles played by certain semantic forms, such as "should," "must," and "ought." He suggests that most important irrational beliefs can be subsumed under one of three "musturbatory ideologies": (1) that one must perform well and win the approval of others; (2) that one must be treated considerately and fairly at all times; (3) that one must have one's needs met without undue difficulty (Ellis, 1977a).

In helping clients identify and alter irrational beliefs, Ellis (1977a) has extended the A-B-C framework to include Point D, at which the client *disputes* irrational thoughts, and Point E, which represents the eventual cognitive, behavioral, and emotional *effects* of the revised belief system.

Contributions to Our Understanding of Human Experience. Like the other theoretical systems previously discussed, Ellis's emphasizes our active role in mentally interpreting events in our lives and shaping our psychological reactions. Whereas Kelly provides ideas on the structures of cognitions and the attributionists concentrate on the processes, Ellis has contributed to an understanding of the content of cognitions likely to be involved in dysfunctional emotions and behavior and has demonstrated that individuals can consciously identify and rethink unproductive beliefs.

Contributions to Our Understanding of Cognitive Change. According to Ellis, the therapist's role, in leading clients to examine and alter irrational beliefs, is to be active, confrontative, and persuasive. Since, in Ellis's view, clients can be swayed by logic, the therapist sometimes plays the role of debater—actively disputing the validity of irrational beliefs. Like behaviorists, Ellis recognizes the strength of habit—both in behavior and in cognition—and encourages repeated efforts to monitor cognitions and dispute irrational beliefs. Particularly in recent years, Ellis (1977a) has emphasized multimodal change methods, giving particular attention to the value of behavior change interacting with new cognitions. In this position he seems to suggest that we can think ourselves into new emotional and behavioral patterns but that the whole change process is facilitated when cognitive change is augmented with targeted behavioral changes.

The Cognitive-Behavioral Approach

The body of technique, research, and theory called "cognitive-behavioral" has evolved as three trends have occurred. First, behavior therapy has moved in the direction of emphasizing self-control and incorporation of mediating processes, such as expectancies and coping strategies, into techniques for effecting change. Second, behavioral researchers and therapists have begun to draw on the contributions of cognitive theories, including the theories of Ellis and Aaron Beck. As cognitive techniques have been found useful in areas such as anxiety management, they have gained more acceptance in the empirically oriented behavioral school. Third, cognitive psychology has come to receive greater attention among empirically oriented researchers, such as those studying attribution theory. As a result, therapists such as Arnold Lazarus and Marvin Goldfried, who formerly considered themselves behavior therapists, have moved in the direction of a therapy that is still grounded in scientific method but is oriented to self-control and incorporation of methods such as "cognitive modification" and "cognitive restructuring." In fact, a split has occurred among those who are committed to a narrow conception of behavior therapy and those who accept mediational processes and multimodal methods. This split is best represented by the ongoing debate between former coauthors Wolpe (1984) and Lazarus (1983).

Review of the Theory. The cognitive-behavioral movement actually consists of the ideas and research findings of a number of individuals and can probably best be considered a body of related ideas and findings on therapy rather than a cohesive theory. Many of the cognitive-behavioral premises are similar to those proposed by Ellis, and many therapists make use of Ellis's A-B-C framework. One difference may be that cognitive behaviorists consider the cognitive and behavioral domains to be equally important as sources of disturbance and points of intervention, while Ellis more strongly extols the virtues of cognitions. The cognitive behaviorists have probably put slightly more emphasis on scientific method and have been quite creative in empirically studying various intervention techniques. Another difference is that the cognitive behaviorists have emphasized the importance of cognitive coping methods in addition to irrational beliefs. Meichenbaum (1976) has asserted that normal and clinical populations differ more in the effectiveness with which they can apply cognitive coping mechanisms in response to irrational thoughts than in the actual incidence of irrational beliefs. Perhaps the greatest contribution of the cognitive behaviorists is in development of methods by which cognitions can be changed. While Ellis initially relied greatly on didactic presentation and persuasion, the cognitive behaviorists have incorporated behavioral and social learning principles. They emphasize the teaching of cognitive skills in a sequential, stepwise manner, with reliance on effective schedules and methods of reinforcement. More important, they utilize observational learning and have developed effective modeling techniques for teaching cognitive processes.

One individual who has been influential in the cognitive-behavioral movement is Aaron Beck. His basic theory is similar to Ellis's; however, Beck uses a more varied method of identifying maladaptive cognitive processes, emphasizes coping, and prefers an educative rather than a confrontative style. Much of his work has been with depression (Beck, Rush, Shaw, and Emery, 1979), although he has also addressed other emotional difficulties to some degree (Beck, 1976). He advocates analyzing cognitive processes progressively, using three levels: (1) conscious "automatic thoughts" that contribute to depression or other emotional consequences; (2) patterns of "faulty thinking" that are represented in the automatic thoughts and lead to distortion; (3) basic underlying assumptions, or "schemas" (that is, basic rules learned for processing information). This stage is similar to Ellis's identification of irrational beliefs; however, in Beck's system clients are not thought to be ready to focus on this level until they are familiar with levels 1 and 2.

Another central figure in the cognitive-behavioral movement is Donald Meichenbaum. Meichenbaum (1977) has been an integrator of cognitive-behavioral concepts and a proponent of the responsible use of empirical methods in examining the constructs and efficacy of the techniques. He has applied cognitive techniques to an impressive range of problems, including test anxiety (Meichenbaum, 1972), speech anxiety (Meichenbaum, Gilmore, and Fedoravicius, 1971), stress management (Meichenbaum, 1975), anger and pain (Meichenbaum and Turk, 1976), schizophrenic thinking (Meichenbaum and Cameron, 1973), and impulsivity in children (Meichenbaum and Goodman, 1971). Meichenbaum has perhaps contributed less than Ellis or Beck to our understanding of the nature of maladaptive cognitions; however, he has contributed perhaps more than any other to emphasizing coping processes and to the use of sound social learning principles in effecting cognitive changes. His treatment programs follow a carefully constructed sequence of procedures: identification of maladaptive cognitions, presentation of a smorgasbord of coping techniques, modeling of techniques, and individualized shaping and practice with selected coping methods.

Many others in the cognitive-behavioral tradition have made useful contributions. Marvin Goldfried has experimented with cognitive restructuring in the context of self-control methods to effect cognitive and behavioral changes (Goldfried, 1971; Goldfried and Goldfried, 1975). Jeri Wine (1971, 1974) has presented a stimulating analysis of the role of focus of attention in evaluative anxiety (incapacitating feelings suffered in tests, speeches, and other "evaluative" situations) and has developed an effective treatment based on training subjects to redirect attention to immediate tasks. Michael Mahoney (1974, 1977) has also served as an integrator of cognitive-behavioral concepts and has contributed a treatment approach based on the learning of personal problem solving.

Contributions to Our Understanding of Human Experience. Cognitive-behavioral theorists view cognition as one very important link in the chain of maladaptive responses. While Ellis emphasizes the role of irrational beliefs, cognitive behaviorists, with concepts such as Meichenbaum's "self-talk" and Beck's "internal dialogue," emphasize the maintenance of belief systems with ongoing, dynamic thought processes. These theorists have also been instrumental in portraying human thought as a balancing act—between initial cognitive reactions and cognitive coping processes. It is "normal" to entertain a variety of thoughts about a situation, including self-defeating and irrational ones. Those who function well are able to cope more effectively with the thoughts and feelings originally elicited than are those who do not function well.

Contributions to Our Understanding of Cognitive Change. In keeping with the optimistic view of human nature inherent in the behavior therapy tradition—that most unproductive responses can be altered through learning—the cognitive behaviorists emphasize that cognitive coping processes and more adaptive beliefs can be learned. Furthermore, cognitive processes are subject to many of the principles under which behavioral responses are learned, particularly observational learning. Thus, an important role for the counselor or therapist is to direct this learning by offering an appropriate sequence of steps and effective stimuli for learning.

Cognitive Development Theory

None of the theories thus far reviewed have given much consideration to the development of cognitive processes and skills. Kelly believes that constructs are acquired and reordered more or less continuously; he does not seem to recognize the possibility that different kinds of learning may occur at different stages. Ellis and the cognitive-behavioral theorists assume that many cognitive processes are learned and learned early; however, they too give little attention to the interaction of environmental events with maturational or stage differences in the person. The cognitive development perspective, therefore, represents a different way of exploring the role of cognitions in our lives.

Review of the Theory. Beginning with Piaget (1964), who studied the cognitive development of children, researchers interested in cognitive development view humans as taking an active role in information processing—attending to and interpreting events and developing rules in an effort to give meaning and order to the world. Cognitive structures filter our experiences. As cognitive activity becomes more complex, distinct stages—

representing qualitatively different kinds of functioning—can be identified. A sequential order is required for development; that is, an individual must develop adequately at one stage before being equipped to progress to the next. This process is fueled as the person interacts with the environment and encounters "disequilibrium" caused by events that cannot be adequately processed with existing cognitive structures. The individual, being unable to *assimilate* the new events into the present cognitive system, must *accommodate* the system and make the cognitive structures more complex. This concept is similar to Festinger's (1957) cognitive dissonance theory (Widick, Knefelkamp, and Parker, 1980).

Several researchers have applied these concepts to older individuals. Kohlberg (1971) studied cognitive aspects of moral development. Harvey, Hunt, and Schroeder (1961) have addressed cognitive development in university students, and Hunt (1966) has modified this work into a description of four conceptual stages. However, the work that has been most influential in student development has been that of William Perry (1970).

Perry studied the cognitive processes of students from Harvard and Radcliffe and identified a developmental progression across nine positions, which have been simplified to four stages: (1) dualism, characterized by rigid, dichotomous, either-or thinking; (2) multiplicity, a shift to the belief that there are multiple interpretations of the truth; (3) relativism, the realization that many possible answers exist (at this stage, however, the individual is capable of more organized thought and analysis than at earlier stages); (4) "commitment in relativism," the ability to accept relativism and, at the same time, to form strong commitments to values and personal beliefs. (Perry's stages are discussed in more detail in Chapter Two.) Perry's original conception was that students enter university in the "dualism" stage and progress to the "commitment in relativism" stage by graduation. Further research has upheld the sequential nature of this progression; however, college seniors are more often measured in the high "multiplicity" or low "relativism" stages than in the most advanced stage (King, 1978).

Contributions to Our Understanding of Human Experience. Perry's scheme must be considered tentative and incomplete at this time, as are the other theories of cognitive development of adolescents and young adults. One aspect that is not fully addressed is the obvious observation that individuals may apply more advanced and sophisticated cognitive processes with certain subjects than others. Another notable deficiency in Perry's research, as in Kohlberg's, is that his samples were predominantly male. Questions have been raised regarding the degree to which concepts derived from research with unrepresentative samples are generalizable to the population at large and applicable to women in particular (Gilligan, 1982).

In spite of the difficulties with research to date, the cognitive development perspective adds to the previous theories discussed by suggesting that improved cognitive functioning is not simply a matter of learning but proceeds in a developmental sequence. An implication is that a person may need to be ready to progress in cognitive development—whether the readiness is a function of maturation or attainment of necessary skills.

Contributions to Our Understanding of Cognitive Change. The developmental perspective suggests that counselors must be more than simply trainers of new cognitive patterns. They must be astute observers of the client's present level of functioning and developmental readiness to make certain kinds of progressions. The skill of "timing" becomes important. Another implication is that the process of encountering environmental problems, subsequently experiencing cognitive dissonance, and accommodating the cognitive system will continue naturally, given conducive environmental circumstances. Developmental theorists have used Sanford's (1962) concepts of challenge and support to describe environmental conditions that facilitate cognitive growth. A certain amount of challenge is required in order to increase the complexity of cognitive systems, in that if disequilibrium is not experienced, there is no motivation to change. On the other hand, too much challenge can be overwhelming and cause regression. The proper levels of support are also required; too little support can render the challenge overwhelming, while too much can make cognitive change unnecessary.

Representational Theory

A recently conceived approach that has had a large impact on counseling and cognitive psychology is the metacommunication model of Bandler and Grinder (1975). Based on the study of language structures, this theory is similar to others previously discussed in asserting that we construct "models" of our experiences and that these models guide our behavior. The use of language concepts in understanding human information processing has led to some useful ideas.

Review of the Theory. Bandler and Grinder assert that we form models, maps, or representations of our experiences. "The map is not the territory," however, in that any model is an imperfect representation of the data being modeled. A model of an experience is created in the "deep structure" of our language system, which consists of the data as encoded and organized by the nervous system. The representation in the deep structure is an imperfect map of the original experience, since selective perception and idiosyncratic organization can occur. In other words, our organized mental constructs do not fully reflect what we have experienced. The deep-structure information is in turn represented in a "surface-structure" model, which consists of an individual's verbalizations and other observable communications. One's outward communication is an imperfect model of what one actually "knows."

These representational processes are important in interpersonal and intrapersonal communication. In order for one person to be well understood by others, surface-structure communications must be relatively good representations of deep-structure information. The counselor's first task is to facilitate the translation of the client's deep-structure model into surface-structure communications. In order for a person to enhance self-understanding and undergo cognitive development, deep-structure representations must continually grow in the accuracy with which they model the original experiences. Therefore, the other major role of the counselor is to help clients incorporate more pieces of information into the organized map with which they think about their experiences.

Another important deviation from other cognitive theorists is Grinder and Bandler's (1976) concept of multiple representational systems. Ellis and the cognitive-behavioral theorists have primarily considered verbal cognitions. Grinder and Bandler maintain that there are "other maps for the same territory" and that these correspond to our sensory channels. Most important information is represented in one or more of three channels: auditory, visual, and kinesthetic (internal feedback from muscles and organ systems). The presence of more than one representational system means that more than one model of the same experience can be constructed and that these models may differ. If they differ in important ways, "incongruity" exists. For instance, in auditorily represented verbalizations, a parent may have constructed a model of a child as mature and considerate; however, visual models of an impulsive, inconsiderate "brat" may still exist. According to the theory, an important role of the counselor is to help clients examine and integrate models from different representational systems.

Grinder and Bandler (1976) also speculate that an individual has a "primary" representational system. One person may be more likely to encode information visually and manipulate visual representations, whereas others might rely on auditory or kinesthetic channels. According to the theory, the favored representational system tends to be reflected in an individual's choices of predicates. For instance, visualizers are more likely to use expressions such as "I see . . ." or "It appears . . . ," while auditory representers may use phrases like "I hear . . ." Therefore, the counselor needs to learn to tune into the system used and "talk" to clients in the language of the most used mode.

Contributions to Our Understanding of Human Experience. As some of the other theories have suggested, we are "model builders." Our feelings, behavior, and reactions emanate from the models we have constructed of our experiences. If our surface-structure models are impoverished, we will find communication with others difficult. If our deep-structure models are impoverished, we will be unable to understand ourselves and our reactions and therefore will be unable to cope effectively with events. The theory also suggests that we are "multichanneled" information processors and that we can encounter confusion and dissonance when models constructed in different channels differ from one another.

Contributions to Our Understanding of Cognitive Change. The theory suggests that cognitive and other psychological changes occur as models are enriched—made more accurate "maps" of the territory they represent. Bandler and Grinder (1975) propose a number of questioning techniques derived from their metamodel of communication. Counselors can use these techniques in helping clients represent deep-structure models in their surface-structure communications. While these methods are developed with language analysis concepts, they are consistent with what counselors generally learn in interviewing techniques. Bandler and Grinder also propose various experiential techniques, including Gestalt methods, as ways of enriching deep-structure models and exploring incongruity among representational systems.

Unfortunately, much of the research dealing with assumptions regarding sensory mode representations and potential counseling applications has been disappointing. Research by Dowd and Pety (1982) and Ellickson (1983) has cast doubt on the value of using the primary representational system to match clients' predicate styles. Fromme and Daniell (1984) did not find support for the hypothesis that preferred representational systems would predict predicate selection or that subjects similar in visualization ability would communicate designs more effectively than mismatched subjects. However, the general concept of talking to clients in their "own languages" seems to be viable. In studying brief counseling interactions, Hammer (1983) found that clients' perceptions of counselor empathy were increased when the counselor matched clients' predicates; however, the predicate matching was based on tracking immediate disclosures rather than identifying a primary representational system. In all probability, we are not as restricted to use of one channel as Grinder and Bandler suggest; instead, our information processing is likely to consist of fast-paced interweavings of different sensory representations.

Other Influential Theories

A review of several other theories is warranted, since they have made important contributions to our understanding of cognitive processes. While these have influenced the Cognitive Intervention Planning Model less directly than the ideas discussed previously, readers should be aware of these concepts and may want to seek further information on one or more of them.

Decision-Making and Problem-Solving Concepts. Several theorists have addressed a very important aspect of cognitive functioning: How we go about actively making decisions and grappling with the problems that we face. Some of the earliest work concerned the ways in which groups can address problems creatively (Osborn, 1963; Parnes, 1967). The technique of group brainstorming was developed as a way of helping people keep an open mind to possibilities and discover novel solutions. Several individuals have applied some of these concepts to the fields of counseling and psychotherapy.

D'Zurilla and Goldfried (1971), who worked within a self-control behavior therapy model, reasoned that the difficulties of many clients can be traced to deficient cognitive skills in problem solving. Using ideas of Parnes (1967) and Osborn (1963) and others, they developed a therapy based on teaching clients effective problem-solving skills. The proper cognitive set for problem solving must be shaped, because clients have tendencies to avoid problems or to make impulsive decisions. The problems must then be formulated and defined. All potential solutions must then be generated. Brainstorming principles involving suspension of judgment can be used with this phase. After elimination of obviously unworkable solutions, the outcomes of potential alternatives should be generated and then weighed. In subsequent steps a decision is made, implemented, and evaluated.

Another adaptation of problem solving to therapy is the "personal science" approach devised by Mahoney (1974, 1977). Mahoney parallels Kelly's "every man a scientist" concept by suggesting that clients learn coping strategies and solve problems through application of a scientific process to their personal difficulties. His model is particularly well suited to attacking intrapersonal difficulties, such as emotional reactions. Mahoney views the counselor or therapist as a "technical consultant" or "coach" who takes the client through a systematic process of addressing problems and developing coping skills. Clients are to be "apprentices" in this endeavor. The goal is for them not only to learn specific skills but also to assimilate the personal science model as a widely applicable set of coping skills. The steps of this process are represented by the mnemonic "science": S, specify general problem area; C, collect data (including assessment of cognitive status); I, identify patterns or sources of the problem (the physical and social environments, cognitive factors, skills); E, examine options; N, narrow and experiment; C, compare data (evaluate effects of various experiments); E, extend, revise, or replace.

Others have explored the roles of decision-making and problem-solving processes in counseling. Janis and Mann (1977) conducted research with decision making and endeavored to define decision-making processes. Among other interesting contributions, they identified some of the anticipated outcomes that influence people's decisions. Anticipated outcomes, both positive and negative, can be internal phenomena, such as feeling proud of oneself, or external, such as obtaining praise from one's friends. People are also influenced by anticipated effects on important others, as well as effects on themselves. Janis and Mann believe that greater awareness of various facets of the decision-making process can guide an individual in dealing with life's problems. Janis (1982) has edited a book of articles focusing on the use of good decision-making strategies in counseling and their effects in intervening in various difficulties. Heppner has studied the appraisal of personal problem solving and has related this dimension to cognitive variables (Heppner, Reeder, and Larson, 1983) and psychological adjustment (Heppner and Anderson, 1985).

Those studying problem solving and decision making remind us that certain important cognitive processes are complex skills. These are consciously and actively employed and can be improved through systematic training. They point out that many cognitive, behavioral, and emotional difficulties experienced by clients involve an inability to decide and solve problems. The cognitive skills of problem solving can be learned through direct, didactic methods, observational learning, and experiential applications. Mahoney states that his personal science method is intended for developmental purposes as well as for remedial goals. This wide applicability seems to be possible with the other perspectives as well.

Social Learning Theory. This theoretical area is closely akin to cognitive-behavioral theory in its insistence on empirical method and validation of precisely defined constructs. In fact, many cognitive behaviorists ascribe to social learning theory as the model for psychological processes that underlies their treatment techniques. Social learning theory departs from stimulus-response learning theory by asserting that constructs within the organism, such as expectancies, mediate an individual's response to a stimulus. These constructs imply a cognitive, information-processing perspective. Social learning theorists also believe that the most meaningful source of learning of cognitive sets and behaviors is the behavior of others.

One of the earliest proponents of the social learning approach was Julian B. Rotter. An interesting historical fact is that Rotter and George Kelly were both mainstays of the Ohio State clinical psychology training program during the period when both produced their major works (Sechrest, 1977). Rotter's (1954) *Social Learning and Clinical Psychology* was published one year earlier than Kelly's volumes. The theories have many differences, although they are bound together by the concept of humans as active construers of their experiences. In Rotter's view, people respond not to objectively real stimuli but to their perceptions of them. He emphasizes the effect of "expectancies" on individual behavior. It is not so much whether a reinforcement will occur that influences a person's response but whether it is *expected* to occur. One of the most enduring of his concepts is expectancy regarding locus of control of reinforcement. Those who develop an internal locus of control have a general expectancy that reinforcement will come to them through their own efforts. Those with an external locus of control believe that whether or not they receive reinforcement is dependent on external forces. One's locus of control would therefore mediate the effects of any reinforcement schedule.

A more comprehensive theory of personality development is offered by Albert Bandura (Bandura, 1977b; Bandura and Walters, 1963). Like Rotter, he views humans as processors of symbols. Through observation of events and construction of symbols, they form expectancies that guide their responses in situations. Bandura asserts that learning can occur and be maintained symbolically without the learned behavior's being executed. One of Bandura's chief contributions is his elaboration of the important role of observational learning—that is, cognitive, behavioral, and affective responses as learned from models. Subjects do not simply learn isolated responses but assimilate the context in which responses are appropriate. Bandura and others have attempted to discover the conditions under which effective modeling occurs. They have found, for instance, that an observer's decision to emulate a model's response will depend on the results of that response. By observing others and creating cognitive models of their responses, we are capable of learning myriad concepts and responses. Whether or not we act on this learning will depend on how we view a situation and our expectancies for the outcomes of various responses.

According to Bandura's theory, the person and the environment are in continuous interaction. One's map of the environment, reflected in expectancies, affects one's choices of behavior, the consequences of which in turn shape the expectancies. Bandura (1977a, 1977b) has recently elaborated on the kinds of expectancies that are important. *Outcome expectancies* involve predictions regarding the consequences likely to follow certain responses. Even if outcome expectancies are favorable, people are unlikely to implement responses if they are unsure of their abilities to execute the necessary actions. These determining factors are called *self-efficacy expectancies*. Goldfried and Robins (1982) offer guidelines for helping clients process information regarding self-efficacy.

Interpersonal Influence Theory. Drawing on some of the

concepts from social psychology previously described, Stanley Strong (1968) proposed a social influence theory of counseling. His conception of clients' difficulties is that significant amounts of misattribution are often involved. The counselor's role is to help clients rethink and reorganize important attributions. Since individuals often manifest opposition to the content of the counselor's offerings and resistance to the process of counselor influence, the counselor must understand and use the social psychological dynamics of the client-counselor dyad (Strong and Matross, 1973). Strong suggests that the degree to which the counselor can influence the client depends on the degree to which the client perceives the counselor as trustworthy, expert, and attractive (defined as being similar to and liking the client). Numerous researchers have investigated the basic validity of these concepts and the counselor factors related to clients' perceptions of the three key dimensions (Heppner and Dixon, 1981). The ideas have been continually refined as a result of these research findings (Strong and Claiborn, 1982). Strong's theory is important to counselors because it indicates that cognitive change is partially dependent on the counselor's attaining "social power" and that development of certain perceptual and cognitive sets is crucial in setting the stage for change.

Ego Psychology Theories. One of the earliest reactions to Freud's psychoanalytic theory was that it placed too much emphasis on the unconscious and the instinctual motives of the "id." Beginning with Alfred Adler, a number of theorists have retained some Freudian concepts but have given greater emphasis to the adaptive nature of humans through conscious processes controlled by the "ego." They have also tended to favor the influence of the social environment over instinctual strivings in accounting for important psychological processes. Harry Stack Sullivan, Eric Fromm, and Karen Horney extended their theories along these lines. These approaches were developed from a rich clinical tradition. While their constructs lack the precision and the testability characteristic of those in some of the other theories from the empirical tradition, their focus on conscious processes offers useful ideas on cognitive functioning.

Value of Cognitive Approaches for
Student Development Interventions

In this period of financial contraction and increasing demands for accountability, counselors and other student development professionals have particular need of theoretical models that guide design and delivery of effective interventions. The body of theory, technique, and research concerning cognitions appears to offer a useful basis for effective and efficient programs. Many of the concepts and techniques have been well researched and validated, particularly in the rational-emotive, cognitive-behavioral, and social learning schools. In addition to their empirical value, the cognitive ideas reviewed appear to be particularly well suited to use in college and university settings. Reasons for this suitability include the following:

1. *Applicability to Different Kinds of Program Goals.* Morrill and Hurst (1971) and Morrill, Oetting, and Hurst (1974) have advocated that counselors venture beyond the traditional one-to-one counseling role and design services that use different modalities and accomplish different kinds of goals. Cognitive theory offers guidance not only for remedially focused counseling and therapy but also for psychoeducational interventions with preventive and developmental goals. It also contains concepts that can be used in group counseling and interventions using media, as well as in individual counseling.

2. *Compatibility with a Humanistic-Educational Model of Intervention.* Counselors and others on university campuses have tended to favor a humanistic-educational model of psychological need in preference to an illness/medical model. Perhaps because the psychological processes of most university students are relatively healthy, a concept that emphasizes personal strengths and the capacity for growth and learning is often favored over one emphasizing psychopathology. The cognitive perspective is compatible with this view, in that it advocates development of self-control and coping processes and emphasizes the individual's responsibility for his or her mental life.

3. *Compatibility with Theories of Student Development.*

The cognitive ideas reviewed are compatible with cognitive development theory as it has been applied in higher education settings. Less obviously, they are intricately involved in ego development. Chickering's (1969) vectors of development can be analyzed from a cognitive perspective, since cognitive gains are required in order to progress on any of the dimensions. Crystallizing identity requires development of more complex constructs about oneself, including one's interests, preferences, needs, values, and skills. Achieving instrumental autonomy requires improvement in cognitive skills necessary for living one's life independently, including problem solving. Achieving emotional autonomy entails an improved cognitive differentiation of one's own responsibilities and values from those of others, including parents.

4. *Compatibility with Higher Education Goals.* One of the most important goals of universities is the enhancement of students' intellectual development in academic disciplines. This mission is closely paralleled by a focus on improving cognitive skills useful in understanding and managing thoughts, emotions, and behavior.

5. *Applicability to Immediate Problems.* Many university students are quite practical in the ways they conceptualize their needs and favor addressing significant, immediate problems rather than more abstract matters. Use of some of the cognitive concepts can help counselors intervene in practical, immediate ways.

6. *Compatibility with Students' Levels of Cognitive Functioning.* Students are capable of using cognitive approaches quite well—even creatively. Furthermore, their developmental stage—in conflux with an environment stressing intellectual curiosity—disposes them to exercise their "cognitive muscles" in reexamining long-held beliefs.

7. *Suitability for Short-Term Interventions.* Many of the cognitive concepts presented can be incorporated into interventions that are problem focused and time limited. Many focus on the learning of coping strategies, for which goals can be defined, versus the unraveling of layers of insight, which can potentially be a never-ending process. Such short-term methods are often sought by students, encouraged by accountability-conscious administrators, and necessitated by the time constrictions imposed by the university calendar.

TWO

The Model and Its Use in Assessing Developmental Needs

In this chapter a tentative model useful in enhancing the cognitive complexity of late adolescents and young adults will be outlined. This model represents my most current effort to integrate some of the ideas reviewed in Chapter One into a single framework. In particular, two bodies of concepts about cognition have been incorporated: ideas from cognitive-behavioral approaches and concepts from cognitive development research and theory. It is my hope that this model will prove helpful to counselors and student development specialists who wish to consider the cognitive dimension in planning and conducting a range of interventions, including individual and group counseling, structured groups, and workshops.

Overview of the Model

Figure 1 is provided to help readers follow the model, which consists of eight sequential steps or phases. In actual counseling practice, however, counselor and client seldom proceed through the phases in orderly fashion. Addressing two or more phases concurrently and recycling to earlier phases are to be expected and encouraged.

In Phase 1 important *cognitive events*—discrete information-containing elements that make up an individual's stream of

33

Figure 1. Cognitive Intervention Planning Model for
Use in Individual Counseling and Program Development.

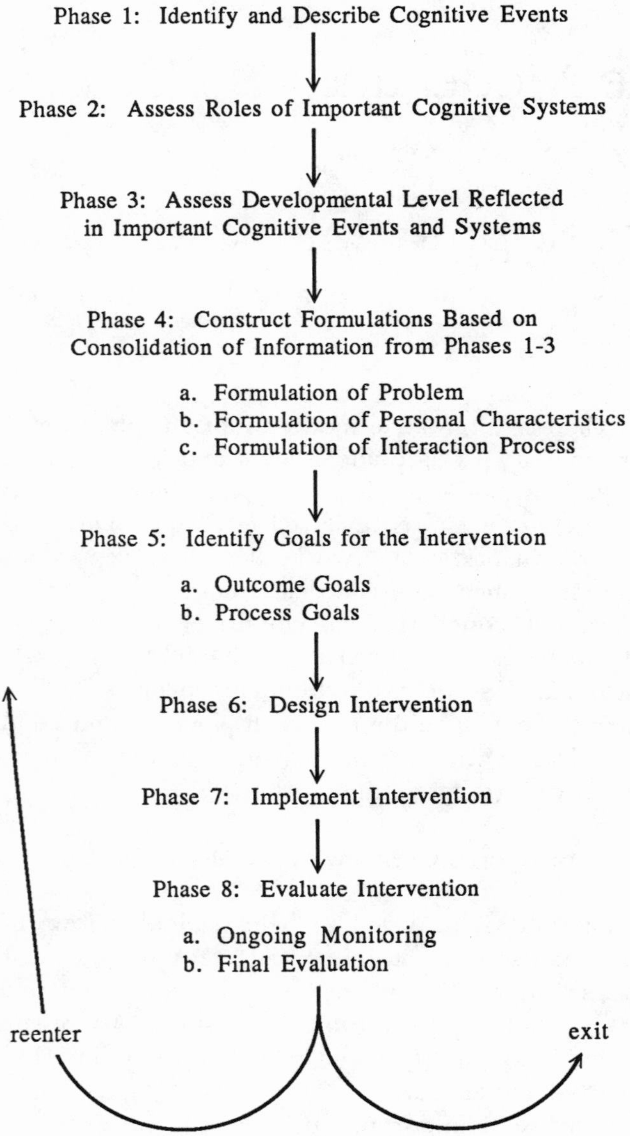

Phase 1: Identify and Describe Cognitive Events

Phase 2: Assess Roles of Important Cognitive Systems

Phase 3: Assess Developmental Level Reflected
in Important Cognitive Events and Systems

Phase 4: Construct Formulations Based on
Consolidation of Information from Phases 1-3

a. Formulation of Problem
b. Formulation of Personal Characteristics
c. Formulation of Interaction Process

Phase 5: Identify Goals for the Intervention

a. Outcome Goals
b. Process Goals

Phase 6: Design Intervention

Phase 7: Implement Intervention

Phase 8: Evaluate Intervention

a. Ongoing Monitoring
b. Final Evaluation

reenter   exit consciousness at a particular moment—are identified and described. These events might then be categorized in some fashion —for instance, under the headings "Self-Talk," "Nonverbal Cognitions," "Conflicting Cognitions," "Cognitive Content," and "Cognitive Processes." Note that these categories are not mutually exclusive. The individual counselor can use these dimensions to specify and understand the problematic aspects of a client's immediate cognitive activity. Student development professionals planning preventive or developmental interventions can also benefit by identifying relevant cognitive events common in the target population.

In Phase 2 important *cognitive systems*—integrated networks into which isolated cognitive events are organized—are assessed. A limitation of the cognitive-behavioral and rational-emotive schools is that they focus predominantly on discrete cognitive events rather than broader organizational structures. Kelly's (1955) personal construct theory and cognitive dissonance concepts suggest that individual cognitions are often integrated into larger systems. Once counselors have identified important cognitive events, they can then consider the cognitive systems important in the client's difficulties (in remedial interventions) or the systems to be targeted for development (in proactive interventions).

In Phase 3 the *cognitive development* of clients or members of the target population is assessed. Concepts from cognitive-behavioral, rational-emotive, personal construct, and social psychological theories do not address developmental change in cognitions. Cognitive development concepts, such as those proposed by Perry (1970), are incorporated into the Cognitive Intervention Planning Model in an effort to address this facet. An effort is made to understand cognitive functioning on a developmental continuum for specific cognitive systems as well as for overall cognitive functioning.

In Phase 4, the culmination of the assessment process, formulations necessary for effective intervention planning are constructed from the information gained in Phases 1 through 3. At Phase 4a a formulation of the problem of the client or target population is constructed. The problem definition would include a description of the problematic cognitive events, systems, and developmental issues. The second formulation, devised at Phase 4b, is of the personal characteristics of the client or target group. The effectiveness of the cognitive intervention depends on its compatibility with the client's personology as well as with the problem. The third formulation, Phase 4c, is of the interaction process, which also affects the success of the intervention. In individual counseling the process formulation would be made of the counselor-client dyadic interaction, whereas the group process would be conceptualized in group counseling.

On the basis of these formulations, the goals for the intervention are specified at Phase 5, the initial phase of planning the intervention. At Phase 5a outcome goals are determined, consisting of the cognitive outcomes necessary for solving the problem (identified in Phase 4a). Outcome goals may reflect needed changes in cognitive events, systems, and developmental functioning. Process goals are then identified at Phase 5b. These reflect aspects such as the kind of relationship established between counselor and client. The process goals identified are likely to depend on the problem and person formulations and particularly on the formulation of the process (Phase 4c). Careful setting of outcome and process goals is important in individual counseling, as well as in proactive interventions, such as designing structured groups and workshops.

In Phase 6 the intervention is planned, based on the problem, person, and process formulations and the goals identified. In individual counseling this phase would take the form of counselor and client agreeing on a contract for counseling. Phase 7 consists of implementing the intervention.

In Phase 8 the intervention is evaluated. Phase 8a represents continual monitoring of degree of success in meeting process goals, the client's progress toward outcome goals, and the client's reactions to aspects of the intervention. The information from this monitoring is reentered in earlier phases, particularly Phase 4, in which the formulations of problem and person are refined. Thus, a Phase 8 to Phase 4 feedback loop is an important facet of the model. Phase 8b represents the final evaluation of the intervention. Did the intervention bring about the desired outcome goals and resolve the problem formulated at Phase 4a? Were the desired changes in cognitive events, systems, and developmental level achieved? The evaluation can include clients' subjective appraisals, counselors' observations of changes, and/or use of assessment instruments.

Phase 1: Identifying Important Cognitive Events

In using the cognitive dimension with people in the late adolescent–early adulthood stages, the counselor should be sensitive to a broad range of potentially influential cognitive events and processes—a broader range than is covered by any one of the theories previously discussed. In order to identify the important cognitions occurring with clients or students, assessment of several categories can be useful: the presence of "self-talk," or what we say to ourselves in words; the presence of visualizations and other "nonverbal" cognitions; conflicting cognitions; the cognitive content involved, as well as the processes; the proportion of observations to inferences; the time perspective displayed; expectancies; the involvement of self-awareness cognitions; metacognitions; and the level of awareness of the cognitive events.

Self-Talk: Speaking to Ourselves. Cognitive events that are important in our lives include covert self-verbalizations or "self-talk"—instances in which we consciously think in words, as though we are listening to an inner voice. This concept may seem humorous at first, in that "hearing voices" and "talking to oneself" are associated with eccentricity at best and serious mental illness at worst. Nevertheless, all of us must admit that we do in fact talk to ourselves. We may instruct, reward, harangue, punish, warn, console, worry, soothe, and amuse ourselves and perform many other functions through engaging ourselves in internal conversation.

As we gain awareness of the streams of conscious thinking that are part of our everyday lives, we learn that we talk to ourselves in many different ways. As well as consisting of words, our self-talk often contains vivid auditory imagery. We

may talk to ourselves in our own voices, or our voices may assume a timbre characteristic of people significant to us. If we
listen closely, we may hear the high-pitched voice of a whining
mother or the cutting tone of a critical parent or teacher. How
something is said aloud can have a greater emotional impact
than the actual ideas expressed. The haughty manner of a request to turn down a stereo may elicit more anger than the suggestion itself. In a similar way, the tone of voice or loudness in
our auditory imagery may influence the impact of self-talk on
emotional responses.

Our self-talk may take the form of an *internal mono-
logue,* in which one voice discourses on a theme. Or the cognitive activity may more accurately resemble an *internal dialogue,*
in which two or more different perspectives are debated, perhaps by two or more distinguishable voices.

As Meichenbaum (1977) has noted, well-learned self-
talk can become internalized, so that the meaning is transmitted
even though a person is not conscious of thinking the words.
Perhaps the information is encoded in a kind of mental short-
hand for the self-talk. We do not have to think the words consciously in order for the meaning to be conveyed. Meichenbaum's example is that of a person learning to drive a car. For a
while the commands are consciously delivered in self-talk, sometimes even aloud: "Put in the clutch slowly!" As the concepts
become well learned and the responses to the self-instructions
become second nature, the consciously perceived self-talk may
be used less and less. Nevertheless, the self-instructions are re-
trievable if one is asked to reflect on the knowledge used in
driving. In the same manner, clients may have internalized self-
statements such as "I must not get angry!" or "If I mess up, I'm
no good." Such messages may be encoded and become operative without being consciously thought.

Some of the more problematic cognitions are ones in
which this automatic process has occurred to such a degree that
the person is unable to retranslate them into words. In a verbal
sense, the individual has "lost touch" with these cognitive connections. The words applied to the situation may even outline a
different or a conflicting theme. For instance, a student may

take the conscious position that "It's OK not to be liked by every important person in my life." Yet the well-learned theme, which is still operative even though denied, may be "If I am not liked by someone important to me, that's *awful!*"

Nonverbal Cognitions. "People not only think about what happens to them in words, phrases, and sentences but also do so by images, fantasies, dreams, and other kinds of pictorial representations" (Ellis, 1979, pp. 193–194). Many of us use such *visual cues* extensively and are able consciously to construct pictures in our minds—vivid, full of motion, and in living color. We can retrieve images of past events, including ones that were traumatic for us. We can also construct completely new and original movies based on our hopes or fears for the future. We can mentally project ourselves into the future and see ourselves in failure as well as in mastery. Other individuals rely heavily on auditory cues in representing events and might thus be expected to engage extensively in the kind of internal dialogue described. It is therefore important for the cognitively oriented counselor to focus on visualization as well as on self-talk as a mediator of feelings and behavior.

What about the other three modes of receiving external information: taste, smell, and touch? Is information from these senses also encoded and consciously retrieved and manipulated, as Grinder and Bandler (1976) suggest? It seems quite possible that it is, in that I can recreate in my mind the taste, smell, and texture of a favorite spicy meal. While representations of taste, smell, and touch do seem to occur, however, they have little to do with most of our consequential mental distortions. Eating-related problems may be exceptional in the degree to which taste and smell play crucial roles. The most important role of these representations may be to supplement and enhance the impact of auditory and visual imagery. For instance, the visual image of a traumatic experience may be more powerful if amplified by taste and/or smell imagery. In light of the possibility that taste, smell, and touch enhance the effects of other representations, counselors should stimulate multiple-imagery modes when doing imagery exercises with clients.

What about information from within—feedback from our

muscles and other organs? Are these encoded, retained, and retrieved? As mentioned in Chapter One, Grinder and Bandler (1976) assert that the kinesthetic sense provides a representational system that some use as a primary mode of "remembering" events. I have found, however, that people rarely reexperience kinesthetic sensations without accompanying thoughts and/or imagery. Clients may at first claim that they do not "think or imagine anything" when they reexperience the physical sensations common to depression or some other feeling state. However, after they have developed greater awareness, they often become cognizant of self-talk or imagery that had been occurring unobserved. Kinesthetic feedback is obviously an important process, in that it is a component of our experience of emotion. I therefore encourage clients to be sensitive to kinesthetic cues. Rather than assuming that the kinesthetic data have been encoded and retrieved, I prefer to encourage clients to study the fabrics of their internal dialogues and visualizations for cognitive processes that are actively eliciting the kinesthetic responses.

Conflicting Cognitions. One possibility presented by the existence of more than one representational system is that conflicting perspectives of the same event can be encoded. A student may engage in realistic self-talk about a calculus test and yet be besieged by visual imagery of a previous test "failure." The visual representation, which may fuel the intense anxiety, may be less available to awareness than the benign verbalizations. Therefore, the counselor should carefully assess the variety of cognitive mediating modes active in a client's problem and intervene effectively with each.

Cognitive Content and Processes. It is helpful to divide cognitive events into the categories of *content* and *processes.* Content refers to the makeup of a thought or image. Meichenbaum's anxiety-arousing self-statements represent an example of cognitive content. Ellis's rational-emotive approach focuses on irrational beliefs and is therefore also directed at the content of the client's thoughts. Recognition of cognitive content is often helpful in conducting counseling or educative interventions.

Ellis (1977a) has presented several versions of the irrational beliefs that he regards as most important. Most of these beliefs relate to one of four patterns: (1) thinking that someone or something ought to be different than it is, (2) finding this state of affairs "terrible," (3) deciding that this situation is unbearable, and (4) damning oneself or other people for making the horrible errors contributing to the undesirable situation. As mentioned in Chapter One, he has also identified three related "musturbatory ideologies": (1) maintaining that one *must* do well and win approval for one's performances or deserve devaluation as a person, (2) believing that others *must* treat one considerately or deserve blame and punishment, and (3) assuming that one *must* get practically everything one wants.

Other approaches have attempted to focus on ongoing, dynamic processes more than on content. Beck's identification of faulty thinking styles is one example (Beck, Rush, Shaw, and Emery, 1979). Clients may engage in dichotomous thinking, overgeneralization, or other faulty processes, which can be summarized as follows:

> *Arbitrary Inference:* Arriving at an erroneous conclusion —one that is not supported by the evidence available.
>
> *Selective Abstraction:* Attending selectively to only one or more pieces of information and ignoring other relevant pieces.
>
> *Overgeneralization:* Forming a conclusion based on one or more isolated incidents and applying this generalized conclusion to more situations than would be warranted.
>
> *Magnification:* Distorting the processing of an event by attributing more significance to it than warranted.
>
> *Minimization:* Distorting the processing of an event by attributing less significance to it than warranted.
>
> *Personalization:* Relating external events to oneself when there is no basis for this connection.
>
> *Absolutistic, Dichotomous Thinking:* Placing events into one of two opposite categories or polarities, instead of recognizing that differences can occur on a continuum.

By engaging in these processes, clients may arrive at a number of instances of irrational cognitive content.

Wine (1971, 1974) identified an attention-focusing process, in which clients direct attention either to immediate tasks or to themselves. "Self-focused" cognitions are related to evaluative anxiety in performance situations. "Task-focused" attention is related to decreased anxiety and improved performance. She found that students can be trained to control this attention-focusing process and learn to shift attention from self to task, thereby reducing and managing their anxiety levels.

Identification of both content elements and problematic aspects of cognitive processes is helpful with many clients. However, I often prefer to tune into processes of thoughts and imagery. A specific content statement is a simplification of what actually occurs in our minds. We rarely maintain a specific thought in our consciousness for very long. Our mental life can be more accurately characterized as a dynamic ebbing and flowing of different thoughts and images. The chaining of one thought to another and the leaps and spirals of thoughts and images are often more significant than the content of any particular thought. Furthermore, it may be more economical to intervene in cognitive processes rather than in content. If students can learn to alter the processes by which they deduce irrationalities, they can come to rethink and avert a number of instances of irrational thinking. If the content were the focus, each instance would have to be addressed separately.

Cognitive Observations Versus Inferences. Our cognitions often take the form of monitoring and describing data, both external and internal: "This question is the longest one on the test." "I'm thinking about Mom again." In an observation we merely note something as it is represented without making judgments or conclusions about it. In an inference we form conclusions from the data: "I don't think it's fair to ask a question this long! He must be trying to confuse us." "I must really miss Mom to be thinking so much about her."

Determining whether errant cognitive activity involves observations or inferences can be important in designing an intervention. When an observation is problematic, the difficulty is often in whether the process is overused or underused. An obsessive-compulsive style is marked by overuse of cognitive observations. Underutilization of certain kinds of cognitive observations can also present difficulties. Clients can engage in selective attention by cognitively observing certain events and ignoring others. It is common for students to have periods of seeing their parents as "all bad." During these times they may rarely think about instances when their parents were understanding and supportive. Enhanced cognitive complexity will enable them to observe a more balanced representation of events.

Cognitive inferences are at the root of many problems involving overemotionalized responses. A person leaps to a harsh and restrictive interpretation of an event. Kelly's (1955) concept of "constructive alternativism" reminds us that multiple ways of construing an event are possible. Students prone to jumping to conclusions can benefit from becoming more aware that they engage in inference and cautioning themselves to slow down their reactions: "Hold on! I have a tendency to jump to conclusions. I'd better reserve judgment until I know more about this."

Time Perspective of Cognitive Events. Another helpful distinction is whether cognitive events involve labeling and interpreting past experiences, processing present data, and/or anticipating and predicting future experiences. Events that have occurred are given meaning and integrated into our systems of thought. Both observations and inferences about past data are made, as the experience is labeled. Once our minds have looked backward at the event and constructed its meaning, these conclusions are then stored for future use in decision making or problem solving. The expectations and anticipations may be kept alive through self-talk or visual imagery.

The counselor may want to determine whether cognitive observations are misapplied with present or past data and whether mistakes in cognitive inferences occur in processing present, past, or future events (see Table 1). Admittedly, I am presuming that we are incapable of actually observing the future, although believers in clairvoyance would disagree with me.

One client's selective attention may occur more often when events are remembered than when they are registered in the present. Another person may make more inferential mistakes when processing present data than when thinking about events after they have occurred.

Table 1. Cognitive Observations and Inferences
for Three Time Perspectives.

	Past	Present	Future
Cognitive Observations	Retrieving Remembering Reflecting Recalling Imagining	Observing Attending Monitoring Labeling Identifying Sorting Describing	
Cognitive Inferences	Attributing Interpreting Generalizing Concluding Synthesizing Analyzing	Attributing Interpreting Generalizing Concluding	Anticipating Predicting Expecting Planning Imagining

Expectancies. An expectancy, a concept developed by social learning theorists, is a cognition based on processing of past experiences and used in anticipating future events. Bandura (1977a, 1977b) distinguishes two kinds of expectancies important in predicting whether behaviors within an individual's repertoire will be enacted. The first of these is the "outcome expectancy," an individual's perception of the consequences likely to follow a particular response. If desirable outcomes are expected to occur, emitting the response is made more probable. For instance, students are more likely to write extra-credit papers if they believe that the professor will give high grades. On the other hand, if the outcomes anticipated are negative, the person is less likely to carry out a response.

In addition to his concept of outcome expectancies, Bandura has described "self-efficacy expectancies." These are beliefs about one's ability to complete the necessary actions in a situation (Bandura, 1977a, 1977b; Bandura and Adams, 1977). Students who expect that a professor will give high grades for good extra-credit papers will still be unlikely to write the papers unless they believe that they can perform at the needed level. Emotional responses are also affected by self-efficacy expectancies. If a male is unsure of his ability to make interesting conversation with females, he is likely to avoid dating and to feel anxious when conversation with females is required.

Self-Awareness Cognitions. Many of our cognitions, including self-efficacy expectancies, concern ourselves. Two self-awareness dimensions important to assess are self-monitoring cognitions, which consist of observations, and self-evaluating cognitions, which require inferences. *Self-monitoring cognitions* occur when our attention is devoted to ourselves and what is happening to us. In a sense, a part of us—our "observing self"—stands aside and views, hears, and comments on our feelings, actions, and thoughts. We label our internal data. We may note certain of our responses, such as increased heart rate and muscle tension, and suggest to ourselves that we are excited. We may observe ourselves arriving late for a meeting and state something like "That's the third time today I've been late."

We can engage in self-monitoring too frequently or not frequently enough. With overfrequent self-monitoring, we can overload our circuits with cognitions about internal data. The effect is well encapsulated in the word "self-consciousness." We can become so absorbed with monitoring internal data that we are insufficiently attentive to external data and may therefore not engage the outside world in a productive manner. A student anxious about public speaking may become immobilized with the inner sensations of fear. A depressed student may become too absorbed with internal data to attend adequately to schoolwork or relationships. Insufficient self-monitoring can also be problematic, in that a person may "lose touch" with important internal processes. Stress-prone students may have misplaced the ability to monitor internal physiological cues and may unconsciously maintain muscle tension at high levels. The first step in the self-statement coping approaches of Meichenbaum (1977) and others is to help individuals improve in monitoring their inner thoughts and sensations. These can then be used as cues to initiate coping activities.

Self-monitoring cognitions are often followed by *self-evaluating cognitions,* in which we grade ourselves on the dimensions observed: "What's wrong with me that I get anxious so often?" "I've got to start getting to places on time. That's terrible!" We may observe ourselves entertaining unflattering thoughts about a revered parent and scold ourselves: "I shouldn't even think things like that!" A condemnatory negative judgment delivered to oneself in a severe internal voice is likely to have a negative impact on emotions and behavior.

Some self-evaluative thinking is necessary if we are to learn from our experiences. It is often productive to ask "How well did I do?" as a prelude to asking "What might I do differently the next time?" However, self-evaluating cognitions can produce problems if they are offered too frequently. We then become overabsorbed with self-evaluation. Burns (1980b) and Barrow and Moore (1983) have noted that perfectionistic thinking, in which one's goals are unrealistic and rigidly held, can be detrimental to one's performance and emotional state; and Ellis has shown that irrational demands can lead one to become excessively self-critical (Ellis, 1977a; Ellis and Harper, 1975).

The degree of cognitive complexity represented in self-evaluation is likely to be important. Discriminating assessments of specific responses can be helpful, provided the individual does not focus exclusively on negative instances. Global self-indictments, in which an individual generalizes from "I did poorly" to "I am no good," are likely to lead to problems of lowered self-esteem and heightened anxiety and depression. Insufficient self-evaluation can also be a problem. A person who is overly defensive may need to learn to confront the question "Are there aspects of my behavior that could be improved?" For example, a student who has been unmotivated to study may blame a precarious academic situation on the unfairness of a professor. An extreme example of insufficient self-evaluation might be someone with a sociopathic personality, who has no regard for standards of right and wrong.

Metacognitions—Cognitions About Cognitions. It is possible to have self-monitoring cognitions about our thoughts and mental processes—cognitions about cognitions. For instance, we may catch ourselves thinking about a friend with whom we have had an argument and observe, "I've sure been thinking about Susan a lot lately." Several cognitive theorists have outlined the importance of "metacognitive variables," referring to awareness of cognitive processes (A. L. Brown, 1977; Heppner, Neal, and Larson, 1984; Meichenbaum and Asarnow, 1979). For instance, we can be aware of our own cognitive abilities ("I have success-fully worked a lot of math problems") and can monitor our thoughts ("I'm getting off the track here"). Approaches such as those of Meichenbaum (1977) and Beck (1976) encourage the development of metacognitions that monitor thought processes.

Like self-monitoring cognitions, self-evaluating cognitions can be directed toward other cognitive processes. For instance, Butler and Meichenbaum (1981) found that the metacognition of appraisal of one's problem-solving ability is related to prob-lem-solving performance. A test-anxious student might begin to think, "I'm not thinking straight. What's wrong with me?" Or the self-evaluation could be more positive: "I'm remembering things well and moving along fine."

Levels of Awareness of Cognitions. A favorite sensory awareness exercise of mine comes from a book by Stevens (1971) and likens awareness to a searchlight. This metaphor of a searchlight is helpful in discussing the three levels of aware-ness that can pertain to cognitions. At the first level, a person is consciously aware of certain thoughts or images; these are illu-minated by the searchlight, in that attention is directed toward them. "Internal dialogue" or self-talk occurs at this level. Indi-viduals vary in their abilities to register and remember these cog-nitions. The first stage of structured cognitive therapy is to help clients become more sensitive to their streams of consciousness. For instance, early in Beck's cognitive therapy of depression, clients learn to identify and monitor their "automatic thoughts" (Beck, 1976; Beck, Rush, Shaw, and Emery, 1979).

The second level of cognitive processing includes events that are known but are not currently in words or pictures in a person's immediate consciousness. These can be easily retrieved if the individual chooses to shift the searchlight. Some of the cognitive events that fit this category are beliefs, expectations, and assumptions. Sometimes cognitive activity at level 1 may not reflect all of a person's information available at level 2. In these cases the counselor may be able to help by asking questions that lead the client to retrieve more comprehensive data about a situation. In the terms of our metaphor, the counselor may help widen the focus of the client's searchlight. This concept is akin to Bandler and Grinder's (1975) idea of helping clients translate the "deep structures" represented into the "surface structures" that are verbalized.

Level-3 cognitions operate beyond self-observation; they can be illuminated, but only with effort, examination, and cognitive development. The counselor can help clients slowly recognize these underlying cognitions by becoming aware of their internal dialogues. Beck (1976) and Burns (1980a) teach clients to question themselves so that they penetrate beneath the automatic thoughts (level 1) to the underlying assumptions and schemas (level 3). As level-3 cognitions are identified and recognized, they become level-1 or level-2 cognitions.

"Ah-ha," you say, "now the cognitive guy is getting himself into a position of having to admit that there is an unconscious." However, the unrecognized process that is operative at level 3 can be distinguished from unconscious events as posited by psychoanalytic and psychodynamic theorists. A person can be "unconscious" of level-3 cognitions in the sense of being "unaware" of them at the moment. However, no "unconscious" as an entity need be assumed to account for this phenomenon. Adler deviated from Freud by using "unconscious" as an adjective but not reifying the construct by using the word as a noun (Mosak, 1979). Similarly, Ellis (1979) suggests that cognitions can be unconscious but that there is no entity called "the unconscious." Rather than unconscious events containing a life and energy of their own, they are simply encodings of information awaiting the illumination of the person's attention. For example, a person may maintain an idealized concept of a parent and may deny any negative feelings or thoughts. A psychodynamic theorist might interpret this situation as a case of repression of unwanted memories into the unconscious. In contrast, a cognitive theorist will attribute the unrealistic concept to the person's level of attention; that is, more frequent and complete attention has been given to the positive information, and attention has been diverted from the negative thoughts and images. With cognitive development an underlying schema stating "I should not think any negative thoughts about my father" can be illuminated.

Phase 2: Assessing Cognitive Systems

We generally have relatively consistent attitudes toward concepts, such as "authority," "counselors," and "art." Our concepts are made up of many individual cognitions that reflect the way in which our experiences have been encoded. Within the concept of "authority," there lie a number of memories, observations, interpretations, conclusions, and expectations. Included are elements of what we have experienced, what our parents and others have told us, and what we have heard, read, and otherwise observed. We organize these elements into a cognitive system dealing with the concept. In general, the individual cognitions within a system reinforce other cognitions in the system and the system as a whole.

Cognitive systems can improve the efficiency with which we predict future events. Making predictions based solely on the individual cognitive elements would be an extremely complex, overwhelming, and time-consuming task. In order to make predictions, judgments, and decisions more quickly, we integrate the elements into an overriding organization. In the process, we may simplify our data and delete or reinterpret events in order to make them congruent with the system.

A cognitive system that is rigid and unidimensional is more likely than a complex system to encounter incoming information that conflicts with it. While a rigid system is more likely to be challenged than a complex one, it is also more likely to resist change, since its elements are more consistently supportive of one position. The dualistic thinking described by Perry (1970) is marked by rigid, simplistic cognitive systems, in which polarities such as good-bad and right-wrong are used extensively. A more complex cognitive system allows finer discriminations to be made about events. "Authority" is not viewed simply as "oppressive and malevolent." A person's cognitive system may take into account a wide range of authority figures and structures; some authorities may be judged as "oppressive and malevolent," but these can be discriminated from others with other qualities. The "authority" system may be divided into a number of subsystems, including "young authorities," "authorities over thirty," "empathic authorities," and "harsh authorities." In more complex cognitive systems, the subsystems are divided into further subsystems. "Female authorities" might then contain subsystems such as "female authorities in large organizations" or "female authorities with families." Typically, general constructs are subdivided into more specific subsystems.

The more complex cognitive systems with many subsystems and qualifiers afford quicker judgments than the method of individual consideration of each element. They do not provide the speed of judgment offered by a unidimensional system; they do, however, provide improved *accuracy of future prediction*. While the major motivation for developing cognitive organization is the speed with which judgments can be made, the motivation for developing complexity is the accuracy of prediction. When encouraging clients to develop more complex systems of thought, it is important for the counselor to recognize that there are both benefits and losses in progressing. A person leaves a simpler assumptive world where quick decisions and judgments can be made to enter one in which greater accuracy of predictions can be achieved, *if* the maze of subsystems can be negotiated.

Three kinds of potential problems with cognitive systems can be identified. First of all, *the system may not have developed a sufficient degree of organization* to enable the person to deal with the demands provided by the environment. A shy male student's system of social expectations might be so diffuse and unorganized that he feels overwhelmed by the social world and does not have an adequate framework for deciding how to act. Further life experiences and productive reflection upon them can, however, lead to increased organization.

A second problem occurs when the *cognitive system is insufficiently complex* to include all relevant experiences. The campus Romeo who sees himself as irresistible to women may experience cognitive dissonance and confusion when he is rejected. The dissonance can promote cognitive growth if he is able to amend his view of himself so as to encompass the new data.

The third potential problem concerns *the flexibility of the system*—how amenable it is to being altered by new information. Some cognitive systems are rigidly maintained, whereas others adapt flexibly to new events. Persons with low self-esteem may adhere rigidly to the notion that others do not respect them, even in the face of evidence to the contrary. Rather than accommodating their systems, they are more likely to discount the evidence.

Counselors must remember that each individual has a unique network of cognitive systems. It is therefore important to identify the most salient systems for a particular student. At the same time, some cognitive systems seem to be operative in all of us and serve as cores for the organization of large numbers of subsystems and cognitions. These are the self system, the world system, the self-in-world system, the self-in-time system, and systems that comprise cognitive skills.

The Self System. One of the first distinctions that infants begin to make is between the "me" and the "not me." From this point in development on, experiences related to the "me" are encoded as cognitions in the self system. The self system is a very large system, composed of a great many memories, images, beliefs, assumptions, expectancies, and attributions. It is also relatively complex, with many subsystems and, often, conflicting cognitions. The related construct of "self-concept" has been discussed by a number of phenomenological theorists, most notably by Rogers (Rogers, 1951, 1959; Meador and Rogers, 1979), Wylie (1968), and Hamachek (1985).

Rogers (1951, 1959) has distinguished between the "perceived self" and the "ideal self." These concepts can be considered subsystems of the cognitive system of self. The "perceived self" subsystem is composed of cognitions reflecting our views of ourselves: "I am angry at my brother." "I get anxious easily." *Insufficient organization* in the "perceived self" subsystem is related to Erikson's (1968) concept of identity diffusion. A person's self-awareness cognitions might not have been organized into a cohesive system allowing clear articulation of identity, including personal values and interests. *Insufficient complexity* in the system implies that a person has encoded a number of self-relevant experiences that have not been integrated into the system. Students who view themselves as people who do not get angry may quickly dismiss self-monitoring cognitions that convey that they are experiencing anger. Such individuals are often described as not "knowing themselves very well." How quickly self-understanding can progress will depend on the *flexibility* of the perceived self subsystem—the degree to which it is amenable to changing in light of new information.

The "ideal self" subsystem consists of self-talk and images of the person we would *like* to be. As Rogers (1959) has noted, the ideal self evolves, and becomes different from the perceived self, in accordance with a child's perception of "conditions of worth"—conditions that must be met if the child is to be valued by one or more significant adults. The adults in question might explicitly define these conditions with direct statements, such as "Stay away from me when you cry like that." Or the conditions can be transmitted behaviorally, when parents or others consistently reinforce certain kinds of behavior and punish or ignore other kinds. The conditions can also be conveyed vicariously, as children hear and see adults expressing or displaying certain value positions. If external love and acceptance are perceived as conditional, the child can come to believe that self-worth depends on meeting these conditions.

The ideal self subsystem contributes greatly to feelings of anxiety, guilt, and depression. Any number of people or societal forces can play a role in the development of this system, including teachers, ministers, friends, siblings, perceived community standards, and models presented in mass media. Not surprisingly, many ideal self cognitions have been learned through interactions with parents. This contribution has been recognized in other theories, including the psychoanalytic concept of "superego," the psychodynamic construct of "parental introject" (Blanck and Blanck, 1972; Kernberg, 1976), and the transaction analysis idea of the "Critical Parent" (Berne, 1961; Dusay and Dusay, 1979).

Deficient *organization* in the ideal self system can lead to various difficulties, including inability to articulate goals. The *complexity* of this system can be deficient if relevant data have not been integrated. For example, children may have incorporated instances when parents were highly critical into their ideal self systems; however, they may not have integrated other pieces of data, when their parents were more forgiving. The *flexibility* of the ideal self system can also be problematic. In entering college students, this system is often resistant to being altered by new experiences. Still in Perry's (1970) dualism stage, they may cling to old perceptions of right and wrong, especially regarding their own conduct.

Cognitions from the ideal self subsystem may be in conflict with ones from the perceived self subsystem. For instance, a young woman who perceives herself to be plump may not conform to her ideal body type. As a number of such incongruencies are perceived, we erect a concept of our overall value or "self-esteem." The degree to which our self-esteem is positive probably depends on three factors: the number of conflicting cognitions involved, the degree of the disparity between perceived and ideal self cognitions, and the importance attributed to the dimensions on which there are differences. In the late adolescent–early adulthood stages, self-esteem issues are common, partly because adult identity is not yet crystallized and autonomy is not yet fully developed. It is therefore important for counselors to note discrepancies between the perceived self and ideal self subsystems of clients.

The World System. Adler envisioned that a person evolves a "picture of the world" in the course of development (Mosak, 1979), and Frank (1961) has referred to our "assumptive world." As already noted, an infant begins to distinguish between the self and the rest of the world. A great many bits of information begin to be encoded as "This exists outside of me." The amount of information about the outside world that enters our nervous systems in a single hour is staggering. We make a great many decisions about what information is relevant or meaningful and what is not. The formation of cognitive systems and subsystems helps us filter and process the massive amounts of information, which would otherwise be overwhelming. Gradually, on the basis of specific experiences, we begin to form generalizations about what can be expected from the world as a whole. Some may view it, for instance, as unfair or cruel; others, as an exciting and bountiful place.

Lack of sufficient *cognitive organization* in the world system can lead to difficulties, in that an individual will not have an adequate map for processing events. When the world system is insufficiently *complex,* the person is unable to make enough meaningful distinctions regarding external reality and may resort to dichotomous and dualistic thinking in classifying external events. When the system contains insufficient *flexibility,* individuals are unable to adapt their cognitive maps to changes in the world. Data about the world are therefore negated or distorted. Tolerance increases as the complexity and flexibility of systems pertaining to people improve. With added complexity, distinctions can be made among those in a social classification, such as a racial group. This more complex system is likely to afford better prediction than ascribing stereotyped qualities to all members of the group.

The Self-in-World System. Just as we develop cognitions pertaining to ourselves and to the world, we also entertain cognitions that encompass the juxtaposition of the two—our perceptions and assumptions regarding our interactions with the world. What is our special place in the world? What roles do we assume? How do we expect others to treat us? As with the other cognitive systems discussed, the self-in-world system can be problematic if it is insufficiently *organized* and provides an inadequate cognitive map of what might happen in our interactions. Insufficient *complexity* of the system, such that it cannot account for important events, can also be problematic, particularly when the system is rigidly maintained.

Kelly's (1955) concept of role is related to the self-in-world system, since it illustrates the interdependence of our cognitions about ourselves with our social experiences. We enter into many roles, including those of child, parent, teacher, student, supervisor, supervisee, spouse, and friend. To some degree, the roles that we maintain are consistent with the ways we conceive of ourselves. However, our ways of viewing ourselves are continually altered by our experiences in the roles we have assumed. For instance, a college student might change his self system as a result of assuming the role of fraternity brother.

Bandura's self-efficacy concept is also related to the self-in-world system. Although Bandura refers to expectancies about specific situations and behaviors, it seems possible that more general expectations regarding one's capacities would be made from these specific expectancies. For example, a female student who has done poorly on several speeches may decide that she is a poor speaker. She may actually be a reasonably accomplished speaker, whose below-par performances resulted from some unusual aspects of the speaking situations. Nevertheless, because of her generalized view of herself as a poor speaker, she probably will feel undue anxiety regarding speaking and therefore will avoid speaking situations. Her overgeneralizations about her speaking abilities also will decrease her confidence and inhibit risk taking.

Finally, Rotter's (1954) notion of locus of control is relevant to a person's self-in-world system. Clients or workshop participants who perceive their locus of control of reinforcement to be external may feel resigned to problematic aspects of their lives and be unmotivated to attempt to make changes. At the other end of the continuum, individuals with an internal locus of control believe that they can extract rewards from the environment through their own efforts. Even though the research with this concept has suggested that a more complex set of variables is involved, it is often helpful for the cognitive counselor to consider the degree of internality of a client's locus of control.

The Self-in-Time System. While we are all capable of focusing attention on the past, present, and future, one kind of focus may predominate—sometimes as part of an individual's overall cognitive style but more frequently in one domain of an individual's experience. Obviously, focusing attention on one time frame to the exclusion of the others can produce difficulties. Sometimes a depressed person will think mostly about the past—about past failures or about how the past was more satisfying than the present. Students experiencing difficulties in adjusting to new situations may also display this excessive focus on the past. For instance, a homesick freshman who has not yet adjusted socially to the new environment might spend a lot of time thinking about the comforts of home and high school. Such an individual may need to learn to refocus attention on present and/or future possibilities.

An excessive focus on the present can lead to a lack of planning as well as to an inability to learn from the past. Some students avoid attending to cognitions regarding the past because these thoughts are painful to them. This denial process makes it difficult for them to deal productively with cognitions that need to be examined. Avoidance of cognitions about the future can be a way of managing anxiety; however, if carried to extreme, this pattern can present a hindrance to planning and preparing oneself for challenges. Career counselors are familiar with the college senior who has treated college as a stay-in-the-present time warp and who has consequently done little reality testing of images of a future career.

A common problem in our society is for individuals to be focused on the future to the exclusion of the present. The Type A personality as described by Friedman and Rosenman (1974) is compulsively busy meeting future deadlines and goals. The future-focused cognitions may contribute to the driven quality that makes such people vulnerable to the negative effects of emotional stress. Future-focused cognitions are often characteristic of the perfectionists described by Barrow and Moore (1983) and Burns (1980a, 1980b); these individuals often magnify the hurdles that loom in the future and ignore the hurdles recently cleared. The results can be anxiety and the inability to feel proud of accomplishments.

As mentioned, in most instances only one domain of

someone's experience is treated with an excessive attention to one of the time dimensions. The homesick freshman may be past focused in the social domain but future and present focused in the academic realm. A person who is extremely future focused and planful in academic and career activities may consider only the present in the social realm. Someone who has lost a loved one may be able to balance past, present, and future cognitive activity in most areas and yet retain a focus centered in the past in regard to cognitive systems where the loved one was included.

Systems for Manipulating Cognitions: Cognitive Skills. A very important kind of cognitive system provides guidance as we manipulate or think about symbols and other cognitive events. We develop cognitive systems about objects in the external world. As our thought systems become more complex, we can entertain increasingly abstract concepts regarding ourselves, the world, and our interactions with it. We also can develop cognitive systems of *processes,* including ways to think through situations or solve problems. Development of these systems gives us the "know-how" or skills necessary for proceeding through complex sequences of steps in processing encoded information. In essence, we form a cognitive map of what to do with data.

One kind of skill system is made up of cognitive coping skills—skills developed to help an individual cope with difficult situations. In effect, mental rules and procedures for processing cues are learned. Another skill system—one that is extremely important for late adolescents and young adults—pertains to solving problems. Many young people are still in the process of developing sound maps for defining problems, generating alternative solutions, analyzing outcomes of possible alternatives, weighing alternatives, deciding on courses of action, making plans for implementing decisions, and evaluating actions. The acquisition of these kinds of cognitive skills parallels cognitive development during university years as described by Perry (1970). As mentioned in Chapter One, both D'Zurilla and Goldfried (1971) and Mahoney (1977) have developed forms of therapy based on helping clients improve in such skills.

In assessing problem-solving skills, we can ask the same

three questions considered in relation to the other systems discussed. Is the problem-solving system sufficiently *organized*? Certainly, many in the adolescent–young adult stages have vaguely defined or poorly organized ideas of how to attack and solve problems. Is the problem-solving system sufficiently *complex*? In these stages individuals often undertake problems with a simplistic cognitive map that does not provide adequate guidance. Is the system sufficiently *flexible*? Someone with a rigid concept of how to manage problems is unlikely to assimilate new ideas on possible ways to proceed. For example, many male college students seem to view personal problem solving as something they should accomplish by themselves and are therefore opposed to exploring solutions by confiding in someone else.

Phase 3: Assessing Cognitive Development

Cognitive development involves acquiring increased complexity in our cognitions and cognitive processes, so that we can quickly make meaningful discriminations regarding ourselves and our world. In order to survive, we must predict the future quickly and accurately. The most adaptive cognitive system is one that is well organized and complex and remains open to new information. Rather than remaining static, the levels of organization and complexity inherent in cognitive systems change, partly due to a developmental process.

Our cognitive processes at infancy are not at all complex. The cognitions are only loosely organized. Initially, we develop some concept of "the me" and "the rest," which enables us to begin extracting what we need from the world. As we continue to develop, we evolve relatively simple concepts for important basic events, such as "food" or "warmth." As our language develops, we begin to attach symbols to more and more of the events in our lives. Luria (1961, 1969) noted the importance of a modeling process in language development, in which a child mimics the verbalizations of a parent or other person. In one stage children are likely to repeat aloud these "adult verbalizations" as they negotiate their world. As they begin to feel ownership of the symbols, the overt verbalizations give way to covert ones.

As we gain competence with greater numbers of symbols, we become better equipped to manipulate these symbols in our heads—projecting them into the future and weighing events, analyzing, synthesizing, and deciding. As we assimilate more information and entertain feedback about the accuracy of our predictions, our cognitive processes become more complex. By the time we reach late adolescence, our thoughts reflect a great deal of complexity. We can generally negotiate the physical world successfully; however, our cognitive systems relating to the social and affective worlds may have attained less sophistication.

Stages of Cognitive Development. Cognitive development is difficult to measure and research. Therefore, our understanding of this area is incomplete. Student development professionals must choose from a number of models, none of which are fully developed or validated. One meaningful framework for attempting to understand late adolescents and young adults is the scheme devised by Perry (1970), discussed briefly in Chapter One. As noted, Perry's original description contained nine positions; however, these have been simplified into four categories. Many undergraduate university students evidence thinking characteristic of the first stage, *dualism*, in which a black-white, dichotomous view of the world is taken. Dualistic individuals tend to look for yes-no, clear-cut answers, cling rigidly to their positions, and find ambiguity difficult to manage. They are also oriented to seeking "truth" and standards of "correctness" from external sources. Many of the irrational beliefs described by Ellis, the cognitive errors outlined by Beck (Beck, Rush, Shaw, and Emery, 1979), and the perfectionistic thinking identified by Barrow and Moore (1983) and Burns (1980a, 1980b) evidence dualistic thinking.

The second stage is that of *multiplicity,* in which individuals discover that there are many truths. They swing from the rigidity of dualism to an almost chaotic state, in which they are confronted with a multitude of possible interpretations about any fact. They are freed from the rigidity of their dualism but have not established an alternative organizational framework for dealing with all the data available to them. They have not yet established criteria by which alternatives can be judged. Students at this stage may sometimes feel overwhelmed by the world and the necessity for decisions: "There are so many possibilities. How can I choose?" These kinds of questions can surface in regard to career planning, relationships, sexuality decisions, and other issues.

In the third stage, *relativism,* the existence of many answers is acknowledged, but more organization to the chaos is provided than in the multiplicity stage. Students in the relativistic stage are better able to identify assumptions, analyze events, evaluate points of view, and consequently make choices, with the assumption that each situation may have its own unique solution. While thinking at this stage is productive in dealing with many external physical and even interpersonal problems, it is insufficient for forming commitments to basic values. The young adult in the relativistic stage may for the first time be troubled by existential questions.

In the fourth stage, *commitment in relativism,* the individual develops personal values and takes moral/ethical positions without denying others the right to form different beliefs. They feel strong commitment to their beliefs, yet they recognize that other truths might exist and are consequently tolerant of others. As students form their identities, including their priorities and beliefs, they are then in a position to commit themselves to value systems, career directions, and relationship decisions. The more complex thinking evident at this stage can encompass the multiplicity of inclinations within the individual. Students are able to accept and establish a balance of polarities within them, such as active versus passive or self-controlled versus impulsive (King, 1978).

As noted in Chapter One, Perry proposed that many entering undergraduates are in the dualistic stage and progress to commitment in relativism by graduation. Development of greater complexity occurs as cognitive dissonance is produced by events that cannot be *assimilated* into their cognitive structures. If sufficient support is available and the challenge is not too great, *accommodation* of the system will occur; thinking will be made more complex in order to incorporate the new information. If insufficient support is available or the challenge is too great, further development might not occur. Perry describes the phenomenon of "retreat," in which an individual regresses to dualistic thinking at a time of intense stress. Further research with Perry's system has supported the sequential nature of the stages; however, students' progression through the stages is more modest than originally envisioned. Rather than evidencing Stage-4 thinking, college seniors usually function in the high "multiplicity" or low "relativistic" stages (King, 1978).

Perry's ideas are presented as one framework for assessing cognitive development. Counselors may choose to apply other concepts in Phase 3. One further comment that should be made about Perry's work is that recent questions have been raised regarding how representative the scheme is, in that the research samples were predominantly composed of males. Gilligan (1982) contends that females reason "in a different voice." Rather than emphasizing laws and principles in their judgments, as do males, they accord greater attention to maintenance and enhancement of relationships. Since a disproportionate number of males have been used in research, the resulting measurement methods have contained a bias in favor of the male approach. The Perry scheme should thus be used flexibly, and student development professionals should be aware of the possibility of divergent reasoning systems favored by males and females.

Developmental Differences for Different Domains of Experience. Cognitive development is likely to be more advanced in one aspect of a person's life than in another. Our social learning experiences and the blend of challenge and support factors are unlikely to be equivalent for different domains. We are likely to have had better models, more nurturance, and more experience for enhancing the complexity of some cognitive systems than others. For instance, some students may have developed at an accelerated pace in the intellectual-academic realm and progressed much more slowly in other areas, such as in emotional awareness and social interaction. This lack of complexity in the social domain may have been less evident in high school, where these students had the support of family members and long-held friends, than in college, where the demands are greater and initial support levels lower. Other students may be advanced in social development and human relationships but have not attained the same level of cognitive sophistication in the academic realm. Such students probably were popular in high school but experience adjustment difficulties on entering college, where more emphasis is placed on their intellectual skills than on their social abilities.

Cognitive development can also be situation specific. Many students use dualistic thinking more extensively when processing information about their families than when others are the subjects. This kind of regression to a less sophisticated form of thinking can also occur with other important people, such as romantic interests and friends.

There seem to be three reasons for levels of cognitive complexity to vary from one domain to another. First, certain cognitive skills may be more relevant to one domain than another. The analytical skills that are adaptive in philosophy class may have little to offer in socializing at a loud party. Second, a person may have learned to apply cognitive skills in one situation and may not yet have learned to use the same skills in other situations. Third, because of emotional interference, the cognitive skills applied in one situation may be more difficult to use in another. Thus, a sophisticated thinker may resort to dichotomous thinking when interacting with a parent.

Relationship Between Psychosocial Development and Cognitive Development. While ego and psychosocial development concepts have somewhat different emphases than cognitive development, improved cognitive functioning is an integral part of progression on Erikson's (1959, 1968) stages and Chickering's (1969) developmental tasks. Widick, Knefelkamp, and Parker (1980) note that intellectual development and identity development represent "two sides of a coin," since one needs sophisticated intellectual skills in order to develop a workable concept of personal identity and commitment. Progression in cognitive complexity is necessary for improved mastery on each of Chickering's tasks: developing competence, managing emotions, developing autonomy, establishing identity, freeing interpersonal relationships, clarifying purpose, and developing integrity. In each of these areas, one must make fine discriminations and complex interpretations of one's own internal processes and events in the external world. For example, developing autonomy involves improved problem-solving and decision-making skills as well as increased differentiation of one's own values and priorities from those advocated by influential others. Establishing identity requires increased complexity within the self system of cognitions.

Assessment of Phases 1-3

Counselors must develop assessment skills that allow them to obtain good information regarding Phases 1, 2, and 3. In cognitive counseling, assessment and intervention are highly related processes. Questions important for the counselor to ask in assessment are likely to stimulate client thought and cognitive development. In fact, self-assessment by the client is often one of the goals of counseling, particularly in developmental counseling. Moreover, since continual monitoring of a client's progress and reactions occurs at Phase 8a, information obtained during the counseling intervention is periodically used to refine and revise conceptualizations.

Collaborative Assessment Versus Private Assessment. Two processes of assessment usually occur simultaneously. The first is a mutual exploration of the client's difficulties and related cognitive systems. In this process the counselor explicitly joins the client as a collaborator in the task of understanding the client. The picture of the client that emerges from this exploration is known to both counselor and client. The second process is undertaken privately by the counselor. The information obtained from the client and observations and inferences made by the counselor contribute to the counselor's cognitive map of the client. This map is consulted at Phases 4, 5, and 6 as the counselor makes decisions about specific questions: What kinds of cognitive development are needed? What methods are likely to help the client move toward the needed development?

How will the client respond to certain intervention approaches? What kinds of approaches will the client perceive as supporting and what as challenging?

Both of these assessment processes are continuing and ongoing. The first continues throughout the counseling, as counselor and client explore important issues. The private assessment processs is often concentrated in the early stages until formulations are constructed, goals are identified, and an overall intervention direction is defined. However, this private process is also ongoing, in that the counselor's tentative hypotheses about the client and the directions chosen for the counseling are continually examined in light of the ways the client responds to what is done.

Assessment Goals. As well as eliciting information about affective and behavioral processes and about environmental situations, cognitive counselors are particularly intent on discovering how cognitive variables enter into clients' problems and personal characteristics. Phase-1 information, cognitive events, can often be elicited directly from clients. As counseling continues, clients often become more sensitive to their ongoing internal dialogues and can contribute more of this information. Phase-1 data are therefore often primarily descriptive of what clients think and visualize. Clients are less likely to directly express Phase-2 (cognitive systems) and Phase-3 (developmental level) information. Awareness of these variables is more likely to occur as the client is helped to integrate cognitive patterns and as the counselor forms inferences about cognitive systems and development. Assessment of Phases 2 and 3 is therefore more inferential than assessment of Phase 1.

Assessment Methods. In the collaborative assessment process, clients develop better-organized and more complex cognitive systems as a result of the self-exploration done with the counselor. Cognitive-focused reflections, summaries, integrations, and questions are the most frequently used methods. (These exploration-facilitating techniques are described in Chapter Four.) Test results also can be incorporated into this collaborative assessment, although tests themselves are used sparingly in cognitive counseling; interview information is often a richer source of information on cognitive variables, except in career counseling, where testing instruments are often helpful in enabling clients to clarify and organize their cognitive systems of themselves so that these "maps" can provide better guidance in career exploration. Other techniques—such as feedback, self-disclosure, interpretation, and confrontation—can be useful when the counselor makes observations or formulates hypotheses that are unknown to the client. The counselor's decision to bring these observations into the discussions will depend on the privately conducted assessment of the degree of challenge appropriate for the client. In the assessment process conducted privately by the counselor, the interview is most often the primary source of information. (The techniques discussed in Chapter Four and the questions listed in Chapter Three can be useful in the course of the interview.)

Ellis's A-B-C system provides an excellent framework for asking questions that help explore the interactive roles of cognitions, actions, and feelings (Ellis and Harper, 1975). At Point A (Activating Event), clients can be asked to describe specific situations that are troubling and to clarify their unwanted affective and behavioral reactions at Point C (Consequent Reactions). Then the counselor helps them carefully explore the intervening cognitive activity occurring at Point B (Beliefs). It is often helpful to list the A-B-C's on a pad as they are identified. In order to help clients discover cognitive patterns that operate beneath awareness, counselors can employ the "vertical arrow" technique (Beck, Rush, Shaw, and Emery, 1979; Burns, 1980a), whereby layers of Point-B cognitions are revealed. When a cognitive pattern is identified, such as "They might notice that I was anxious," the counselor asks what makes that possibility so disturbing. The clients then may discover an underlying cognitive pattern that has been less apparent to them, such as "I need to appear in control to others." Discussion of the A-B-C's during the session can be followed by homework assignments in which clients write down their reactions to difficult situations.

In the process of interviewing the client, the counselor is also sensitive to observable nonverbal cues that provide information beyond what the client has consciously disclosed. Nonverbal behavior that accompanies a verbalization is often a clue to a schema that guides information processing of the topic, particularly when the verbal and nonverbal messages are incongruous. For instance, a client who smiles gamely while describing serious problems may be assuming, "I have such an investment in what you think of me that I need to try to look pleasing even when I am falling apart."

Interview assessment of cognitive events, systems, and developmental levels can often be supplemented by use of homework assignments in which clients monitor cognitive activity. This approach is particularly helpful when problems related to specific situations are addressed, such as evaluative anxiety regarding exams. Beck has also found this approach useful with depressed clients. They are asked to write down "automatic thoughts" together with descriptions of the situations that elicit them (Beck, Rush, Shaw, and Emery, 1979). Ellis often encourages clients to write down irrational beliefs, along with the situations and resulting affective and behavioral consequences. As well as providing cognitive content helpful in assessment, clients' responses to requests to complete homework monitoring assignments can provide additional information on cognitive systems and developmental level.

Interview information about cognitive events, systems, and developmental level can be supplemented in several other ways. Imagery exercises can be based on recent situations that illustrate aspects of clients' problems. Clients can be asked to "run the movie" of a situation in their heads, in order to recapture some of the internal dialogue that occurred (Meichenbaum, 1977). Role playing can be used in the assessment phase with some clients. Client and counselor can enact a typical situation and then explore the cognitive activity that was elicited. Reviewing the role plays on audio- or videotape can sometimes provide additional stimuli that help clients retrieve cognitions; however, it would be unwise to suggest using this method until the client feels relatively comfortable with the counselor. Rather than using role playing, the counselor can sometimes identify a relevant, close-at-hand situation to consider in exploring cognitive activity. For instance, the counseling contact itself or contact with a receptionist regarding the appointment might arouse self-questioning internal dialogue in a client concerned about shyness. It can also be effective to contract with clients to engage in prescribed activities and observe their internal dialogue processes. For instance, a shy student can be asked to offer a greeting to a bank teller during a transaction and to observe cognitive processing before, during, and after the task. Assessment techniques developed for research may be useful to the practicing counselor. Cognitive data have been generated by asking subjects to "think aloud" or list thoughts in problem situations (Blackwell, Galassi, Galassi, and Watson, 1985; Stone, 1980). With more global developmental difficulties, reading assignments can be given—relevant articles, books, novels—and clients can be encouraged to clarify their thoughts about the reading.

Certain assessment instruments can be helpful on occasion to supplement interview information. The Myers-Briggs Type Indicator (Briggs and Myers, 1976), which is sensitive to styles of processing information, is useful in considering how clients will respond to certain approaches and what they will perceive to be challenging and supportive. One scale measures the degree to which subjects use a "sensing" style of absorbing information versus an "intuitive" style. A second scale focuses on preferences for processing information and making judgments. Individuals oriented to a "thinking" style rely on rational, logical reasoning; in contrast, "feeling"-oriented individuals rely on their gut feelings and values in arriving at judgments. A third scale measures the degree to which subjects are "judging," meaning that they prefer a planned, orderly life-style and like to make decisions quickly. Persons oriented toward the other dimension, "perceiving," prefer a spontaneous, unplanned life-style and like to keep decisions open-ended. The other scale on the Myers-Briggs measures introversion-extraversion. An extraverted person may be challenged by being asked to think introspectively and supported by discussions of interpersonal behavior. An introverted person may be supported by a reflective, introspective discussion and challenged by encouragement to "take risks" in interactions with others. The scales are discussed in more detail in Chapter Three, since they can be useful in arriving at formulations of clients' personal characteristics.

Counselors may often choose *not* to administer the Myers-

Briggs but to use the dimensions as a cognitive map for eliciting relevant cognitive information and thinking about clients' cognitive styles. The dimensions can also provide a cognitive framework for clients to use in better understanding their interactions with important individuals. It can help them organize their self-in-world cognitive system in a way that improves their abilities to understand conflicts and other experiences with people, including roommates, friends, parents, and romantic interests.

Another instrument that can be useful in crystallizing and understanding Phase 1–3 variables is the Student Development Task Inventory (Prince, Miller, and Winston, 1974). This inventory is designed to provide indexes of some of Chickering's psychosocial developmental tasks; however, its use may help counselors better understand cognitive development issues related to clients' maturity on the psychosocial dimensions. Discussion of this instrument can help students understand the developmental nature of many of their concerns and appreciate themselves as growing and developing rather than as static individuals. This awareness may enhance the complexity of their self systems of cognitions, alter their self-in-time systems, and allow them to be less critical of themselves.

Another potentially useful instrument is the Role Construct Repertory Test (Kelly, 1955). It provides an interesting way of discovering the constructs used by clients in their interpersonal functioning and would thus help in assessing cognitive systems of self, world, and self-in-world. Subjects select individuals who fill different roles in their lives, examine three of these at a time, and identify constructs that distinguish one of the three from the other two. This proces is continued until all possible groups of three have been examined. Having clients go through this process can be enlightening; however, it is also time consuming. Counselors can often discover clients' important role constructs by simply discussing their interpersonal experiences. The time-consuming testing method would be an approach to consider with clients who find it difficult to remember or disclose cognitive processes related to their daily interactions with important people in their lives. Without using the test, counselors can make use of the basic principles in interviewing clients. I often ask questions along the lines of "What made this experience different from the other ones we have discussed?"

Unfortunately, an easily used instrument for measuring cognitive development has not yet been fully developed. Erwin (1983) has constructed an objectively scored Scale of Intellectual Development; however, it has not yet been well studied. The most frequently used methods require obtaining written or tape-recorded responses from subjects to sample situations and using trained judges to make ratings. Examples include procedures for arriving at ratings of Perry's cognitive development positions (Widick, Knefelkamp, and Parker, 1975) and the related concepts of reflective judgment (Kitchener and King, 1981) and conceptual level (Harvey, Hunt, and Schroeder, 1961). While these instruments do not offer the convenience of objective scoring, counselors might want to use one of them in assessing certain clients. An alternative is to become familiar with one or two of these systems and use the principles and rating criteria in obtaining and evaluating interview data.

Personality assessment instruments can be useful on occasion, in that they may give counselors more insight into cognitive systems and developmental aspects and may stimulate clients to think about, organize, and clarify their cognitive systems of themselves. Examples include the California Psychological Inventory (Gough, 1956) and the Sixteen Personality Factor Questionnaire (Cattell, Eber, and Tatsuoka, 1967). This kind of instrument is most useful in cognitive counseling if the counselor is having difficulty in formulating a picture of a client and determining how counseling approaches would be received. A self-concept instrument, such as the Tennessee Self-Concept Scale (Fitts, 1965), might help counselors tune into cognitive systems of self and self-in-world.

Instruments that are frequently helpful in cognitive counseling are ones designed to measure affective states, such as anxiety or depression. With depressed students, the Beck Depression Inventory (Beck, 1978) is useful, particularly in assessing cognitive dimensions. The Zung Self-Rating Depression Scale (Zung, 1965) is also easy to administer and score. The State-Trait Anxiety Inventory (Spielberger, Gorsuch, and Lushene, 1970) is excellent for general anxiety. Instruments for measuring anxiety and/or skill levels in specific situations, such as social interactions or tests, are discussed in Part Three. These can be useful in gauging the severity of the problem, helping clients and counselors better define the problem, identifying problematic cognitive factors, and indexing changes from pre- to postcounseling.

Summary and Conclusions

The model for counseling and programming with adolescents and young adults that is presented in this chapter represents an integration of some of the concepts discussed in Chapter One, particularly those of social learning and cognitive-behavioral theorists and cognitive development proponents. Obviously, I do not find these concepts contradictory but think that they have different emphases and can therefore complement and enrich one another. Using the Cognitive Intervention Planning Model, counselors can consider a sequence of questions, including the following: What are the important cognitive events and processes in this case? How well organized, complex, and flexible are important systems of cognitions? How developmentally advanced is a student's cognitive functioning? What are appropriate goals for the intervention? How can productive cognitive change and development be fostered? The information-gathering stage of assessment, Phases 1–3, has been described, along with methods used in this assessment. In Chapter Three the culmination of the assessment stage, Phase 4, will be discussed, along with Phase 5, the first step in intervention planning. The model will serve as a basis for the remaining chapters, which focus on interventions for facilitating cognitive development, including individual counseling, group counseling, and outreach educational programming.

THREE

Completing Assessment and Planning the Intervention

Frank is a third-year graduate student who has come to the counseling center at the suggestion of his major professor. He wants help in dealing with the intense anxiety he experiences before and while speaking to groups, including discussions in his seminars. He has become so afraid of such situations that he has begun to avoid them whenever possible. Furthermore, he has developed the irrational fear that, because of his extreme anxiety, he might faint during a talk. He is particularly dreading a presentation that he must make at a national conference when the current semester is over. Although he has never been completely comfortable with public speaking, he thinks that this intense reaction developed after he began his graduate program. Because he was in an accelerated program in high school and graduated early from college, he is two to three years younger than his graduate school peers.

In order to formulate problems and define goals that lead to effective interventions for problems such as Frank's, the counselor must not only review and integrate the already collected data pertaining to Phases 1–3 but also consult a cognitive map of how change can occur. Knowledge of change methods can help counselors formulate problems in ways that can be directly translated into interventions and identify goals that are realistic.

Ways of Creating Cognitive Change

Two major sources of ideas for how cognitive change occurs are particularly useful: those presented by proponents of social learning and cognitive-behavioral approaches and those discussed by cognitive development theorists. A brief introduction to these concepts was provided in Chapter One; here, the discussion will be more complete and detailed.

Social Learning and Cognitive-Behavioral Concepts. One of the most important principles from behavioral and social learning theory is that we can learn from the consequences of our behavior. We are likely to increase the frequency of responses that are followed immediately by the introduction of events shown to be desirable (positive reinforcement) or the removal of undesirable events (negative reinforcement). Likewise, we are likely to decrease the frequency of a response that is followed by the introduction of undesirable or the removal of desirable circumstances (punishment). Cognitions that are coupled with behavioral responses are also likely to be reinforced or punished by the immediate consequences. Children who are repeatedly scolded for playing with their genitals may refrain from this activity and may conclude "I shouldn't even think about such a thing."

Student development professionals need to be aware of the consequences they present to different kinds of student expressions. A counselor's unruffled, accepting style of responding to a client's tentative disclosure of embarrassing material may serve to reinforce continued exploration of this theme. A counselor can also positively reinforce a verbalization that displays growth of cognitive complexity: "I like the fact that you questioned your original either-or way of thinking about that situation." By the same token, a counselor can gently punish clients' destructive cognitions: "There you go, putting yourself down again." Counselors rarely like to think of themselves as using "punishment." Nevertheless, some counselor responses are designed to decrease the frequency of certain behaviors or thoughts and thus fulfill the definition of punishment. To be sure, punishment is rarely sufficient and should be used in a timely way in conjunction with a great deal of positive reinforcement of other responses. If all the counselor in our example did was punish self-putdowns, the student might not develop alternative thought systems.

The behaviorists have been extremely helpful in emphasizing that *immediate* consequences have the greatest effect on behavior. The immediate consequences may also influence cognitions. Students engaged in an internal debate regarding the merits of going for ice cream or beginning study for a test may experience different immediate consequences of these thoughts. The thoughts about going for ice cream are likely to be fueled by very vivid imagery, while rewards for initiating the study may seem vague and distant by comparison. In order to attain long-range goals, we have to learn to make more distant consequences seem graphic and immediate. Mature and complex cognitive processes help us accomplish this task.

Just as cognitions can be conditioned by consequences, they can acquire the powers to reinforce or punish through association with reinforcing and punishing events. The negative self-talk entertained by a child when being spanked by a parent may acquire punishing properties. Self-statements such as "I'm bad" or "I'm dumb" may be used to punish useful initiatives. Covert events, such as imagery and cognitions, can be used to condition responses, as evidenced in the covert conditioning procedures developed by Cautela (1970a, 1970b, 1971).

The principles of behavioral discrimination learning seem particularly important for development of cognitive complexity. Greater cognitive complexity is achieved when one situation is discovered to differ from another in that the same response is met with a different consequence. For instance, as we learn that a raucous joke may be reinforced in a casual social gathering but not in a formal meeting, a cognitive construct allowing discrimination of these situations is developed. Stimulus discrimination learning is a crucial aspect of progression on developmental tasks. We can help students develop cognitive complexity by assisting them to become better observers of what they think and do, what results from their responses, and what situational nuances account for different patterns. We thus help them construct a better differentiated cognitive map of the world and their interactions with it.

Another important concept from social learning theory is that learning often occurs through observation. As Bandura (1969a, 1977b) and others have discussed, we do not have to rely solely on our direct experiences for what we learn. We can observe a friend get scolded by the teacher for talking excessively and recognize that we will suffer the same consequences if we talk too much in class. In other words, we can form an outcome expectancy without directly experiencing that outcome ourselves. Students can learn new cognitions and more complex cognitive processes by observing different kinds of models, including the actions of others, visual media, and even printed materials (books, handouts, and others). In particular, students need to be provided with models of more complex cognitive processes, so that they can develop new cognitive organizations to deal with the challenge of cognitive dissonance. Since student development professionals serve as models for students with whom they interact, they must recognize the importance of displaying flexible, tolerant, and discriminating cognitive processes in their own actions and expressions of thought.

Certain conditions facilitate learning from models. People are more likely to alter their thoughts and behavior in response to models with whom they can identify and whom they respect (Bandura, 1969b; Bandura, Ross, and Ross, 1963; Rosenbaum and Tucker, 1962). Thus, in some cases a forty-year-old professional may be perceived by college freshmen as too far removed from their life circumstances to serve as a meaningful model. Group interventions, use of media portraying students as models, and peer counseling programs are good ways to present models whom students can respect and identify with. The consequences occurring after thoughts or actions by a model are also important (Bandura, 1965; Bandura, 1969b; Liebert and Fernandez, 1970). A subject is likely to adopt the behavior of a model who receives reinforcement and to avoid adopting behavior that is punished. For example, if a participant ventures a comment in a group discussion and is embarrassed by the group leader, other participants will be less likely to risk making disclosures. A modeling videotape that shows a satisfying conclusion to a series of cognitive coping efforts is likely to be more effective than one portraying negative or no consequences.

Observational learning is also dependent on whether a "coping" or a "mastery" model is presented. Particularly when learning to manage stressful situations, people can learn more effectively from a coping model than from one who has mastered the situation from the beginning (Meichenbaum, 1971). A coping model displays initial difficulty in confronting a situation, although the difficulty is eventually overcome. This kind of model may provide easier identification for someone who has not developed the necessary behavioral and cognitive skills. The learning may also be more successful because crucial coping steps are displayed by a coping model and not by a mastery model (Kornhaber and Schroeder, 1975).

Cognitive-behavioral theorists have stressed that cognitive learning can best occur when sequential steps are used. Beck (1976) has identified three steps in learning new cognitive processes: (1) altering "automatic thoughts"—self-verbalizations and images that one is conscious of using; (2) recognizing and altering error-producing cognitive processes, such as dichotomous thinking, arbitrary inference, and overgeneralization; (3) discovering and altering underlying, previously unrecognized "schemas" (basic rules used in encoding and processing incoming information). This kind of sequential system can be extremely helpful in providing the kind of support necessary for cognitive change.

Cognitive Development Concepts. Cognitive development theory complements social learning ideas by suggesting that an individual must be in a state of readiness to progress to a higher level of cognitive complexity. In earlier development, readiness is largely dictated by physical maturation. In the late adolescent and early adulthood stages, physical maturation is less of a factor. However, a person may have to fully "own" processes at one level before being ready to proceed to the next. Perry (1970) has introduced the concept of "temporizing," in which an individual consolidates cognitive functioning in one stage as a prelude to making the qualitative leap to the next stage. Piaget (1964) identified a "readiness phase," in which a person is preparing for the next stage. He also noted a period of shakiness in performing the cognitive operations. This slippage, or "horizontal décalage," occurs after the leap to the next stage as the individual is expanding the situations to which the new skills can be applied.

Student clients frequently go through periods of seemingly circular thinking about new concepts before making a relatively sudden advancement. I can recall a female student who maintained dichotomous thinking about her mother and other significant people for about a year in spite of my best complexity-facilitating efforts. Then, all of a sudden, she became willing and able to recognize that her mother was "not necessarily trying to put me down all the time." This experience helped me appreciate that students may need to feel in command of their present levels of functioning before they are ready to risk a qualitative change.

Another thesis from cognitive development theory is that cognitive development is likely to progress according to a sequence of steps. Students functioning at a dualistic level probably cannot engage in the complex reasoning of the relativistic stage; first, they must be confronted with a variety of different points of view and helped to become more multiplistic.

One of the most important ideas emerging from cognitive development theory is that complex cognitions emerge from cognitive dissonance. Development is fueled by an interaction of the person with the environment. As long as the environment is understandable, predictable, and solvable with our present cognitive structures, we need not examine or change them. In light of this aspect, it can be stagnating for people to spend too much of their time with a homogeneous group of like-minded people. If a sorority or residence hall section is composed of people who think virtually alike, the environment can be navigated without thought systems being challenged. Fortunately or unfortunately, our world is almost infinitely complex. The young woman from the like-minded sorority may find the environment of her philosophy class bewildering. Even within groups of like-minded people, events will occur that cannot be incorporated into a person's cognitive systems. The disequilibrium of cognitive dissonance is then experienced—the uncomfortable sense that the world with which one is interacting is inconsistent with the world as accepted in the mind. Only then are we challenged to examine and perhaps alter our cognitive structures. We can deny the disparate information or distort it so that it can be assimilated. Or, more productively, we can accommodate our system and make it more complex, so that the new information can be incorporated without denial or distortion.

Those of us in helping professions, who like to reduce suffering, sometimes find it difficult to accept the fact that our role at times is to increase discomfort by introducing cognitive dissonance into a student's system. We need to be careful that, in our efforts to be supportive and empathic, we do not provide protection from the complexities of the world. We must, in short, be able to balance the elements of challenge and support —to produce cognitive dissonance at times, but not too much dissonance at the wrong times and under the wrong conditions. The proper ingredients of challenge and support and the kinds of conditions likely to be challenging or supporting will vary with the individual. Some aspects, such as a trusting personal relationship, are probably supportive to almost all people who are free from severe emotional deficiencies. Other conditions will depend on the preferences and cognitive style of the individual. A highly analytical student I counseled found it comfortable to analyze events rationally; however, he was challenged when asked to identify his gut feelings and global impressions. The level of functioning on the Perry scheme also determines whether a person will regard an intervention as supportive or challenging (Widick, Knefelkamp, and Parker, 1975). A dualistic person will be challenged by being asked to detail various interpretations of a situation, whereas a multiplistic person will find this activity relatively supportive. In turn, the multiplistic person is challenged by being asked to analyze a problem, whereas this analytical activity is supportive for a relativistic person.

Phase 4: Formulations of Problem, Client, and Process

All counseling interventions are likely to include some attention to cognitive variables, whether or not the counselor observes them consciously and systematically. However, the degree of attention appropriately directed to cognitions, the kind of cognitive intervention selected, and the ways it is implemented are likely to depend partially on the formulations of the problems, the personal characteristics of the client, and the interaction process between client and counselor. As the Phase-1 data regarding cognitive events are gathered and impressions about Phases 2 and 3 are developed, the individual counselor is continually erecting and revising tentative formulations of the problems, the client's personal characteristics, and the process. At Phase 4 the information about cognitive events, systems, and developmental level is consolidated and the tentative formulations are refined into working models to be used in intervention planning. Naturally, no effective counselor will construct hypotheses that are impervious to new data; therefore, the working models may be refined as new information is learned and clients' reactions are monitored at Phase 8a.

Applying Phase 4 in group counseling and workshop design is similar to its application in individual counseling. In group counseling, formulation of the problem (Phase 4a) and of the person (Phase 4b) takes place for each prospective member, perhaps on a somewhat more limited scale than in individual counseling. Instead of forming a cognitive map of a dyadic encounter at Phase 4c, the group counselor constructs a formulation of the group interactions. In workshop planning, the nature of the target population or audience, rather than that of individual members, is likely to be considered in Phase 4b. It is also necessary to make formulations of the group or audience dynamics once the workshop has begun (Phase 4c). Applications of the intervention-planning model to group counseling and psychoeducational workshops are discussed in depth in Chapters Seven and Eight.)

Phase 4a: Formulating the Problem. Some counselors tend to define a problem solely in terms of affect. Purely affective statements, however, imply little about what can be done to bring about change. Therefore, counselors need to make a cognitive-behavioral-affective formulation of the problem. They also need to identify environmental factors, such as situations that serve as eliciting or discriminative stimuli and interpersonal systemic influences. The following questions can help counselors make this kind of problem formulation:

1. What are the most important cognitive events involved in the problem? The counselor consolidates and organizes the information obtained in Phase 1.

2. What important cognitive systems are involved in the problem; are they problematic in organization, complexity, and/or flexibility? Phase-2 information is consolidated.

3. Is the client's level of cognitive development problematic in overall cognitive processing or in thought related to specific domains? The counselor consolidates Phase-3 information.

4. Do the client's problems entail relatively specific situations and cognitive or behavioral skill deficits, or are more global and pervasive issues of normal development or pathology involved? The answer to this question, which may take several sessions to formulate, will determine whether the counselor proceeds in a problem-focused way, similar to the methods described in Chapter Five, or whether a more exploratory, open-ended approach is taken in the counseling, described in Chapter Four. In Frank's case, specific cognitive and behavioral skill difficulties regarding coping with anxiety in speech situations were present. At the same time, the cognitive pattern related to these skill deficits was also ingrained in broader issues of social development.

5. How do behavioral, cognitive, and affective processes interact in the problem? Behaviorists are probably correct in asserting that almost any psychological problem has important observable behavioral manifestations. For problem specificity,

it is helpful to identify these. Clearly specified behaviors are easily translated into intervention goals. Among others, Goldfried and Davison (1976) have provided an excellent description of how the counselor or therapist can go about eliciting behavioral data. Unlike the strict behaviorist, however, a cognitive counselor is also interested in clearly defining cognitive and affective correlates of problematic behaviors: "How were you feeling when you gave in to your roommate's demands?" "What was going through your mind when you decided to leave the party?" By the same token, affective responses can be more fully understood when information about accompanying behaviors and cognitions is elicited. In a case of severe anxiety, for instance, avoidance and escape behaviors and observable physiological manifestations—such as muscle tension, blanching, and constricted breathing—may be present. Likewise, severe depression often is accompanied by behavioral manifestations, such as social withdrawal and disturbance to appetite, sleep, energy, and sexual responsivity. The kind of cognitive activity accompanying disruptive affect can help one decide whether and how to use cognitive methods. Worries regarding one's performance, the consequences of poor performance, one's adequacy, and one's image in the eyes of others are characteristic of evaluative anxiety (Liebert and Morris, 1967; Wine, 1971). These kinds of worries were operative in Frank's difficulties. Serious depression is generally associated with a depressive cognitive triad, consisting of negative thoughts about the self, world, and future (Beck, Rush, Shaw, and Emery, 1979; Beck and Shaw, 1977).

When a client conveys cognitive information, the counselor can assess its relevance and degree of disruptiveness by learning about related feelings and behaviors. Excessive worry about the outcome of an examination is more problematic if it leads to debilitative anxiety (affect) and/or efforts to avoid the exam (behavior). The presence of these kinds of consequences may indicate that systematic cognitive coping skills training would be indicated.

6. What processes seem to be primarily responsible for the problem? Behavioral, affective, and cognitive processes are equal and interacting aspects of some problems. In such cases,

efforts to intervene in all three aspects might be made. It can also be assumed that a significant change in one domain could lead to changes in the others. In other cases, one of the components seems to be the cornerstone of the problem and should therefore be the primary target of change. A good example is a performance problem, such as taking an exam. It is important for the counselor and client to discuss the cause of undesirable performance (behavior). Perhaps the client lacks the skills necessary for performing well and may not know how to study or to take tests or to speak in public. The intervention of choice in this case would be to help the client learn these skills, probably through modeling, didactic teaching, practice, and reinforcement procedures. Suppose, however, that the client has a relatively high degree of mastery of instrumental performance skills, as did Frank with public speaking? A second possible reason for the inadequate performance would be failure to assimilate the necessary information, a cognitive factor. This failure could in turn be related to an insufficient amount of study time (behavioral) or insufficient motivation (cognitive and affective). If insufficient study time proves to be the problem, the counselor might adopt a cognitive-behavioral approach, focusing on time management; a motivation problem might be approached through developmental counseling, in which needs, priorities, goals, plans, and motivations are clarified.

A third possible reason for the undesirable performance is that the instrumental cognitive and behavioral responses are being blocked by debilitating affective processes. The question that must be answered is "Does anxiety interfere with the client's ability to employ instrumental skills?" It can be helpful to consider whether the client would be able to perform more satisfactorily under other circumstances. For instance, could Frank deliver an effective speech to a trusted friend or by himself? As it turned out, the major contributor to Frank's performance difficulties seemed to be evaluative anxiety. Therefore, cognitive coping skills training to develop increased self-control over these affective processes seemed to be indicated.

7. How aware is the client of cognitive aspects of the problem? The role that cognitions play in the chain of events,

experiences, and responses that constitute the problem needs to be elucidated. Some clients are readily aware of this role, particularly as patterns are explored in assessment. With these clients cognitive processes can quickly and explicitly be explored. On the other hand, Frank experienced his anxiety reactions as "just happening" and insisted that he "was not thinking about or imagining anything particularly." Therefore, the counselor decided to place greater emphasis on open-ended exploration and to use behavioral self-control techniques (relaxation training) in the intervention. As the treatment progressed, Frank began to realize that some assumptions and expectations were operative "in the back of my mind," even though these assumptions did not take the form of conscious self-verbalizations. With this understanding, he became more receptive to the idea that cognitive strategies using the focus of his attention could "short-circuit" the buildup of anxiety.

8. How incapacitating is the problem? The frequency and intensity of the problematic responses must be gauged. Clients who are in crisis states may require an active, structuring role on the part of the counselor. At the same time, they may be unable to maintain sufficient focus on the intervention. If the anxiety or depression experienced is too overwhelming, the client might not be able to concentrate on acquiring new skills. In such cases a period of crisis intervention might be required, in which the client is helped to mobilize already existing resources and effect changes in environmental circumstances. Rather than learning new cognitive skills, such clients may need help in applying the skills they have already developed. An example is a student who came to me requesting a structured approach aimed at learning stress management techniques. After about a week, he became extremely panicky about his academic situation. It became necessary for us to pull back from the cognitive coping skills training and shift to a very supportive approach focusing on structuring strategies for addressing daily problems.

9. What are the situational determinants of the problematic responses? Where, when, with whom, and under what circumstances do problems occur? The exploration of these questions is valuable as treatment because the exploration helps cli-

ents become aware of external "triggers" of problematic responses. These can serve as cues to the client to initiate cognitive strategies for coping with the situations. Answers to these questions also help in deciding what kind of cognitive counseling intervention to use and how to apply it. If the unwanted responses are restricted to a very specific set of situations, cognitive coping skills procedures that closely follow a systematic desensitization model—where the client is confronted with gradually more challenging aspects of a single theme—may be indicated. On the other hand, if difficulty is experienced in a broader range of situations, training procedures that focus more generally on the application of coping skills are advised. Still, if the range of situations is especially wide—for instance, if a person becomes unduly anxious in a large number of different situations—the problematic cognitions might be quite pervasive and deeply rooted in basic cognitive systems. A problem-focused approach, such as coping skills training, may not be effective in this case. Instead, or in addition, awareness clarification and supportive therapy are likely to be required. Therefore, the counseling methods characteristic of developmental counseling, described in Chapter Four, and experiential cognitive dissonance counseling, described in Chapter Six, probably will prove helpful.

10. How unusual and compelling are the situational determinants? If a client's problematic feelings are brought about by some unusual and powerful events, self-exploration cognitive counseling may not be indicated; a more productive direction might be to help the client effect a change in the circumstances. For instance, if Frank's anxiety had been elicited by the behavior of several sarcastic students in a seminar, helping him develop ways of dealing with them would be a more productive course than coping skills training. In some overwhelming situations, however, counseling can be directed toward integrating a new experience into important cognitive systems, so that the client can cope more successfully. For example, a student whose depression was precipitated by the death of a close family member might receive benefit from counseling that facilitates productive grieving.

11. What environmental circumstances (consequences) af-

fect the maintenance of the problem and how strong is their influence? The consequences of responses can have a subtle but profound impact on the continuation of a problem and its resistance to change. Efforts to cope with the problem or to change patterns may meet with punishment and be rendered less likely to persist. The punishment can be self-administered internally, as when negative affect results from cognitive processing of a response. For instance, a client's action of visiting a counseling service may be punished by feelings of embarrassment or anxiety elicited by negative perceptions of talking with a counselor. Punishment can also occur externally. In the previous example, the student might be teased by a roommate for "seeing a shrink" and therefore be less likely to follow through with further appointments.

Problematic responses may be reinforced and made more persistent when they bring about desired consequences. For instance, what if a student secretly dislikes college and wants to leave but is unable to confront her parents with this preference? Poor academic performance could conceivably lead to desirable consequences, in that she might be able to leave school without overtly going against her parents' wishes. This reinforcing contingency might seriously undermine her motivation to learn coping skills.

In addition to identifying punishers and reinforcers, counselors must pay attention to the pattern in which the punishment or reinforcement occurs. It is well known that a "variable ratio" schedule of reinforcement—when the reinforcer is gained in an unpredictable way—produces learning that strongly resists extinction. Problems learned according to this schedule will prove very stubborn in counseling.

In analyzing important consequent events, a counselor using a cognitive approach would be interested in a greater range of reinforcers and punishers than the strict behaviorist. Whereas the behaviorist would focus on observable, externally presented conditions, the cognitive counselor would also inquire into the presence of internal events. Cognitions can be important reinforcers or punishers. The internal dialogue of depressed patients, for instance, often includes minimal amounts of self-reinforcement and a great deal of self-punishment—contingencies that can lead to withdrawal and passivity (Beck, Rush, Shaw, and Emery, 1979). Affective processes can also serve as reinforcers or punishers. The panic that Frank experienced when he attempted to express ideas to a group served as a punisher of that behavior and made him less likely to "stick his neck out." The pleasurable feelings associated with self-control and mastery of tasks serve to reinforce productive coping behavior, as taught in cognitive coping skills training.

Affective processes can also bring about negative reinforcement, in which a response is followed and thereby encouraged by the cessation of something that is aversive. One student whom I recently counseled had great anxiety regarding academic performance. His anxiety was lowered when he was able to involve himself in something nonacademic. Therefore, avoidance of and escape from his studying seemed to be negatively reinforced by the lowering of this aversive internal stimulus. The counseling was therefore directed at altering the perfectionistic cognitions that resulted in the performance anxiety.

12. To what degree are the problematic responses related to roles that the client fills in important interpersonal systems? Certain thoughts, behaviors, and feelings are integral parts of a role that an individual plays within an interpersonal system, such as a family, a peer group, or a romantic dyad. Since the responses of the members of such a system tend to be interdependent, an alteration in one person's behavior will produce imbalance in the system and require either a realignment of the system or restoration of the individual's behavior to its original form. For this reason, other parties in a system can exert pressure for the status quo in the form of subtly reinforcing the problematic responses and punishing efforts to change. When a client's problem is imbedded in such a system, the counselor can anticipate resistance and may want to prepare the client to cope with the system's influence.

The cognitive counselor must also remember that an interpersonal system can exist on a cognitive level even when it is no longer operational in fact. Cognitive systems instilled by our families of origin often remain with us throughout our lives.

Anxiety- and depression-stimulating thought patterns engendered by parental expectations may outsurvive the parents themselves. For instance, the cognitive aspects of Frank's speech anxiety were related to his role as the eldest child and "academic achiever" in his family. This role seemed to exist in juxtaposition to two siblings, who filled other niches in the family patterns. Frank continued to experience the burden of this role, even though he had not lived with his family for several years. In conducting cognitive coping skills training with him, I was aware that implementation of these coping strategies challenged family-reinforced concepts and required an implicit reevaluation of his perceived role in the family.

13. What important historical influences contributed to the development of the problem? Identifying past events is not as much a part of cognitive methods as of psychodynamic approaches; however, assessing the nature and degree of influence of certain kinds of past experiences can be helpful. One important kind of historical influence is traumatic experience, in which debilitating emotions such as anxiety become conditioned to certain situations. For instance, early interactions with a highly critical parent can lead to anxiety in performance situations. This kind of conditioning seems to have occurred in the case of Frank's public-speaking anxiety. A second kind of influence is observational learning, in which the client has assimilated cognitive and affective responses and adopted behavior patterns observed in important models.

Knowledge of relevant historical factors may help the counselor assess how deeply ingrained cognitive patterns are and therefore how intensive the counseling intervention will have to be. With this understanding, realistic goals can be formulated. Awareness of these historical factors can also facilitate the course of cognitive interventions by increasing clients' understanding of themselves and their problems. This improved self-understanding enhances their sense of control over their lives and motivates them to proceed with the intervention. Awareness of historical elements may also provide fodder for imagery exercises used to explore self-views and problems and to shape coping skills. Imagery exercises incorporating past traumatic events or models may provide more powerful stimuli than ones dealing only with present situations.

Phase 4b: Exploring Clients' Personal Characteristics. A number of aspects of clients' development and self-views and world views can affect the likelihood of success of any therapeutic approach. The following questions are important to consider in arriving at a formulation of a client's personal characteristics:

1. How do important cognitive systems that constitute clients' self-views and world views influence their receptivity to change? Counselors should try to determine how changeable their clients' important cognitive systems are. Obviously, students who believe that they must maintain their self-images at all costs will require longer and more intensive interventions in order for change to be effected. It may also be necessary to set more limited goals with such students. One dimension of the cognitive system of self-in-world that is relevant to the conduct of cognitive counseling, particularly coping skills training, is Rotter's (1966) concept of perceived locus of control of reinforcement. The degree to which clients assume that they can control much of what happens to them is an important factor that can affect a number of aspects of counseling, including client motivation. Counselors would be ill advised to launch into direct cognitive skills training with clients who believe that "It does not matter much what I do to try to improve my life." These basic self-in-world beliefs may need to be identified, discussed, and perhaps challenged before coping skills training is undertaken. If unyielding, this belief system might have to be approached with some of the experiential cognitive dissonance techniques that work indirectly toward change. On the other hand, perceived locus of control can be changed in the course of effective counseling, including cognitive skills training. The experience of attaining more self-control over one important aspect of one's life may challenge the generalized construct that one is relatively powerless and thereby may produce cognitive dissonance. The counselor can be conscious of nurturing a favorable assimilation of the new information or resolution of the dissonance. With Frank, I repeatedly made clarifications and

summarizations that integrated evidence of enhanced self-control. Ordinarily, assessment of this dimension via interview is sufficient; however, Rotter (1966) has constructed a scale for measurement of perceived locus of control of reinforcement.

2. How does the client's cognitive development level, either in overall functioning or in thinking regarding specific domains, influence receptivity to change? The cognitive counselor should keep in mind that problematic cognitions may reflect the client's cognitive development. Perry's (1970) model, described in Chapter Two, can be useful. Dualistic thinking is almost always inherent in the negative self-talk that produces undue levels of anxiety and depression. Frank tended to view his speeches according to a rigid success-or-failure dichotomy, which severely restricted the degree to which he was likely to gain in confidence from his experiences.

With some clients the dualistic thinking may be largely confined to one kind of emotionally charged situation. In such cases the gaining of cognitive skills can probably proceed relatively rapidly and may constitute sufficient intervention. The client can quickly learn to apply more complex thinking patterns used in other situations to the troublesome events. Frank's dualistic thinking was somewhat more pervasive, in that it entered into his thinking about a range of interpersonal and performance situations. Thus, the coping skills training was conducted slowly, and exploratory counseling was included in the intervention. In other instances the dualistic thinking is a generalized, pervasive quality that is manifested in almost all aspects of a person's life. The cognitive pattern characteristic of depression is often applied in almost all areas of endeavor. Coping skills training is not necessarily contraindicated when dualistic thinking is widely applied; however, counselors and clients should be prepared to make greater time commitments, since the complex cognitive responses have to be learned rather than simply transferred from other situations. Also, more emotional support and attention to a greater variety of situations are likely to be required. Beck's carefully structured program for depressed patients illustrates the need for carefully sequenced training.

3. To what degree has the client mastered important developmental tasks of young adulthood? Chickering's (1969) description of tasks provides a useful framework. The degree of development on some of the vectors can influence the degree to which the counselor encourages self-awareness exploration and the pacing of problem-focused techniques, such as cognitive coping skills training. In the assessment phase with Frank, "becoming autonomous" was identified as a developmental issue related to his public-speaking anxiety. Insufficiently developed autonomy was partially manifested in his overreliance on others' evaluations of him and his performance. Because he needed to master this developmental task, the coping skills training was conducted slowly, and a considerable amount of open-ended discussion time was included in the sessions. In addition to the structured training, such aspects as his relationships with his father and extended family and his dating and social experiences were discussed. While formal measurement of developmental tasks is often unnecessary in counseling, the Student Developmental Task Inventory (Prince, Miller, and Winston, 1974) can be used.

4. What is the client's cognitive style, and how might it affect receptivity to different cognitive counseling interventions? A number of ways have been conceived for considering stylistic differences in how individuals process information. While I rarely administer the Myers-Briggs Type Indicator (described in Chapter Two) in assessment (Briggs and Myers, 1976), I often use its dimensions as a frame of reference. Clients oriented toward a "sensing" style of information assimilation attend to objective facts and probably are well equipped to attend to specific situational elements and sensations important in the first stage of coping skills training. However, if they are deficient in the other pole of this scale, "intuiting," they may find it difficult to make inferences about the underlying meaning system—a task that is important later in the treatment.

Clients strong in the "thinking" mode are often attracted to coping skills training because it seems rational, analytical, and systematic. Frank was highly thinking oriented and responded well to the training from the outset. Clients who are deficient in the thinking mode and are "feeling" oriented in making their judgments may be less attracted to the techniques. Nonetheless, coping skills training is often advisable with "feeling" types, although the training may have to be paced more gradually and the counselor may need to make sure that a particularly warm, supportive relationship is maintained. Such clients are more likely to need to know that their counselor cares about them. They may also need to explore and express their feelings in some depth before being ready to link them to cognitions and undertake structured, systematic training.

Clients with "perceiving" styles may be reluctant to commit themselves to specific goals and a planned, orderly process. Counselors might have to be particularly diligent and creative in such aspects as keeping the client from wandering unproductively in the sessions and gaining compliance with homework assignments. On the other hand, clients who are excessively "judging" are often impatient with any type of counseling or psychotherapy, including coping skills training. They can expect too much too quickly and become disenchanted.

5. How can the client's cognitive system for solving personal problems be characterized, and how might this orientation influence receptivity to various cognitive counseling directions? Counselors should attempt to tune into clients' cognitive sets regarding how personal problems should be solved. Some clients are likely to attack personal problems by exploring and clarifying their reactions and experiences and are therefore "made to order" for exploratory, developmental counseling. Clients who are drawn to systematic problem solving are likely to be attracted to more structured cognitive skills training. However, D'Zurilla and Goldfried (1971) summarize some problem-solving tendencies that can undermine this kind of counseling approach. Some people, classified as problem avoiders, can tolerate long periods of having their heads in the sand, hoping that the problem will disappear. They may feel threatened by coping skills training, which requires directly acknowledging and challenging a problem. Developmental, exploratory counseling that is highly empathic may enable such clients gradually to acknowledge and then confront the problem. Other people are im-

pulsive deciders who will arrive at premature decisions without really grappling with the issues. Clients with this kind of problem-solving set may be more inclined to latch onto a series of superficial and inadequate solutions than to commit themselves to either in-depth exploration or an ongoing sequence of coping skills training. Other problem-solving styles might make it difficult for clients to embrace particular methods. Those who prefer to make decisions purely intuitively and those who seek solutions from external sources may not be receptive to structured cognitive skills building.

6. What characteristic defenses does the client use, and how might these defenses influence receptivity to different cognitive counseling strategies? Clients' defenses are dictated by schemas that control the processing of information regarding situations or feelings. Clients who characteristically repress feelings and conflicts are likely to conclude prematurely that they have mastered their difficulties. These clients may also be more resistant to the counselor's probes to discover the substrate meaning system beneath the surface cognitions, particularly if these systems are related to painful experiences. On the other hand, clients who are oversensitized to their feelings are likely to overreact to their life circumstances. Counselors may feel that they are constantly attending to series of isolated crises rather than focusing on an important theme. Such clients may greatly need cognitive coping skills training; however, because of their inability to focus on the necessary training, it is likely to take longer. Also, the counselor may need to structure a counseling format that allows for at least some attention to coping skills after the flames from the latest crisis have been dampened. For instance, the counselor might suggest a contract of preserving at least the last fifteen minutes of the session for this purpose.

Clients with rigid obsessive-compulsive defenses also present interesting problems for the counselor using cognitive methods. Some would argue that a cognitive approach is inappropriate for these clients, because it "plays into" the defensive structure and enables the client to avoid changing. I disagree with this position and think that it is generally unrealistic to expect such clients to abandon these defenses. "Hot" cognitions—ones that have emotional impact—can be pursued and discussed in developmental counseling. Through flexible cognitive coping skills training, the client's perfectionistic cognitive system can be redirected into a perhaps still obsessive but more effective coping system. To be sure, the counselor must work hard in encouraging adequate attention to internal sensations and affective cues. In effective cognitive coping skills training, clients must allow themselves to experience both the cognitive events and the accompanying affect. It can also be difficult to help such clients discover the assumptions that underlie their surface thoughts about troubling situations. The obsessive-compulsive client, with an intellectualized, overly rational style, may be unable to recognize irrational elements that fuel unproductive emotional responses. For this reason, the counseling may require more time than with other clients, particularly in the later stages.

7. How accurate are the client's reality-processing abilities? Clients whose perception of events is grossly distorted—sometimes to the point of hallucinations and delusions—will probably require treatment other than counseling and psychotherapy in order to gain control. Cognitive interventions with such individuals can probably be best directed toward thought processes in immediate problem solving and coping. A great deal of structure is ordinarily required, as opposed to open-ended self-exploration. Clients who show scattered, disordered thought processes are also likely to respond best to a structured cognitive approach focusing on problem solving. Self-awareness counseling or coping skills training can probably best be introduced with such clients after these processes have been stabilized through pharmacological or other methods. Meichenbaum and Cameron (1973) have used a form of coping self-talk training with schizophrenics, to help them ground their thinking more fully in reality.

8. What are the client's resources for focusing attention on the counseling intervention? Some clients may experience considerable stress or anxiety; yet their levels of generalized emotion and agitation may be so high that they cannot main-

tain a focus on skills building. Because they feel overwhelmed by a number of troubling situations, their minds may spin from one aspect to another. With such clients a period of crisis intervention counseling, in which one or more of the environmental stressors are removed or altered, is often necessary before unstructured exploration can be undertaken or cognitive coping skills developed. For instance, a recent client was experiencing a great deal of stress and expressed interest in structured stress management training. However, he was preoccupied with several converging themes, including indecision regarding his educational plans, unresolved feelings of resentment toward his father, confusion regarding his role in his family, feelings of isolation in the university community, and poor academic performance. His preoccupation and confusion were such that he was unable to settle on the training. It became necessary to work out intermediate steps to simplify his environment, including a reduction in his academic load.

9. What are the client's expectations of counseling or therapy, and how might these influence the effectiveness of various cognitive approaches? Lazarus (1971) has noted that the therapeutic approach must be adapted, at least to some degree, to what the client initially expects. Some clients enter counseling with a diffuse or flexible set of expectations and are likely to be reasonably receptive to any well-founded approach, provided they receive appropriate orientation and education from the counselor. The expectations of some are made to order for exploratory developmental counseling—a fortunate occurrence if their problems can be resolved with this method. Others may have expectations compatible with a more structured cognitive skills training, which can be paraphrased "I don't expect any magic, but I thought our talking might help me learn to cope more successfully with ____ situations and ____ feelings." The set of expectations held by still other clients may be inconsistent with exploratory developmental counseling or cognitive coping skills training or, for that matter, with any responsible counseling approach. One example is the "all I want is a caring sounding board" set. Some clients expect the counselor simply to listen and offer sympathy, and they perceive efforts to struc-

ture the counseling as indications of disapproval or judgment. Reflective listening is often the best initial approach, with more active methods being introduced gradually. Experiential cognitive dissonance techniques to circumvent resistance may be useful. Coping skills training may still be an option with some of these clients; however, a listening-reflecting stance may be necessary at first. The counselor may be able to plant seeds that cognitive coping skills training would be helpful by making such reflections as "It sounds as though you are feeling frustrated because you are unable to control yourself when you get anxious."

Another potentially problematic set of expectations is the "anything less than in-depth analysis is superficial" belief. Since Freudian psychology has been so widely promoted in literature and media, many people have the expectation that therapy will involve a couch or, at the very least, free association, dream analysis, and the uncovering of deeply hidden secrets. Rather than butting heads directly with this belief system, the counselor can begin with an exploratory, historical approach and then branch into other areas of exploration. If coping skills training appears to be the most productive intervention, the counselor can attempt to lead the client toward a more problem-focused stance: "We've discovered that from quite early in your life you have felt very frightened of your father, because he was such a powerful, critical figure, and that you still carry around a lot of the 'recordings' you learned from him. In a sense, you absorbed this very critical streak and have made it a part of you, so much so that you are overly fearful of putting yourself on the line in a test. The fact that you now realize this should help you in your academic work; however, learning ways of coping directly with the self-criticism and anxiety can sometimes be helpful. We could also do some of this kind of work in our sessions." If the client is not attracted to this additional direction, the counselor can continue the historically focused work, if appropriate, or begin a referral process. Again, experiential cognitive dissonance methods might help in widening the latitude that the counselor has.

A third example of difficult expectations is the "I don't want drugs but give me a pill" set. Some clients believe that the counselor should be able to bestow immediate relief, without the client's having to exert much effort. Obviously, any counseling approach requires work on the part of the client. Some clients with this orientation are impatient with exploratory counseling, even if it is relevant to their concerns. They may be initially attracted to cognitive skills training, perceiving it as a "solution package." Unfortunately, if they are not helped to make this set of expectations more complex, they will quickly become disenchanted with skills training, which requires practice and, often, homework. Counselors can combat these expectations by providing education on the nature of counseling and offering positive reinforcement for instances of client initiative.

10. How motivated is the client and for what kinds of counseling activities? Since coping skills training requires homework, commitment to specific strategies, and follow-through on the part of the client, a relatively high degree of motivation to commit time and energy is required. Clients' perceived reasons for changing may have to outweigh their reasons for not changing. Clients likely to attend only one or two sessions and unlikely to comply with suggestions regarding practice may not benefit from this method and might get more out of a here-and-now self-awareness focus. On the other hand, there are clients who are motivated to commit time and energy to the treatment but not to risk personal self-disclosure or examination of painful thoughts and feelings. Such clients might be willing to submit to structured skills training but may resist exploratory developmental counseling.

11. What internal "reasons" not to change does the client have? (This concept of reasons not to change was first expressed to me in conversation with Raymond Bergner of Illinois State University.) Counselors must assess whether the client's motivation is affected by the presence of secondary gains. Questions 8 and 9 under "Formulating the Problem" focus on external reasons for the client *not* to change. The status quo might be reinforced by external circumstances, or other individuals within an interpersonal system may exert influence on the client to remain unchanged. In addition, a client may harbor internal reasons for not changing—reasons that the client usually is

not aware of. One client, a test-anxious student, was embroiled in a covert control struggle with his domineering mother. He did not want to be in the engineering curriculum or the ROTC program; however, he had not developed sufficient independence to go against the family script. He therefore had something to gain by demonstrating through poor grades that these programs were not for him. Understandably, he felt ambivalent about learning to control his stress and thereby improving his academic performance. Rather than dealing extensively with the test anxiety, his counseling centered on his sense of independence, his relationships with his parents, and his life planning.

Clients may have unrecognized underlying assumptions that influence them to avoid certain changes. A male student may consciously want to engage in more self-disclosure with his girl friend; however, this kind of activity may be discouraged by a schema that identifies such activity as "unmanly."

Phase 4c: Considering the Interaction Process. In individual counseling, the counselor must also form a cognitive map, which is ever changing, of the interaction process occurring in the client-counselor dyad. From the beginning of the first session, the counselor monitors the rapport established, the client's responses to counselor initiatives, and the counselor's reactions to the client's presentation and behavior. The overall openness of communication is important to monitor. Does the client seem to withhold information? Is communication more open with certain topics than with others? How comfortable and/or warm are exchanges between counselor and client? Does the client display resistance or defensiveness? Is this a general reaction or a reaction that is more specific to certain topics or counselor initiatives? How compliant is the client when offered suggestions and interpretations or asked to do homework? How does the client react nonverbally to counselor responses? Are nonverbal reactions congruent with verbal responses? The nature of the counselor-client dyadic process will influence the initial goals identified for counseling and the intervention planning. At Phase 8a the counselor monitors information about the process and may use this information to revise the Phase-4c formulation, make specific intervention decisions, alter goals, or revise global intervention strategy.

Phase 5: Identifying Goals

In order to develop a good intervention plan, complete with overall strategies and techniques, the counselor and client must decide on goals for the counseling. Well-formulated goals provide direction for the counseling and serve as valuable reference points for gauging progress. However, unrealistic, vague, or otherwise misguided goals are not helpful at all and may offer only the illusion of direction.

In order to be effective, goal setting must evolve directly from the formulations of problem, person, and process at Phase 4. Clearly, the nature of the problem will directly affect the goals negotiated. Also, different goals are sometimes appropriate for two clients with the same problem but different personal characteristics. With Frank, who was open to self-exploration and was psychologically minded, a goal of increasing self-awareness of developmental issues was identified in addition to goals of learning to use coping skills. For other clients with public-speaking anxiety, those whose thinking is more dualistic or who are resistant to exploring feelings, the coping skills goal might be the only one identified, particularly if time is limited. Thus, in identifying goals counselors should keep Phase-4 formulations firmly in mind.

Outcome Goals. Outcome goals (Phase 5a) focus on changes that clients desire in their perceived problems and can include alterations in thoughts, feelings, or behaviors in relation to themselves, others, or important aspects of the world. A client entering counseling has generally made a decision that a "problem" is unacceptable and that counseling has potential as a method of solving the problem. Often, precipitating circumstances have altered the client's perception of the problem and/or of its acceptability. The "problem" can be relatively specific, such as an inability to study effectively or to decide on a major. Or it can be diffuse and difficult to identify. Some clients may feel "depressed all the time" or may experience vague dissatisfaction. For the client, the initial outcome goals involve solution or reduction of the problem, however it is experienced. The counselor may find that the outcome goals as identified by the client are realistic and sufficiently comprehensive or may find it necessary to reframe the client's goals.

Counselors will be in a better position to help clients if they consider the role of cognition in the particular outcome goals identified. Improved self-understanding, for instance, is often one of the goals in developmental counseling. It is hoped that the counseling will help clients improve their cognitive maps of themselves. Increased cognitive complexity may be needed, so that the client is able to improve the number and accuracy of discriminations regarding internal processes. A student may thus become able to separate feelings of anger from those of depression. Or cognitions related to the self system may need to become more meaningfully organized, as when a student's rather diffuse concept of identity begins to be crystallized. Or perhaps a rigid self system, characterized by dualistic cognitive processes, needs to become more flexible and open to new information.

In addition to improved self-understanding, the outcome goals may include development of a better understanding of the problem, its context, and its resolution. In order to meet this goal, cognitive development may be required in the self system and/or the world system. Since most psychological problems involve the interactions of an individual with others, an improved cognitive map of self-in-world is particularly important. Improved complexity may be needed to enable a client to make finer discriminations regarding interactions. Improved organization of this system may also be needed. A shy male may have a number of different impressions about how one is supposed to act in the social world; however, he might not have organized these into a cohesive map that provides effective guidance. The flexibility of the self-in-world system may also be targeted. The same student may benefit by reopening his thinking on the question of whether the male should always be the initiator in a relationship with a female. Clients may need to develop self-efficacy expectancies—that is, the confidence that they can perform certain actions required in solving their problems. They may also need to enhance their overall sense of control in the world and become more internal in their perceived locus of control of reinforcement.

Progression in one or more of the developmental tasks of

young adulthood, such as those identified by Chickering (1969), is often a goal of exploratory counseling. As noted in Chapter Two, increased maturity on these tasks is at least partially achieved through improved cognitive complexity. In order to help students progress in developmental tasks such as autonomy and identity, the counselor should consider the kind of cognitive development necessary for achieving progress and should set cognitive goals. One of Frank's goals was to become more autonomous. To achieve this goal, he needed to differentiate his cognitive systems of self and self-in-world from those he perceived to be held by family members.

Another goal sometimes associated with counseling is for clients to become better problem solvers. An improved cognitive map for solving problems most often develops indirectly, as clients make generalizations from the specific problems discussed. Often, the skills are learned through observation, as the counselor's approach is used as a model for how to explore and think through personal problems. Sometimes, however, a more direct, structured approach is used (D'Zurilla and Goldfried, 1971). It can be useful to identify the degree to which the problem-solving cognitive system must become more complex, organized, or flexible.

When the client's problem is formulated as an inability to control emotional processes in certain situations, a goal of developing the client's cognitive system of coping skills is identified. Again, the counselor may want to consider whether clients' coping systems need to become more complex, better organized, or more flexible.

Process Goals. Process goals (Phase 5b) refer to changes that are desired in the interaction itself, including alterations in how client and counselor think about, feel about, and act toward one another. Establishing "trustworthiness" in the client's eyes (Strong, 1968) is often an important process goal of the counselor. Achieving this goal contributes to attaining other process goals, including increasing the client's self-exploration and self-disclosure. If these process goals can be met, it is assumed that clients will be more likely to meet outcome goals. Counselors can better articulate these process goals by determining the cognitive changes involved. In order for the client-counselor relationship to be strengthened, clients must become familiar and comfortable with the *roles* of client and counselor. Many students enter counseling with vague or erroneous expectations of how they and their counselors are to act in counseling. Counseling is "unwalked ground," and they have no cognitive map for what is to occur. In order for trust in the counselor to develop, clients must come to construe the counselor as a trustworthy individual. This conception requires their developing sufficient cognitive complexity to discriminate the counselor and counseling situation from other individuals and situations in which the same level of trust would be unwise. Clients may also need to acquire outcome expectancies that the counselor will respond to self-disclosures with acceptance and will not betray confidences.

In order to develop trust and engage in increased self-exploration, clients may have to encounter cognitive dissonance and enhance the complexity of certain cognitive systems so that the dissonance can be reduced. One form of dissonance occurs when the counselor differs from the client's previous expectations. For instance, the counselor may not conform to the client's stereotyped image of "shrink" or may be older, younger, more formal, or less formal than the client had expected. Cognitive dissonance can also be produced for clients by inconsistency between cognitions in their self systems and the act of entering counseling. Many students, often males, believe that they should solve their problems on their own and that "Real men would eat quiche long before they would go see a counselor!" Such students can use counseling productively only if their cognitive dissonance is resolved. Since time may be required for the dissonance to be resolved, the process goals may develop slowly with some clients. Counselors can help in this adjustment phase if they recognize the occurrence of the cognitive dissonance phenomenon and provide the support necessary for its successful resolution.

Counseling directed at the learning of specific cognitive skills can best proceed if the client perceives the counselor as ranking high on Strong's (1968) expertness dimension—as someone who is knowledgeable about problematic processes and techniques for overcoming them. Counselors may also hope to establish themselves as relevant models of coping skills and cognitive processes and as creditable teachers.

When formulations of clients' personal characteristics suggest that they may be resistant or that verbal channels may not mediate the difficulties, counselors' process goals may be somewhat different from those already discussed. Counselors may still be interested in establishing the expertness perception; however, less attention may be directed to building an image as warm and accepting in clients' views. With some quite resistant clients, it may even be necessary to work toward a process goal of "keeping them guessing" about directions and methods. This idea will be developed further in Chapter Six.

Terminal and Intermediate Outcome Goals. In some cases, particularly when it is appropriate to focus directly on a relatively clearly defined set of problems, two sets of outcome goals—terminal and intermediate (Mager, 1962)—should be identified at Phase 5a. *Terminal* goals are the client's major outcome goals. Frank wanted to be able to speak more spontaneously, fluidly, and effectively in group communication and public-speaking situations. *Intermediate* goals are the goals that must be achieved before terminal goals can be met. For instance, an important intermediate goal in cognitive coping skills training is to increase clients' control of unwanted affective processes that interfere with their attainment of the terminal goals. Frank needed to develop skills for controlling anxiety, including early detection of anxiety signals and use of relaxation and cognitive control techniques. The identification of intermediate goals can also be helpful in addressing developmental issues. For instance, before clients can behave in a more autonomous manner, they may need to achieve greater complexity in their self-in-world cognitive systems. Explicit discussion of the intermediate *learning* goals that must be achieved can increase clients' awareness that success requires work on their part.

Three Individual Counseling Strategies

The nature of the problem, person, and process formulations at Phase 4 and goals identified at Phase 5 can lead to myriad decisions in the intervention-planning phase (Phase 6). A number of specific decisions must be made. Many of these specific decisions are made as the counseling unfolds, sometimes even on the spot during a session. In making these decisions, the counselor recycles to Phase 4 to review the formulations, to Phase 5 to review goals, and to Phase 6 to make the intervention decision.

In addition to specific decisions, counselors must construct an overall "game plan" at Phase 6. A number of overall directions are possible. Neither these global decisions nor the more specific ones can be made in cookbook fashion. In light of the complexity of the variables to be considered, Phase 6 must represent individualized planning rather than exact prescription based on the Phase-4 and Phase-5 information.

Those of us in the counseling field recognize that our counseling interactions have a dynamic, flowing, ever-changing quality. It is difficult and sometimes arbitrary to make categorizations about the nature of different counselor-client interactions or stages in the same interaction. Nevertheless, I have found it convenient to divide the nature of counseling directions into three categories and to discuss each separately. A brief description of these three global strategies follows; however, each is discussed more thoroughly in a succeeding chapter. A counselor usually would not implement one of these strategies in its purest form. More often, techniques characteristic of different categories are intermingled. Nevertheless, the overall attitude represented by counseling often is more representative of one of these three strategies than the others. In addition, one direction may be used predominantly for one phase of counseling, while another is used in another phase. For instance, an exploratory method may be used in the early stages of counseling, when rapport is being established and assessment accomplished, and a more structured skills training method used in the later stages.

The *first category of counseling* is often applied when the client's problem formulation includes incomplete self-awareness, when insufficient development of specific cognitive skills is *not* particularly problematic, and when the client is motivated and relatively able to engage in self-exploration. Outcome goals for this style of counseling often focus on increased complexity of the self, self-in-world, and world cognitive systems. A major process goal is development of rapport between counselor and client, so that the exploration of the client's problems, views, feelings, and thoughts can occur. The counselor attempts to cultivate an atmosphere in which the client feels accepted and may be particularly concerned with establishing the trustworthy perception identified by Strong (1968). The counselor's primary role is that of *facilitator* of communication between counselor and client and of self-exploration by the client. The counselor is likely to do a lot of careful listening and reflecting, along with asking open-ended questions. This kind of counseling, which often takes place during the early stages of a counseling relationship, is described in Chapter Four.

The *second category of counseling* is most often applicable when the client needs to develop a specific set of cognitive skills, such as those used in anxiety or depression management, and is relatively free to learn these skills—is not severely blocked by unacknowledged needs, overwhelming emotions, or other processes. In this method—for which Strong's (1968) expertness dimension is important—counselor and client form a mutual contract to address one or more specific problems and then proceed in a direct, relatively straightforward manner to evolve strategies and apply techniques that work toward agreed-upon goals. The best example is the cognitive-behavioral approach of training clients to develop skills for coping more successfully with errant feelings and reactions, such as depression, anxiety, and stress. In this approach the counselor guides the client through a systematic sequence of steps designed to help the individual *learn* new cognitive and behavioral responses. This approach, which I call a *training* method, is described in Chapter Five.

The *third category of counseling,* like the second one, also involves counselor and client working toward changes in specified problem areas; however, the direct, training approach is not used. Perhaps it has been tried unsuccessfully. Or perhaps the counselor has decided that one or more of the problem and person formulation questions at Phase 4 contraindicate use of such an approach. For instance, clients with a highly introspective cognitive style may view a problem-focused method as "too cut and dried" and therefore offer resistance. Or perhaps unacknowledged needs lead the client to avoid changing, and severe resistance is noted in the Phase-4c process formulation. The counselor may therefore decide to work toward cognitive changes by using an *experiential* rather than a training approach. The outcome goals addressed with this method can be global development, as with developmental counseling, or cognitive shifts regarding specific troubling situations, as with the training approach. However, the process goals of this kind of intervention differ from those used in the developmental and training methods, in that more attention is directed to elucidating or creating cognitive dissonance. Like the second category of counseling, this approach places greater emphasis on use of change-producing strategies and techniques than on relationship development dimensions. However, the techniques are not designed to directly train clients in new skills. Rather, the counselor attempts to lead clients to reassess old experiences or encounter new ones that conflict with constrictive views, expectancies, or assumptions. Approaches typical of this category are strategic therapy (Haley, 1976), some of the neurolinguistic programming ideas of Grinder and Bandler (1976), and concepts from Gestalt therapy (Perls, 1969; Simkin, 1979) and transactional analysis (Berne, 1961; Dusay and Dusay, 1979). Use of the cognitive dimension in this experiential change approach is discussed in Chapter Six.

Summary and Conclusions

In designing effective cognitive interventions, counselors must integrate the intervention design phase with the assessment phase. Phases 4 and 5 are therefore crucial in the Cognitive Intervention Planning Model. In applying these phases, counselors need to be aware of how cognitive change can take place. Phase 4 represents a consolidation of assessment data and an attempt to "make sense" out of the information that has been obtained. Formulations are constructed of the problem

(Phase 4a), the personology of the client (Phase 4b), and the counseling interaction process (Phase 4c). Intervention planning is then begun with identification of goals at Phase 5. It is helpful to define both outcome (5a) and process goals (5b). Some outcome goals can be divided into terminal and intermediate goals. Based on the formulations and goals, decisions regarding the intervention are made at Phase 6, intervention design. Decisions may apply to specific aspects of the intervention or to the global "game plan." Individual counseling intervention plans often approximate one of three general counseling strategies: exploratory-developmental counseling, cognitive skills training, or experiential cognitive dissonance counseling.

The problem formulation for Frank included two aspects: the presence of developmental issues of autonomy requiring clarification and the need to further develop cognitive skills used in coping with anxiety stimulated by speaking situations. The formulation of his personal characteristics revealed him to be motivated both to explore his thoughts and feelings and to learn new skills for coping with the difficult situations. While he was at first not highly aware of anxiety-arousing cognitive processes, the formulation of the counseling process indicated that good rapport had been established and that he was thoughtful and relatively open in the sessions. There seemed to be no major contraindications to approaching his difficulties in a direct manner. Two sets of outcome goals were established: first, to help him make his self and self-in-world cognitive systems more complex and to differentiate these systems from expectations held by family members and others; second, to enable him to improve his cognitive system of skills for coping with anxiety. Process goals included attempting to build trust and establish the counselor as expert in the content of the problem and in specific treatment techniques. The direction established for the intervention was to pursue two courses. Time in each session would be spent in structured work to help him develop cognitive coping skills. However, considerable time would also be devoted to open-ended discussion of his social experiences and family relationships in order to address the broader developmental implications of his difficulties.

Part Two

Using the Model
in Counseling
with Individuals
and Groups

~~~~~~~~~~~~~~~~~~~~~~~~~~~~~~~~~~~~~~~

FOUR

Counseling Individuals: Building Rapport and Encouraging Self-Exploration

Marie, a nineteen-year-old sophomore, had originally come to the counseling center to discuss her boyfriend, whose parents had just announced that they were getting divorced. She was concerned that he was denying his feelings and was drinking more than usual. When she returned in three weeks, she indicated her interest in receiving counseling herself. Her boyfriend, with whom she had gone steady since her junior year in high school, had told her that he was confused and thought they should "go out with some other people." While she had become aware of areas of incompatibility in the relationship, she was still quite dependent on him and was hurt by his decision. Marie's freshman year had been satisfying at first. However, in the second semester, she was not accepted into the sorority she had hoped to pledge. Since she had always been socially successful, this rejection had shaken her confidence. In the first semester of her sophomore year, she had struggled with her organic chemistry class, to the degree that she decided to change her premed major. This experience was also difficult for her to accept, since she had always been quite successful academically. Further, a good friend had developed serious emotional problems and was eventually hospitalized. Her boyfriend's family difficulties and subsequent decision to date other people were the last in a series of troubling events that had left her confused and moderately depressed. In the initial session, she also alluded to her own family concerns, including lack of resolution regarding her parents' divorce and difficulties with her domineering, overprotective father. In addition to her concerns, Marie seemed to have a great many strengths, including intelligence, a good sense of humor, good judgment, and a high degree of social sensitivity. She was engaging and expressive in the counseling.

After the intake interview session, the counselor thought that enough information had been obtained to make tentative formulations at Phase 4 of the Cognitive Intervention Planning Model, to specify intervention goals at Phase 5, and to then devise a tentative intervention plan at Phase 6. Marie's difficulties, as tentatively formulated at Phase 4a, included frequent instances of self-critical internal dialogue and a lack of complexity and organization in her self-in-world cognitive system. Partly because of her relatively sheltered past, she had developed unrealistic expectancies about the way in which the world "should" treat her. The challenges directed toward these cognitive systems had caused her to feel overwhelmed by cognitive dissonance. Insufficient development of emotional autonomy was also present, in that her self and self-in-world systems were not yet sufficiently differentiated from the expectations of others, particularly her parents. At Phase 4b the formulation of Marie's personal characteristics included the judgment that her important cognitive systems were relatively flexible and her overall cognitive development relatively advanced. Also, her expectations for solving personal problems were quite compatible with an exploratory approach. In the formulation of the client-counselor interaction process at Phase 4c, it was noted that excellent rapport was quickly established. While feeling somewhat overwhelmed, Marie was willing and able to explore sensitive areas productively.

In light of these Phase-4 formulations, outcome goals of helping Marie explore, clarify, and make more complex her views of herself and her place in the world were identified at Phase 5a. The process goals chosen at Phase 5b included establishing trust, communicating understanding, and facilitating self-exploration. Based on these goals and the Phase-4 formulations, a strategy of exploratory, developmental counseling was planned at Phase 6. Marie did not appear to have significant deficits in specific coping skills and therefore did not require the coping skills training methods to be discussed in Chapter Five. At the same time, she seemed open to examining her thoughts and feelings without undue resistance and therefore did not appear to need the experiential cognitive dissonance methods discussed in Chapter Six. Naturally, as the intervention progressed (Phase 7), her responses to this approach would be continually monitored at Phase 8a, with the possibility of Phases 4, 5, and 6 being reentered and another form of intervention devised.

How can the counselor help clients such as Marie achieve the desired process and outcome goals? A number of verbal methods will be described in this chapter; however, the counselor's nonverbal behaviors also are important in this kind of counseling. Nonverbal communications, such as attending skills (Ivey, 1971), may be particularly useful in achieving process goals in this mode of counseling. Research by Kaul and Schmidt (1971) suggests that the counselor's manner is more influential in establishing the trustworthiness perception than is the content of verbalizations. Lee, Uhlemann, and Haase (1985) found that clients' perceptions of a counselor's trustworthiness were related to the clients' judgments of the counselor's nonverbal behavior (although not to ratings made by judges).

In Chapter Two the concept of balancing challenge and support factors was introduced as an important consideration in facilitating cognitive development. The methods discussed in the following sections are presented in something approximating an ascending order of the degree of challenge introduced in the counselor's response: facilitating communication, seeking new information, and interjecting new perspectives.

Facilitating Communication and Self-Exploration

Cognitive development can often be enhanced by the counselor's reflecting and summarizing a client's communications without introducing a different perspective into the discussions. Several kinds of counselor responses are effective.

Facilitative Conditions and the Cognitive Dimension. The core conditions of empathy, genuineness, and respect (or warmth) were suggested by Rogers (1957) as "necessary and sufficient" for positive change to occur in counseling. Although many have disputed the sufficiency claim, most agree that these conditions are important regardless of the kind of counseling practiced. In spite of Ellis's (1979) assertion that a "warm relationship" is neither necessary nor sufficient, I believe that these conditions are important in the conduct of cognitive counseling, particularly in promoting the trustworthiness perception and, therefore, the client's willingness to verbalize his or her ideas.

Saying something aloud can foster cognitive development, because concepts can thereby be crystallized, inconsistencies identified, and experiences better understood. In short, I contend that "articulation breeds development." By verbalizing ideas, we present our experiences to ourselves in a form that is somewhat different from the ways that data are encoded in our minds. We can then observe these verbalizations and perhaps notice discrepancies, oversights, or distortions that we had not noticed before. We may also be able to synthesize information, discover patterns, and form conclusions that would have been difficult to formulate on the basis of our thoughts alone. When someone with whom we have a dialogue can react to our verbalizations, there is even more opportunity for growth of our perspectives and ideas.

Rogers's core conditions are important partially because

we are more likely to talk under certain circumstances than others. The depth of self-disclosure is likely to be based largely on our expectations of the consequences likely to follow certain kinds of verbalizations. In general, we are more likely to self-disclose, particularly about aspects that are central to our self systems, if we believe that what we say will be met with acceptance. Cognitions in our self-in-world system must tell us that we will not be humiliated, punished, criticized, or ignored if we reveal sensitive information. The communication of respect and genuineness helps establish this climate.

The dimension of respect or "nonpossessive warmth," as described by Truax and Carkhuff (1967, p. 58), can range "from a high level, where the therapist warmly accepts the patient's experiences as part of that person, without imposing conditions; to a low level, where the therapist evaluates a patient or his feelings, expresses dislike or disapproval, or expresses warmth in a selective and evaluative way." This kind of attitude is important for encouraging increasingly personal self-disclosure. Truax (1966) analyzed a tape of one of Rogers's counseling sessions. He found that counselor responses were offered selectively and served to reinforce certain kinds of client verbalizations. For instance, greater counselor attention followed client statements suggesting productive grappling with problems. As time passed, the reinforced classes of statements were voiced more frequently. The concept of "reinforcing meaningful self-disclosure" need not be viewed as mechanistic or inhumane. In fact, this cognitive map might enable the work of the counselor to proceed more smoothly, particularly with clients whose self-in-world cognitions discourage them from disclosing sensitive information.

Genuineness is described by Truax and Carkhuff (1967, p. 69) in the following way: "At the moment the therapist is really whatever his response denotes. It does not mean that the therapist must disclose his total self, but only that whatever he does show is a real aspect of himself, not a response growing out of defensiveness or a merely 'professional' response that has been learned and repeated." In other words, they point out, the therapist must not adopt a "professional façade." Particularly in the first stages of counseling, most clients are sensitive to non-genuine behavior by the counselor. In order for us to serve as effective models of the communication process, we should avoid sending the double messages that can occur when we are not genuine. If we say to a client, "Oh, no! I wasn't worried about you," in a tentative, somewhat halting voice, our tentativeness may be observed and noted.

In my experience, genuine behavior counteracts some of the prevalent negative cognitions that students have about counselors or therapists—their preconceptions of counselors as humorless voyeurs, overprofessionalized "caring machines," or mind readers. These kinds of expectancies breed resistance and distrust. I think it is important for my behavior to convey that I am human as well as professional and that I am engaged in talking with clients, not just playing the game of counselor. Genuine behavior is inconsistent with some clients' stereotyped concepts of counselors and would stimulate cognitive dissonance, which might be resolved as they amend their views of counselors.

Accurate empathy—the third of Rogers's core conditions —has been defined as "understanding the world of the client *as he* [the client] *sees* it. . . . The therapist attempts to 'get into the shoes' of his client, to 'get under his skin' " (Meador and Rogers, 1979, pp. 151-152). The condition of empathy is regarded by many as the cornerstone of rapport building and developmental counseling. By empathizing with clients' reactions and perspectives, counselors can reflect aspects of their experiences and enable them to reexperience and perhaps reinterpret these aspects. Also, by appreciating clients' internal frames of reference, the counselor is in a good position to ask questions that guide clients in productive exploration of experiences.

The cognitive map that many counselors have of empathy is extremely limited; that is, they seem to emphasize empathy of affect over other aspects of experience. The "phenomenal world" of the client, discussed by Rogers, does not seem to be restricted to any dimension of experience. Yet the concept of empathy reflected in the Truax empathy scale (Truax and Carkhuff, 1967) is almost completely directed at "feelings." I have begun to wonder if the rallying call of the practicum supervisor is "Sure, that's what he is thinking (or say-ing), but what is he *feeling?*" (said with an emphasis that com-municates bemusement if not disdain for the thinking formula-tion).

An often used technique that emerges from and commu-nicates empathy is the *reflection.* I think that reflecting feelings is extremely important, in that many clients need to enrich their cognitive maps of their affective responses. They may fail to attend to internal sensations or may have insufficiently devel-oped cognitive systems for interpreting these sensations. Clients may also lack the necessary cognitive framework for making fine discriminations among their feelings. Fruitful counseling can center on helping clients better identify different feelings they have, including differentiating guilt from fear or anger from depression. These activities require exploring the inter-actions of cognition and affect rather than the affective domain exclusively.

Cognitive-Focused Reflections. Reflection of cognition can be as important as reflection of affect in communicating empathy. Any of the cognitive events discussed in Chapter Two can be recognized in a client's expression and reflected by the counselor. In an effective cognitive reflection, the counselor is able to pull the client's thoughts into a succinct formulation that better labels the experience and the client's manner of pro-cessing it. When cognitive patterns are reflected, clients can bet-ter recognize problematic cognitions, understand errant pro-cesses, and identify irrational aspects of thinking. Cognitive reflection can stimulate clients to incorporate the full range of their experiences more completely and accurately into impor-tant cognitive systems. The cognitive reflection is therefore one of the foremost tools in enhancing the complexity of cognitive development.

The following example illustrates a counselor's reflection of important cognitive *content.* Marie is discussing an interac-tion with her boyfriend.

Client: And then I worried what would happen if Fred blew up at me, and got really mad, and all. I really

can't stand it when he gets mad at me. I'm just
sure he's going to leave me.

Counselor: At times like that, this belief that he'll leave you—
or something bad will happen—if he gets angry at
you is pretty strong.

Client: Yes, it's really strong. I know it's silly. I mean,
he's been mad at me before and hasn't left, but I
feel it really strongly then. I've always been real
afraid of having people get mad at me.

The reflection of cognitive content offered by the counselor enabled the client to identify more clearly a problematic
aspect of her experience—the belief described. It also stimulated
her to examine the validity of the belief and to relate her present experience to an ongoing pattern of difficulty with others'
being angry with her.

The next example, occurring later in the same session
with Marie, illustrates the counselor's reflection of cognitive
processes.

Client: So by the time I'd gotten back that C on the poly
sci test and had that horrible talk with Fred, I was
really feeling lousy.

Counselor: Sounds like you were feeling depressed and down
on yourself. [*Note the reflection of feeling.*]

Client: That's for sure. I started remembering everything
else that had gone wrong this week, and got to
thinking that I've had so many frustrations in this
relationship that I won't ever be able to get involved in another one.

Counselor: It also sounds like you got into a "mental spiral"
and started remembering only the bad and making
a lot of assumptions.

Client: I did. And the more I thought, the more depressed
I got. I do that a lot when I get down on myself.

The reflection of the mental spiraling process enabled the
client to crystallize in her mind the problematic aspects of her

thinking. It also helped her appreciate the interaction of her thoughts and feelings.

Cognitive-Affective Reflections. Counseling need not be thought of as an either-or process in which the counselor is sensitive either to affect or to cognitions. Both dimensions can be valued and explored. In fact, a reflection of cognition often can be combined with a reflection of feeling. Sometimes, empathy is better established if the counselor reflects a surge of strong affect and then goes on to make a cognitive reflection.

The following example occurred with an intelligent graduate student who had entered counseling in hopes of improving his confidence and reducing his anxiety in group communication situations. He is describing an experience in which he became anxious in anticipation of doing a reading in a church service.

Client: I couldn't, uh, I just couldn't believe it. It was so weird! All of a sudden I got so anxious, ya know. I started thinking, "What if I mess this up," uh, "in front of all these people," ya know. I could feel my, uh, feel my heart pounding and I was so tense. And then I worried about they'd see how tense I was and think I was a, uh, loser or something.

Counselor: Sounds like you got to feeling really panicky. Once those feelings and thoughts get to spiraling, it can be kind of overwhelming. [*Reflection of feeling.*] Your internal dialogue got into an "expect the worst" kind of thing—"What if I mess up? What if they see me get tense?" [*Reflection of cognition.*]

Client: Yea, "expect the worst" is right. You're right. I'd probably be all right if I just didn't think ahead so much [*pause*] and didn't worry about what others thought so much. But it's so hard to not do that, ya know. I mean, it just happens so fast.

In the above example, the counselor's beginning with a

reflection of feeling was important. The client was so intensely emotional in his expression that he might not have felt understood if the counselor had not acknowledged his feelings immediately. The reflection of feeling communicated empathy more effectively than a reflection of cognition would have. However, once the counselor acknowledged the strong feelings and communicated his understanding of the client's affect, he could direct attention to important cognitive aspects by making a cognitive reflection. The cognitive reflection in this case stimulated the client to explore his internal dialogue further. In other situations it may be more productive for the counselor to respond with the cognitive reflection first and then offer a reflection of feeling. This type of dual reflection can sharpen a client's awareness of the relationship of feelings to cognitions.

Cognitive-Focused Summary and Integration. In a reflection the counselor presents the client with a synopsis of important aspects contained in one or more very recent expressions. In summarizing and integrating, the counselor presents a synthesis of elements that have been communicated over the course of a session or even over a number of sessions. While a reflection is most amenable to identification of cognitive events, a summary/integration can often highlight important cognitive systems or developmental patterns.

The client in the following example is a sophomore university student. She has been feeling somewhat depressed, has low self-esteem, and is in general unsatisfied with her life at school. During the session she has described several situations with which she is dissatisfied, both academic and interpersonal. However, she has "yes butted" several attempts by the counselor to pursue ways of dealing with problems.

Client: I don't know. I just don't think it would do any good to talk to him about it. You know how these professors are around here. They're not going to reconsider a grade just because a student asks them about it. Are you kidding?

Counselor: Let me summarize for a moment what I think you are saying. With your friend Nancy and your boy-

friend and your English professor, you believe that
they are going to treat you the way they're going
to treat you no matter what you do. Is this how
you're thinking about those situations?

In this example the counselor was able to integrate different instances in which the client's system of self-in-world contained the external locus of control pattern. This more integrated picture may enable her to develop a more accurate and
detailed cognitive map of her role in relationships.

Sometimes the counselor can tune into the client's level
of cognitive development and make summary/integrative responses that enhance awareness of this dimension. In the following discussion with Marie, the counselor integrates several
events that suggest she has progressed from dualistic thinking to
a more complex level.

Client: I'm realizing that the kind of thing that happened
                   to Jean can happen to people, whether they bring
                   it on or not. Maybe I'm getting cynical in my old
                   age [*laughs*], but I'm learning that life's not al-
                   ways fair.

Counselor: I guess you're right—it isn't always fair. And I'm
                   realizing that the way you're thinking about Jean,
                   and the way you're thinking about Fred, is differ-
                   ent from the way you were thinking about them
                   about a month ago. Then you were thinking "This
                   isn't fair!" and you couldn't accept it, whereas
                   now your thinking is a lot more flexible about the
                   way things are *supposed* to be.

Client: I know. Is that bad? [*Still looking for external
                   verification of what is right.*]

Counselor: What do you think?

Client: I don't think it's bad. I think it's just being realis-
                   tic.

In this exchange the summary/integration response by
the counselor helped the client become aware of progress she

had made in her cognitive development during the course of counseling. It can be easy for clients to take their present status for granted and fail to observe themselves making progress across time.

Cognitive-Focused Interviewing

In addition to offering cognitive reflections, summaries, and integrations, a counselor engaged in rapport building and in developmental counseling can greatly help clients by asking effective questions. Good questions interspersed with other counselor responses can provide the counselor with important information for assessment purposes. They can also guide clients in examining experiences and cognitions and in enriching what Bandler and Grinder (1975) call their "models" of experience.

In attempting to be aware of cognitive elements and the ways in which clients process information, I have found the behavioral interviewing described by Goldfried and Davison (1976) particularly useful. These methods stress specificity in identifying important problematic behaviors, their antecedents, and consequences. Global recollections of situations are often overly limited models of what has actually been experienced. Helping clients recognize the specific relationships between their responses and events in the world can lead them to a more complex cognitive system of self, world, and self-in-world and can provide them with a clearer cognitive map of their difficulties.

Another system for interviewing that is particularly useful is the metamodel approach developed by Bandler and Grinder (1975). Their method is founded on the belief that clients' verbalizations constitute a metamodel; that is, they are *representations* of clients' encodings of their experiences, which are models of the outside world. A counselor's interviewing is guided by two tasks: first, to enable clients' verbalizations to be fully representative of their conscious formulations about events in question; second, to enable these conscious formulations to be fully representative of encodings of relevant experiences, some of which may not have been integrated into awareness.

The reader is encouraged to consult the books mentioned above and other resources dealing with interviewing. Rather than offering a detailed discussion on this topic, I will discuss aspects of interviewing that are important in attending to cognitive variables.

Open-Ended Questioning. Most discussions of interviewing suggest that open-ended questions are generally preferable to closed-ended questions (yes-no, multiple choice). Open-ended questions are particularly valuable in assessing cognitive systems and in determining how they are organized. The information that first comes to a client's mind in response to an open-ended question may be one of the most important elements in the cognitive system. Closed-ended questions do not permit the counselor to note the decisions that clients make about what to say first, which provide clues about their ways of processing information. Open-ended questions are therefore often preferable for clients who are reasonably comfortable and verbal.

In certain instances, however, closed-ended questions are preferable. Someone who is embarrassed by and uncomfortable in the counseling interaction might be able to respond to yes-no and multiple-choice questions more easily than to open-ended ones. Likewise, someone whose verbal skills are limited may require some yes-no questioning in order to make the differentiations that are important. In addition, clients who are highly verbal but not very introspective can benefit from a kind of multiple-choice questioning regarding their cognitive processes; for instance, they might be presented with several possible self-statements and asked whether any "strikes a chord" and seems related to the internal processes that occurred.

One kind of closed-ended strategy that is particularly useful in cognitive development counseling is "Please indicate, on a scale of 0 to 5, your degree of belief in the following statements." Beck has suggested that asking clients to make such ratings of experiences can counteract tendencies toward dichotomous thinking (Beck, Rush, Shaw, and Emery, 1979).

Specification of Clients' Responses. In order to empathize with clients and accurately assess them and their difficulties, the counselor must have as complete and accurate a picture of their experiences as possible. Language often contains shortcuts or globalized categorizations that do not convey a sufficiently specific meaning. Counselors need not fear that asking for specification of these experiences is antithetical to an empathic relationship. If sensitive questions are interspersed with other types of counselor responses, they can contribute to the communication of empathy. Questions that challenge clients to describe their responses more specifically can also be valuable in helping them improve their cognitive maps of themselves and how they "tick."

Asking clients to *specify their behavior* in important situations is often necessary. Such questions as "What exactly did you do when your mother made those accusations?" can enable the counselor to get a more complete picture of how clients behave in important situations. Clients frequently use verbs, adverbs, and adjectives that provide insufficient information about their actions. A college student may say that he has been "lazy" about his studying. The counselor may need to ask him to elaborate: "In what ways have you been lazy?" Asking for examples can help give general terms a meaning that is more concrete.

In some cases the kind of precision stressed by behaviorists regarding the frequency, duration, intensity, and other dimensions of behaviors is important. For instance, a client who claims that she and her boyfriend have been arguing "all the time" might be asked, "About how many arguments have you and Jack had this week?" The answer would provide the counselor with a better picture of the relationship. It might also lead the client to a productive reassessment of her concept of this situation, in that "all the time" is no doubt an overgeneralization.

Clients' descriptions of their *affective responses* frequently require specification. Words such as "depressed," "anxious," "angry," and "frustrated" can mean different things to different people and can be used differently by the same person in reference to different situations: "What are your feelings of depression like?" "What do you notice about yourself that tells you that you're depressed?" It can be especially important to stimulate clients to "tune into" sensations that are involved: "When you get real anxious, what kinds of physical changes do you notice?" Again, the resulting information is important for the counselor's cognitive map of the client and is also useful in helping clients clarify their cognitive maps of themselves. Questions regarding the frequency and duration of affective responses may also be important.

Counselors can also help clients *specify cognitive events and processes* that are involved in their difficulties: "What kinds of things were you saying to yourself as you were on your way to see Professor Jones?" Clients are often aware of conflicting inclinations and find it helpful to conceive of different "parts" of themselves engaging in self-talk: "Remember that 'whining, fearful part of yourself' that we identified last week? What was that part saying to you as you started the trip home?" The frequency and duration of cognitive events can also be important to specify: "During the course of an average hour of studying, how many times do you think your mind gets caught up in thoughts about home?"

Specification of Circumstances. Just as specification of clients' responses helps them enrich their cognitive maps of themselves, specification of circumstances can help them develop more accurate cognitive maps of the world and their interactions with it. When, where, with whom, and under what circumstances do they act, think, or feel in certain ways? It is tempting to adopt a "trait" explanation of events and assume that "aggressiveness" accounts for a bully's behavior. Mischel (1968) and others believe that these trait inferences are often overgeneralizations. Rather than being generally "aggressive," an individual may act aggressively only around certain kinds of people and in certain situations. A counselor's questions might be directed toward detecting the situational determinants of the troublesome responses. This line of questioning could lead to a more complex concept of self-in-world, in which aggressive feelings and behavior are known to occur in some interpersonal situations but not in others. The improved identification of the problem could lead to a more effective exploration of possible solutions.

As well as exploring the situations in which certain behaviors, feelings, or thoughts occur, the counselor can ask about the circumstances under which the same responses do *not* occur: "Are there certain courses in which you do not get anxious during the tests?" Clients are often selective about what they remember and report, and therefore their presentation can be incomplete. If asked to specify when problematic behaviors, feelings, or thoughts do not occur, they might be able to provide clearer information and to formulate more balanced pictures of themselves. Bandler and Grinder (1975) suggest testing whether clients have encoded experiences that are inconsistent with generalizations they have made. For example, in response to a young female client's statement "My mother disapproves of everything I do lately," the counselor asked, "Can you recall any times during the last month when your mother was not critical of you?" The elements that differentiated situations in which her mother was critical from ones in which she was not were then explored. The result was a clearer understanding of the nature of the client's interactions with her mother, an important component in her self-in-world cognitive system.

Exploring Consequences. One of the most important contributions of learning theory to counseling practice has been identification of immediate consequences as important determinants in whether responses are repeated. Our behavioral, affective, and cognitive responses are affected by the immediate "payoff" they elicit. This very important but simple factor can easily be overlooked by counselors and clients as they struggle for a complex understanding of clients' motivations. Yet awareness of these contingencies will increase the complexity of the self-in-world cognitive system.

Cognitive counselors can help clients explore *external consequences* of important responses: "What was the result of your tirade to Steve?" *Internally administered* consequences, including cognitions, can also affect learning and the persistence of learned patterns. For example, "What did you think about right after you blew up at him?" As language-using animals, humans carry important reinforcers and punishers in their heads. Exploring cognitive reinforcers and punishers is an important part of understanding self-world interactions and the self-in-world cognitive system.

Sorting Experiences. Developing more complex cognitive systems requires formation of constructs that permit finer discriminations among experiences. Cognitive-focused interviewing can sometimes appear similar to administration of Kelly's (1955) Role Construct Repertory Test, in that the counselor may ask the client to contrast experiences: "You have gotten along well with Herb and Joanne but not with Sue. Are there some important ways that Sue is different from the other two?" Exploration of this kind of question can lead to greater awareness of the aspects of the world that bring about different responses in the client.

Exploring the Meaning of Events. After clients have described important or difficult events, particularly ones that elicited a great deal of emotion, the counselor might ask what the event meant to them: "What does it mean to you that you and Fred had such a good time last night?" It is often productive to ask clients the meaning they attribute to their *behaviors* and *feelings*: "What does it mean for you that you are feeling so angry at Mary?" This kind of question often can help both counselor and client become aware of cognitive dissonance produced by a powerful or unexpected occurrence. Exploring the meaning of *cognitive events* is also important. In Chapter Two the concept of "metacognitions" was introduced—thoughts about thoughts. The meaning of certain thought patterns to clients' self and self-in-world systems should be explored. For example, a client struggling with his reaction to his girl friend's decision to break up with him was asked, "What does it mean to you that you're so preoccupied with her?" The question led to an explanation that he had always assumed he had "the upper hand" in the relationship and that he had always equated his present reaction to "acting like a wimp."

Exploring Relationships of Cognitions to Affective and Behavioral Responses. Interviewing can help clients become more aware of how their actions and feelings can be influenced by their cognitions. Counselors can use questions such as "What was going through your mind when you first began to get anxious?" or "What was your perfectionistic, taskmaster part saying to you when you were avoiding working on your paper?" It is often effective to guide clients toward juxtaposing problematic feelings or behaviors with cognitive processes and to allow them to form their own conclusions about whether the nature of their cognitions influenced these responses.

Ellis's A-B-C system is used extensively in problem-focused cognitive counseling, as discussed in Chapter Five; however, it can also be useful in developmental counseling. With situations that are particularly disturbing or otherwise important, clients can be asked to specify important elements of the situation (Point A: Activating Experiences) and their problematic behavioral or affective responses (Point C: Consequent Emotions and Behaviors). They can then be asked to identify the cognitive events and processes (Point B: Irrational Beliefs) that might be occurring in self-talk or visual imagery form. I often find it useful to represent Ellis's system visually on a pad, as the interrelationships of cognitions with the behavioral and affective responses are discussed. A form on which clients write the A-B-C's of significant situations is sometimes used with "homework" assignments. It is often productive to ask clients to write the A-B-C's of difficult situations that do *not* elicit unwanted reactions, as well as ones that do.

The following segment illustrates the use of Ellis's A-B-C system in exploring the relationship of affective responses with cognitions. Marie is reflecting on her reactions when she did not receive a sorority bid.

Counselor: This situation was really troublesome for you. Remember the A-B-C scheme we used last session? Let's think through this situation using it.

Client: OK.

Counselor: So, you've already defined point C, your feelings. You were feeling really rejected and depressed, right? [*Counselor begins sketching A-B-C chain on a pad of paper.*]

Client: Yea, right.

Counselor: And Point A, the situation, is that you didn't get a

Client: bid from the sorority you wanted. So let's think about Point B, what was going on in your mind about not getting the bid.

Client: Well, I was feeling real rejected—thinking those girls must not like me. And I was kind of thinking that other people would know I wanted to be in that sorority and all.

Counselor: What seemed so bad about the possibility that other people would know?

Client: Well, I guess I thought that they'd think I was a loser or maybe feel sorry for me or something and that my friends wouldn't think as much of me any more.

The last counselor response in this interaction is an adaptation of the "vertical arrow" technique (Burns, 1980a). The client is taught to uncover a deeper layer of cognition. In effect, the meaning the client attaches to self-talk is investigated. Through this mode of questioning, core irrational beliefs can be identified and then examined.

Exploring Historical Factors. Cognitive-focused developmental counseling is generally directed at expanding self-awareness through examination of current experiences. Counselors using this approach assume that meaningful personality change does not necessarily require working through memories and fantasies from the first few years of life. Nevertheless, clients can often gain by discussion of historical aspects that are related to current experiences. A clearer concept of how maladaptive patterns were formed can increase the complexity of the self system and sometimes enhance internality of locus of control. Understanding of cognitive patterns can sometimes be facilitated by exploring important source influences of those patterns. Early interactions with parents and others are often capsuled into problematic thoughts and imagery. A counselor might ask, "Where do you think you learned to talk so critically to yourself?"

Exploring Interpersonal Systems. Our interpersonal systems help create, maintain, and change our cognitive systems, which in turn affect the ways in which we approach our inter-personal worlds. When a client and I discuss problematic cognitive events or processes, I may ask, "How do you think you came to view things this way?" Peer groups and friends often exert a powerful influence on the ways that university students think and behave. The family system continues to be extremely important, even though students may be somewhat more re-moved from their families than in earlier stages of life. They are learning to assume roles in their families that are more independent than ones they have filled in the past. They may be challenged to examine old values and in the process may encounter more conflict with parents.

One of the liabilities of the human power to think is that our interpersonal systems remain operative on a cognitive level long after they have ceased to exist in the world. In our heads we may still hear the voice of a mother who is no longer living. We can also maintain the mental model of a parent's behavior after the behavior itself has undergone change. Thus, family systems are not just of historical significance, even if they no longer exist in the outside world. They are a part of our present worlds—the ones we maintain in our minds. The roles we learned to play in our families are often related to more generalized concepts of how we should live our lives with other people. Cognitive interviewing focused on family systems can help clarify the assumptions we use in initiating and interpreting interactions with others.

Perspective-Challenging Responses

With reflections, summaries, and integrations, the counselor is attempting to present clients with cohesive formulations of their experiences. These formulations consist of pieces of information that the client has already communicated and that the counselor has pulled together. In these kinds of responses and in questioning, the counselor is not presenting clients with new inferences about themselves. The responses described in this section entail the counselor's interjecting a perspective that is new to the client.

Cognitive-Focused Interpretations. Interpretations are generally used more sparingly in cognitive developmental counseling than in a medical, clinical method. Nevertheless, interpretations that are sensitively and respectfully offered can contribute to clients' cognitive development. In an interpretation a counselor is offering a hypothesis that seeks to explain some aspect of the client's feelings, behavior, or cognitions. Counselors should remember that interpretations are based on inferences and should therefore be offered as *tentative possibilities.* When clients reject interpretations, many of us in the counseling profession are quick to make another inference—that they are "resisting." There is no doubt that resistance occurs. It can be a response to cognitive dissonance produced by an accurate interpretation that cannot be assimilated into important cognitive systems. However, in some instances the interpretation itself may be off the mark.

Interpretations are helpful for enhancing clients' cognitive development in several ways. They can help clients become aware of cognitions that are at level 3 of awareness—ones that require some degree of cognitive development before they can be elucidated. For instance, an interpretation was helpful in a session with Marie. While she was fully aware that she frequently felt anger toward her father, whom she blamed for her parents' divorce, she denied negative feelings toward her mother. However, with some gentle confronting by the counselor, she acknowledged feeling irritated at her mother for often being late. The counselor commented that this was the first time Marie had disclosed any negative feelings at all about her mother and added, "I'm wondering if you've been operating with a rule along the lines of 'My mother *must* be absolutely wonderful and I must not let myself have any negative feelings toward her.'" The interpretation of this schema led to Marie's productively exploring her unacknowledged reactions to her mother.

Notice that the tentative nature of this interpretation was conveyed by its "I-message" form. Rather than saying "You've been operating . . . ," the counselor said, "I'm wondering if you've been . . ." The I-message phraseology labels the interpretation a tentative inference the counselor has made.

As well as being used to increase awareness of level-3 cognitions, interpretations may help clients better understand the role of important cognitive systems or developmental aspects of their thinking. The client in the following segment was a graduate student who was doing extremely well academically but was continually frustrated in her social life. She was unable to maintain interest in males who liked her and treated her well. Further, she was unable to control her attraction to males with "love-'em-and-leave-'em" reputations.

Client: I guess I should have known Ted would turn out that way. He's a lot like Mike and Burt. They all really like having a lot of girls around them and flirting. I should know better. But those other guys seem so boring to me.

Counselor: You know, we've talked about a number of guys you've dated or known. It seems to me that you've got two categories in your mind for placing guys: the handsome lady killers who'll turn out to be louses but are interesting and the well-meaning but boring guys. Am I overdoing this?

Client: No, not much anyway [*laughs*]. I guess I do see guys pretty much that way. Guys who are eligible, anyway.

Cognitive-Focused Self-Disclosure. While it is generally unwise for counseling to be an existential encounter in which both client and counselor make major personal revelations, selectively used self-disclosure by the counselor can contribute to cognitive development (Carkhuff, 1969). Late adolescents and young adults who are in periods of great change and uncertainty can easily form idealized concepts of older adults who are helpful to them. It can be a useful learning experience for them to realize that counselors and other adult models have had, do have, and will continue to have uncertainties and unresolved issues. This knowledge can help them make their self-in-time and self-in-world cognitive systems more complex and realistic. I therefore think it is permissible for counselors to reveal human vulnerability at times with some clients. This approach is best taken with clients who are functioning at reasonably advanced developmental levels and implemented when these clients are in a growth/enhancement phase rather than in crisis. Also, counselors should in most cases refrain from disclosing issues that might make them appear emotionally needy to the client.

One form of counselor self-disclosure occurs when counselor and client share and compare relevant cognitive systems. The client's model may become more complex as the counselor's vision is processed and integrated. The following interaction occurred toward the end of counseling with Marie:

Client:	But something I've noticed is that even those people who seem to have it so together don't, ya know. There's always some part of their lives that is out of kilter, somehow. You know what I mean?
Counselor:	I know what you're saying. I've known a lot of people who I thought had everything going for them. Yet, when I've gotten to know them, I learn that they have their vulnerabilities too.
Client:	I find that idea really depressing.
Counselor:	I can appreciate that that could seem discouraging. In a way, though, I find that idea kind of comforting.
Client:	You do?
Counselor:	In a way. I think it helps me realize that having things incomplete and imperfect is part of the "human predicament."

Self-disclosure also can be used as a method of presenting clients with models of coping skills. In discussing an experience or a situation that the counselor has personally encountered, the counselor can convey cognitive coping processes that he or she has evolved. For instance, the student in the next segment has been working on controlling his speech anxiety. He has made quite a bit of progress but is still preoccupied with how he appears to others.

Client:	So I'm doing better. I can tell that. I've eliminated, pretty well, the anticipatory anxiety, and I can be

OK right before the talk. And I'm doing better in the talks, but I've still got a big part of my mind on what they think about me. I just can't stand the idea of making a fool of myself!

Counselor: I think it's good you're keeping in focus how you have improved and that you're not too discouraged that you're not where you'd like to be completely yet. What you're describing is very familiar to me. I have gotten really caught up in how others are judging me at times. The kind of thing that has evolved for me is to remind myself—particularly before I start off on a speech—to pay attention to saying what I have to say to the audience and that I'll do the best I can and I'll just have to let them form their own opinions. I say to myself, "No need thinking about how they're going to like me. I just need to pay attention to what I'm doing and do my job and let the chips fall where they may."

Self-disclosure can also be used as a kind of nonthreatening interpretation. If the counselor has had a schema or an irrational belief that contributed to a difficulty similar to the one the client is facing, this cognition can be disclosed as a way of presenting it for examination by the client. For instance, suppose a counselor is working with a very shy male client who has felt extremely awkward and anxious at a couple of parties. The counselor might say, "I can recall feeling uncomfortable when I first started going to parties and thinking about dating. One of the things I used to do a lot was play mind games with myself—worry a lot about how 'cool' I'd look and whether I'd look like I knew what I was doing. Of course, the more my mind got caught up in that, the more anxious I'd get." This self-disclosure presents the client with a description of a cognitive process that could be involved in his difficulty. He may be able to recognize the process, even though he had not previously been able to articulate it.

Another advantage of the self-disclosure offered in the

above example is that it conveys the developmental nature of the social concern. It implies that the counselor has made progress with difficulties encountered at an earlier stage of life and that the client may also be able to make progress. The self-disclosure might also serve to universalize the client's experience. The peer atmosphere among students often discourages them from being very candid about feelings of social insecurity. They therefore perpetuate the illusion that almost everyone navigates social situations confidently. The self-disclosure by the counselor might help this client become aware that others have similar reactions.

Cognitive-Focused Immediacy. Immediacy refers to the degree to which the counseling discussion is focused on the present situation (Carkhuff, 1969). Discussing the present interaction between client and counselor is the highest form of immediacy. The counseling relationship should ordinarily be well developed and the client should be functioning at a relatively high level before the counselor encourages a great deal of immediacy. Under these circumstances selectively used immediacy-encouraging responses can promote cognitive development.

Asking clients to reveal thought processes regarding the counselor and the counseling interaction can be instructive. Information regarding the way in which the client is responding to the counseling can be obtained and used in conducting the intervention. Also, clients' cognitive responses in counseling may be similar to their ways of processing information in other important interactions. The following example occurred with a student who was concerned about a lack of confidence in socializing, particularly meeting new people. Although somewhat reticent at first, he seemed to have become reasonably comfortable with the counselor, who therefore decided that he would not be overwhelmed by a more immediate discussion.

Client: I don't know why. I just don't feel that comfortable with a lot of people. As far as I can tell, most people seem to like me OK when they get to know me. I'm not sure what happens that I get to feeling so uncomfortable.

Counselor: As we've already mentioned, sometimes the ways we think about things—that "little voice" in our heads—has a lot to do with how comfortable we feel. One thing I've been wondering is how you've been feeling talking to me. I'm a new person to you.

Client: Yea, but you're a professional person, so I kind of expect you to be understanding and all. I have to admit, though, I did feel uncomfortable at first. Before I came in, I was really wondering what it would be like. But I feel pretty comfortable now.

Counselor: So you did feel some discomfort. And that's pretty much gone away. If you feel OK about it, it would be interesting to look at what you were thinking—what your little voice was saying to you about coming in here.

The client was able to discuss his self-talk regarding the counseling situation and how it had changed from the beginning of the session. This clarification led to a better understanding of the self-talk process in other important interactions.

Cognitive-focused immediacy is also useful if the counselor has questions about the client's response to something that has occurred in counseling. Perhaps the client's nonverbal communication suggests confusion or unspoken disagreement. As well as exploring affective and behavioral reactions, the counselor might ask, "What was going on in your mind when I was . . . ?"

Cognitive systems of self and self-in-world can sometimes be made more complex when counselors provide immediate feedback on patterns observed during sessions. As with the other active counselor dimensions discussed, feedback should be offered selectively. I-message phraseology is preferable, because it labels the feedback as a reaction of the counselor, not an objective presentation of "the truth." During early sessions with Marie, the counselor pointed out that she repeatedly maintained a smile when discussing emotionally difficult material: "I've been noticing that as we've discussed your sadness about

Fred and the sorority you've kept smiling." The feedback resulted in her exploring her overdeveloped needs to be polite and make a good impression on others.

    Cognitive-Focused Confrontation. According to Carkhuff's (1969) definition, a confrontation occurs when the counselor points out "discrepancies" noted in the client's behavior—discrepancies between clients' expressions of what they wish to be true and what they actually perceive in themselves ("ideal self" versus "perceived self" cognitive systems), between information they have presented verbally and their nonverbal messages, and between clients' self-views and the counselor's views of them. A *cognitive*-focused confrontation consists of the counselor's pointing out two or more conflicting cognitions or new information that conflicts with existing cognitions. In effect, this kind of confrontation focuses attention on preexisting cognitive dissonance or stimulates new dissonance. A well-timed and well-formulated cognitive confrontation clearly presents the conflicting data to clients and increases the likelihood that they will grapple with the cognitive dissonance rather than automatically dismiss the unsettling information.

    The client in the following example had undergone an unusually stormy relationship with her mother, particularly for the past three years. She had come to engage in a great deal of dichotomous thinking regarding her mother and would infer negative motivations in whatever her mother had done.

Client:	I got a letter from my mother yesterday, and she seems to really want me to come home fall break. It wasn't like most of her letters. She even seemed to appreciate the problems I'm having in chemistry. The sarcasm wasn't there either. So I guess I'll go home. Anyway, what I wanted to talk about was this guy who seems to want to go out with me.
Counselor:	Sounds interesting about the guy. Let's talk about it. But I don't want this thing about the letter from your mother to pass us by. You know, the picture you've been building up for me of your mother is someone who only thinks of herself and

is conniving and doesn't care about you. And yet
this letter you got evidently seemed pretty understanding about things. What do you make of this
difference?

Client: To tell you the truth, I don't know. Maybe she's
plotting something and just wants to get me up
there for some reason and is just being nice to me
for that. It didn't seem that way, though. I don't
know. I guess we'll see what happens.

Remembering the Principles of Challenge and Support

Counselors need to keep in mind the importance of balancing support and challenge factors in planning (Phase 6) and
implementing (Phase 7) developmental counseling. Widick, Knefelkamp, and Parker (1975) have incorporated Sanford's (1962)
concept of support and challenge into "developmental instruc-
tion," designed to enhance students' cognitive development.
The degree of challenge must be great enough to stimulate
growth and yet not sufficient to overwhelm the learner. We as
counselors should carefully consider how challenging to make
our interventions. For a period in my professional development,
I took a simplistic "honesty is the best policy" position in counseling. I thought that any observation, question, interpretation,
or confrontation was likely to be helpful for almost any client,
as long as I was being "honest with myself." There were times
when the degree of challenge I provided was too great for clients and resulted in their leaving counseling, "resisting," or
avoiding their problems. Earlier in my career, I had functioned
in a more nondirective manner, and there were no doubt instances when I provided insufficient challenge for clients to
examine and work toward changing problematic cognitions.

Counselors must also regulate the amount of support provided to their clients. As counselors we are often taught to provide as much support as possible, as opposed to gauging the
amount of support that would be optimal. There may be times
when we need to allow clients to endure cognitive dissonance
until they themselves are able to find a resolution. Important

self-efficacy expectancies may be developed more successfully if clients attribute achievements largely to their own efforts instead of being "shown the way."

If counselors are to balance challenge and support factors, they need to know what clients find challenging and supporting. The sections in this chapter have been ordered according to the degree of challenge that would be presented to most clients by the counselor's using a particular kind of response. Cognitive reflections, integrations, and summaries are likely to be less challenging than cognitive interpretations, self-disclosure, immediacy, and confrontation. While these generalizations are accurate for many clients, counselors should not assume that they apply in all cases. The degree of support and challenge appropriate and the kinds of responses likely to be perceived as supportive are dependent upon the client. The formulation made of the client at Phase 4b is thus quite important. Some clients may have extremely low trust levels or may be extremely afraid of closeness in relationships. They might therefore find themselves very uncomfortable with a counselor who exudes a great deal of warmth and perhaps elicits warmth within them. I can recall counseling a university sophomore who was relatively isolated from other students and lacked supportive relationships. Partly because of several unsatisfactory experiences in the past with mental health practitioners, he was extremely wary of counseling. Sensing his great need for supportive relationships, I concentrated heavily on communicating the core conditions and attempting to develop closeness. In retrospect, I suspect that he would have found a more distant relationship more supportive, at least in the early stages of counseling. After only three sessions, he elected not to return.

In balancing support and challenge factors, counselors must be sensitive to clients' unique characteristics (as judged in Phase 4b). As mentioned in Chapter Three, cognitive style is one important variable to assess. Allowing clients to approach problems and self-exploration in ways that capitalize on their most familiar styles is likely to be supportive, while asking them to operate in a different way will be more challenging.

Perry's (1970) stages of cognitive development also pro-

vide a useful framework in assessing what clients may find challenging. Allowing clients to attack problems that are amenable
to their present level of functioning is generally supportive, in
that they can comfortably master the tasks involved. However,
challenge is presented when they are asked to deal with questions that are not "answerable" with their present cognitive
arsenal. In general, an appropriate amount of challenge is presented when they are at times asked to apply cognitive skills at
the next highest position on Perry's scheme. For instance, a client who is primarily dualistic in appraising the social world
might be asked, "Why don't we see how many different interpretations for Bill's behavior we can come up with?" This intervention would challenge such a client to use thinking that is
more multiplistic. Clients who are primarily multiplistic in their
cognitive development concerning problematic areas might be
asked to struggle with an issue at the relativistic level, with a
question such as "How about trying to think through this situation in a systematic way and see if we can make sense out
of it?"

Summary and Conclusions

The kind of counseling intervention I have called "rapport building, exploration, and developmental counseling" is
particularly applicable in the early stages of counseling. It can
serve as the primary thrust of the intervention with many clients. With nine sessions of developmental counseling, Marie was
able to make substantial progress in better understanding her
reactions, developing more complex cognitive systems of self
and self-in-world, and differentiating her expectations of herself
from those of her parents and peers.

Two central ideas have been developed in this chapter.
First, counselors should be sensitive to *cognitive* aspects of clients' experiences as well as to affective dimensions and should
regard *cognitive development* as one of the goals of counseling.
Second, counselors should balance ingredients of support and
challenge in order to help clients develop cognitively and not
avoid or be overwhelmed by cognitive dissonance. The order in

which the methods characteristic of this counseling approach have been described reflects the degree of challenge likely to be presented by different kinds of counselor responses. In many cases the more challenging kinds of interventions should be offered later in the counseling process, since the counseling relationship will then have developed sufficient supportiveness to allow clients to deal successfully with the challenges. Counselors must remember, however, that individual factors account for clients' perceptions of what is supportive and challenging. Therefore, in assessment and Phase-4b formulation, counselors must identify individual characteristics that are likely to influence a client's responsiveness to different counseling methods.

❧❧❧❧❧❧❧❧❧❧❧❧❧❧❧❧❧❧❧

FIVE

Helping Clients Develop Cognitive Coping Skills

Susan is an eighteen-year-old freshman who has come in for counseling because she is concerned about her academic performance. She had always been a straight-A student in high school; however, she is having difficulty in her first university semester. The primary problem is in her history course, her intended major. She currently has a D average on history tests, whereas she is making B's and C's in her other courses. Her major concern is that she becomes extremely anxious before and during these tests and consequently does not concentrate as well or think as clearly as she normally would. In fact, sometimes she cannot think of an important point during the test but is able to remember it afterward. Susan is somewhat shy and, like many freshmen, dependent; however, in general, she seems to be adjusting well to other aspects of university life.

What would you do if you were Susan's counselor? Would you tell her that she needs to develop a greater understanding of the conflicts hidden beneath the symptoms of anxiety? Or might you try to create an accepting interpersonal climate, in which she can conduct her own exploration and arrive at her own solution? Would you help her understand the role that cognitions play in her difficulties and train her to use cognitive strategies in coping with her feelings and situations? Probably your answer to the above questions is a resounding "I can't say without further information!" and you would undoubtedly be correct. The secret to conducting effective counseling is to remain flexible and to make discriminations regarding what approach will work with what kind of problem experienced by what kind of client under what circumstances. Admittedly, we need to know more about Susan before committing ourselves to an approach; however, I believe that training in cognitive coping skills would be worthy of consideration.

The counseling methods described in Chapter Four remain applicable with clients such as Susan. In addition, however, the counselor can include techniques directed at helping clients develop cognitive systems that enable them to prevent and reduce debilitative feelings, such as anxiety and depression. I refer to this direct, relatively structured approach as a "training" model of counseling, in that the counselor is attempting to train the client in the use of specific skills.

Cognitive coping skills training can be included in the treatment plan for a wide number of difficulties that students are likely to experience. Susan's test anxiety and Frank's speech anxiety (described in Chapter Three) were approached with this method. Several kinds of "evaluative" anxiety—including speech anxiety (Meichenbaum, Gilmore, and Fedoravicious, 1971; Weissberg, 1977; Weissberg and Lamb, 1977), test anxiety (Denny and Rupert, 1977; Holroyd, 1976; Meichenbaum, 1972), and social evaluative anxiety (Barrow and Hetherington, 1981; Glass, Gottman, and Shmurak, 1976)—have been treated successfully with cognitive methods. Beck has developed an effective cognitive treatment for depression (Beck, 1976; Beck, Rush, Shaw, and Emery, 1979; Rush, Beck, Kovacs, and Hollon, 1977). Anger and chronic pain have also been targeted with a cognitive modification procedure called "stress inoculation training" (Meichenbaum and Turk, 1976). Guilt is another unproductive feeling with which cognitive coping skills training can be used.

Other unwanted behaviors and feelings experienced by students may merit cognitive coping skills training as one component in the intervention. For instance, a perfectionistic cognitive network often underlies common student problems, including procrastination, ineffective study habits, obsessive-compulsive symptoms, underachievement, stress, guilt, and low self-esteem. Barrow and Moore (1983) have developed a group program for students with this difficulty that makes extensive use of cognitive methods.

This chapter focuses on cognitive coping skills training methods that can be incorporated in Phases 6 (Planning) and 7 (Implementation) of an intervention. Susan's test anxiety difficulties will be used to illustrate these training methods, as will Frank's speech anxiety problem (introduced in Chapter Three). The problem formulations constructed at Phase 4a for both clients identified cognitive coping systems that were inadequate for the demands they faced. At the same time, their person formulations (Phase 4b) revealed no contraindications for undertaking coping skills training. The cognitive development and cognitive style features of both students were amenable to a cognitive skills approach, and neither appeared resistant to a direct, problem-focused method. While both were concerned about their difficulties, neither was in a crisis state likely to impede attention to the intervention. In the formulation of the client-counselor interaction process at Phase 4c, it was noted that both responded well to problem-focused exploration and to a structured method.

The outcome goal identified at Phase 5a for Susan was to help her develop a cognitive system for coping with the troublesome test situations. Process goals (Phase 5b) included molding an atmosphere conducive to learning and practicing coping skills and establishing the counselor as expert in Susan's eyes; however, in light of the limited outcome goals and the fact that only three sessions could be held prior to the end of the semester, it was not thought to be crucial to establish the degree of trust necessary for exploration of extremely sensitive personal issues. A brief intervention of three sessions of cognitive coping skills training was planned at Phase 6. For Frank, the problem-focused goal of developing coping skills was identified at Phase 5a, as were more far-reaching goals pertaining to development of autonomy and identity. In light of these more extensive outcome goals, the process goals identified at Phase 5b included development of high trust levels and facilitation of extensive self-exploration in addition to enhancing Frank's perception of the counselor as expert and establishing an atmosphere conducive to learning. Cognitive coping skills training was again included in the intervention planned at Phase 6; however, the overall approach also included developmental counseling focusing on broader social development issues.

Several definable steps are usually followed in implementing cognitive coping skills training (Phase 7). These will be discussed in the order in which they are usually introduced; however, in actual counseling practice, two or more steps are often addressed concurrently rather than sequentially, and frequent recycling through the steps is common as new experiences are discussed and client progress is monitored at Phase 8a. While the description may give the impression that a "lock-step" approach is used, the steps are undertaken in a fluid manner in counseling practice. The steps include helping the client formulate the problem, developing commitment to the intervention, setting goals for the intervention, early detection training, analyzing cognitive processes, developing cognitive coping strategies, helping the client "own" coping methods, and terminating.

Helping the Client Formulate the Problem

Unlike the frequent practice in psychodiagnostic assessment, clients in cognitive coping skills training are not left in the dark regarding the significance of information they provide in assessment. Instead, counselors describe the problem to clients, perhaps in a more organized form than the clients have been able to formulate it. Clients who can cogently articulate their problems are likely to maintain motivation for an intervention plan based on the formulation.

The cognitive events, systems, and developmental features identified in Phases 1, 2, and 3 are integrated into the problem formulation. What are the problematic affective, behavioral, or cognitive responses? What situational factors contribute to the problem? What cognitive processes create or accentuate the difficulties? Other aspects of problem formulation reviewed in Chapter Three are to be considered. Ellis's A-B-C analysis system provides a useful framework for helping clients understand their difficulties (Ellis and Harper, 1975). This system can be used as the basis for an integrated summary of the problem for the client. A visualization of the problem also can be presented, as the A-B-C's are sketched on a pad by the counselor. Figure 2 contains the representation shown to Frank in conjunction with the following summary: "As we talk, it appears that in certain situations at Point A—situations requiring public speaking and the potential of some kind of judgment—you become extremely anxious at Point C, to the degree that you cannot think or speak effectively. An important contribution comes from Point B, your self-talk, in which you are extremely preoccupied with not wanting to make a mistake or to be judged negatively by others." Frank found this formulation "on target" and therefore was amenable to the recommendation that cognitive coping skills training be attempted.

Figure 2. Problem Formulation for Frank.

Point A:	Point B:	Point C:
Activating Event	Belief System	Consequent Feelings
Public speaking	"What if I mess up?" "I *must* make a good impression on people in the audience!"	Extreme anxiety

Another model that is useful in formulating evaluative anxiety difficulties—such as may occur in tests, public-speaking assignments, or social interactions—is based on the factor analytic research of Liebert and Morris (1967) with test anxiety and on Wine's (1971) analysis. Using this model, counselors help clients identify the elements of an unproductive "anxiety spiral." First, the eliciting situations are defined. Second, elements of the two components of evaluative anxiety are identified: *emotionality,* the physiological component, consisting of autonomic arousal experiences such as "butterflies," increased heart rate, cold and sweaty hands, and constricted breathing; and *worry,* the cognitive component, consisting of thoughts about performing poorly, being judged negatively, or other negative consequences. The emotionality and worry components tend to interact with one another in a spiraling fashion. The physiological manifestations augment the worry, which further stimulates the emotionality reactions. If this anxiety spiral proceeds unchecked, consequences include mental immobilization and inhibition of expressive behavior.

Like the A-B-C system, the "anxiety spiral" model can be used to diagram a client's problem. A formulation of Susan's test anxiety difficulties was sketched for her on a pad (see Figure 3). In test situations, particularly timed exams, she would develop an uncontrolled anxiety spiral, consisting of emotionality experiences (feeling her heart racing, butterflies) and worry ("What if I fail?" "I *must* get an A!" "I *should* be able to score as high as anybody in the class"). As these components interacted, she would feel more and more anxious and less and less in control, to the degree that her ability to retrieve information and to think clearly would become hampered. This formulation

Figure 3. Problem Formulation for Susan.

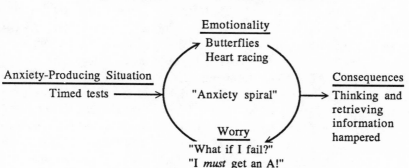

helped her better understand her reactions, enhanced her sense of self-control, and began the process of building her commitment to the coping skills intervention.

Assessment instruments are available for many of the kinds of difficulties targeted with cognitive coping skills training. When used to assess problem status before and after counseling, they can be discussed in the problem formulation stage in order to sharpen clients' awareness of their difficulties.

Developing Commitment to Coping Skills Training

Another title for this section could be "Selling the Rationale." If clients are to follow through with the structured procedures of coping skills training, they must agree with the problem formulation and understand and believe in the intervention plan. Kirsch and Henry (1977) found that the credibility of the treatment to speech-anxious clients was related to treatment outcome.

Clearly formulating the problem greatly helps in achieving commitment to the treatment. In eliciting information from clients regarding A-B-C chains or the anxiety spiral process, counselors can write down the responses and organize them into a diagram of the model without labeling the components. They can then insert labels as the formulation is summarized. Clients are often impressed by how easily the model parallels their reactions. This effect increases the "face validity" of the model and strengthens commitment to interventions that emanate from the formulation.

Bibliotherapy early in the intervention can often contribute to enhanced client commitment. In Beck's therapy of depression, a brief article on the role of cognitions in depression is prescribed after the first session (Beck, Rush, Shaw, and Emery, 1979). Ellis and Harper's (1975) book can be helpful in illustrating the importance of cognitive events. Another resource that is particularly useful when a perfectionistic cognitive system underlies evaluative anxiety and other problems is an article on "perfectionism" by Burns (1980b). Burns's (1980a) book *Feeling Good* provides a clear description of cognitive therapy and can be very helpful, particularly with depressed clients.

Clients who have read one or more of these materials often return to the next session with a heightened sense of anticipation because they have recognized and identified with the processes described and no longer feel alone with an inexplicable problem. This more hopeful stance is generally reflected in enhanced motivation to undertake a structured, cognitive-focused intervention. Clients' responses to these readings can also be useful data in the assessment process. The minority who do not seem to identify with the themes discussed or who react negatively to the models or interventions described are either unlikely candidates for cognitive coping skills training or will require considerable education regarding the principles.

Commitment to the training is heightened when clients come to understand the role of cognitive events. Most readily embrace a cognitive formulation. In introducing the concept of the role of cognitions, counselors can offer an explanation similar to the following: "We all talk to ourselves, inside our heads, in one manner or another. In talking to ourselves, we monitor things that happen, interpret what they mean to us, and evaluate ourselves and our performances. These cognitive processes have a lot to do with how we behave and feel." In order to establish commitment to the training, counselors should keep in mind that a broad definition of "cognitive" is likely to be more effective than one that includes only verbal mediators. As noted in Chapter Two, some individuals may be more conscious of visual images than words in their reactions to troublesome situations. As well as becoming more aware of "audiotapes" that affect behavioral and emotional responses, they can be encouraged to notice "videotapes" that exert influence.

Most clients can readily identify self-talk and/or imagery that mediates their unwanted reactions, and these clients generally can quickly commit themselves to the coping skills training. Yet some clients are unaware of thought or imagery patterns precipitating emotional reactions: "I didn't think anything particularly; I just all of a sudden felt panicky!" It is rarely profitable to try to convince such clients early in the intervention that an internal dialogue underlies their emotional reactions. Most are receptive to an initial explanation along these lines: "The thoughts, images, or perspectives may not be consciously in your mind at the time that you become panicky, but certain connections or assumptions have become so much a part of your basic view of yourself that they are in the back of your mind." Meichenbaum's (1977) analogy to the way in which instructions become internalized when one learns to drive a car is often convincing (see Chapter Two). Many clients discover the phenomenon of an internal dialogue as counseling unfolds and as cognitions that are at level 3 of consciousness move to level 1.

Setting Goals for the Intervention

As the problem is formulated and the client's commitment to a problem-focused intervention is built, counselor and client are ready to clarify goals for the intervention at Phase 5. As with the problem formulation, the setting of outcome goals (Phase 5a) in cognitive coping skills training is a collaborative activity between counselor and client, not simply unilaterally prescribed by the counselor. While the setting of concrete goals may not always be possible or productive in the early stages of developmental counseling, it is generally accomplished within the first two or three sessions in cognitive coping skills training. Discussion is often a sufficient method; however, use of goal attainment scaling (Paritzky and Magoon, 1982) can be helpful in clarifying outcome goals and can also contribute to evaluation of the intervention at Phase 8. In this approach, clients write out their goals early in counseling and then rate their attainment of these goals when counseling is completed. An explicit clarification of goals contributes to the intervention in several ways. It provides a clear "road map" of the direction of the counseling and can thereby increase the client's understanding of and involvement in the intervention process. It can also increase client motivation and strengthen compliance with activities prescribed in the treatment. Further, clearly defined goals specify what can be achieved and therefore promote realistic expectations by the client. Unrealistic client expectations often surface in discussions of treatment goals and can then be addressed. Finally, clearly defined goals are benchmarks by which client and counselor can monitor their progress (Phase

8a) and eventually evaluate the effectiveness of the counseling (Phase 8b).

Clients may need to learn that "coping" outcomes are more realistic for short-term interventions than "mastery" outcomes. Rather than expecting to become completely relaxed in public-speaking situations, Frank accepted the goal of being able to keep his level of anxiety under control by using coping strategies. The goal of cognitive coping skills training is to help clients develop cognitive systems that can enable them to detect unproductive feelings and thoughts, use these signals as cues to initiate coping strategies, and thereby cope more successfully with a situation. It is often helpful to discuss with clients the importance of their *continuing* to monitor thoughts and feelings and apply coping strategies. For instance, Susan found that simply getting her anxiety under control before a test was insufficient. She had to check cognitive and physiological cues continually and sometimes bring anxiety-reducing strategies into play during a test.

At the end of treatment, the client may still be apprehensive about the situation. However, there is evidence that clients who learn self-control methods can continue to improve in their ability to apply the strategies (Goldfried and Trier, 1974). Clients may be able to enhance coping skills through continued practice after treatment. Also, an important shift in the cognitive system of self may occur as mastery of the once problematic situation is integrated into one's self-perception. Frank and Susan may eventually progress to a stage where they no longer are anxious about speeches or tests. However, this degree of improvement is more likely to occur after counseling. Developing coping skills and learning how to use them to control maladaptive feelings are realistic goals in the kind of short-term intervention characteristic of university counseling settings.

While cognitive coping skills training addresses cognitive self-control goals, additional goals can be identified for certain clients. Developmental issues, such as gaining autonomy, crystallizing identity, and improving one's sense of competence, often undergo change as clients improve their abilities to cope with previously difficult situations. The cognitive processes that stimulate behavioral and affective problems, such as evaluative anxiety, are often related to one's cognitive systems of self and self-in-world. Cognitive coping skills training may stimulate re-evaluation of some basic beliefs and assumptions. With clients for whom developmental issues are particularly pronounced, changes in important cognitive systems may be identified as additional intervention goals: "As we work on how you can cope with your speech anxiety, our goal at times might be to help you separate your own expectations of yourself from those your parents had for you." Goals pertaining to cognitive systems of self and developmental issues are often slower in being formulated than those related to learning coping strategies. For instance, it was not until the third session that Frank's interest in understanding more about how his view of himself had been shaped by family experiences was identified as a goal of the counseling.

Early-Detection Training

In order to apply coping skills successfully, clients must develop more complex cognitive maps of their own reactions to situations. As Meichenbaum (1977) has noted, clients need to recognize sensations associated with the early stages of anxiety and use these as cues to initiate coping strategies. Development of this skill suggests that a very subtle cognitive shift has occurred. The sensations, once viewed as reasons for panic, come to be interpreted matter of factly as signals to implement coping strategies in order to regain or maintain control.

There are several kinds of cues that clients can incorporate into their "early-detection cognitive maps":

1. *Situational Cues.* Via assessment interviewing and homework-monitoring assignments, clients can improve their abilities to discriminate the conditions under which the problem occurs. Awareness that they are entering a troublesome situation can then cue them to begin using or preparing to use coping strategies.
2. *Physiological Cues.* Discussion, homework monitoring, role

playing, and imagery exercises can help clients learn to "tune into what happens early in the anxiety spiral that can tip you off to the fact that anxiety is mounting." Physiological cues of anxiety, known collectively as the "fight-flight" response, emanate from activation of the sympathetic nervous system. Cues most often useful to clients in early detection include "butterflies" in the stomach, increased heart rate, cold hands, perspiration, dry mouth, and tense skeletal muscles, particularly those in the face, neck, shoulders, back, or stomach. Most clients are able to detect these cues; however, they may not consistently remind themselves to "tune into" them. They therefore need to develop a cognitive set that instructs them to monitor the changes carefully. Relaxation training can help clients enhance awareness of muscle groups or other physiological systems that are most reactive to stress.

3. *Cognitive Cues.* Clients can also use awareness of cognitions associated with spiraling emotions as coping cues. These metacognitive cues are quite important to early detection. Unproductive thinking patterns can often be detected before physiological sensations are sufficiently pronounced to permit their being discriminated from baseline levels.

4. *Behavioral Cues.* Certain behavioral patterns are the result of spiraling emotions. For instance, anxiety regarding evaluation might lead to avoidance of or escape from anxiety-arousing situations, such as speeches, tests, or writing assignments. Through association with these evaluative situations, other activities, such as studying, can also produce avoidance and escape behavior. With some clients, awareness of the avoidance/escape responses can serve as cues to initiate coping strategies. For instance, a student might learn that flight away from studying to the snack machine is motivated by heightened tension regarding an upcoming test. The student might then learn to interrupt the snack seeking and implement anxiety management strategies. In most cases it is the impulses or fantasies associated with avoidance/escape behavior that can be used as cues to initiate coping. The actual avoidance behavior may not occur early

enough in the chain to allow for early detection. A student taking an anxiety-arousing test may fantasize about a trip to the beach, or one about to begin a speech to a class may become aware of an impulse to leave the room.

Most clients can become aware of "early signals" of anxiety and other debilitative emotions relatively quickly. These clients simply need to learn to consciously monitor the signals by incorporating attention-focusing reminders. Clients who cannot easily develop an awareness of early signals need to develop new cues. Such clients can be asked to keep written records of their physiological, mental, and behavioral reactions to troublesome situations. Also, role plays or guided imagery exercises of previous or anticipated situations can be conducted and followed by discussion of the client's internal reactions. With role playing, reviewing audiotapes or videotapes can sometimes help clients recapture their immediate physiological and cognitive reactions.

Analyzing Cognitions and Developing Coping Skills

The thoughts on cognitive analysis and coping skills development of Meichenbaum, Wine, Ellis, and Beck are presented in this section. In recent years proponents of cognitive therapy, including these four theorists, have borrowed extensively from one another. The ideas offered in this chapter represent the *initial emphases* of these influential authors. Taken together, they illustrate the subtly different directions that counselors can adopt for these two steps of cognitive coping skills training.

The primary differences among these four approaches center on the "depth" of the cognitive analysis and the degree to which active disputing and rethinking of underlying irrationalities are taught as coping skills. The approaches initially developed by Meichenbaum (1977) and Wine (1971) require primarily a descriptive kind of cognitive analysis. Self-talk is labeled as anxiety arousing, or attention focusing is observed to be self-oriented; however, no effort is made to uncover irrational beliefs at level 3 of consciousness. More of an inferential approach is taken with Ellis's and Beck's methods of cognitive analysis, in that the counselor helps clients identify level-3 cognitions that are implied in initial verbalizations. Likewise, Meichenbaum and Wine emphasize the learning of specific coping skills—coping self-talk and task-focused attention. In contrast, Ellis and Beck encourage addressing the irrational thoughts and rethinking them.

Meichenbaum's Pragmatic Approach. In Meichenbaum's (1977) approach to cognitive analysis, the "self-statements" that promote and/or maintain anxiety are identified. In his view, it is enough for clients to recognize that these cognitions increase debilitative feelings and are therefore self-defeating. It is not necessary for them to understand the irrationality of their thoughts. The goal is to improve the client's cognitive map of the immediate, conscious thoughts that flood a person's mind in difficult situations. This step can be accomplished through discussion of previously encountered difficulties, role playing, and homework thought-recording assignments.

Meichenbaum's ideas on developing coping skills follow the pragmatic, straightforward philosophy represented in his cognitive analysis methods. He has speculated that the rationality of the initial cognitive reaction to a situation is *not* what distinguishes those who manage the situation successfully from those who do not (Meichenbaum and Cameron, 1974). In effect, having irrational thoughts related to troublesome situations is commonplace. What is more important to the success of the encounter is whether the individual has an effective repertoire of cognitive skills for coping with the initial internal dialogue. Therefore, in Meichenbaum's stress inoculation approach —a model that has been used with stress, anger, and pain—little emphasis is given to reevaluating or disputing irrational thoughts (Meichenbaum, 1975; Meichenbaum and Turk, 1976). The approach can best be described as a coping self-statement smorgasbord, in which clients are exposed "cafeteria style" to a range of coping methods.

One of Meichenbaum's greatest contributions to developing cognitive coping skills is his application of sound learning principles. In stress inoculation training, models of the use of coping self-statements are presented to help clients develop coping skills for four phases of dealing with a stressor: preparing for the stressor, initially confronting it, feeling overwhelmed by it, and reinforcing one's efforts after coping successfully. Through presentation of these models, clients come to internalize the process of talking to oneself in a helpful way. In addition, they begin to integrate some of the modeled self-statements into their own language styles.

As potentially valuable coping self-talk patterns are evolved, clients are drilled in making their use habitual. Meichenbaum (1977) has incorporated some of Luria's (1961) concepts regarding the development of thought into the procedures. Clients may be asked to go through a stage of repeating the coping self-statements aloud in order to assimilate them better. They then are asked to repeat the statements silently. In the final phase, they have integrated the meaning of the self-statements and do not have to consciously recall the statements themselves. In stress inoculation training, the counselor has the client practice and test coping skills under stressful circumstances. Homework assignments can be used—graduated so that less threatening situations are attempted first. Meichenbaum has also suggested exposing clients to a variety of ego- and pain-threatening "laboratory" stressors, such as electric shock, immersion in cold water, stress-inducing films, failure and embarrassment situations, and stress-producing imagery. Many counselors, including myself, do not feel comfortable about inducing physical pain as a part of counseling. Nevertheless, it is important to devise ways by which clients can come to associate internal cues and threatening situations with initiating the coping strategies. The use of coping imagery is an attractive alternative. Clients visualize threatening scenes, monitor their internal signals of anxiety, and imagine themselves using their coping strategies (Meichenbaum, 1972). For example, a sequence of several test-related situations was presented to Susan in imagery during her last counseling session.

Meichenbaum's approach, consisting of pragmatic cognitive analysis and employment of learning principles to help clients learn coping self-statements, is preferable to other methods under several circumstances. Clients can often learn coping skills quite quickly with this approach, making it a good choice when brief treatment is desired. Perhaps there are only several weeks before the end of a semester, as was the case with Susan, or a waiting list necessitates working with students in a time-efficient manner. Meichenbaum's approach is also a good method to use with students whose limited psychological sophistication is best suited to a concrete focus. Also, some students are less likely to be resistant to this straightforward approach than to approaches that require them to uncover underlying irrationalities—although, in some instances, a more probing method might be adopted later in the counseling. The stress inoculation model is probably also most helpful when clients need to learn to cope with one particular kind of emotional response (anxiety, stress, anger, pain) elicited by identifiable situations (such as tests, social contacts, or public speaking). A more involved method may be preferable when clients' coping difficulties occur in a broad range of situations and when development of "insight" into less obvious cognitive processes is important. Also, when the coping difficulties are embedded in more general developmental issues, an approach emphasizing in-depth cognitive analysis and rational reanalysis may lead to greater resolution of the developmental aspects.

Wine's Focus-of-Attention Approach. Wine (1971) distinguishes between self-focused attention and task-focused attention. She notes that the self-talk of an anxious person is almost exclusively *self-focused*: "What if *I* miss this question? What will *my* grade be? What if *my* GPA goes down? What will *my* parents think of *me*?" This kind of focus heightens anxiety and interferes with intellectual performance. In contrast, *task-focused* attention reduces anxiety and enhances performance. This concept, elegant in its simplicity, is surprisingly effective with many clients. As well as identifying cognitions that are anxiety producing, clients can make a further analysis by noting whether their thinking is self-focused or task focused.

Wine's (1971, 1974) method of developing coping skills consists of training clients to follow detection of self-focused attention processes with self-instructions to return their focus of attention to immediate tasks. Like Meichenbaum, she uses modeling and rehearsal procedures to ensure that clients learn the skills. For several reasons this method of developing coping skills is well suited to helping clients cope more successfully with evaluative situations. First of all, the coping skill of attention shifting can be employed very rapidly, unlike a more involved rational analysis. It is difficult to imagine someone carefully thinking through alternative assumptions during a timed exam. Second, the notion of task-focused attention provides a positive, concrete direction for one's attention, as opposed to creating the paradoxical task of trying *not* to think about a negative theme. (Have you ever tried *not* to think of a pink elephant? This task can best be achieved by positively fixing one's attention on another stimulus, such as a green elephant.) Third, employment of attention refocusing does not require as much psychological sophistication or openness to exploration of underlying assumptions as does rational reanalysis. Resistance to this method is encountered only rarely. Fourth, the client is given more guidance than in Meichenbaum's process of exploring self-statements until workable ones are identified. Consequently, coping skills can sometimes be taught even more quickly with this method than with Meichenbaum's.

Wine's cognitive analysis and coping skills development system can most effectively be used in circumstances similar to those in which Meichenbaum's method is effective. Clients with rigid, intellectualizing defenses are often more accepting of this level of analysis than of uncovering irrational beliefs or assumptions. Likewise, clients who are psychologically unsophisticated and concrete in their thinking may be able to grasp this kind of analysis more easily than a more abstract analysis of assumptions. The Wine approach is also excellent when time is limited. In fact, I have used it effectively with clients whom I have been able to counsel for only one or two sessions. While superbly geared to helping clients quickly learn to cope, Wine's method is probably insufficient with clients whose coping difficulties are closely related to important psychosocial developmental problems.

Ellis's Irrational Beliefs and Disputation Approach. In

Ellis's system (described in Chapter One), clients are sensitized to the use of such words as "should," "must," and "ought." These words tend to exaggerate the emotional response. Their use implies a demand on the part of the client that something *should, must,* or *ought* to be different and that the party at fault should be condemned. Frank's public-speaking anxiety was heightened by his perfectionistic demands of himself, such as "I *should* be able to perform at high levels in everything I attempt." Ellis has identified 259 different irrational beliefs that are relatively common. However, he believes that the great majority of these beliefs can be classified as one of three "musturbatory ideologies": "I must do well and win approval for my performances, or else I rate as a rotten person"; "Others must treat me considerately and kindly, in precisely the way I want them to treat me; if they don't, society and the universe should severely blame, damn, and punish them for their inconsiderateness"; or "Conditions under which I live must get arranged so that I get practically everything I want comfortably, quickly, and easily, and get virtually nothing that I don't want" (Ellis, 1977a, pp. 12–13).

In using Ellis's cognitive analysis system, the counselor discusses problematic situations with the client and listens for evidence of irrational beliefs, which can then be presented in cognitive reflections. The uncovering of such a belief system is profoundly helpful for some clients; however, some resist the impact by intellectualizing that "Of course no one would believe that; it doesn't make sense." Some have even commented, "That would be irrational," as though they were incapable of such imperfect thinking. This kind of response is common from clients with obsessive-compulsive styles who often use denial and intellectualization in managing their feelings. Ellis (1977a) has noted that clients may sometimes hold contradictory beliefs simultaneously. One may be purely intellectual, while the other evokes powerful emotional responses. A helpful tactic with this kind of client is to suggest that each of us has a rational, intellectual side and a side that is at times emotional and illogical. The positions that both sides express in self-talk and visual imagery can then be explored: "That sounds like what your intellectual side might be saying. What is your emotional side telling you about this situation?" If clients do not respond to this suggestion with an effort to explore affect-arousing cognitions, it is often more productive for the counselor to retreat temporarily than to continue the probing style. The client may be more receptive when future openings are explored.

Some of Ellis's ideas can be quite helpful in developing cognitive coping skills; however, because his approach was developed before the cognitive-behavioral self-control movement had begun, the concept of coping skills is more explicitly incorporated into Meichenbaum's and Wine's approaches. While adaptable to a coping skills framework, the rational reanalysis process was initially seen as a way of changing basic personality patterns.

Once the irrational beliefs (iB's) have been identified, Ellis's rational-emotive therapy focuses on helping the client shape rational beliefs (rB's) that can be substituted for the irrational ones. In order to achieve this goal, Ellis and his colleagues have extended the A-B-C (*A*ctivating Event, *B*elief System, *C*onsequent Feelings) model to include steps D and E. Ellis (1977a) refers to Step D as "disputation" of the irrational beliefs and lists three substeps. "Debating" consists of actively questioning the irrational beliefs in the internal dialogue. For instance, Frank came to ask himself whether "aceing" all assignments was as necessary as he had once thought it to be. In Ellis's terminology, he conquered his "musturbation" by debating his assertion that he *must* ace every assignment. "Discriminating" consists of differentiating irrational premises from rational ones and distinguishing wants from genuine needs and desires from demands. Finally, "defining" means carefully describing the actual elements of a situation, so that one is reacting to facts rather than inferences and assumptions.

Maultsby (1977) has devised other techniques that can be used in disputing irrational beliefs. Step "Db," which consists of rationally disputing Point-B thought systems, is preceded by step "Da." In this step the client performs a "camera check" of the troublesome situation at Point A. The client is to imagine that a sound camera is trained on the situation and is to review precisely what would have been recorded. This technique is helpful for clients who overreact because they read too much into events that occur. A similar strategy was used in a session with Frank, who was describing a high degree of frustration (Point C) brought about by his less than perfect delivery of a speech (Point A). Cognitive activity at Point B included perfectionistic demands and the presumption that others would judge him negatively for his behavior. In place of the camera analogy, he was asked to assume the perspective of someone in the audience and to imagine what he would have seen and heard and how he would have processed the data. Through this exercise Frank concluded that, although his performance was in fact not perfect, he had done an adequate job and had probably been perceived as competent by members of the audience. This cognitive shift led to a more balanced emotional reaction.

Point E in the rational-emotive therapy system refers to "new effect." As an individual becomes more and more proficient at detecting irrational beliefs (iB's) and implementing disputation at Point D, the cognitive system becomes more complex and "rational." A permanent cognitive effect (cE) is achieved. Also, new behavioral effects (bE's) and emotional effects (eE's) occur. As Frank was able to soften some of his perfectionistic demands and evolve a more self-accepting cognitive system (cE), his anxiety became reduced (eE), and his public speaking (bE) could become more spontaneous.

Ellis's ideas are particularly useful when clients can devote more than three or four sessions to examining their thought processes regarding important themes in their lives. The method provides less specific guidance in the development of coping skills than Meichenbaum's or Wine's approaches do. However, it affords structured procedures for helping clients explore broad cognitive systems. It is therefore a good choice when clients' difficulties involve issues of psychosocial development and overall self-acceptance.

Beck's Three-Tiered Analysis. In Beck's approach to cognitive analysis, attention is successively directed toward three different levels of cognitions (Beck, Rush, Shaw, and Emery, 1979; Beck and Shaw, 1977; Shaw and Beck, 1977). While developed primarily as a treatment for depression, the procedures are applicable to other emotional reactions, such as anxiety. The treatment is directed at the cognitive triad in depression: negative views of the self, the world, and the future. In the first tier of the treatment, clients are taught to record and monitor "automatic thoughts" that are associated with depressed feelings. To facilitate this process, a "double-column" technique is often used, in which clients record problematic situations in one column of a sheet and then write their automatic thoughts in the other. The goal is for the client to learn to recognize the automatic thought patterns. This part of analysis is similar to Meichenbaum's pragmatic approach.

In the second tier of the treatment, the therapist helps clients learn to identify faulty reasoning patterns inherent in the automatic thoughts that stimulate the unwanted emotional reactions. (These are summarized in Chapter Two, in the section headed "Cognitive Content and Processes.") For example, the internal dialogue of a depressed male student was found to contain a great deal of *dichotomous thinking,* in which he insisted that without complete success in a situation he was a failure. He therefore felt depressed, even at times when he performed relatively well. The pattern that Susan identified as the most problematic for her was *overgeneralization.* When she encountered difficulty with one question on a test, her mind would race to the conclusion that she would be unable to contend with the rest of the questions. While Ellis's effort to discover irrational beliefs focuses on the content of thought, Beck's detection of thinking errors pertains to thought processes. Some clients who are initially resistant to examining irrational beliefs are more likely to commit themselves to identifying errors in thinking patterns.

In the last tier of Beck's therapy, the focus shifts from the automatic thoughts and thinking errors to the identification of basic "depressogenic assumptions." Themes observed in the automatic thoughts and faulty thinking patterns can suggest "schemas," which are assumptions or perspectives that have become "structuralized" as permanent formations of the cognitive organization. Schemas underlie automatic thoughts; determine whether one accepts, rejects, or distorts incoming information; and affect interpretations of situations, expectancies, evaluations, and memories. The process of identifying schemas is much like Ellis's method of determining irrational beliefs, except that Beck's system is more individualized and flexible. Rather than reducing the client's automatic thoughts to one of the predefined irrational beliefs, the therapist attempts to uncover the idiosyncratic cognitive patterns involved. Burns (1980a) describes the "vertical arrow" technique for this type of analysis. The therapist teaches clients to deepen analysis of Point-B cognitions by asking, "What would it mean to you if . . . ?" In homework assignments in which clients monitor their cognitions, a vertical arrow placed below an automatic thought signifies this question. The answer, presumably representing cognitions at a deeper level, is then written. This process is repeated until a basic schema is identified. Figure 4 displays the analysis of Frank's cognitions relating to his public-speaking anxiety.

Figure 4. Use of "Vertical Arrow" Technique in Cognitive Analysis with Frank's Speech Anxiety.

Point A:	Point B:	Point C:
Activating Event	Belief System	Consequent Feelings
Anticipating having to read at a religious gathering	"What if I get nervous and can't function well?" ↓ "They might notice that I am nervous." ↓ "They might think badly of me--think I look like a fool." ↓ "That would be awful, because I need to look competent to others at all times."	Extreme anxiety

Much like Ellis's rational-emotive therapy, Beck's method of developing coping skills seeks to help the client analyze emotion-producing automatic thoughts and underlying assumptions (Beck, Rush, Shaw, and Emery, 1979; Shaw and Beck, 1977). A Socratic method of questioning is often used, in which clients are led toward identifying their irrational assumptions themselves. This questioning approach is more consistent with my own style than is the flamboyant, argumentative method associated with Ellis.

In practicing internal dialogue that analyzes thought processes, clients graduate from the double-column technique, already described, to the "triple-column" method. Troublesome situations are described in the first column of a handout, and automatic thoughts that lead to unwanted emotions are written in the second column. The third column is then devoted to clients' analyzing the facts of the situation and testing the reality of their assumptions. The facts of the situation are carefully analyzed (Shaw and Beck, 1977). Burns (1980b) has discussed the "horizontal arrow" technique, in which an arrow placed to the right of a description of cognitions in column 2 signifies that a rational analysis is to be written in the next column. This horizontal arrow can become a discriminative stimulus for the initiation of reality testing of one's thinking.

Another cognitive coping skill taught by Beck and his colleagues is the "alternative" technique, in which clients are instructed to generate alternatives to original interpretations of situations. The degree of believability of various alternatives can then be rated as counseling proceeds, and clients can be asked to list advantages and disadvantages of alternatives. Clients are often so committed to a limited mental set that they are unwilling or unable to consider alternatives. Use of "reverse role playing" may help stimulate awareness of alternatives. In this method clients are asked to reflect on their actions from the vantage point of an external observer (Shaw and Beck, 1977). As in Maultsby's camera technique, clients must momentarily remove themselves from their usual perspectives.

An interesting method for combating self-defeating cognitive processes involves helping the client design an experiment to test a core irrational assumption (Beck, Rush, Shaw, and Emery, 1979; Burns, 1980a, 1980b). For example, one of my clients and I concocted an experiment to test a belief that "important people in my life will be greatly disappointed in me if I mess up, particularly if I don't give absolute effort." She decided that she would take half a day off from studying on the weekend before exams, even though she might not perform quite as well on them. When she told her mother about this decision, to her surprise her mother said that she was not disappointed at all. In fact, she was relieved that her daughter was "letting up a little" and "learning to enjoy life."

For clients with specific difficulties, such as evaluative anxiety experienced in one kind of situation, Beck's method is probably less preferable than Meichenbaum's or Wine's, since clients can learn specific coping skills more quickly with these approaches. On the other hand, Beck's system is ideally suited to clients whose difficulties involve a broad and intricate web of self-defeating cognitive processes and systems, as is often the case with depression and "free-floating" anxiety. Beck's three-tiered attention to cognitions and Socratic style of exploration are often acceptable to clients who might be resistant to Ellis's approach, which would attempt to sensitize them to irrational assumptions more quickly and would rely more heavily on confrontation.

Integrating Different Ideas into the Counseling Intervention. The four approaches described have somewhat different emphases. Nevertheless, drawing on two or three of the approaches is often helpful with a client. A flexible format of analyzing cognitions and developing coping skills can allow the intervention to proceed smoothly and still benefit from inclusion of various ideas. Ellis's A-B-C framework is the most helpful device for initial exploration of cognitive processes and their relationships to emotional and behavioral consequences. I have therefore used this framework in conjunction with techniques drawn from the other approaches. In order to ensure that the client explores cognitive processes and practices cognitive analysis, prescribing daily written homework for at least two weeks is often advisable. A handout on which clients analyze situations in three columns (*A,* Activating Event; *B,* Beliefs or Self-Talk; and *C,* Consequent Feelings or Behaviors) is used. One situation per day is to be submitted to analysis; however, clients are encouraged to complete this written exercise for any situations that are particularly troubling. The vertical arrow technique can be sequenced into this exercise, if the intervention is to emphasize attaining better understanding of underlying assumptions.

Clients who experience difficulty in the analysis stage can be helped by other techniques. Rather than relying solely on discussion, one can use guided imagery. When previously difficult situations are made more accessible to clients, they sometimes becomes more aware of their internal dialogue. Role playing a difficult situation can have the same benefit. Videotape or audiotape feedback combined with role playing can help clients better tune into their cognitions. In an interesting twist on the usual role-playing method, the counselor can play the part of the client and invite the client to speculate on what might be going through the counselor's mind.

In the development of coping skills, an extended concept of "cognitive" is advisable. The counselor can never be sure what clients will find helpful as coping strategies or what sensory mode will be most effective. As well as using coping self-talk, clients might develop more powerful coping arsenals if they also incorporate visualizations and even kinesthetic stimuli into their strategies. For instance, a self-inflicted pinch on the leg may help a client refocus attention from anxiety-arousing self-perusal to immediate tasks in a testing situation. Counselors need to encourage clients to explore a range of cognitive mediating strategies that can interrupt and decrease self-defeating cognitions. One student who recently consulted me for test anxiety was able to make greatest use of visual strategies. Between our first and second sessions, she was surprisingly successful at coping with her anxiety about an important test. When I asked what, specifically, had helped her cope, she explained that she had visualized the anxiety spiral diagram I had shown her in our first session (similar to the one drawn for Susan in Figure 3). This imagery had enabled her to "short-circuit" the chain of "worry" self-talk and refocus her attention on the task of taking the test. I was unaware that the sketch of the diagram had made such an impact on her; however, she was more visually oriented than is usual.

Rather than the counselor's simply prescribing certain coping self-statements, clients need to experiment with different coping methods. They can be encouraged to "window shop" for ideas and to "try some things on" to gauge their fit. Lange and Jakubowski (1976) suggest that the client be encouraged to look for internal physiological validation of the potential effectiveness of coping self-statements. As clients listen to or think different phrases—or try out images—they should observe whether they experience a slight but perceptible physiological relief. If so, the cognitive process eliciting the relief can be incorporated into the coping repertoire.

In summary, the in-depth analytical methods of Ellis and Beck are particularly useful when coping problems are related to general issues of self-concept and psychosocial development; however, they do not lend themselves as efficiently to the limited problem of coping effectively with immediate situations as do the methods of Meichenbaum and Wine. The coping difficulties of many students are both specific to certain situations, such as tests or social interactions, and related to developmental tasks. With these individuals, both kinds of approaches can be incorporated. For instance, Wine's task-focused attention concept was used in imagery training with Frank to help him improve his skills for coping with public-speaking anxiety; however, in-depth rational analysis was also used in discussing events during the sessions in order to extend cognitive development to issues of autonomy and identity.

Using Humor in Developing Coping Strategies. Most of the theorists discussed in this chapter have discussed the value of humor as a useful instrument in identifying and puncturing unproductive belief systems. By definition, humor involves a reorienting of a common perspective. Skillfully used by the counselor, it can facilitate self-questioning, broadening of perspective, and making useful cognitive shifts. When used by clients in reference to their own cognitive knots, it often signifies that cognitive coping skills are being applied (Beck, Rush, Shaw, and Emery, 1979). The growth of benevolent humor toward oneself is often indicative of a more complex concept of oneself as adaptable and enduring.

Counselors need to take care not to use humor carelessly or abusively. When used with due caution, however, humor can play a valuable role in coping skills training. Counselors who can occasionally "poke fun" at themselves may be good models for self-centered and perfectionistic clients. Sensitively carrying clients' frames of reference to their logical extremes can enable them to recognize the self-defeating and arbitrary nature of their cognitions. Humorous metaphors, analogies, or stories can help clients recognize their "mental games." Finally, humorous "one liners" woven into internal dialogue may greatly enhance coping self-talk.

Relaxation Training as a Cognitive Coping Skill. Relaxation is frequently used as a coping skill with anxiety problems. Although it is often considered a behavioral strategy, Rachman (1967) has suggested that its contribution in systematic desensitization is primarily mental. Since the use of relaxation as a coping skill has been well described in other sources (Goldfried and Davison, 1976; Jacobson, 1938), I will not discuss it in detail here. However, I want to discuss ways in which relaxation can act as a powerful "cognitive modifier." Relaxation techniques can help still the frenetic "worry" self-talk by focusing clients' attention on relaxation instructions, relaxation cue words, slow rhythmic breathing, or the kinesthetic sensations of relaxation. This present-centered focus of attention is incompatible with the future-centered, self-oriented worrying characteristics of anxiety. For this reason, relaxation is often a beneficial strategy for clients to learn to use as a prelude to using coping self-statements. Both Susan and Frank were trained in a two-stage strategy of taking deep breaths and engaging in breathing meditation followed by task-focused coping self-talk.

Relaxation skills can also contribute to cognitive development in the self-in-world system by enhancing the internality of a client's perceived locus of control. Clients learn that they can in fact maintain some control over their internal physiological reactions and consequently over their responses to troublesome situations. As this confidence develops, the mastery of re-laxation can lead to a cognitive shift from a perspective of "I get overwhelmed and can't cope" to one of "I have means by which I can regain control."

Helping the Client "Own" Coping Methods

Once effective coping strategies have been developed, the client must integrate them so that they become almost auto-matic responses to the desired situational, cognitive, and physio-logical cues. It is one thing for a client to shift attention from self to tasks or recite coping self-talk in the sanctity of the counselor's office and another to initiate these strategies when the client begins to feel overwhelmed in a threatening situation.

Imagery exercises—with images sometimes presented in hierarchical fashion, as in systematic desensitization—can be used to give clients repeated practice in confronting difficult situations, detecting cues signaling emotional reactions, and im-plementing coping strategies. In coping skills training, a "self-control" model (Goldfried, 1971) is often used. Clients are in-structed to assume an active to assume an active role as the scenes are imagined. They are to "tune into" internal reactions, detect early signals of anxiety, and implement coping strategies in order to control and reduce the debilitative feelings. This use of imagery is more compatible with the goals of fostering self-control and developing an internal locus of control than is the traditional systematic desensitization approach, where clients assume a generally passive role and signal the therapist to termi-nate imagery if they experience anxiety. In an adaptation of this model developed by Goldfried, Decenteceo, and Weinberg (1974), clients rationally reevaluate their reactions as they visu-alize the situations.

Although a hierarchy is sometimes useful in imagery exercises, on many occasions it is preferable to present se-quences of scenes. Research has suggested that careful calibra-tion of a hierarchy is really not important and that providing exposure to the feared stimulus is its primary value (Goldfried and Goldfried, 1977). A sequence of events related to an anxiety-arousing final exam was presented to Susan: (1) She looks over the material several days before the exam and realizes how much she has to learn. (2) On the night before the exam, she studies the material and realizes that she does not understand an important section. (3) She enters the classroom on exam day. (4) She receives the test. (5) She encounters confusion as she tries to answer a difficult question. With each event she was to imagine herself in the situation, first detecting cues of anxiety and then implementing coping strategies.

Imagery practice for developing coping skills should contain "coping models" rather than "mastery models." Research has suggested that observers can better identify with and learn from models who eventually cope successfully but initially show self-doubt and imperfect behavior than from models who function perfectly (Kazdin, 1974; Meichenbaum, 1971). For this reason, I ask clients to imagine themselves detecting the beginnings of debilitative feelings and self-focused worrying and then implementing coping strategies to regain control.

In order to integrate the techniques, a great deal of repetition in using coping skills to grapple with difficult situations is needed. The counselor can provide repeated exposures by making an audiotape of imagery practice in a session and asking the client to listen to it at least once a day during the next week. This method provides more exposure to scenes than could be offered in the sessions alone. Those familiar with the rationale for systematic desensitization might fear that clients would not terminate visualizations when anxiety began and would therefore recondition anxiety to the stimulus. However, in the self-control rationale, it is helpful if the scene produces some anxiety, so that the client can practice coping strategies to reduce it. Clients who have learned workable coping methods and are able to cope successfully in the session with feelings evoked by the imagery rarely experience any difficulty. On the rare occasions when clients do report difficulty, further in-session work should be done before tape practice at home is prescribed.

In addition to imagery methods, graduated *in vivo* assignments can be used to help clients incorporate the strategies. The term "graduated" means that the client undertakes less difficult situations first and then progresses to more difficult ones. Graduated speaking tasks during sessions can be arranged for clients with public-speaking anxiety. For instance, clients might begin with an informal two-minute presentation to the counselor, progress to a more formal stand-up speech to the counselor, then progress to an informal talk to the counselor and one other person, and so on. In planning *in vivo* exposures, the counselor should determine how well clients have learned the coping skills and whether the next task is sufficiently manageable for them. A speaking task for one recent client evidently presented too much of a jump from the previous step, in that she became overwhelmed with embarrassment. For this reason, it is often advisable to conduct some imagery work before starting *in vivo* exposures.

In *vivo* assignments that the client undertakes as homework are often more practical than exercises done in the session. Graduated interpersonal tasks can be useful for clients with social evaluative anxiety. For instance, a shy student might be asked to use coping strategies to control anxiety while initiating conversation in a cafeteria line and then progress to more difficult interactions. A test-anxious client might be asked to experiment with coping strategies while studying for a test rather than in the test itself. I suggested to Frank that he first use his strategies in a test, which aroused some anxiety but not as much as was produced by public-speaking situations.

A role-playing technique useful in helping clients internalize cognitive coping strategies is called the "mind game" (Barrow and Hetherington, 1981; Barrow and Moore, 1983). After a troublesome situation is identified, the clients can be asked to be the "anxiety-arousing part" of the mind and to verbalize worry self-talk about the situation. The counselor assumes the role of the "coping part" of the mind (Point D) by countering the worry statements with coping self-talk. After several minutes of modeling cognitive coping skills, the counselor reverses roles with the client.

Use of cuing techniques can help clients incorporate coping skills into their automatic responses to situations. When a meaningful way of disputing a core irrational thought or a particularly salient coping self-statement has been identified, the client can be asked to write the thought on an index card. Several years ago I counseled a young physical therapy student who was overanxious about academic demands. Her anxiousness was largely related to self-imposed perfectionistic standards. The statement "It doesn't have to be perfect!" seemed quite reassuring to her. She was instructed to write this message on an index card, to keep the card with her books, and to read it frequently throughout the day. She used the card a great deal initially, and it helped her remember to use her coping strategies. As she internalized the message, she began to use the card less and less.

Another type of cue is used to help clients become more aware of self-monitoring and self-control strategies. After one student had learned relaxation and task-focused attention as coping skills, she was instructed to purchase some bright paper stickers and to place them in different locations in her room, study cubicle, and books. When she noticed one of the stickers, she was to monitor her thoughts and feelings and to initiate coping strategies if she detected anxiety or irrational thoughts. This step is *particularly* useful with students who frequently repress their feelings and compulsively drive themselves. Such students habitually avoid attending to their internal signals.

As clients develop ability in identifying their cognitions and reevaluating them, an Ellis (1982) technique can help them solidify cognitive coping strategies. Clients are asked to picture a disturbing situation and to describe the debilitative feelings experienced. They are then told to continue imagining the situation and to bring the feelings to a more moderate level. Clients almost always use cognitive strategies to achieve this result and are often surprised at how easily the feelings can be altered. The effect is to strengthen confidence in existing strategies and/ or suggest new coping ideas. I used this method with a shy female student who reported to one session in a panic about a presentation she was to make in a seminar that afternoon. I asked her to imagine herself sitting in the classroom immediately prior to giving her presentation and to bring her level of anxiety from "extremely anxious" to "only somewhat anxious."

She did so by directing her mind into relaxing and focusing on the present and later reported that she was also able to use these strategies successfully in her seminar.

Unproductive cognitive patterns often are closely related to earlier experiences with certain people or situations. Not surprisingly, parents are often influential in the development of irrational beliefs or self-defeating schemas. Imagery or other experiential exercises directed at these "source influences" may be particularly effective because such imagery is unusually vivid. The method may also serve to anchor coping strategies more firmly in the client's network of self-defining cognitions than would focusing exclusively on immediate situations. Attention to source influences can be particularly helpful in facilitating exploration and growth in developmental tasks. A good example of this technique occurred with a medical student who had "swallowed whole" her father's extremely perfectionistic attitudes and had difficulty being flexible and nurturing with herself. After several sessions during which we discussed her relationship with her father and worked on developing coping skills, I asked her to write a letter to him that was not to be mailed. She was to explain her own criteria and values and to indicate how they differed from his. Partially through this exercise, she was able to differentiate her own goals and beliefs from his and to surrender some of her perfectionistic precepts.

It is often helpful to go beyond standard verbal exchanges and to encourage clients to make use of other sensory modalities. Imagery exercises incorporating visualization and other sensory representations can contribute in this way. *In vivo* practice is perhaps partly successful because it allows the client to use all sensory modalities in encountering the situation. Clients can also be asked to make something that represents what they have learned about coping with difficult situations. In a perfectionism group, I gave students paper and pencils and asked them to draw pictures or make paper sculptures. Students can also be asked to design a logo that connotes what they have learned about coping. Ellis (1982) has written a number of "rational songs" that satirize irrational beliefs. The singing of these would entail a richer sensory experience with the concepts than would simply thinking or talking about them. Many counselors, myself included, may be reluctant to impose loudly singing clients on our colleagues in adjoining offices; however, other related options—such as asking clients to compose mottos, poems, or slogans—are less intrusive and perhaps just as effective.

Termination of Counseling

In embarking on cognitive coping skills training, clients can benefit from a road map of the rationale for the approach and the steps involved. At termination, counselors should assess the status of clients' cognitive maps of where they have been as they progressed through counseling. Clients can be asked to explain how they have progressed and what they have learned about coping with problematic situations. My reasoning for this step may be naive, but I simply think that there is a better chance that they will "own" and remember coping strategies if they can explain them to me than if they cannot. In essence, I strive to "anchor" the coping skills in the client's conscious cognitive systems. My position is different from that of strategic therapists, who are less inclined to encourage a client to formulate an explicit understanding of a change (Haley, 1976).

The counselor can begin this review process by summarizing clients' presenting problems and then asking them to describe the current status of the problem, the degree to which outcome goals have been attained, and their reactions to the counseling. It is important that clients understand the specific coping techniques they have learned. However, I am also hopeful that they have generalized the implications of the coping methods beyond the immediate situation and have altered important views of themselves and others. In order to test the degree of generalization, the counselor can ask, "What have you learned about yourself as we have gone through this process?"

It is difficult to gauge how newly learned cognitive coping strategies will weather the storm of further life experiences. In many ways it is simpler for clients *not* to change than to make substantial changes. A number of motivations can combine with the strength of old habits to encourage clients to sabotage their change efforts. Counselors can suggest that clients speculate about cognitive, affective, and behavioral aspects that could contribute to their sabotaging implementation of the coping skills. Once identified, these impulses can be submitted to the intervention model; assumptions can be identified, questioned, disputed, and so forth. Irrational beliefs about making changes often surface in this phase. As sabotage-encouraging cognitions come to light, they can be converted into cues for renewed efforts to cope.

New learning can also be eroded by the influence of students' interpersonal systems, since these often helped create the unproductive cognitive patterns. Counselors can take two steps to deal with this reality. First, further sessions can be suggested for clients who are coping successfully but still seem a little shaky. Among other directions, these sessions can focus on preparing students for the expected "regressive suck" of interpersonal systems. They may need to devise coping strategies for dealing with these sources of influence. Second, effort can be made to "keep the door open" for further counseling in the future if problems recur. This step is particularly important when time limitations bring about the termination earlier than the counselor would ordinarily advise. Because she began counseling just before the ending of the semester, Susan received only three counseling sessions. While the intervention enabled her to cope successfully with some difficult exams, the period of the intervention may not have been long enough for the coping methods to remain in her repertoire at full strength. Two years later she returned to the counseling service with a rekindled level of anxiety regarding tests in two courses. She might have benefited from some "booster" sessions, perhaps a couple at the beginning of the following fall semester and then two or three others spaced about three months apart. The use of booster sessions may be particularly worthy of consideration with clients whose counseling is particularly brief as a result of time restrictions.

Discussions with clients during the termination phase of counseling provide important data for evaluating the intervention (Phase 8b). Responses to pre- and postintervention assessment instruments or goal attainment scaling procedures can help clients clarify the status of their difficulties and formulate postcounseling goals.

Summary and Conclusions

Cognitive coping skills training proved to be relatively successful with both Frank and Susan. Frank's intervention was conducted for eleven sessions and included structured training of coping skills and less structured developmental counseling directed at his cognitive systems of self and self-in-world. Initially, he was unaware of a great deal of cognitive activity related to his public-speaking anxiety. Nevertheless, he recognized the value of learning cognitive and behavioral coping skills to "short-circuit" his reactions. He was trained in using relaxation as a prelude to using coping self-statements and task-focused attention. Imagery practice was conducted, both with a hierarchy he had constructed and with sequences related to specific speeches he had to give, including the presentation at the national conference. *In vivo* practice of the coping skills was also undertaken, first with a test and then with less formal speech tasks. As the training proceeded, Frank began to tune into his internal dialogue and was able to identify more of the self-defeating cognitive activity. The first four sessions focused on assessment and structured coping skills training. In subsequent sessions coping skills were discussed and practiced during the second half of the session, and the broader implications of Frank's self-defeating cognitions were explored in the first half. Developmental counseling centered on his overall social development and the influence of his family system. As he gained confidence with the coping strategies and began to have success with them, the implications of these gains for his self-concept were explored. One outcome of the intervention was that Frank was successful in coping with his anxiety before and during the conference presentation and felt quite good about his performance. He also acquired a better understanding of the perfectionistic cognitive system related to his autonomy and identity development.

The scope of the intervention used with Susan was more limited than Frank's, partly because she was seen for only three sessions and partly because her coping difficulties seemed more specific to one situation and less related to broader developmental issues. By midway through the first session, enough information had been obtained to suggest that she was an appropriate candidate for coping skills training. Thus, a relaxation exercise was conducted with her in the first session; and she was instructed to practice the technique once a day, using an audiocassette recording. In the second session, the relaxation training was reinforced, her self-defeating cognitions were discussed so as to sensitize her to the patterns, and she was introduced to task-focused attention as a coping strategy. In the third session, the relaxation and task-focused coping strategies were further discussed; and imagery practice of these techniques was conducted, in which sequences pertaining to two of her upcoming exams were used. The imagery practice was tape-recorded, and she was encouraged to listen to the tape several times during the three days before her exams. Upon completion of her exams, Susan telephoned to say that she had done well. She had begun to feel anxious on several occasions but had been able to employ her coping strategies and reduce the anxiety. As previously noted, her gains might have been made more resilient with booster sessions offered the following fall semester.

SIX

Focusing on Old and New Experiences in the Change Process

Harvey was a twenty-year-old college student from a rural community. On the basis of a referral from a dean, he entered counseling with complaints about his academic functioning. It soon became apparent, however, that he was deeply dissatisfied with a number of other aspects of his life, particularly his relationships with others. He felt isolated and lonely and complained that he was victimized, neglected, or rebuffed by others. He seemed obsessed with the need to find a girl friend and was continually thwarted in his efforts to do so. While these difficulties had become particularly acute since he had entered the university and partially involved adjustment to the new situation, the basic interpersonal style and degree of involvement with others seemed to be long-standing problems. He had been the object of ridicule for his odd manner by other children in junior and senior high school. His relationships with his parents had been characterized by authoritarian rule and criticality on their part and obedience with simmering resentment on his.

176

Clearly, Harvey's social behavior was very poorly developed, and his cognitive systems for viewing himself, the world, and his interactions with the world were limited and rigid. He consistently denied his feelings, externalized responsibility for his difficulties to "idiotic" classmates or professors, and perceived the locus of control of his reinforcement to be external. His general attitude toward problematic situations was "I'm angry as hell at these people and want to complain about them at length; however, I'm an innocent victim, and they're the sole cause of the trouble, so there's nothing I can do about this."

How can Harvey, with his limited cognitive systems, be helped to develop more cognitive complexity? My first formulation in Phase 4 of the Cognitive Intervention Planning Model was that Harvey needed to learn to trust someone and experience a relationship in which he was not judged, victimized, neglected, or rebuffed. He obviously had deficits resulting from a long-standing history of receiving double messages and criticism. Perhaps by offering high levels of the facilitative conditions, I could provide him with a "corrective emotional experience." So I tried. And tried and tried. He seemed to become quite comfortable talking with me. In fact, the dean reported that he had extolled my virtues. However, he did not seem to be broadening his views or interacting more successfully with the world.

What then? Having returned to Phase 4 to reformulate Harvey's problems, personal attributes, and our interaction process, I decided that a more active stance on my part might be necessary in order to help him gain a more complete understanding of himself and his difficulties. I therefore gave him feedback on the limited nature of his conceptions of situations, interpreted some of the patterns I had observed, and gently presented him with challenges in the form of alternative maps of reality. I also tried to help him pinpoint important skills that would help him interact more successfully with others and cope more effectively with his feelings. What were the results of these efforts? He began to regard me as one of his enemies and held doggedly to his rigid beliefs.

Why was Harvey not more receptive to my efforts to help him change? He said that he wanted to feel more satisfied with his life, and sometimes he seemed to recognize, deep down inside, that he did share some responsibility for his problems with the culprits of the world. In short, there seemed to be good reasons for him to change, even from his limited perspective. What I had not clearly identified in Phase 4b of the first two stages of my counseling with him was that he had substantial reasons for *not* changing (see Chapter Three). Primarily, his victim role served as a "face-saving" defense, and he was fearful of being without the protection that it provided. His implicit guidelines as he processed new information were along the lines of "I *must* persist in seeing myself and my world in the way that I do. This is the only way I know to escape despair and protect myself from the harshness and cruelty in the world." In his mind, the loosening of these rigidly constructed systems would render him defenseless and expose him to intolerable ambiguity. In short, change was not worth the risks. Naturally, Harvey was not fully aware of all his reasons for not changing. Most of his guiding assumptions in operation were at the third level of awareness (see Chapter Two).

So what did I do then, as I reentered Phase 4 of the model for the third time? I considered several options including termination of the counseling or referral of the case back to the dean who had started the whole thing. Fortunately, I did come up with an approach that seemed to be more effective with Harvey. The approach, which I call "experiential cognitive dissonance counseling," entails approaching the client in a less direct way than the counseling methods previously described and searching for ways to stimulate cognitive dissonance.

Working toward cognitive change in a less direct manner is one cornerstone of experiential cognitive dissonance counseling. The other important characteristic is that the counselor attempts to use modes of experience other than verbal representations. If clients' reasons *not* to change are encoded in nonverbal channels, developmental counseling, as described in Chapter Four, and coping skills training, as described in Chapter Five, may not deal adequately with important constraints to change, since these approaches rely extensively on verbal exchanges. The experiential approach differs from the two counseling strategies already discussed in that an intermediate step of disrupting or confusing existing cognitive processes is often seen as a necessary process goal in order to increase cognitive complexity.

When and with whom is this kind of approach indicated? The following guidelines can help counselors answer that question:

1. If the outcome goals (Phase 5a) can be achieved through direct, exploratory interchanges, as described in Chapter Four, and if the client is open and motivated to engage in these interchanges (Phases 4b and 4c), rapport-building and developmental counseling methods should be used predominantly.

2. If achieving the outcome goals requires learning new cognitive skills that are unlikely to be developed through developmental counseling and if the client is open and motivated to engage in this learning process, the cognitive coping skills training approach, discussed in Chapter Five, should be used alone or in conjunction with developmental counseling. This approach might also be advisable if it would significantly shorten the time needed to attain the cognitive changes.

3. If the outcome goals are unlikely to be achieved through one or both of the first two approaches and/or if the client does not appear to be open and motivated toward engaging in the activities required, then indirect and subtle influence methods might be advisable. Such an approach might also be permissible if it would significantly reduce the necessary duration of the counseling.

It must be remembered that I have somewhat arbitrarily chosen to divide counseling interventions into these three categories. With most clients, counselors are likely to intersperse methods characteristic of two or more of these categories during the flow of counseling. The guidelines I have offered apply to the overall attitude assumed in counseling (how collaborative should counseling be?) and the relative frequency with which different methods are used (how often should the counselor be indirect?). It must also be remembered that clients may differ in the developmental levels they have attained in different domains of experience. A client might be open to direct exploration of one set of experiences and yet defensive regarding another. For instance, I can recall a student who was open to discussing his family and peer relationships but was extremely reserved about exploring his male-female interactions, particularly when sexuality was implied. I could directly suggest that we explore the former but had to be subtle and indirect in dealing with the latter.

Experiential cognitive dissonance counseling would be the preferred "game plan" identified at Phase 6 under several circumstances. First, this approach can be used when methods from the other two approaches have resulted in insufficient progress and/or resistance. With Harvey, both developmental and direct problem resolution counseling had been attempted unsuccessfully. Second, some of these methods are indicated when emotionalized reactions are insufficiently understood through exploratory discussions that are primarily verbal. Third, the approach can be tried when emotionalized reactions seem to be insufficiently influenced by direct cognitive exploration and skills training. In these situations the meaning behind the emotions may not be encoded exclusively in verbal channels. Therefore, predominantly verbal techniques are only partially capable of influencing the associations.

Methods used in the implementation (Phase 7) of experiential cognitive dissonance counseling can be organized into three categories. First, counselors may need to develop ways to deal with a client's resistance and control maneuvers, so that they can achieve or maintain a position of influence with the client. Second, counselors may take actions designed to help clients recognize and resolve cognitive dissonance that is already present. Third, counselors can attempt to lead clients to have new experiences that will create cognitive dissonance, in that the new information will conflict with previously held beliefs.

Managing Issues of Resistance and Control

The fear produced by the challenges of exploring sensitive information can be so intense for some clients that they resist direct efforts to help them confront important issues. They may resort to various maneuvers in order to establish control of the counseling and thereby avoid the threat. Harvey's oppositional behavior in response to my efforts to conduct active developmental counseling and pursue problem solving is a good example. In order to establish a position of influence that can be used to foster cognitive complexity, the counselor needs an effective cognitive map for dealing with these maneuvers.

Sidestepping and Using Resistance. A counselor is often tempted to continue direct interventions when resistance is elicited. Perhaps the "heat" apparently felt by the client is a good indication of the salience of the issue. However, many clients intensify resistance as the heat of cognitive challenge is increased. A confrontational approach can result in termination of counseling, withdrawal from the counselor, and/or an unproductive spiral of stubbornness. I often try direct feedback the first time or two that an issue should be explored or examined. If the client is able to deal constructively with this direct method, I am likely to continue with it.

Unfortunately, clients are often unable to benefit from direct confrontations about sensitive issues, even after they are given time to "get used to the ideas." In these instances, as Milton Erickson has noted, the counselor can attempt to make use of the client's resistance (Haley, 1973). Erickson has emphasized that resistive stances contain a great deal of emotional energy. If this energy, currently directed toward self-protection and preservation of the status quo, can be redirected, it can fuel productive grappling with difficulties.

A helpful way of conceptualizing resistance is as a method by which clients attempt to resolve cognitive dissonance stimulated by threatening or confusing information. If the counselor presents a point that conflicts with a key cognitive system, clients can resolve the dissonance by declaring the counselor's point invalid. They may further buttress this resolution by construing the counselor as an antagonist who does not understand them. They may then expect that the counselor will attempt to assert dominance over them, as others have often done. One of the best ways for the counselor to deal with resistance is *to avoid confirming clients' expectancies of an antagonistic encounter.* For example, the counselor can invite clients to avoid discussing any topic when the wisdom of their gut instincts urges caution. This kind of response places the counselor in the "one-down" position described by Fisch, Weakland, and Segal (1982). They believe that this position is preferable to a "one-up" position in enabling the counselor to elicit information and obtain compliance from the client.

After a number of unsuccessful attempts to directly engage Harvey in an exploration of his part in his interactions, I began to respond as illustrated in the following exchange. He had complained at length about unfair treatment he thought he had received from a professor.

Counselor: Would it be worthwhile to think about how you approached Dr. Jones?

Client: I don't know why [*speaking very animatedly and loudly*]. If you mean did I do anything to deserve him dumping on me, I didn't.

Counselor: OK, you have strong feelings that that direction wouldn't be a good one for us. I think it's important that you listen to your insides and steer us away from those areas.

This kind of response can take the wind out of a client's sails, produce confusion, and create cognitive dissonance. The counselor's behavior may differ from the client's expectations of the counselor and perhaps of people in general. Paradoxically, rather than wrestling with clients for control of the session, the counselor may be more effective by overtly handing them control. Haley (1976) and others have suggested that this kind of counselor response presents clients with conflicting messages. Since the clients are coming to an expert for help, they are likely to perceive that the counselor is in a position of some control. But the counselor's verbalizations negate this position. The disruption of rigid cognitive processes may help foster productive cognitive reorganization.

This kind of counselor response may conflict with the client's cognitive systems of the world and of self-in-world. Clients may develop the self-in-world belief that "everybody gets on my case sooner or later." The counselor's remaining calm in the face of resistance and extending control to the client may subtly and indirectly challenge these restricted cognitive systems. With the support of a consistent, dependable relationship with the counselor, clients may be able to resolve the cognitive dissonance by expanding their views of themselves and their interactions.

Reinforcing Growth Rather Than Confronting Deficits. Sidestepping resistance maintains the workability of the counseling relationship and disrupts narrow cognitive systems. However, this response alone is generally not sufficient to help clients develop cognitive systems that are appreciably more complex. Counselors can help defensive clients move toward greater cognitive complexity by positively reinforcing instances of more flexible or mature thinking. In my work with Harvey, I tried to highlight instances where he evidenced more flexible cognitive processes, rather than attempting to explore his deficits. The following exchange occurred when we were discussing an interaction with a classmate:

Client: So I just decided that I wasn't going to get into that kind of thing with him. Maybe what he said was pretty harmless, I don't know. Anyway, I didn't even pay attention to it. I just kept on working on my math problems.

Counselor: Good for you. You know, that can be a hard thing to do—to say to yourself "Well, I don't really know what he's up to, so why worry about it" and to keep yourself from getting drawn into some sniping. But I think that way of dealing with it shows real strength.

The importance of showing "strength" was a key element in Harvey's "ideal self" cognitive system, so I thought that the use of this term would be particularly reinforcing. In using the tactic of providing positive reinforcement, the counselor must learn to be attentive to small alterations, because major changes are ordinarily too infrequent.

Refusing to Play the Client's Games. Harvey was accustomed to playing a "wrestling" game with others and therefore expected me to follow this pattern—to play "controlling parent" to his "rebellious child." Proponents of transactional analysis define "games" as interactions in which "players transact on an *open* (overt) level and at the same time transmit a *hidden* agenda (covert level)" (Dusay and Dusay, 1979, pp. 393–394). If the client is successful in drawing the counselor into playing certain games, the counseling is less likely to be productive in the long run. The client may be able to avoid responsibility and manipulate the counseling interactions so that important areas are not addressed. Through their games clients may assume positions in which they are supported too extensively and challenged too insufficiently for cognitive development to occur.

If the counselor avoids being drawn into the client's favorite games, confusion and cognitive dissonance may occur. The client may be left in an unfamiliar "where do I go from here" state and may be more receptive to proceeding in productive directions. A client's cognitive map of self-in-world can often be paraphrased "In order to get along with people and get what I need from them, I *must* have our interaction go according to my game." This precept may be challenged if the counselor does not allow the game to be played *and* the interactions continue to be perceived as productive by the client. The cognitive dissonance produced by the discrepancy between the client's perceived need for the game and experiences in counseling without the game can be resolved by revising the restricted schema.

One game discussed by transactional analysis proponents is the "drama triangle," in which individuals unwittingly play roles of victim, persecutor, and rescuer (Dusay and Dusay, 1979). Most commonly, clients will present themselves in the victim role and expect the counselor to play rescuer. This game can often be successful in counseling, because many of us in the counseling profession like to help others. We must be careful that we do not confirm a helpless approach to life or assume too much responsibility for helping clients make changes. Becoming a rescuer may also be appealing because we may accurately sense that the client is likely to label us a persecutor if we do not assume the rescuer role. Cognitive dissonance is produced if the counselor can avoid being cast in the rescuer role and continues to be seen as supportive by the client. Thus, resolution may be stimulated, culminating in the client's surmising "Maybe it is possible for someone to be on my side and not bail me out all the time."

Many victims are so skillful in this role that they are rescued frequently; and each time they are rescued, they become more firmly convinced that they cannot deal independently with problems in their worlds. Cognitive dissonance regarding perceived locus of control can be stimulated if the counselor can avoid the rescuer role and thereby force the client to grapple with the problem. Clients are often surprised at their effectiveness when forced to take an active part in problem solving and may conclude, "Maybe I'm more capable of handling things on my own than I thought."

How can this tempting role of rescuer be avoided by the counselor in a way that maintains or enhances the client's view of the counselor as a supportive influence? One option would be directly presenting the client with immediate feedback: "From the way you are presenting me with so many questions, I'm getting the impression you'd like me to take you under my wing and lead you out of this mess." With many clients this direct approach would be effective. With others it could easily lead to a reconstruing of the counselor as a persecutor. A second option would be to ignore the ploy and lead clients toward acting as their own rescuers. The following interaction occurred with a college junior who seemed to have one melodramatic crisis after another and was constantly viewing herself as the victim in her relationships. On a previous occasion, the counselor had interceded with her academic dean and had helped her obtain an extension on an assignment.

Client: I'm just not in any shape to get anything done! My mother was so horrible when I called her on

Saturday. I've got this paper today and two exams tomorrow. I'm just gonna crack if something doesn't happen.

Counselor: You know, Ellen, you've proven yourself to be a pretty resourceful person a number of times. You're pretty smart, and I'm not all that bad either, so I bet if both of us put our minds to this we can come up with a good plan for how you can pull through.

Client: I was thinking maybe I could get an incomplete in one of them—that maybe you could write my professor a note or something.

Counselor: And say what?

Client: That I'd crack up or something if I don't get the incomplete.

Counselor: You know what? I'll bet you're too resourceful to let that happen. I've seen you pull things together pretty fast when you've had to. I don't think the note is the best option. What is your game plan for getting the paper done and studying for the exams?

Client: [*Sits quietly for a few seconds, looking disappointed.*] I don't know. I guess I could try to finish up the paper by around 2:00 this afternoon and then start reviewing.

The counselor avoided the client's ploy to be rescued and at the same time maintained a supportive posture by aligning with her resourcefulness.

Another option would be to use humor to deflect the client's efforts to secure the counselor as rescuer. This option has to be used with a great deal of caution, because humor rendered without sufficient support in the relationship might well be interpreted as persecution. Yet a humorous response that remains empathic can enable the counselor to avoid the unwanted role and to comment on the game itself. One such game is the "reassure me" game. Some clients defensively run themselves down as a way of getting others to provide them with what transactional analysis counselors call "strokes." Their self-in-world cognitive system is such that they expect to be judged negatively or criticized by others. Their defensive response is to criticize themselves first. This tactic generally enables them to avoid external criticism and obtain reassurance. Unfortunately, the reassurance is often discounted, even if it is genuinely offered, because on some level these individuals realize that it was secured manipulatively. The following discussion occurred with a very capable female student who lacked self-confidence in her social skills and had developed a self-deprecatory style:

Client:	Jean is so pretty and nice. It's surprising any of the guys will give me the time of day with girls like her around.
Counselor:	Yea, I guess it's a lost cause—with you being such an eyesore and being up for the "Worst Personality of the Year" Award.
Client:	Hey, you're not supposed to talk to me that way! [*Laughing.*]
Counselor:	Oh, what am I supposed to say?
Client:	You're supposed to tell me that I have all those nice qualities and remind me of all the good things my friends see in me. [*Still smiling.*]
Counselor:	You seem to be catching on to those things. Do you still need me to do that?
Client:	It wouldn't hurt. [*Said good-naturedly.*]

Two considerations regarding the use of this kind of humorous response are important to mention. First of all, the counselor would not have used this kind of humor if a good counseling relationship had not been established. The line between good-natured humor and sarcasm is quite fine, and the counselor should not risk saying something that the client might take as demeaning. Second, the humorous response was offered when the client was maintaining and enhancing her cognitive gains, not at a time when she was in crisis.

Transactional analysis counselors also discuss the "kick me" game, which is a favorite among many clients. Such clients expect to be punished by others and may attempt to maneuver the counselor into fulfilling this expectation. The communication stances identified by Satir (1972) provide another framework for identifying clients' games. The role of her "placator" is to try at length to please, build up, and cater to the counselor, perhaps in exchange for being treated protectively. The "blamer" will attempt to induce the counselor to accept too much responsibility for the counseling and the blamer's state. The "computer" will try to converse in an ultracool, reasoned manner in an effort to keep things from becoming too emotional. The "distractor" is adept at using irrelevancies, charm, and a dramatic flare to distract the counselor from focusing attention on significant vulnerabilities.

Satir's communication styles and the games outlined by transactional analysts can be helpful. However, the counselor needs to be sensitive to the individual nuances of clients and the games they play. It is often better to "start from scratch" in assessing the game dynamics of a client than to use a preset repertoire of games in conceptualization.

Giving Paradoxical Directives. Strategic therapists such as Haley (1976) make a great deal of use of paradoxical suggestions and directives, particularly with clients thought to be resistant. In this approach the counselor presents two conflicting messages. One is usually conveyed by the counselor's words, while the other may be contained in nonverbal cues or in the context of the situation. It is difficult for clients to resist paradoxical interventions successfully, because if they defy one directive they abide by the other. For instance, the context of being in counseling contains the message "talk about your problems." A counselor might send a paradoxical message by suggesting, "Let's agree not to discuss anything too personal for the rest of the session."

From a cognitive perspective, one of the benefits of the use of paradox is that it often disrupts clients' habitual cognitive patterns and produces some confusion. Rigidly maintained cognitive boundaries can thereby be loosened, at least momentarily. If clients are subtly disengaged from their familiar and characteristic methods of processing information, they may be able to arrive at new formulations. However, since paradoxical interventions are rarely sufficient, the counselor should be prepared to follow the use of paradox with other methods discussed in this chapter and in Chapters Four and Five.

Use of paradoxical methods can be illustrated by the problem of low study motivation. Frequently, students seek counseling only after their procrastination has placed them in a difficult situation, and they hope that the counselor can provide a quick, simple solution to what is often a long-standing and relatively complex problem. The counselor may therefore be wary of being placed in an impossible position and can use a paradoxical ploy to avoid being saddled with responsibilities that should remain in the client's hands. For instance, I suggested to one student, "I'm not sure we ought to work toward your doing a lot more study right now. When people are ready, they usually know it, and there don't seem to be any signs that you're really ready to change your habits. Maybe we should concentrate on helping you feel better about not working very much." If clients protest that they do indeed feel ready, I may respond, "Well, maybe you are, but it still seems pretty inconclusive. What convincing reasons can you come up with?" The counselor may also suggest that the client should avoid trying to do "too much too fast" and attempt only a very small amount of change before the next session. This method will sometimes result in clients' increasing their commitment to changing. Even if the results are not as conclusive, the counselor has maintained maneuverability by avoiding responsibility for coming up with a way to get the client to study.

The use of paradox is a delicate technique that requires careful discrimination on the part of the counselor. In my judgment, a more explicit, direct approach is preferable, if such methods seem to work with a client, since clients who are fully aware of the directions of counseling can contribute valuable information regarding their needs. Readers should acquaint themselves more thoroughly with paradoxical methods before attempting to use them extensively in counseling. Haley's (1963, 1976) work provides a more complete description of the use of these techniques.

Focusing on Cognitive Dissonance
Contained in Previous Experiences

Much of experiential cognitive dissonance counseling is based on helping clients more completely process events they have previously experienced.

Mirroring Cognitive Distortions. A relatively simple yet effective technique is for the counselor to mirror a phrase used by the client that suggests that information has been distorted. Clients often engage in cognitive distortions so habitually, both in speech and thought, that they are unaware of doing so. The mirroring by the counselor can provide immediate feedback of the presence of distortions. Clients can then examine their speech and thought for distortions, review their encoded experiences, and perhaps emerge with a new cognitive construction of the problematic situation. The following example occurred with a college sophomore who was prone to dichotomous thinking, particularly regarding herself:

Client: I bungle things like that every time. I'll swear, I do it every time.

Counselor: *Every* time?

Client: Well, not every time, but a lot.

Counselor: Have there been some times the last week when you didn't bungle?

Client: Well, sure, a few. I mean, I'm not a total loser. I handled this one thing pretty well actually.

Asking for Negative Evidence. The above example illustrates another approach the counselor can take to bring clients' thoughts and verbalizations into conflict with previous experiences. Clients can be asked whether instances exist that are not consistent with an assertion that has been made. They can then examine their encoded experiences more carefully and perhaps revise their formulations. Bandler and Grinder (1975) have discussed similar methods of encouraging clients to compare their cognitive representations and verbalizations with encoded experiences or "reference structures."

Humorously Exaggerating Cognitive Distortions. Along lines similar to mirroring, counselors can sometimes call attention to maladaptive cognitive processes by humorously and gently exaggerating them. As with any humorous approach, this method should be used in a sensitive manner and ordinarily should not be used until client and counselor have established a reasonably good relationship. The interaction presented previously to illustrate avoiding the "reassure me" game can also serve as an example of exaggerating a distorted cognitive process.

Shifting the Client's Vantage Point. Another way of getting clients to review their experiences and determine the degree of consistency of these reference structures with their verbalizations and thoughts is to ask them to consider a situation from another vantage point. This step can sometimes be accomplished through imagery, in which the client is asked to visualize a situation from the eyes of another person. For instance, a client who had been denigrating himself for bungling a conversation was asked to visualize his behavior as if he were the other person. The perceptions and cognitions he offered were then explored and submitted to reality testing. An empty-chair technique can also be used. For instance, a client who is overcritical of her qualities as a mother can be asked to assume the role of her daughter. As the daughter, she can then be asked to describe her mother, who is supposedly seated in an empty chair across from her.

While imagery, empty-chair, and role-playing techniques can be useful in asking clients to appraise situations from another point of reference, they are not always necessary. Some clients are made uncomfortable by such techniques. Also, the shift in vantage point sometimes can be made in less time without the use of such techniques. Clients can be asked to "suppose" that they are viewing themselves from the eyes of another person privy to a situation. By describing their own behavior as seen by another, they can often arrive at a more balanced appraisal of their performance and a more complex view of themselves. This technique, which is sometimes used in coping skills training, was used with Frank and described in Chapter Five.

Experimenting with Different Classification Frameworks. With a black-and-white television set, we are more limited in discerning shades of light than with a color set. In the same manner, a limited classification construct leads us to a less differentiated understanding of our experiences than does a more complex construct. When a counselor senses that a client is classifying or evaluating experiences too simplistically, the client can be asked to experiment with a more complex framework. Burns (1980a, 1980b) has suggested asking clients who are prone to dichotomous thinking to make ratings of experiences rather than either-or determinations. Instead of allowing clients to maintain a dichotomous position, such as "I know she thinks I'm a complete loser now," the counselor can suggest a rating scale: "On a scale of 0 to 10, with 0 meaning complete and absolute loser and 10 meaning complete winner, where do you think she sees you?" It can also be helpful to experiment with different reference points for the rating: "Where did she see you on the scale before you put your foot in your mouth?" "Where do you think she saw you right at that moment when you goofed?" More complex classification systems, such as percentages and frequencies, also can be used.

Beck and his colleagues have designed an interesting approach that combats the tendency for clients to assume the truth of one alternative interpretation (Beck, Rush, Shaw, and Emery, 1979). This technique was applied with a student who had an extremely stormy relationship with her mother and had become convinced that her mother's actions toward her were always negatively motivated. Over the course of several sessions, the counselor asked her to clarify assumptions she was making about actions taken by her mother, generate other possible reasons why her mother might have taken a particular action, and then specify the percentage of "believability" of each option. This exercise helped her realize that she did in fact make assumptions about what her mother was thinking and that she might be better off restraining her tendency to jump to conclusions.

Using Metaphors. Preexisting cognitive dissonance can sometimes be highlighted through the use of metaphors, a method pioneered by Milton Erickson (Haley, 1973; Rosen, 1982). He saw metaphors as means of planting ideas in clients' minds without their being aware of it. I am more likely to use metaphors as colorful, memorable ways of communicating concepts to clients in language patterns they can understand. A metaphor that "hits home" may activate more cognitive modes and emotional reactions than the same idea presented in didactic form. For example, I made use of a metaphor in a session with a shy student who experienced anxiety in social situations. In the two previous sessions, we had worked on his developing anxiety management coping skills, as discussed in Chapter Five. While he had been able to make some use of these methods, he had not yet developed a comprehensive cognitive map for bringing them into play. In previous sessions he had mentioned that he enjoyed playing basketball, so I used a basketball metaphor to enhance his understanding of the coping strategy. Regarding social situations, I suggested that we think in terms of a "game plan" in which he tried to prepare himself by focusing on what he wanted to do rather than on how he was being judged. During the "game" he would need to keep his mind on the tasks, just as a basketball player needs to think about aspects such as moving and following through. With this positive focus, he would be "playing to win" rather than "playing to keep from being beaten." This metaphor allowed him to apply a more complex cognitive system, which had been developed regarding basketball, to the less familiar domain of socializing.

In a session with a college junior who was struggling with a series of disappointing experiences, both academic and social, I made use of a metaphor that she herself had initiated. This client had developed a self-in-world cognitive system based on the assumption that she would eventually be thwarted in almost anything of importance. A metaphor she used for her perspective was that she had written a book on each disappointing experience and placed the books on one shelf. Whenever something new happened, she added the new book and then read them all from start to finish. As we continued to explore her feelings and cognitions from within the bookshelf metaphor, she developed increased understanding of her cognitive processes regarding her old wounds and her new experiences. Because of her pessimism and external locus of control of reinforcement, she would write the final chapter in her mind before events had run their course. Not surprisingly, the final chapter continued the theme of inevitable failure. We then continued with the metaphor in considering "what kind of rewriting of these books would be helpful." She began to consider the possibility of holding off on rewriting the final chapter until events had actually transpired. Also, she thought that she might need to think back over the books and determine whether she had chronicled all her experiences. She thought she had probably preserved only the more negative events.

Cognitive Reframing. Applying a method that advocates of brief therapy have called "reframing" (Fisch, Weakland, and Segal, 1982), the counselor attempts to produce a subtle shift in the client's frame of reference. Generally, the counselor strives for small but significant shifts rather than major ones, which are likely to conflict too intensely with important cognitive systems. Successful reframing often entails integrating two familiar concepts rather than forming a new one. In other words, the counselor attempts to help the client expand a cognitive system by applying previously developed cognitions to new situations.

The following discussion ensued with a graduate student who was experiencing frustration regarding his dissertation:

Client: I just can't believe it took me that long! I spent all that time getting registered, and then had to call four people to get this meeting changed, and it took me several tries to get ahold of each of them. And then I had to get a time set up with a statistics consultant. So here it is midweek, and I haven't really gotten to work on my dissertation, just messed with all these hassles.

Counselor: That kind of thing is so frustrating. [*Note reflection of feeling.*]

Client: Is it ever!

Counselor: You know, it's interesting you said you hadn't done any work. I can think of some times when I

went through similar periods where all I did was
mess with red tape. I remember really going crazy.
But it happened so much, I finally decided that
messing with these hassles and red tape is part of
the "work" of being a student. It helped me when
I began to view those things as a necessary part of
my "job," not just extra hassles.

Client: Ah, that's a better way of looking at it. Here I've
been feeling so frustrated because I didn't think
I was getting anything done, but I guess I've been
doing what I had to do.

In this interaction the reframing was accomplished through
self-disclosure. Perhaps this self-disclosure method of presenting
an alternative frame of reference was less likely to produce resistance than a more interpretive method might have.

Experimenting with Language. Another way to help clients confront preexisting cognitive dissonance is to focus on the
language patterns that they use. One language pattern to examine is pronoun selection—for instance, the use of the pronoun
"you" in referring to one's own experiences: "You can never
tell what Joe will do." "You get to feeling sorry for yourself
when those things happen." The effect of this pattern can be to
distance oneself from the experience and to avoid acceptance of
responsibility for one's feelings and thoughts. The counselor can
sometimes suggest that the client make the same statement but
with "I" (or another derivation of the first-person pronoun)
substituted for "you": "Try saying that again, just the way you
said it; however, this time say 'I' or 'myself' instead of 'you' or
'yourself.'" Any differences in thoughts or feelings associated
with the two patterns can then be explored. Rather than asking
the client to change the pronouns, the counselor can respond to
statements such as "You always feel . . ." by asking "I always
feel . . . ?" Clients will generally then make the substitutions on
their own. This approach can be used in a good-natured, humorous way, most often after the counselor has developed a good
relationship with the client.

Another significant language pattern is the use of overinclusive qualifiers. In light of the human need to take linguistic short-cuts, many of us are prone to exaggerate events when describing and thinking about them. When something rarely occurs, we say that it "never" does. When we frequently feel a certain way, we claim that we "always" do. Obviously, these overinclusive statements are not accurate cognitive maps of the experiences we are representing. It is important for the counselor to recognize these patterns and take steps to help clients examine them. The best response is often a question that requires a more specific assessment of the experiences: "How often has that happened?" "What percentage of the time would you say that occurs?" These kinds of questions can be followed by asking for negative evidence, as previously discussed: "Can you recall times when things haven't worked out that way?" Another method is to use the mirroring technique by simply repeating the overinclusive qualifier: "Always?"

Still another language pattern to observe is the inclusion of words such as "must," "should," "ought," and "can't" in the predicate of statements. Ellis has pointed out that these verb forms are often indicative of irrational beliefs (Ellis and Harper, 1975). "Must" and "can't" imply that some outcome is *necessary* for the individual, while "should" and "ought" imply that some moral precept will be violated if something is not done. One counseling strategy is to conduct questioning that aids clients in reality testing: "Why *must* you get a good grade?" or "What would happen if you did not get a good grade?" "What makes facing them seem so bad?" With "should," it is often helpful to ask "Who says you *should* . . . ?"

The language patterns mentioned are some of the most common and most problematic; however, many others may be significant. The counselor must therefore listen for other linguistic presentations that indicate problematic cognitive development. The work of Bandler and Grinder (1975) is an excellent resource for developing sensitivity to clients' language patterns.

Suspending Rules for Information Processing. Good rapport building and developmental counseling should enable clients to suspend certain rules that they have habitually followed when interacting with others. For instance, many people probably operate with a rule against conveying information that might leave them in vulnerable positions. As counseling proceeds and they develop trust in their counselor, they revise this rule. In experiential cognitive dissonance counseling, it can be useful to find ways that enable clients to suspend other rules pertaining to how one talks about or processes data. One approach is to suggest that counselor and client engage in brainstorming. This method was developed for group decision making (Osborn, 1963; Parnes, 1967); however, the rules also can be applied in the counseling dyad. The rationale behind the technique is that people tend to be prematurely critical in problem solving and thus stem the flow of ideas. Therefore, the evaluation phase should be separated from the idea generation phase. Knowing that an evaluation phase will follow, people can then use their full creative powers in generating ideas. The rules of brainstorming are as follows: (1) judgment of ideas is not allowed during this phase; (2) participants (client and counselor) should strive for *quantity* of ideas rather than for quality; and (3) creativity, spontaneity, and unusual ideas are welcomed.

A brainstorming process can be especially valuable with competent but unconfident clients who use a great deal of self-censorship. Through this process they may gain a greater appreciation of their own problem-solving abilities. Other advantages of brainstorming are that it calls on clients to take an active rather than a passive role in searching for solutions and that it reinforces the concept of counseling as a collaborative venture. As well as having clients brainstorm strategies for solving problems, I have often asked them to brainstorm about the different cognitive formulations possible for an event.

There are other ways of encouraging clients to suspend long-standing rules for exploring experiences. The counselor might be able to set up a hypothetical situation that requires new rules. For instance, a well-meaning but retiring client who had declared himself a failure for his shy, "uncool" social behavior was asked to imagine how someone from another planet would interpret his interactions with others.

Some schools of psychotherapy use interpretations of dreams. While I do not regularly ask clients for dreams or deal with them in a highly interpretive way, I have gained a new appreciation for the value of discussing dreams. It is generally recognized that with dreams "all rules are out the window." Clients are sometimes more spontaneous in exploring their feelings, thoughts, and motivations when discussing dreams than in other counseling interactions. I do not believe that most dreams have one correct interpretation or even that all dreams have significant meanings. However, whereas I formerly tended to discourage discussions of dreams in favor of events "based more firmly in reality," I am now more likely to explore clients' conceptions of their dreams. These discussions provide an opportunity for clients to explore feelings and cognitions with their usual rules for processing information suspended.

Enhancing the Vividness of Conflicting Cognitions. Clients often experience themselves as having two or more organized networks of cognitions, feelings, and inclinations that are in conflict: "Sometimes I want to study hard, go to med school, and be really successful. At other times I just want to do my job, have fun, and not get all caught up in the rat race." Gestalt therapists, Grinder and Bandler (1976), Satir (1972), and others have developed ideas for helping clients clarify and work with polarities. In the past I have been leery of encouraging clients to "reify" these kinds of experiences. I have since concluded that, when clients become more vividly aware of these conflicting systems, they are better able to explore and alter them. However, the counselor should be aware that the polarity model may sometimes be too simplistic.

I often help clients develop awareness of different cognitive subsystems by referring to the "parts" or "sides" of themselves that are evident in their experiences. It can then be helpful to name these parts, so that they can be more easily discussed, explored, and incorporated into interventions. Rather than relying on names such as "ego," "superego," or "parent," I try to fashion names from the client's own ideas and language style. Thus, clients and I have discussed such polarities as the "Big Me" and "Little Me," the "Whiner" and the "Problem Solver," and "My Wimp Side" and "My Strong Side." The use of labels that arise from clients' own language structures ensures that the concepts are central to their self and self-in-world cognitive systems.

Another way of making conflicting cognitive systems more concrete is to identify source influences and to use them in developing labels. As unproductive cognitive processes are discussed, many clients are able to relate certain influential individuals to these processes. The cognitions may be in the form of encoded verbal teachings, such as maxims that parents have frequently used ("Never put off until tomorrow what you can do today"). Or they may be in the form of auditory or visual images. As noted in Chapter Five, unproductive cognitive processes can often be related to reactions of parents. However, other influential individuals—siblings, other relatives, teachers, and unaccepting peers—can also play important roles. One client maintained active visualizations and thoughts about instances of being bullied by his brother. These cognitions were important ingredients in his self-in-world cognitive system, which was predicated on the belief that people are in general untrustworthy.

When source influences are identified, they can then be incorporated into descriptions of the client's conflicting cognitions. For instance, I made the following statement to a college sophomore who was struggling to develop a sense of competence in order to overcome experiences with her highly critical mother: "On the one hand, you've still got the voice of your mother inside you—nagging you, sometimes shrieking at you that you've failed. Then on the other hand, you've got your 'growing-up part' that's buttressed by all the good feedback you're getting from your friends."

Discovering conflicting cognitions and labeling them in a way that allows them to be more vividly experienced can heighten the degree of cognitive dissonance encountered. At the same time, the structure of this framework can provide support for clients to confront and resolve the dissonance. Once the cognitions are organized into the polarities or "parts" discussed, a number of methods—such as guided imagery, role playing, and empty-chair techniques—can be used in helping clients explore these influences and work toward resolution.

Guided Imagery. Guided imagery can be particularly helpful when the counselor believes that a more complete exploration of a problem can be achieved by deviating from a purely
verbal discussion. Imagery exercises activate visualization and
other imagery modes that might be important in the problem.
Sometimes clients are so well schooled in what they say that
they can successfully fool themselves in identifying feelings and
other processes. Imagery may enable them to retrieve aspects of
their experiences that differ from ones most often elicited
through verbal channels, which emphasize well-considered responses.

Imagery can be used as a way of implementing some of
the approaches already mentioned, such as altering the client's
vantage point. In experiential cognitive dissonance counseling,
imagery is most commonly used as a way of exploring and attempting to resolve conflicting cognitions. The "parts," "sides,"
or "polarities" can be incorporated into imagery exercises to
help sharpen awareness of their roles and to facilitate development of a more complex cognitive system that reduces the dissonance. Several years ago I counseled a master's student who
was attempting to become less perfectionistic. Her father had
been extremely successful, both as a professional and as an ath-
lete, and had preached a dichotomous "be the best or be a failure" philosophy. In the course of the counseling, we identified
two "parts" to her cognitive processes. One part was extremely
self-critical and perfectionistic and often spoke to her in the
voice of her father, while the other part was "more independent
and able to think for itself" and was more balanced in its approach to tasks. She was asked to envision a dialogue in which
her "balanced side" and her father discussed her welfare. This
exercise led to some productive insights about both her father's
influence and her more independent side.

With imagery exercises and other approaches that deviate
from interview dialogue, I have found it best to suggest the
technique in a matter-of-fact manner rather than to explain it
elaborately. Counselors I have supervised have sometimes been
uncomfortable with suggesting imagery and have been inclined
to overexplain the approach and the rationale. I may say some-

thing like "Let's try something a little different for a minute. Let's see if we can get some new ideas by using your imagination. What I'd like you to do is to close your eyes and picture yourself . . ." Naturally, I am likely to use these approaches with clients who have appeared to be relatively open to a variety of ways of exploring their difficulties. It is also important to observe nonverbal behavior indicative of embarrassment or discomfort.

The Unmailed-Letter Approach. A method briefly described in Chapter Five can also be used to help clients better understand and begin to resolve conflicting cognitions related to a powerful source influence. They are asked to write a letter to the influential person, which is not to be mailed. I may ask them simply to write the letter themselves or to write it from the perspective of the "part" that is in opposition to the cognitive system related to the source influence. Clients are asked to discuss their goals and thoughts about the teachings of the influential person. After conducting and processing this exercise, I sometimes ask clients to answer the letter as they think the influential person might.

This method was used with the female master's student previously described. After the imagery exercise mentioned, she was asked to write a letter to her father in which she explained what she had learned about her conflicting inner parts, described both positive and negative aspects of how his teachings had affected her, and discussed the differences between her goals and the goals he had chosen for himself. This exercise added to the clarity she had developed in the imagery dialogue and increased her resolve to strengthen her "independent" part.

Empty-Chair Approaches. The empty-chair technique was introduced by Gestalt therapists, most notably Perls (1969). While my use of this technique is based on a different rationale, I have found empty-chair work useful in helping clients better understand and attempt to resolve conflicting cognitive systems. Clients can be asked to position themselves in one chair and to assume the role of one of their differing parts. They are then to imagine that the other part is in the other chair and to speak to that part. After a while, they can be asked to position themselves in the other chair and assume the other polarity in answering the comments of the first. A dialogue can eventually ensue, with the client alternately assuming the perspective of one part in addressing the other.

I used this approach with a shy, retiring college student who was concerned about his social skills and undecided about continuing with his computer science major. He was also confused about whether he wished to stay at the university where he was enrolled or transfer to a school near his home. We had identified two "parts" in his cognitions about himself—a "creative" part that liked to explore different ideas in an unstructured way and a "practical side" that preferred structured activities and definite answers. His practical side led him to feel secure in the computer science major and to be concerned with "saying the right thing" in social interactions; however, his creative side, which he was just discovering, was dissatisfied with the limitations on conducting creative thought in the computer science major and sometimes stimulated him to be overabstract in his discussions with others. He was asked to sit in one chair and to assume the perspective of his practical side in discussing the differences between home and school. I then asked him to take the other chair and to speak about these issues from the perspective of his creative side. Similar dialogues developed in other sessions focused on his social experiences and possible career directions.

Improving Cognitive Development by Introducing New Experiences

As well as helping clients improve their processing of experiences that have already been encoded, counselors can attempt to foster cognitive development by leading clients to new experiences.

Role Playing as a Cognitive Intervention. Behavior therapists have used role playing or "behavior rehearsal" as a way of developing new skills. I continue to use it in this way but have also come to view it as a way of stimulating cognitive growth. In Kelly's (1955) "fixed role therapy," the construct systems of clients are identified and their problematic aspects assessed. Then the therapist designs a role containing constructs that differ from the problematic ones. The clients are then instructed to enact their roles for a period of time, just as they would if they were given a part in a play. Kelly believed that clients ultimately would come to adopt the new construct. Kelly's approach is similar to Adler's method of responding to clients' wishes that they could be different. He would request that they act "as if" these desired characteristics were true of them for the next week (Mosak, 1979).

Rather than asking clients to enact roles for prolonged periods, I usually ask them to assume a new role during a session and to explore their immediate reactions. For instance, clients who are unassertive may be asked to role-play a situation in an assertive way. They are often surprised to discover that this new mode of behavior does not feel as uncomfortable or alien to them as they had expected. Mild cognitive dissonance is created as their new experiences differ from their expectancies. In many instances their self system of cognitions becomes more complex so as to absorb the new experiences.

One productive use of role playing is as a way of exploring interpersonal difficulties. By actually going through the motions of enacting their roles in difficult situations, clients may become more aware of feelings and important cognitive processes. The role play may arouse immediate feelings and activate cognitive processes that would not be retrieved if they simply discussed the incidents. With the counselor's observations and feedback, the client may be able to develop a more complete cognitive map of the interactions, which can then lead to discovery of ways to resolve the interpersonal difficulties.

Like imagery and empty-chair techniques, role playing can be especially useful in attempting to clarify intrapersonal processes. Rather than having the client interact with an inner "part" imagined sitting in an empty chair, the counselor can assume the role of this part. The counselor must have a good understanding of the perspective, in order to make the role play sufficiently similar to the client's internal dialogue. Role playing can be used after the empty-chair approach is first employed.

The counselor then has an opportunity to learn the kinds of perspectives reflected by the conflicting cognitive systems.

Role playing also can be useful when the counselor wants to strengthen the contribution of one part in the dialogue—for instance, when clients are learning to overcome irrational beliefs and cope more successfully with difficult situations. As described in Chapter Five, the counselor can ask the client to role-play the part voicing the irrational beliefs and can assume the role of the more balanced part that is learning to counter irrationalities. The female master's student struggling with perfectionism (described in the section on guided imagery) was asked to play the role of the "perfectionistic part" internalized from her father's influence, while I played the role of her "more independent part" and countered the cognitive distortions she offered. After several minutes, we switched roles.

Behavioral Contracting as a Cognitive Intervention. Behavioral contracting, when a client contracts with the counselor to complete a task before the next session, was developed as a way of improving behavioral skills. Cognitive use of this method is somewhat similar to Kelly's prescription of a fixed role, except that specific behaviors are identified, as opposed to an entire personality pattern. Clients often have less difficulty carrying out a relatively specific task. For instance, a client might be asked to use someone's name in conversation at least five times during the next week, initiate at least one conversation with someone of the opposite sex, or use I-message terms in discussing a conflict with a friend. When clients have accomplished these tasks, I explore their reactions, particularly whether excessively limited expectations were confirmed or challenged. Profound cognitive changes often occur as a result of clients' experiencing themselves engaging in behaviors that they once avoided. Cognitive shifts in the self and self-in-world systems can result, as well as more positively focused self-efficacy and outcome expectancies.

Designing Cognition-Testing Experiments. The method of designing an "experiment" to test the validity of an irrational belief or schema (Beck, Rush, Shaw, and Emery, 1979; Burns,

1980a, 1980b) was discussed in Chapter Five as a way of developing cognitive coping skills. This approach can also be used to lead clients to new experiences that challenge limited cognitive patterns. For instance, shy clients are often preoccupied with the expectancy that others will think negatively of them if they appear to be anxious or behave at all awkwardly. I have helped several such clients design an experiment to provide them with further information about this assumption. With one student, the experiment consisted of asking a close friend how he perceived individuals when they displayed anxiety or awkwardness. In this case, the friend did not view these as negative indications about the person. This information enabled my client to scale down his preoccupation with how others viewed him.

When using this method, the counselor must be aware that more than one irrational assumption can be tested. In the case mentioned, what would have happened had the friend voiced negative reactions? If this had occurred, the client would have had the opportunity to test the validity of a second irrational assumption—that he *must* be viewed favorably by everyone of importance to him. In developing the experiment, we discussed the possibility that his friend's response could result in a test of this second assumption. He decided that he was prepared for both of the possible experiments.

The "experiment" method has several advantages. It takes a Socratic approach in leading clients toward new experiences and allowing them to evaluate the results for themselves. Many clients are more likely to modify their thinking patterns as a result of direct experience than through didactic presentation of an alternative position. This approach also reinforces a client's sense of independence and competence. Another interesting aspect of this technique is that the "experiment" terminology may help subtly to reframe the client's way of viewing life experiences. Many clients take events too seriously and catastrophize when unpleasant results occur. Thinking of life experiences as experiments to "see what we can learn" conveys a more relaxed attitude that may allow individuals to "roll with the punches" more successfully.

Summary and Conclusions

Counselors can use experiential cognitive dissonance counseling when the formulations of the client at Phase 4b and the counselor-client interaction process at Phase 4c suggest that cognitive systems in important areas will not be responsive to direct and explicit methods, such as developmental counseling or cognitive coping skills training. In order to help clients explore cognitive systems and resolve cognitive dissonance, these techniques attempt to go beyond verbal interchanges in activating a variety of experiential modes, such as visual and auditory channels. Some of these techniques also involve the counselor's being less explicit with clients regarding the directions and purposes of the interventions. The less direct method is helpful in counteracting resistance and leading clients toward shifts in rigidly maintained cognitive systems.

Some methods characteristic of experiential cognitive dissonance counseling were used with Harvey, after developmental and problem-focused counseling were tried in vain. The counselor sidestepped and parried Harvey's resistance, noted and reinforced instances of more flexible cognitive processing, and used a great deal of cognitive reframing in order to interject more complexity while still appearing to accept some of his assertions. In light of Harvey's oppositional nature, paradoxical techniques were used to some degree, usually incorporated into suggestions rather than given as directives. In general, the counselor tried to help Harvey develop cognitive complexity by focusing on already experienced events rather than designing new experiences. Harvey continued to display a relatively rigid cognitive style; however, these methods helped him develop enough complexity that he was able to adapt to the demands of university life and function with fewer disruptive crises.

SEVEN

Applying Cognitive Approaches in Group Counseling

In this day of accountability, shrinking budgets, and cost-effectiveness, counselors are exploring interventions capable of affecting the lives of more people than can be reached through one-to-one counseling. Group counseling is one such approach. During the past fifteen years, the goals and methods of group treatment have become more diverse. Rather than restricting themselves to an unstructured, relatively long-term group therapy approach aimed primarily at intrapsychic insight development, group practitioners have devised other concepts of capitalizing on group interactions.

Group human relations training, including sensitivity and encounter groups, emphasizes the use of exercises and attention to "here-and-now" interactions to stimulate greater awareness of interpersonal styles (Lakin, 1972; Lieberman, Yalom, and Miles, 1973). Support groups have been developed, such as Alcoholics Anonymous and Weight Watchers, in which members with a common difficulty can obtain support and enhance coping skills. The structured group movement (Drum and Knott, 1977), which has been particularly strong on university campuses, represents another direction. While often combining elements of human relations training and support groups, structured groups are designed to help members better understand

and cope with a specific theme or problem in their lives. A psychoeducational approach is taken, in which relatively structured discussions and exercises are used to help participants learn new skills and concepts. It is hoped that the learning will lead to more successful mastery of developmental tasks and in some cases prevent the formation of more serious problems or crises.

While the development of these group approaches was influenced by efficiency considerations, they have also been proposed as methods that are more effective than one-to-one interventions in achieving certain goals. The particular advantages of the group modality stem from the important role that groups play in our lives. As human beings, we are *social* animals. Our most important self-constructs are related to our interpersonal systems. Our parents and other influential adults play crucial roles in the ways we begin to view ourselves and others. In turn, our cognitive systems affect the ways that we behave toward others and undergo continual readjustment in response to our experiences with the social world.

Counselors can expand their capabilities for intervening in the cognitive domain by becoming skilled in the use of group approaches. In light of the importance of peer relationships among university students, small-group counseling and programming would appear to be a particularly effective intervention method. For instance, Oppenheimer (1984) found that group counseling enhanced social adjustment among university freshmen.

Value of Groups in Enhancing Cognitive Complexity

A group milieu can stimulate positive cognitive development for clients in a number of ways.

Promoting "Universalization." Yalom (1975), Drum and Knott (1977), and others have cited the "universalization" phenomenon as one of the major benefits of participation in a group. Persons with problems often consider themselves different from and less adequate than others: "What's wrong with me? Why do I get so anxious when everyone else seems OK? I should be stronger."

Because we are acutely aware of our "private selves," including our innermost insecurities, it is quite easy to construe oneself as different and inadequate because of a personal difficulty. Yet we can only witness the "public selves" of others—only the aspects of their inner experiences that are revealed outwardly. The public selves of others can appear quite competent and serene when contrasted with the vulnerability experienced within our private selves.

An effective group-counseling experience can counteract this tendency for members to accentuate and feel ashamed of their perceived differences from others. As the trust level of the members is increased, they can risk revealing more aspects of their private selves, thus making the public selves they present to other group members a more complete model of their private experiences. Group members frequently express surprise at learning that others have the same thoughts and feelings that they do. Cognitive dissonance is created, with the construct "My problem is unique and shameful" in conflict with evidence that conveys the message "Other people have concerns similar to mine, and some of them seem like OK people." Through support provided by the group leader and other members, the dissonance may be resolved by an expansion of the previously limited view of self and problem: "Maybe it's not so horrible that I have this problem. Maybe others have to deal with similar dilemmas." This cognitive shift often involves a generalization from others in the group to people in general. Members may redefine their problems as emanating from dilemmas or frailties inherent in the human condition. This universalization effect can help reduce excessive self-incrimination and negative affect and enable group participants to focus productively on possible solutions.

Helping Individuals Develop Self-Awareness. Groups provide rich possibilities for learning about oneself. A member can be led to a clearer or redefined view of self by hearing others talk about themselves. As Kelly (1955) suggested, we are continually developing, testing, and altering our theories about ourselves and others. Our self-understanding is always incomplete. It is common to have "a sense" about something, in that an idea has "emotional validity" for us even though it is incomplete and vaguely formulated. Group members can enrich their models of themselves as they listen to others' ideas and interpretations. Some of the other members may have developed more complex cognitive maps of similar experiences.

The ideas of others frequently act as stimuli for original thinking. The group decision-making methods of Osborn (1963) and Parnes (1967) are based on the principle that new ideas can be formed as members of a group react to and diverge from previously expressed ideas. Self system cognitions can be better understood as one person's ideas elicit chains of useful associations by others. This "spinning-off" process can occur in clients' thoughts, even if it is not evident in what they say in the group. Quiet members sometimes reveal in the last session that other members' disclosures stimulated useful flights of ideas about themselves.

Providing Diverse Sources of Feedback. Some group interventions offer the benefit of obtaining feedback from other group members on one's ideas, interpretations, constructs, and behaviors. Human relations training and support groups are generally designed to stimulate feedback among members. Structured groups vary in the degree to which open interchange among participants is fostered.

Group feedback can enable members to contrast their views of themselves with an external view. Hansen, Warner, and Smith (1976) have noted the value of groups for reality testing. People often have the "theory" or expectation that others perceive them as having certain characteristics and therefore judge them negatively. A group can allow them to receive feedback on how members actually view these aspects. Others' views may be more accepting. Cognitive dissonance is established, with the negative and restrictive set of expectations in conflict with the group feedback. To resolve the conflict, group members may begin to reassess their expectations.

Group feedback can also help members discover self-defeating thought patterns or behaviors. Many clients are aware of frequently receiving negative reactions from others but do not understand the specific characteristics that elicit these reactions. Through feedback from other participants, they may be able to pinpoint specific patterns in their behavior or thoughts that bring about the unwanted results. Their cognitive maps of self and self-in-world become more complex, and they can better address the self-defeating patterns.

Group feedback is also valuable in indexing how members are progressing with certain goals. Changes in habitual ways of thinking, feeling, and behaving are difficult to measure concretely, and clients often distrust their own evaluations. Group feedback can help participants judge whether and in what ways they have progressed. The increased confidence that one is making valuable changes can favorably influence self-efficacy expectancies.

Group feedback can often go beyond that provided in one-to-one interactions. First, there are more people to perceive aspects worthy of note. Some members of a group might observe important aspects that a counselor would be inclined to miss. Our "professionally trained" minds are more attuned to certain behaviors or processes than others. Second, feedback from other "just folks" may at times have more impact than from a professional counselor, who may be regarded as "just trying to make me feel better" or as unusually tolerant and accepting. Third, similar feedback from two or more people in a group can have more impact than observations from a single source. Agreement by two or more people is likely to be seen as validation of the feedback. Fourth, one or more members of a group can sometimes convey feedback to a member in a language more likely to be "heard" than the words chosen by the counselor. I must confess that group participants have served as valuable translators for me on many occasions.

Creating a Climate of Support. Exploring vulnerabilities and experimenting with unfamiliar ways of thinking and behaving are challenging tasks. The climate of mutual caring and trust generated by an effective group can be an excellent base of support for members to begin taking the necessary risks. Without this kind of external support, it can be easy to conclude that problems are too overwhelming. Clients can feel "alone" with certain difficulties, even though they appear well surrounded by others who care about them. They may think that their problem would not be understood or accepted by their friends or family members. For example, many bulimic female college students are quite active socially but are extremely secretive regarding their bulimic behavior. Thus, having a well-developed group of friends does not guarantee that one has a support system for dealing with a particular problem.

Like group feedback, group support has some advantages over support provided by an individual counselor. Group support can be demonstrated by different group members in different ways. One member may find the words to convey something helpful to another when the counselor cannot. I have often listened appreciatively—and with relief—to the empathic words of one group member to another when I was unable to come up with a helpful response. As with feedback, the support extended by an individual counselor can be discounted by clients as "part of the job," while support provided by group members may be seen as more genuine.

Increasing Group Members' Motivation. Group support for and acceptance of a counselor's ideas, strategies, and techniques can lead to their being accepted by clients who might otherwise be resistant. When a client with negative expectancies of counseling observes other group members responding with acceptance and enthusiasm to the counselor's ideas, cognitive dissonance is aroused. Resolution of the dissonance may come about by the client's expanding his or her views of the counselor's ideas and techniques: "It looks like other people are ready to give these ideas a try. Maybe they'll work after all." Similarly, clients who may have come to doubt their own judgment are relieved when other group members known to be struggling with similar dilemmas confirm their view that the ideas have promise.

Providing Diverse Stimuli for Change. Another advantage of the group modality is the diversity likely to be present in members' perceptions, interpretations, ideas, experiences, and information. Provided that the leader and group are viewed as supportive, the opportunity to witness varying points of view and absorb data from the experiences of others can greatly contribute to the development of cognitive complexity. To become more cognitively complex, one must question overgeneralizations, stereotypes, and prejudgments and develop finer and more accurate discriminations about oneself and the world. A supportive group interchange can facilitate this process, particularly if the subject matter is rarely discussed openly in day-to-day conversation. If general social norms work against open discussion of a difficulty, such as shyness or a sexual problem, one's thinking is rarely stimulated in interchanges with others. Erroneous perceptions go unchallenged and are therefore more likely to persist.

Group discussion about a problematic theme can fertilize growth of a more complex and adaptive way of understanding self and others. However, as Sanford (1962) has suggested, the challenge of the experience must be balanced by its supportiveness. Counselors must be aware of the level of cognitive development represented in the group. Clients with more complex mental processes can handle a great deal of unstructured discussion, whereas those prone to black-white thinking may need more structure in the presentation of new ideas.

Providing Opportunities for Observational Learning. Bandura (1969a, 1977b) and other social learning theorists have outlined the vast possibilities of learning behaviors and concepts from models. In the group modality, members may serve as models for one another (Hansen, Warner, and Smith, 1976). While the members of a group may share a common difficulty, they generally complement one another in the perspectives and coping skills they are able to apply to the problem. One person may have evolved a helpful way of thinking about one aspect of the concern; another may have developed a particular coping method that is potentially useful to others.

Individual counselors can also serve as models for their clients; however, the modeling possibilities are more limited than in group counseling. Obviously, there are more potential models available in a group than in individual counseling. Certain group members may also be more influential as models for participants than the counselor. Research suggests that optimal learning occurs when the subjects perceive a great deal of similarity between themselves and the model (Bandura, 1969a; Bandura, Ross, and Ross, 1963; Rosenbaum and Tucker, 1962).

Some clients might perceive their counselors as being "above" them in functioning and may therefore resist assimilating their behaviors and ideas. However, they may see certain group members as more like them, although perhaps "a little more advanced," and emulate their actions and ideas.

Group members may be more credible than the counselor as "coping models" for one another. A coping model struggles somewhat in gaining control of a situation, whereas a mastery model immediately produces the desired behaviors and results (Meichenbaum, 1971). The counselor may seem too advanced in dealing with the problem and therefore more a mastery model than a coping model. A useful practice in structured groups is to ask members who have successfully handled a difficult situation to report on their experiences and to outline the thought processes that helped them in coping. Other members may assimilate some of the cognitive coping strategies used.

Potential Negative Effects of Groups on Cognitive Development

While the group modality has many positive benefits, these desirable results do not automatically emerge from a group. In fact, each of the positive benefits has a parallel possibility that is potentially negative. If the trust atmosphere of the group is not sufficiently high for members to disclose personal material, participants' concepts of themselves as alone with a problem can be heightened rather than reduced. Rather than the universalization phenomenon's occurring, the narrow self-view of "I am so different" may be reinforced.

Just as clients might enrich their self-concepts by listening to others in a group, they might also apply others' ideas inappropriately to themselves. Some group members may provide a frame of reference that reflects selective attention to negative elements. This phenomenon is particularly troublesome when the negatively oriented participant is a high-influence member of the group by virtue of attractiveness, assertiveness, humor, or another characteristic. As a consequence, other group members may develop narrowed views of themselves rather than expanded ones.

Rather than feeling "we are in this together," individuals might be scapegoated and become targets for the cohesion of other members. The fears and defenses of some people influence them to gang up on others who allow themselves to be vulnerable.

Just as group acceptance of the counseling techniques can enhance their value in the eyes of members, resistance or lack of acceptance can result in an erosion of the counselor's influence. Resistance by a vocal, high-influence member may be interpreted by others as the "sense of the group." Quieter members who have had positive reactions to the process may come to question their views and suspend them in favor of the other's opinions. A devaluing of the counselor and methods can result from no reaction as well as from a negative reaction. A group counselor's nightmare is to have a description of an exercise greeted with blank stares from all participants.

The diversity of viewpoints in a group can lead to increased cognitive complexity; however, it can also produce confusion and stagnation of cognitive development. The challenge of a number of varied viewpoints can be overwhelming for some group members, particularly those who think dualistically. Unless the level of support is carefully calibrated for these individuals, they may withdraw, drop out of the group, or become resistant.

The variety of models available in a group is generally a benefit; however, people can learn behaviors and cognitions that are self-defeating from observing others as well as patterns that are helpful. There have been many times when I have inwardly cringed at a dualistic conclusion voiced by a group member and prayed that it would not be adopted by other members. Ordinarily, one or more other members in the group recognize the limitations of such concepts; however, the group conditions must be conducive to their voicing their thoughts or questions.

Applying the Cognitive Intervention Planning Model

The planning model can help counselors conduct groups that capitalize on the benefits and avoid the pitfalls of the group modality. The model can be applied in screening assessment and initial planning before the group has begun. It can also be consulted during the course of the group, as decisions regarding directions and techniques are made. In screening assessment, counselors elicit clients' cognitions (Phase 1) and make inferences about cognitive systems (Phase 2) and cognitive developmental levels (Phase 3) relevant to the problems to be addressed and to participation in a group. These data and impressions are likely to be gathered in screening interviews before the group and in the initial stages of group counseling. At Phase 4 an attempt is made to arrive at formulations of a prospective group member's problems (Phase 4a) and personal characteristics (Phase 4b) and to answer the question "Given this client's personal characteristics, is this group likely to be an effective way of dealing with the problems?" Counselors should also attempt to construct a tentative "map" of the overall group composition and anticipate group process issues (Phase 4c). Once the pool of participants has been identified, Phase 5 of goal setting can be completed, with cognitive change goals targeted for members. In addition to outcome goals (Phase 5a), it is particularly important in group counseling to consider the process goals (Phase 5b) and their cognitive implications. The "game plan" for the intervention is then planned at Phase 6.

Once the group has begun (Phase 7), members' progress and group interaction patterns are monitored at Phase 8a. At the same time, Phases 1–3 continue, as new cognitive data are presented in the group discussions. After receiving new information and feedback from monitoring, the counselor recycles through Phases 4, 5, and 6. The formulations, particularly those of the group process (Phase 4c), may be periodically refined, outcome and process goals may be revised, and decisions regarding directions and techniques for the group may be altered. The counselor may have to figure out how to involve an individual in the group activities or how to deal with a monopolizer. When the group is completed, a final evaluation (Phase 8b) should be conducted and can include use of participant reactions to group activities, pre- and postintervention instruments, goal attainment scaling methods, and other approaches.

Assessing and Screening Potential Group Members

Bergin (1963) has noted the "deterioration effect" in psychotherapy, whereby some recipients improve while others become worse. In constructing their formulations at Phase 4, counselors must assess the degree to which particular individuals are likely to benefit from a group experience. They should be aware that the support and challenge aspects of group counseling differ greatly from those inherent in individual counseling. Further, counselors can more directly control the degree of support and challenge offered in individual counseling than in group discussions. It is therefore important to assess whether a client's needs are suited to the support and challenge conditions of a group.

There are several kinds of clients whose cognitive development is unlikely to be favorably influenced in group counseling. These attributes should be considered as formulations of clients' personal characteristics and are made at Phase 4b.

1. Clients who become too anxious in a group situation may require individual counseling instead of or prior to group counseling. Some may be able to tolerate a group situation after improving their coping skills through individual counseling.

2. Clients thought to be particularly oppositional and antagonistic may also do better in individual counseling. The individual counselor may be in a better position to make positive use of the client's resistance. Also, this kind of client can adversely affect the way other group members respond to the counselor's approach. Group counseling may be a more workable option for such clients after their cognitive systems have undergone some development and are less rigid.

3. Clients who are in acute crises may be so emotionally needy that they require too much energy and time from the counselor and/or group and may also be better candidates for individual counseling. Examples include adjustment to a recent loss of a family member or to a trauma, such as being assaulted. Some in a crisis state may benefit from group and individual counseling offered concurrently.

4. Clients who are unable to attend and respond to others in minimally supportive ways may not function well in a group. People who are in crisis or who are out of control emotionally may not be able to tune into others sufficiently. Clients who are emotionally insulated and therefore extremely unexpressive with others or who are socially avoidant may also have difficulty interacting supportively in a group.

5. Clients unable to process reality information in a relatively accurate manner are unlikely to do well in group counseling designed to foster cognitive development.

6. Clients for whom being a member of a cohesive group is not a supportive experience are unlikely to benefit. Some may be too threatened by the atmosphere of a close group.

In addition to determining whether group counseling is indicated or contraindicated for each client, counselors should consider the kinds of supports and challenges needed by each client to foster cognitive development. This aspect of the formulation at Phase 4b is important for the kinds of group goals identified at Phase 5 and the interventions planned at Phase 6. Just as in individual counseling, counselors can assess the client's cognitive systems of self, world, and self-in-world; formulate ideas of the client's particular problems; and consider the kinds of challenges and supports likely to help the client with the problems. In addition, the counselor must assess how well the needed supports and challenges can be provided in a group format. Some of the relevant factors include clients' cognitive development on Perry's scheme, social development, comfort in group situations, problem-solving skills, locus of control, autonomy development, overall self-esteem, and the flexibility of the cognitive systems related to their difficulties.

Methods of conducting assessment for group counseling include the use of screening interviews. Individual interviewing can help in gauging clients' cognitive systems related to themselves and the difficulties to be explored in the group. However, the one-to-one interview is obviously a very different situation from group counseling. The kind of interpersonal behavior elicited in this situation may not be fully indicative of how the person will behave in the group and may therefore be of limited value in arriving at formulations of group process issues at Phase 4c. Yalom (1975) suggests that the more similar the screening conditions can be made to the actual conditions of the group, the better. One possibility is to conduct part of the screening in minigroups of two or three clients. Another alternative is to consider the first group meeting a part of the assessment and screening process, thereby allowing counselors to observe group members interacting with one another.

Once screening is completed, assessment is continued throughout the course of the group. Evaluative feedback is provided (Phase 8a) as the counselor observes how participants progress and respond to the interactions; and Phases 4, 5, and 6 are reentered repeatedly. This ongoing assessment process is helpful as counselors revise group goals, plan activities, determine the kinds of supports needed by individual members, and evaluate the overall effectiveness of the intervention.

Use of Principles of Challenge and Support

It is easy for counselors to underestimate the degree of challenge faced by participants in a group-counseling situation, even one that is relatively structured. Clients are concerned about how they and their disclosures will be accepted by the counselor and other group members. The threat may be enhanced if they are uncertain whether confidentiality will be observed. Further, many people find it more difficult to formulate and express their ideas before a group than with one individual. Another challenging aspect is that group members may see one another as competitors, perhaps for the attention of the group or the counselor or both.

In light of these and other complications of the group modality, counselors must be sensitive to the degree of challenge presented in group counseling and consciously attempt to balance challenge and support factors as the intervention is designed (Phase 6) and implemented (Phase 7). In my opinion, this balance was not well regulated in some of the encounter groups offered in the 1960s, when an "honesty is the best policy" and "anything goes" philosophy served as a guideline for some leaders. The challenges from the group environment and degree of cognitive dissonance elicited may have been overwhelming for some participants, leading them to retreat to the security of oversimple constructs. Lakin (1969, 1970) has criticized some common practices in sensitivity training, including leaders striving for highly emotionalized impacts without attending sufficiently to screening and follow-up considerations.

The balance of challenge and support factors is made difficult in a group by the likelihood that different members will need different amounts of support. Some will be relatively mature socially, while others will have greater dependency needs for counselor and group support. Members are also likely to differ in the kinds of interventions they find supportive and challenging. The dualistic individual will be supported by didactic presentations of "how-to" information but will be challenged by open-ended discussions of topics that elude definite answers. On the other hand, a relativistic person will find support in these open-ended discussions but challenge in discussions dealing with personal commitments.

Effective screening can help counselors attend to the support and challenge needs of individual members. In effect, the range of clients' support requirements can be made more manageable if those who are not good candidates for group interventions are screened out. Procedures that stimulate group trust, cohesion, and self-disclosure (described in the next section) are perceived as supportive by most individuals. Clients who do not regard these methods as supportive may require an alternative intervention.

Once a group is constituted, what can counselors do to respond to differences among group members in challenge-support needs and perceptions? This question is difficult to answer, in that all members are present at the same time and engage in the same discussions. Nevertheless, there are some subtle steps that counselors can take to manipulate the degree of challenge and support presented to different members of a group. Some members can be asked to respond to certain questions or to participate in certain exercises, while others can be allowed to remain silent. When forming dyads or small groups, counselors should avoid compositions that potentially present a member with an overwhelming challenge. Counselors can also play the role of gatekeeper, controlling the degree and kind of feedback the group offers a member. Comments made by other members can be stopped or reframed, and feedback can be balanced with other observations.

Importance of Group Cohesion and Interaction

In my early days of working with structured groups, I concentrated on providing participants with good information and was careful to build in opportunities to practice skills. I made little use of methods designed to help participants feel comfortable and to foster the cohesiveness of the group as a whole. Since these groups were designed to teach cognitive and behavioral skills, I did not consider the group atmosphere particularly important, as long as it was not obviously destructive. However, participants often seemed uninvolved in the sessions, and too much attrition occurred. As time passed, I began to experiment with methods for stimulating group involvement. In evaluating the overall success of a series of group interventions done over five years with social skill problems, I concluded that the later groups, which made greater use of methods to build group cohesion, were better received than the earlier ones (Barrow, 1983).

Building group cohesion is extremely important in less structured groups where self-exploration and awareness are the goals. It is also important in groups that are highly structured and have highly specific goals. As well as enhancing participants' levels of motivation and involvement, group cohesion sets the stage for cognitive development. Clients must develop outcome expectancies that what they say will be accepted by the counselor and the other members of the group. When this kind of expectancy is developed, they are freed from worrying about how others are accepting them and can concentrate more fully on exploring important thoughts and feelings and learning new skills.

Observing, Formulating, and Intervening in Group Process

In order to mold group cohesion, counselors need to have a workable "cognitive map" of group processes that are formulated at Phase 4c. This formulation helps them in setting goals at Phase 5, particularly the process goals. At Phases 6 (design) and 7 (implementation), counselors attempt to facilitate group processes that encourage productive cognitive development. Important dimensions of group process can be noted in these phases.

Pattern of Communication. Most of the communication in my earlier structured groups was leader to group and group to leader. The amount of communication occurring among members, without going through the leader at the hub of the wheel, was negligible. This kind of pattern may be satisfactory for conveying information from the leader to group members; however, it does not increase overall group cohesion and does not allow all the potential benefits of the group to occur. For instance, group members are less likely to experience the universalization phenomenon.

There is certainly a place for leader-to-member communication, particularly in structured groups when the leader is expert in a body of information that is to be conveyed. However, even in structured groups, idea generation, skill enhancement, and self-awareness development will progress more productively if communication from member to member can occur, at least for certain periods of each session. Group members may initially perceive the risk to be greater in member-to-member communication, because it may imply more familiarity and intimacy than the member-to-leader pattern. They must therefore develop the cognitive set that it is permissible to address others freely and the outcome expectancy that others will respond to their communications in a reinforcing manner.

The degree to which communication is two way rather than one way should also be monitored. Is there open give-and-take in a discussion, or does one person present ideas in such a way that others do not seem to be invited to respond? In most cases, group members should be given permission to ask questions, make comments, and express disagreement regarding what the counselor says.

Counselors can be aware of the type of communication pattern established in their groups and identify development of member-to-member and two-way communication as *process goals*. A number of methods for encouraging desirable patterns, such as linking and pairing, process observations, and use of smaller groups, will be discussed later in this chapter. When group members are observed commenting in ways that discourage give-and-take, counselors can take several actions, including summarizing and asking for responses from others or suggesting a dyadic or small-group exercise.

Group Influence. Another variable important to monitor is influence. Whose ideas seem to be ignored? Who receives the greatest amount of attention? The high-influence members of the group are likely to serve as models for other members and can exert influence toward more cognitively complex positions or toward more restrictive ones. They can also influence others to respond enthusiastically to the group activities or to react negativistically.

Understanding the cognitive aspects of group influence can enable counselors to intervene more successfully. The high-influence member often personifies some aspects contained in the "ideal self" systems of a number of participants—aspects such as attractiveness, assertiveness, power, or intelligence, which they perceive themselves as lacking. This person's ideas are therefore given greater consideration as models of thought and behavior and more weight as reinforcers and punishers.

Counselors can capitalize on the presence of cooperative high-influence members by asking them to respond to certain questions or issues. These members can help cultivate expectations in others that it is safe and productive to voice ideas. It is sometimes helpful to elicit their thoughts in response to cognitively limited comments, including those from resistant group members. Cooperative high-influence participants can also be paired in dyadic or small-group discussions with members who are quiet, withdrawn, or even negativistic.

High-influence members who are not cooperative can present difficulties. The counselor may have to work hard at eliciting viewpoints from a number of participants, so that the ideas of the high-influence person do not appear to be the only ones acceptable. When the communication is open and participants feel free to voice their thoughts, the negative influence of any one member is reduced. In addition, smaller groups sometimes can be used, thereby defusing the impact of the uncooperative person. Perhaps the most productive route is for the counselor to try to enlist this individual as an ally. For example, the disruptive person can be given an assignment, such as listing all the reasons why a particular method might not work, so that the group can discuss potential trouble spots. Hansen, Warner, and Smith (1976) and Ohlsen (1970) discuss other ways of dealing with uncooperative members.

Another problem for the counselor is presented by participants who are so low in influence that they tend to be ignored by other members. Research by Lieberman, Yalom, and Miles (1973) suggests that active and influential encounter group members are more likely to benefit than ones who are less involved. The low-influence person may bring efficacy and outcome expectancies into the group that can be paraphrased "I can't relate to people in groups very well. People usually misunderstand or ignore me." These self-in-world cognitions may influence them to withdraw or present themselves in a halting manner, thereby leading others to ignore them. Counselors can align themselves with such individuals, thereby increasing their influence. Attention to their verbalizations can be encouraged by the counselor's clarifying and summarizing their ideas and/or asking for responses from the group. Counselors can also use linking and pairing when they find similarities in the views of these members with others, particularly with high-influence members. Dyadic and small-group activities may also help them gain the confidence to take risks in the entire group. Yalom (1975) suggests helping silent members by making reflections of their nonverbal reactions.

Group Norms. The norms that evolve in a group exert great influence on members' actions (Hansen, Warner, and Smith, 1976; Johnson and Johnson, 1975). In cognitive terms, a group norm is an expectancy, usually unspoken, that group members share regarding the acceptability of certain actions and the consequences likely to follow. Some group norms are helpful for developing cognitive complexity. Examples include norms that all members are entitled to express their opinions and that members should try to be helpful to one another. Other norms are not helpful. For example, group members may think that they should avoid any topic likely to create conflict.

Counselors can take a number of steps in Phase 7 in attempting to develop helpful norms. They can model communication behaviors such as showing interest in others' verbalizations, expressing their reactions in the form of I-messages, and showing acceptance of differing ideas. They can also attempt to ensure that behaviors helpful to the group's functioning are reinforced. When a member deviates from an overcautious norm, the counselor can intervene if the response from other group members is not reinforcing: "Bill had an interesting observation regarding how he felt. Has anyone else ever had similar feelings?" Use of various small-group leadership skills and exercises can help mold productive norms.

Group Process Observations. Group members' cognitive development is often advanced by the counselor's commenting on processes occurring within the group. Dinkmeyer and Muro (1979) have noted the importance of process observation as a group-leading skill. In this technique counselors describe events they have directly observed in the group. This mirror of patterns of group interactions can help participants understand their responses and clarify the influence of group norms. By letting group members know that a process is occurring and perhaps encouraging an alternative one, counselors can shape new norms and give members guidance in how to be productive group members. For instance, if a norm of "don't directly disagree" has emerged, the leader can suggest, "I've noticed that everyone seems to be bending over backward to avoid disagreeing with someone else. I think we'll learn more if we are a little freer with one another about expressing our ideas."

The use of process observations can promote group cohesion and can help participants understand more about group processes. By learning more about interactions in the current group, they can better understand general concepts regarding group functioning. As they learn more about the roles they play in group processes, their cognitive systems of self-in-world can become more complex.

Leadership Style and Cognitive Development

In most group-counseling situations, counselors can facilitate group cohesion and establish an atmosphere conducive to cognitive development by adopting a democratic style rather than an autocratic or a laissez-faire style at Phase 7. Most often, counselors want to promote an egalitarian attitude in the group, so that members feel inclined to express their views and feelings. Many clients devalue their own ideas and expect others to do the same. A democratic style communicates that each person's thoughts are of value. Clients may believe that they are unlikely to have valuable insights and that others are unlikely to respond favorably to their ideas. The democratic group leader can subtly counter these cognitive positions by inviting responses from everyone, treating group members' responses with respect and inviting the group as a whole to make decisions.

At times certain process goals can best be met when the counselor assumes a laissez-faire role in the group. In order to allow member-to-member communication to develop, counselors may have to assume a lower profile in the group during some periods, especially in unstructured groups focusing on self-awareness exploration. Nonverbal strategies can help counselors avoid the role of communication broker. For instance, they can position themselves less prominently in the room or avoid eye contact with participants who have just made comments. There are also times when a more autocratic style is needed. In order to balance the challenge and support factors for a particular member, the counselor may at times assume a role as "gatekeeper" and control the amount of feedback exchanged. A direct, limit-setting response might also be required if a group member is violating one of the ground rules of the group, so that other participants do not come to mistrust the ground rule.

Another facet of group leadership important in enhancing cognitive development is orientation to task or maintenance variables. Task-focused interventions address the work objectives of a group and include setting goals, keeping the group "on task," monitoring the degree to which the agenda is being met, and conveying information. Maintenance-focused interventions address the group processes, including the ways the tasks are accomplished and the feelings of group members. Another shift I have made in leading structured groups is to attend to maintenance dimensions as fully as task dimensions. Effective group counselors should be prepared to exercise varying degrees of both of these dimensions. Appropriate degrees of emphasis on task and maintenance variables will depend on the goals of the group, its duration, its degree of structure, the challenge-support needs of group members, and other factors. Another important consideration is the degree to which task and maintenance roles are played by others in the group, an aspect important to note in the group process formulation (Phase 4c). If several members play strong task-focused roles, the counselor may need to be particularly conscious of maintenance in planning (Phase 6) and implementing (Phase 7) strategies. Are some participants feeling overwhelmed or neglected? If several vocal group members are predominantly maintenance focused, the counselor may need to emit more task-focused responses in order to keep the discussions progressing in productive directions, particularly in structured groups. The task-maintenance concept is thus helpful as a cognitive map for assessing the group character at Phase 4c and for subsequent planning.

Group Leadership Skills

In attempting to establish productive patterns of communication and other group processes and to provide effective and flexible leadership, counselors can use specific group-leading skills in implementation (Phase 7).

Paraphrasing and Summarizing. Paraphrasing, discussed by Dinkmeyer and Muro (1979), is just as useful in groups as in individual counseling. Clarifying and restating what a group member has said provides useful feedback to that particular person, just as in individual counseling. In addition, it provides the other members of a group with another formulation of the concept. The counselor may be able to express the client's idea in a form that is more easily appreciated by the other members than the original formulation, perhaps through providing examples or likening the client's ideas to ones previously expressed. Paraphrasing by the counselor helps counteract clients' negative expectations of the value of their thoughts and the seriousness with which others are likely to take them. It also provides a model to group members of how to communicate attentive listening—a model that may enrich their cognitive maps of how to negotiate the interpersonal world.

Reflecting Feelings and Cognitions. Reflections of feelings and cognitions can be even more effective in group than in individual counseling, particularly in regard to cognitive development. Many clients, particularly late adolescents and young adults, are still developing cognitive systems that allow them to identify and discriminate nuances of affect. When feelings expressed by one participant are reflected, this individual as well as other members can learn more about the conditions that produce the feeling and cues that signal its presence. They may consequently become more adept at identifying it in themselves and others. In order to improve group members' cognitive maps of feelings, counselors can specifically identify the cues observed in making the reflection. Rather than simply saying, "Joe, you looked sad when we learned Susan was leaving the group," a counselor might go on to observe, "Your eyes were downcast, and you were slumped over."

Cognitive reflections, as discussed in Chapter Three, are particularly important in producing cognitive development in group counseling. As a counselor reflects a cognitive process experienced by one member, other group members can obtain a better understanding of the individual and can consequently be more supportive. The reflection can also stimulate them to consider whether they entertain similar cognitions and to examine similarities and differences in their own ways of processing information. Self-defeating cognitions that are reflected can help other members better understand their own self-defeating processes. Counselors should also make reflections of productive cognitions that help clients cope with difficult situations. Such reflections facilitate the process of members' using one another as coping models.

   Linking, Pairing, and Contrasting. The linking and pairing technique, along with its counterpart of contrasting, has been discussed by a number of group-counseling experts (Dinkmeyer and Muro, 1979; Ohlsen, 1970). It is generally seen as a method of reducing clients' feelings of being different from one another and promoting group cohesion. An example of a linking and pairing intervention might be "Fred admits that he feels pretty anxious about speaking in a class. His feelings in this situation seem pretty similar to the ways Joan said she felt at the party last week." This kind of response helps group members become aware of aspects of experience shared with others in the group.

   Contrasting, pointing out differences in the experiences of two or more group members, would at first glance appear to counteract the development of group cohesion. For most people, contrasting probably injects a higher element of challenge than does pairing. Counselors should make sure that sufficient support is present in the group and that the individuals whose differences are noted can respond to this challenge. However, if contrasting is done in a sensitive way that communicates acceptance of both persons' reactions, it can facilitate group cohesion, encourage appreciation of individual differences, and lead to a more complex understanding of human nature. Dichotomous views are challenged by the implication that it is natural for wide differences to exist among people.

   Counselors interested in promoting cognitive development can make effective use of pairing and contrasting *cognitive processes.* For example, "It's interesting that Ted and Ann are both inclined to worry a lot about the impression they are making when talking with someone they really like. Gail doesn't get caught up in that so much and keeps her mind on what is being discussed." This method is similar to the approach taken in Kelly's (1955) Role Construct Repertory Test, where subjects identify their constructs through a process of specifying how two individuals are alike and different from a third. As the counselor pairs and contrasts, clients may become clearer about some of their own attributes and about the constructs they use in reacting to others.

Questioning. As Socrates discovered long ago, questioning is particularly important for stimulating cognitive development. Open-ended questions are generally better than closed-ended ones, in that the person responding has to articulate a concept and therefore think more fully about the subject. As in individual counseling, closed-ended questions are helpful at times. For instance, a counselor may be able to help a reticent group member break the ice and get into the flow of a discussion by asking a yes-no question.

Another issue to consider in tailoring questions is whether to address them to the group as a whole or to individuals. Many of a counselor's questions can best be directed to the group as a whole. This method can subtly enhance the group's sense of cohesion, since members collectively feel the responsibility to respond. In structured groups with several reticent members, such as might occur in a shyness group, it can be effective to set the expectation that each member will respond to questions. The anxiety of deciding whether to risk responding is thereby eliminated. Questions directed to individuals may achieve specific goals. For instance, counselors can direct relatively easy, "soft ball" questions to reticent participants to help them enter discussions. Counselors might also ask certain questions to individuals likely to be good models for topics being discussed. Other reasons for directing questions to particular individuals include eliciting support for a member and keeping the group focused on a topic.

Gatekeeping. The skill of gatekeeping might appear antithetical to most of the other techniques mentioned, which are designed to promote an open communication process. However, in the interests of balancing the challenge and support factors experienced by group members, counselors may have to control the number of questions or the amount of feedback directed to an individual. In their zest to develop new ideas, participants may not be sufficiently attuned to the needs of some members and may unwittingly direct more attention toward them than desirable. Counselors need to be alert to this possibility and redirect the attention.

Reframing. Another group-leading skill that is particularly helpful in facilitating cognitive changes is reframing, previously discussed in the context of individual counseling (Chapter Six). Clients often express opinions or interpretations that are potentially helpful to other participants, except that the concept is simplistically expressed. Rather than letting the limited perspective stand as it is, ignoring the contribution, or directly disagreeing, the counselor can agree with the basic thrust of the client's intent and yet expand the perspective in making a reflection to the group. This method allows the counselor to maintain supportiveness of the member offering the idea and yet present a more complex formulation of the topic to other members.

Group Involvement Exercises

Group exercises can be planned at Phase 6 and used at Phase 7 to promote open discussion and group cohesion. Some are designed to increase participants' levels of cognitive complexity and/or to improve skills. However, simply "getting them interacting" does not ensure that the goals of a cohesive group process and cognitive change will be met. By using the planning model, counselors can apply exercises more effectively.

Icebreakers and Get-Acquainted Activities. A get-acquainted exercise early in the first session of a group can help "break the ice" and enable members to cross the first mental boundary to self-disclosure by beginning to talk to one another. Participants are quite naturally observing events and making predictions about how safe it is to take risks in the group. The get-acquainted activities help participants fill in their cognitive maps of the group and the other members with information rather than anxiety-arousing conjecture. Get-acquainted exercises also contribute to a group norm for member-to-member communication.

Icebreakers at the beginning of sessions can help group

members assume the mind set of being in the group. Participants are likely to enter the group somewhat preoccupied with other tasks or events. The icebreaker can ease them into confronting serious issues and can signal them to turn their attention to the activities.

Pfeiffer and Jones (1974–1979) describe many get-acquainted activities, some of which are rather complex and time consuming. These can often be adapted and simplified, so as to better meet goals and time considerations. Material related to the theme of the group can often be incorporated into the exercises.

It is often helpful to have participants discuss a topic in pairs, particularly as a get-acquainted activity in the first session. Some counselors prefer that this discussion be unrelated to the group content; however, I generally focus it on relevant topics. Talking for a few minutes in pairs can be a good "warm-up" for talking in the group. Most people find it easier to take risks of self-disclosure with one other person. It is often helpful to have each member of the pair then introduce the other member to the group and to summarize the information exchanged. Some members may find it safer to explain someone else's ideas, rather than their own, to the group. Topics for this exercise can include participants' expectations and/or goals for the group. In light of the need to keep get-acquainted activities somewhat light, it can also be helpful to include a humorous topic. For instance, early in the first session of career-planning groups, I often ask pairs to describe their "wildest career fantasies."

Another icebreaking activity that can help members work together is the "name game." In turn, group members give their names, followed by the names of the participants who have preceded them in the exercise. A variation is to have participants repeat members' names and then share an adjective for each individual. "Getting on a first-name basis" signifies the crossing of another mental hurdle in moving toward trusting and deriving support from others.

Dyads, Triads, and Subgroups. As mentioned, dyads can be used successfully in get-acquainted activities. They can also be used in other discussions, particularly when participants are being asked to take a "plunge" to a new level of self-disclosure. Triads can be effective, particularly in activities where two discussants and an observer are needed. For instance, in role playing assertive or communication skills, it is helpful to have two role players and an observer who can note such aspects as non-verbal cues. Subgroups of other sizes can also be useful at times, in order to allow participants to explore topics in situations that may seem safer than the entire group.

Experiential-Learning Exercises. Some exercises generate group involvement and additionally facilitate expanded thinking on an important issue or the practice of skills. An example is the "Mind Game," which I have used in structured groups designed to teach cognitive coping skills. After self-defeating cognitive styles are identified and coping cognitions are explained, the group is divided into two sections. One is to play the "Worrying Part" of the mind, while the other, with the help of the leader, is to play the "Coping Part." Members in the Worrying Part are to voice self-defeating thoughts, which are to be countered and placed in perspective by coping self-talk offered by the members in the Coping Part. After several minutes, the sides reverse roles.

Other forms of role playing can lead to cognitive development. Counselors can use creativity and resources such as the Pfeiffer and Jones (1974-1979) volumes to design ways for group members to experience rather than "just talk about" certain kinds of situations. For example, in leading a social skills group, a coleader and I actually held a brief party. It served as an opportunity for members to practice anxiety management and assertiveness skills and to compare their expectations of how they would think, feel, and behave with their actual experiences.

Using Humor in Group Counseling

Dinkmeyer and Muro (1979) encourage group counselors to use humor. However, counselors should not allow humor to serve as a distraction from matters that are difficult to discuss.

Playful bantering is often used as a way of distancing the individual and the group from fully experiencing negative affect, such as fear or anger. In arriving at formulations of the group process at Phase 4c, counselors should therefore note how humor is used and whether it is used in a defensive way. When the use of humor is judged to be an impediment to group progress, interventions designed to gently redirect group discussion can then be planned (Phase 6) and executed (Phase 7). Readdressing the important issue is often an effective tactic in a relatively structured, task-focused group. If the group is relatively open ended and oriented toward self-awareness exploration, the preferred option might be to invite the group to examine the process of the use of humor. Examination of the role of humor in the group can lead to a more complex understanding of self-functioning and group process.

Counselors should also avoid offering or encouraging sarcastic or judgmental humor. Even if such joking is directed at people outside the group, some participants might infer that the judgmental attitude could easily be turned on them. Further, this kind of humor does not model the empathic appreciation of others that a supportive group is well suited to developing.

In spite of the potential difficulties with humor, spontaneity and playful joking in a group can help build group cohesion and further cognitive complexity. With most groups, it is helpful to encourage humorous interchanges in identifying process goals (Phase 5b) and in planning (Phase 6) and implementing (Phase 7) strategies. Many people have "closet humor" that is rarely shown to others. A supportive group can help them risk disclosing this part of themselves and can lead to their "owning" this strength. A light atmosphere during some periods of group sessions can challenge the validity of negative preconceptions of group counseling—for instance, the idea that it will be an extremely intimidating, imposing experience. A natural, spontaneous atmosphere that includes some joking and laughing may help members view the group as a potentially valuable life experience instead of as a frightening and/or highly unusual one.

Group-shared humor often contains metamessages useful

to clients experiencing difficulties. It can communicate the message that "we're all in this together." Since many jokes play upon the fallibility of human nature, humor can help convey that "it is OK to make mistakes now and then and to have human quirks and foibles." As well as contributing to group cohesion, these messages often help group members become less negativistic and less prone to taking themselves and their life circumstances too seriously.

Counselors can model using humor appropriately—as an empathic way to communicate acceptance and support instead of as a way to defend oneself and denigrate others. Counselors also should be willing to laugh at themselves. To do so provides a helpful model of self-acceptance in the face of mistakes and imperfections. When laughing at oneself is combined with productively addressing one's difficulties, it suggests a self-view that can be paraphrased "I mess up in quite human ways, and I want to improve; however, I am OK as a person." In addition to modeling humor, counselors can warmly reinforce appropriate and helpful humor offered by group members.

Summary and Conclusions

Group counseling offers many advantages for influencing cognitive development. It also has the potential of reinforcing limited, restricted perspectives. The Cognitive Intervention Planning Model can help counselors conduct groups that enhance cognitive development. Use of the model can help in assessing whether group counseling is an appropriate intervention for clients and regulating the challenge and support elements for the group as a whole. In addition, it can aid counselors in recognizing and responding to different support-challenge requirements among individual group members. In order to promote group cohesion and influence cognitive change, counselors can use a number of methods in planning (Phase 6) and implementing (Phase 7) group leadership strategies. These include becoming familiar with group process dimensions, developing their leadership styles and group leadership skills, and learning to use group involvement exercises. Humor can also be used constructively to build group cohesion and facilitate cognitive development.

EIGHT

Designing and Leading
Structured Groups
and Workshops

Many student development professionals have recognized that
they must take a proactive stance in order to have a significant
impact on the campus community. Morrill, Oetting, and Hurst
(1974) have advocated multiple services designed to achieve different goals with different student groups. Two forms of service
delivery that are especially useful in addressing developmental
and preventive goals are structured groups and outreach psychoeducational workshops. Both of these methods use a more
structured format than is typically used in exploratory, self-
awareness group counseling, in that a sequence of predesigned
activities is followed. These predesigned groups or workshops
require less preparation by the leader and can be conducted by
leaders who are relatively inexperienced, such as those in training. Some programs can also be led by peer counselors trained
and supervised by professional staff.

   Structured groups and psychoeducational workshops
both use a structured format, generally consisting of various
exercises, discussions, and lecturettes. The skills involved in developing these interventions are similar. One primary difference
is that structured groups generally meet for several sessions and
thereby allow for learning and practice of skills over time,
whereas outreach workshops are most often "one-shot" pro-

grams and therefore do not provide the luxury of between-session practice or the opportunity for ideas to evolve over time. While workshops can sometimes last several hours, it is more common in university outreach programs for them to last one or two hours. The workshop leader may therefore have considerably less time in which to accomplish goals than the structured group leader. Therefore, workshop goals often have to be more modest, centering on awareness of issues rather than on development of skills. Another major difference is that structured groups are generally conducted with a relatively small group—perhaps eight to twelve participants. Workshops are often presented to larger numbers, often to more than twenty participants and occasionally to groups of one hundred to two hundred. While small-group leadership skills remain applicable in structured groups, the workshop leader faces an audience and must develop a completely different set of skills—those required in making large-group presentations.

This chapter focuses on the use of the Cognitive Intervention Planning Model in designing and leading structured groups and workshops. In addition, brief descriptions of specific types of structured groups and workshops are presented in Part Three.

Enhancing Learning Opportunities in Groups and Workshops

Incorporating principles that enhance learning can increase the effectiveness of group and workshop interventions in producing desired cognitive changes. These principles can be observed at Phase 6, when the intervention is planned, and in the implementation at Phase 7.

Providing Clear Cognitive Maps. Counselors relatively familiar with group processes can easily underestimate the anxiety that group and workshop participants may feel, particularly when they know little about what to expect. If a vacuum of information exists, participants may conjure up fantasies that are far afield from anything the counselor plans. Much of what clients do in a group—what they disclose, when, to whom—is regulated by their outcome expectancies, their ideas about the results likely to be produced by certain actions.

Counselors can help allay anxiety by conveying clear cognitive maps of such aspects as intervention goals and the nature of exercises and activities. Evidence presented by Truax (1961) suggests that setting clear expectations increases group cohesion. It is quite often more confusing to give too little information than none at all. An incomplete, poorly worded introduction to an exercise can stimulate participants to entertain spirals of unwarranted thoughts and images regarding what might happen.

In conveying cognitive maps of what to expect in the group or workshop and from specific activities, counselors should try to provide *complete* explanations. A good rule of thumb is to take nothing for granted regarding participants' understanding of the overall direction or activity. What is clear to the counselor—and would appear to be obvious—may be new to participants and undeveloped in their thought systems.

A second goal for the counselor is to be as *clear* as possible. Abstract statements of group goals may have little meaning for participants. Graphic examples can help them visualize what might occur. As well as providing examples themselves, counselors can ask participants for concrete examples of their own. Counselors also may need to demonstrate activities. A demonstration of a relaxation exercise by the counselor may reduce anxiety and help clients better understand what they will be doing. Role-playing exercises are often best modeled by the leaders before participants are asked to undertake them.

Counselors should also observe participants as the activity is being explained and ask for *feedback* that indicates whether they understand the explanation. Blank stares, puzzled looks, and averted gazes may indicate that they are not "getting it."

Using Small Sequential Steps. In exploring new ideas and learning new skills, participants can progress more quickly if counselors proceed in small steps. What appears to the counselor to be a small progression may seem unmanageable to clients, who are less familiar with the content and with group participation. The counselor must avoid getting too far ahead of the members in pursuing a subject. A helpful technique to use in preparing interventions is to construct a flow chart of activities, beginning with the final cognitive or behavioral skill and working backward in identifying substeps.

Using the "Learn-by-Doing" Principle. In order to perfect behavioral skills, such as assertiveness or the use of relaxation, clients need to try out the behaviors. In the same manner, cognitive skills such as decision making or the use of coping self-talk are better learned if clients can apply them. The group modality provides the creative counselor with greater variety of opportunities to use the learn-by-doing principle than does individual counseling. The kinds of role plays, games, and exercises that can be done in groups allow new cognitive perspectives to develop as a result of direct experiences. While most workshop formats allow for only limited application of skills, the learn-by-doing principle can be extended to "learn by thinking." Rather than simply receiving new information, participants can be asked to actively think about the role of the themes in their own lives.

Providing Reinforcement and Feedback. New behaviors can be shaped through the use of immediate reinforcement. Evolving ideas may also require reinforcement in order for them to be fully formulated and used. Counselors can acknowledge and encourage clients' verbalizations that indicate increased self-awareness and/or more complex thinking. Group members can be encouraged to offer feedback and reinforcement to one another: "Does anyone notice any ways that Mary's perspective on her schoolwork is different from last week?" Negative feedback can also be presented, as long as sufficient support is provided in the group atmosphere. Most brief workshops are not sufficiently supportive to allow for a great deal of feedback exchanged among participants; however, workshop leaders can be conscious of reinforcing instances of creative and complex thinking that are expressed. In both groups and workshops, rather than simply commenting "That was well done," counselors should attempt to specify the exact cognitive events or processes that are being reinforced: "The way you refocused your attention to the other people and off of yourself was good and seemed to help you." This specificity makes clear to other group members the particular process they might try to adopt.

Providing Opportunities for Practice. Clients need to have continued experience in applying concepts and/or behaviors. Role playing, dyadic and small-group discussions, exercises, and games can provide varied practice opportunities during group sessions. The group modality also encourages members to undertake "homework," since participants are often attracted to between-session activities that can be done with one or more others. Practice with new thoughts and behaviors can be incorporated into brief workshops, although on a smaller scale than in structured groups. Leaders can describe ways the ideas can be used by participants after the workshop.

Providing Effective Models of Desired Cognitive Processes. Counselors have three options for providing models to participants: (1) They themselves can model the desired aspects. (2) Media models, such as videotaped or written examples, can be used. (3) Participants can serve as models for other members. Counselors should try to remain aware of their own potential as models. Their listening and attending behaviors, ways of providing feedback, questioning approaches, and other responses can serve as models to participants of ways to interact with others. Counselors can model cognitive processes by retracing their thoughts in difficult situations: "I was thinking to myself when Judy got angry, 'Oh, no, what's this going to do to the group?' But then I said, 'Wait a minute. Let's not panic. The group can deal with this kind of thing.' " When providing modeling themselves or using media, counselors need to remember the principles of modeling as discussed in Chapter Three. For instance, they can make explicit how modeled behaviors are rewarded.

Both large and small groups offer many useful models as members observe one another. Counselors can enhance the natural richness of groups for modeling by drawing attention to members who demonstrate effective behaviors or perspectives. They can also focus attention on the salient aspects of a participant's efforts to understand or cope with a situation: "What I like about how Susan dealt with her parents was that, while she initially catastrophized a lot about meeting them, she got herself calmed down by reminding herself to take things one step at a time."

Building Cognitive Development upon Previous Learning. As stated before in this book, it is easier for someone to extend an old concept to a new situation than to formulate a completely new concept. Similes and metaphors can help clients relate ideas used in other areas to new situations. For instance, the "fight-or-flight" concept can be illustrated in stress management groups or workshops with the metaphor of the "Incredible Hulk," a television character. Stress reactions can be likened to the Hulk's metamorphosis when faced with threatening situations. Concrete examples and anecdotes may help participants achieve visualizations related to the concepts. In addition to providing examples themselves, counselors can ask participants to illustrate their points with examples. Counselors can also try to couch ideas in language familiar to the group members.

Making Covert Cognitive Events Explicit. One of the most effective methods for enhancing learning of more expanded cognitive perspectives in groups and workshops with smaller numbers is to make underlying cognitions explicit. Counselors can ask participants to recount thinking processes that they used in coping with difficult situations within and outside the group. Counselors can encourage a norm for this kind of cognitive sharing by disclosing their own covert thinking processes. Sometimes imagery, role playing, empty-chair techniques, and other methods can be used to help members identify and then articulate their cognitive processes so that they can be explored and/or adopted by others.

The Planning Model in Structured Groups

Drum and Knott (1977) have divided structured groups into those focusing on "life skills," such as stress management; "life themes," such as sex role exploration; and "life transitions," such as midlife career change. Most structured groups focus on exploration of a theme; clarification of self-views related to that theme; and development of skills, both cognitive and behavioral, for coping more successfully with difficult situations. Attention to the cognitive dimension is therefore useful in these kinds of groups. The group leader can benefit from a clear conception of the cognitive processes inherent in the group theme and the kinds of cognitive shifts or changes desirable.

The Cognitive Intervention Planning Model can be particularly useful in designing this structured kind of intervention. The relevant cognitive events (Phase 1), cognitive systems (Phase 2), and cognitive development issues (Phase 3) are often gathered from previous activities. For instance, counselors might form ideas based on the problems of former clients or on insights gained in needs assessments. Counselors can then use these data and impressions in constructing the Phase-4 formulations. Phase 1–3 data can also be elicited from potential participants in screening interviews and assessment procedures and incorporated into a formulation of the problem at Phase 4a. Although structured groups are predesigned, counselors can provide variations in the Phase-4a problem formulation by emphasizing certain activities in some groups more than in others. The Phase 1–3 information obtained in screening is also used at Phase 4b to construct a formulation of the personal characteristics that indicate whether or not the group is an appropriate intervention for the individual.

Once a structured group has begun, modifications can still be made in Phases 4a and 4b. These refinements are more likely to lead to minor adjustments in exercises selected or material emphasized than to major alterations of overall direction, as might occur with open-ended process groups. While structured groups are less likely to incorporate group discussion of group processes, counselors still should make Phase-4c formulations identifying important group dynamics. This cognitive map is necessary in order to foster a group atmosphere that is conducive to development of cognitive complexity.

Based on the formulations made at Phase 4, goals for the group are determined at Phase 5, including goals for the changes desired in participants' cognitive events, systems, and developmental levels. Outcome goals (Phase 5a) normally formulated for structured groups are more specific than those often targeted in open-ended group counseling. The process goals (Phase 5b) are also often different, in that, while group supportiveness is desired, major learning is not dependent on directly discussing group dynamics. Although the intervention planned at Phase 6 is relatively structured, there can be some flexibility in the implementation phase (Phase 7); for instance, decisions are made regarding whether and when to use certain group exercises. Information relative to Phases 1–3 obtained during the course of the group and monitoring of participants' reactions to activities (Phase 8a) can lead to adaptation of specific aspects of the intervention plan. Final evaluation of the group's effectiveness (Phase 8b) is often a built-in component of the group and may include pre- and postintervention assessment, goal attainment scaling, and other methods.

Considerations for Leading Structured Groups

Effective structured groups often go through distinct phases. Group leaders should avoid the rut of rigidly using the same format; however, in designing (Phase 6) and implementing (Phase 7) the intervention, they need to consider whether these steps are being adequately addressed by the group activities. Important phases are discussed in this section.

Identifying and Clarifying Goals. Drum and Knott (1977) emphasize that participants in a structured group must understand the group's goals. At the beginning of the group, clients can be helped to develop cognitive maps of (1) their own current status regarding the developmental issues or problems to be addressed, (2) their goals for progressing in the group, and (3) the general direction and goals planned at Phase 5 for the intervention. Group members who clearly understand these areas are more likely to maintain high levels of motivation over the course of the group. They are also better able to identify discrepancies between their expectations and realistic outcome goals. Ideally, the first session will implant the idea that a solid start toward resolution is more likely to occur than complete mastery of developmental tasks. The group should be seen as part of a journey with an important issue, not the entire journey.

As a combination goal-setting and get-acquainted activity, clients can be asked to describe their goals for the group. Group members can be asked to form dyads and talk about a humorous topic (selected according to the group) and about what they would like to gain from the group. Each person then introduces the other member of the dyad to the rest of the members and summarizes their discussion. After all members have talked, the leaders can present the goals for the group and address instances in which individuals' goals appear to be unrealistic or inappropriate. Participants with unrealistic goals can be encouraged to identify intermediate steps that could be formulated into more realistic goals. A description of the goals and activities of the group can then be given, illustrated by goals mentioned by participants. The leader may need to approach a participant with inappropriate goals after the session and discuss whether the group is the best option and what alternatives could be considered.

Program evaluation procedures (Phase 8b) can be incorporated into this goal clarification phase. If pre- and postintervention instruments are to be used, the preintervention questionnaires can form the basis for participants' attempts to clarify goals. Members can be asked to complete the instruments prior to the group or at the beginning of the first session and to reflect on their responses in the dyadic discussions. The items can stimulate them to make finer discriminations regarding the role of the problem in their lives. Another useful program evaluation approach that can be incorporated at this stage is goal attainment scaling. Participants identify individual goals and then specify criteria for different gradations of change on their goals. They then use these descriptions to rate their changes at the end of the group. I have used a simplified adaptation of the procedures described by Paritzky and Magoon (1982). Participants can generally complete the goal attainment scaling form more successfully after the get-acquainted discussions.

Clarifying Expectations and Formulating Ground Rules. Once goals have been clarified, expectations of and ground rules for the group should be addressed. Participants can be asked what they expect from the counselors in order to work toward the goals identified and what the counselors should be able to expect from the group members. Both sets of ideas can be listed and discussed, and consensus ground rules negotiated. Particularly in brief structured groups, it is wise for counselors to suggest ground rules that participants attend all sessions (unless prevented by illness or another major conflict), arrive promptly, notify leaders if unable to attend, and do their best to participate actively in all discussions and exercises.

Developing a Cognitive Map of the Issue. Participants are more likely to commit themselves to a group when they understand the reasoning behind the activities. After participants are given an opportunity to think about and discuss the issues, the leader can provide a model of the targeted problem or developmental task. Examples from the participants' discussions can be used in presenting the model, thus making it more credible to them. For example, in evaluative anxiety groups, participants are asked to voice what happens to them when they are anxious. Their responses are then plugged into the anxiety spiral model as it is explained (see Figure 3, Chapter Five). Other components of this "selling the rationale" stage can include use of bibliotherapy—perhaps an article given to participants to read between the first two sessions.

Testing Participant Commitment. Once participants have clarified their goals and have some understanding of the rationale of the program, they can be asked to think about the forces likely to inhibit them from making the desired changes. Their reasons for *not* changing might be discussed. They might, for instance, be asked to undertake a "costs-benefits analysis," writing down the costs and benefits of changes they have identified. Group or dyadic discussions can then be directed at ways of dealing with the costs so that they do not inhibit possible changes, including cognitive restructuring of self-defeating beliefs.

Developing Self-Awareness. This step often precedes development of skills; however, they can be pursued concurrently. Much of the first two or three sessions may be devoted to sensitizing participants to relevant cognitive processes. It necessitates their tuning in to themselves and forming a cognitive map of their cognitive responses relative to the problem. The goal clarification exercises can help, as can administration and discussion of program evaluation instruments. A major ingredient is to elicit group discussion so that participants can get feedback on their own thoughts and have their ideas stimulated by the thoughts of other members. Modeling procedures in the form of group leader role plays, written handouts, or media "trigger" materials can encourage this tuning-in process.

Developing Cognitive Skills. In some life skills structured groups, such as stress or evaluative anxiety management, development of specific cognitive coping skills is a goal. In life theme and life transition groups, expanded cognitive awareness is a major goal; however, enhanced skill in addressing and thinking through situations is also desired. Again, modeling can add to the collective creativity of the group members in identifying strategies. In addition to group discussions, dyadic discussions, role plays, imagery exercises, and homework assignments can contribute to the formation of skills.

Integrating New Concepts and Skills. As new perspectives and skills are formed, they must be used so that they become permanently enmeshed in important cognitive systems. This kind of application can be achieved through further group discussion, imagery, role playing, and between-session practice. Groups afford the possibility of simulation exercises that could not be done in individual counseling. For instance, a party can be held for a social skills group, or practice speeches in the group can be arranged for speech-anxious participants.

Change-Resistance Inoculation. Once participants have formed new perspectives and skills in the comfort of the group, they sometimes fail to realize that such changes are difficult to maintain. Their reasons *not* to change often generate internal dialogue that may convince them to procrastinate and maintain old habits. Further, they will be rejoining interpersonal systems that may have in some ways encouraged the unwanted patterns. It is useful for the group to discuss the internal and external forces that may sabotage their good intentions. Once these are identified, group members can brainstorm ways to prepare for and combat these forces, including the use of cognitive strategies.

Postintervention Self-Assessment and Planning. In the last session, group members need to consider how far they have come—specifically, (1) what they have learned about themselves during the group, (2) how they have progressed in the targeted problem or aspect of development, and (3) what steps they can take in the future to solidify gains and further develop. Participants can be asked to reflect on what has occurred in the group and to specify activities that were helpful. The ideas volunteered can be written on a blackboard or newsprint. The process of recalling and evaluating the activities can help anchor concepts in participants' minds.

Participants in a structured group need to compare their present status on the problem or developmental issue with their status at the beginning of the group. It is human nature for many of us to raise our goals and expectations as we ascend a ladder of accomplishment and therefore fail to recognize significant gains we have made. How members think they have progressed with goals stated in the first session can be discussed. They can be asked to imagine themselves in the first session and to recapture their experience of the problem at that time. Feedback from other group members and from the leader can be helpful, particularly when individuals are too self-critical to recognize gains.

Program evaluation procedures can also be useful in this stage of a group. Postintervention instruments can be completed and then used as the basis for a discussion of the ways in which members think they have progressed. If goal attainment scaling is used, participants are given the goals and criteria written in the first session and asked to rate the degree to which different goals have been met. Group or dyadic discussion based on this task can help them clarify gains and solidify related concepts in their minds.

Clarification of what members have learned and how they have grown leads to the question of what they need to do in the future. There is evidence that a change process begun in a structured group can continue afterward (Goldfried and Trier, 1974). Participants are more likely to use the group as a springboard to further efforts to improve *if* they identify one or more specific "next steps" before the group is ended. A good concluding exercise is for group members to identify and discuss one or more "next steps" they plan to implement. They can be asked to complete a humorous contract with themselves or another group member in which they make a commitment to a next step. The exercise can be discussed in dyads and then summarized for the group. As group members hear the ideas of other participants, they can expand and sharpen their own plans. This enjoyable exercise helps consolidate ideas and creates an atmosphere conducive to bringing the group to a close.

Facilitating the Group Process. The importance of facilitating productive group interactions in structured as well as in unstructured groups was discussed in Chapter Seven. My experiences and program evaluation data with social development groups suggest that facilitating a comfortable group process contributes to the effectiveness of these groups (Barrow, 1983). One change I have made since my earlier structured group efforts is the inclusion of more "get-acquainted" activities in the first two sessions and "warm-up" activities to begin sessions. From a cognitive perspective, members have to see the group as a safe and comfortable place to self-disclose. Activities that are fun and involving and that require only low to moderate levels of self-disclosure help "get the ball rolling" and build the perception of safety and support that can lead to more substantive disclosures. Warm-up activities to start a session can serve as cognitive signposts of the transition from daily events to the group activities. As noted in Chapter Seven, *A Handbook of Structured Experiences for Human Relations Training,* edited by Pfeiffer and Jones (1974–1979), is an excellent resource for ideas on group exercises; however, I generally attempt to simplify the activities.

Another change I have made is to reduce the amount of content presented didactically and to increase time available for group interaction regarding what is presented. The meaning of handout material is sometimes enhanced if it is offered to highlight what has already emerged in a group discussion. Dyadic and triadic discussions prior to exploring a theme with the entire group can help members feel more comfortable voicing their ideas. I have also come to incorporate more experiential group exercises, so that participants can use their immediate reactions as data in exploring a theme or developing skills.

Outreach Workshops: A Different Direction

One promising direction in keeping with the multiple-goal approach advocated by Morrill, Oetting, and Hurst (1974) is outreach education, in which counselors take a preventive, psychoeducational product to students in residence halls, organizations, and other groups (Drum, 1984; Drum and Figler, 1973). This method requires counselors to identify developmental and preventive needs, design effective interventions based on an educational model, and leave their offices to deliver programs in students' "natural habitats." Outreach education may be more efficient in meeting certain goals than a reactive stance of waiting until students become acutely distressed and then serving their remedial needs in one-to-one counseling.

The psychoeducational workshop is one of the most used outreach education methods. While well-presented outreach workshops can make significant contributions, these services represent a major shift for the counselor. Most individuals are initially attracted to the counseling profession because they value the very personal and intimate nature of the interactions in individual counseling (Goodyear and Shaw, 1984). Group counseling represents a departure from this kind of focus, in that the interpersonal milieu rather than the private inward quest is emphasized. Even so, the atmosphere is relatively intimate, and counselors can continue to receive the reinforcement of feeling that they have really made "contact" with clients. On the other hand, outreach education workshops are presented for briefer periods and to larger numbers. Rather than having an on-going, personal interaction with an individual or a supportive group, the counselor is suddenly face to face with an *audience*. A qualitatively different and more active stance is required, because the skills of individual empathy and small-group facilitation are insufficient for attracting and holding the attention of an audience. While some counselors have developed teaching skills, which are helpful in outreach education, a more informal and engaging style is required in the residence hall lounge than in the classroom. Some of the skills needed are more often fostered in the entertainment field than in academia or human relations. These skills may not come naturally to many counselors, who tend to be reflective and private.

The goals for outreach education activities are by necessity limited. Accepting these more limited goals is another adjustment for many counselors, who are accustomed to helping clients "work through" conflicts or problems. However, the meeting of limited cognitive goals can initiate a process of examination that can continue after the workshop. This continued cognitive growth is of course dependent on the supportiveness of ongoing environmental conditions. With sufficient support, the limited workshop goals can eventually culminate in major cognitive shifts, emotional growth, and the development of behavioral skills.

The Planning Model in Psychoeducational Workshops

A cognitive focus is particularly appropriate for outreach education activities. While counselors hope that their workshop and other outreach efforts will be affect-engaging, eliciting intense affect is ordinarily not a process goal, as it might be in individual or group counseling. The briefness of the contact and the level of group intimacy rarely provide sufficient support for intense emotional challenges. It is also unreasonable to think that major behavioral change is likely to occur as a result of a brief workshop, since insufficient time is available for practice and reinforcement of behaviors. Thus, the most appropriate goals for workshops are often cognitive. Students can be expected to gain *awareness* of a theme, to receive new information, to have old concepts challenged and new ones fostered, and to examine their constructs of themselves and others.

Student development professionals can better attain the promise of the outreach workshop mode if a good cognitive map guides their intervention planning. The Cognitive Intervention Planning Model can help them design and deliver outreach services that effectively stimulate ongoing cognitive development. Information regarding Phases 1 (cognitive events), 2 (cognitive systems), and 3 (developmental levels) is obtained prior to planning through methods such as needs assessments, analyses of individual counseling cases, or interviews with representatives of the target population. This information is used at Phase 4a, where a formulation of the problem or issue is made. Rather than assessing the personal qualities of individual participants at Phase 4b, as is done in individual and group counseling, the characteristics of the target group are formulated. Relevant aspects to consider include how well acquainted potential participants are with one another and how extensively they have been exposed to the concepts. The interaction to be formulated at Phase 4c is of the presenter-audience dynamics; however, if a group of fewer than twenty participants attend, small-group processes can also be included. Based on these formulations, process and outcome goals are identified at Phase 5. As noted, realistic outcome goals (Phase 5a) will more often include awareness of issues rather than actual development of new cognitive or behavioral skills. Process goals for workshops (Phase 5b) are less likely to emphasize group support and individual self-disclosure than those for group counseling. The pacing of activities is also likely to be faster than in individual or group counseling. The intervention "package" is then designed at Phase 6. The implementation of the intervention (Phase 7) is relatively prescribed by the design; however, new cognitive data from participants (Phases 1–3) and their responses to activities in evaluation monitoring (Phase 8a) can affect decisions about aspects of implementation, such as whether or not to use an optional exercise. When possible, it is advantageous to incorporate postintervention evaluation procedures in the final evaluation (Phase 8b). The results are then used at Phases 4, 5, and 6 in planning the next administration of the program.

Benefits and Liabilities of Outreach Workshop Interventions

Many of the benefits of a group-counseling intervention discussed in Chapter Seven can occur in a well-conducted workshop, although the effects are likely to be more modest. Universalization can occur, provided that enough audience participation can be generated on a sufficiently disclosive level. Participants can also hear new perspectives and learn new ideas from others and can use one another as models for ideas and behavioral strategies. Some group support can develop, particularly when the participants have ongoing interaction, as when they are members of the same organization or residential unit. The level of support rarely approaches the level attainable in group counseling, however, because most workshops are of brief duration. Participants are less likely to be willing to risk disclosing private information in this kind of atmosphere. Workshops can also promote useful feedback among participants—although, again, less of this kind of exchange is likely to occur in workshops than in groups. Another advantage of brief workshops is that some individuals needing more extensive help may become motivated to use other services, such as individual or group counseling.

There are also several potential impediments to enhancing cognitive development in workshops. It is easier for vocal individuals to monopolize the discussions than in group counseling, because participants are likely to have less investment in challenging others' ideas. If the views of vocal participants are limited by rigid cognitive development, their perspectives can dominate the workshop and restrict opportunities for others to entertain a variety of ideas. Another danger is that the intensity of some participants' contributions might exceed the level of supportiveness inherent in the group. They may disclose too much or offer feedback that is too penetrating for the degree of trust established. The counselor is less likely to be able to monitor and regulate disclosures and feedback in a large workshop than in a smaller group. Moreover, participants who need a more intensive intervention, such as individual counseling or an ongoing group, might infer that they have received all the benefits a counselor has to offer on the topic. Students who engage in dichotomous thinking are especially likely to reach this conclusion, in that they may simplistically equate help with receiving specific ideas or suggestions.

Considerations in Conducting
Outreach Education Workshops

In order for outreach workshops to be effective, counselors and those they train must become proficient as workshop leaders, so that the positive benefits of this form of intervention can predominate and the negative possibilities can be avoided. Three perceptions are key to participants' maintaining an interest in and learning from outreach education workshops. Potential for cognitive growth is enhanced if the workshop activities are perceived as *understandable*—students will not "sit still" for very long in outreach settings if they are confused by the presentation; *relevant*—students need to know early in the program how the activities will relate to their situations; and *significant*—workshop leaders need to ensure that students will find the topic and activities "worth learning about."

As they go through the phases of the Cognitive Intervention Planning Model, counselors need to think continually about how these perceptions can be fostered. The steps discussed in this section are helpful in creating these perceptions and facilitating cognitive development.

Learning About the Prospective Audience. In arriving at a formulation of the target group at Phase 4b, counselors should consider certain characteristics of the participants. First, qualities of the individuals in the group should be noted. What are the participants like—in terms of age range, class standing, gender composition, and other demographic factors? How knowledgeable are they likely to be about the topic? What kind of cognitive development can be expected—are participants likely to be open to varying points of view? How much might they have thought about the issues? Second, participants' attitudes about the workshop should be considered. Has the group itself indicated an interest in the topic, or is it the pet project of the president or program chairperson? How highly motivated are potential participants for the particular topic? Do they expect a relatively serious, educational experience or casual, light entertainment? Are they particularly interested in the topic or merely satisfying an obligation to have a speaker at a meeting?

The kind of audience or group dynamics that can be expected can be formulated at Phase 4c. Will participants have known one another prior to the workshop? If so, how well? How openly have participants discussed similar issues in the past? To what degree has the group discussed the topic? What kind of leadership structure is used, and to what degree are individuals in formal and informal leadership roles supportive of the workshop?

Obviously, the amount of this kind of information that can be obtained prior to beginning a workshop will vary. In university settings a representative of a living unit or organization may request a program. These representatives can be asked to complete a form that elicits basic information about the organization and the group's interest in the topic. Representatives should be discouraged from making unilateral decisions that particular topics are needed by members of the group. When their perceptions are ill founded, as they sometimes are, attendance may be poor and interest levels low. In order to prevent this waste of resources, representatives can be required to conduct a "needs assessment" to clarify others' interests in the program. Other students' views can be surveyed through discussions at meetings and informal polling. It is also helpful for a student service to establish a minimum number of participants required for an outreach program to be offered and to make sure that group representatives are aware of this expectation. The appropriate number will vary with the setting.

Defining Workshop Goals. Once counselors have an understanding of the target population for a workshop, they need to clearly define the goals at Phase 5. The *outcome goals* should be considered: What specific gains is the workshop designed to produce? As previously noted, the outcome goals of many workshops, particularly brief ones, are cognitive in nature. Counselors should also consider their *process goals* for a workshop: To what degree do they want to stimulate member-to-member communication? Are they hopeful that an atmosphere of group support can be established or enhanced?

Getting and Keeping Attention. Getting participants' attention is a more important and more difficult step in leading workshops than in conducting individual or group counseling. Attention to relevant stimuli is a prerequisite for cognitive development to occur. Because less effort is required in attending an outreach workshop than in entering individual or group counseling, the degree of commitment participants feel to the activities is likely to be less. They may experience lower levels of need and may have goals for participation that are less clearly formulated than those of clients in individual and group counseling.

In light of these difficulties, individual counseling and small-group facilitation methods may not be sufficient. Specific methods for getting and maintaining the attention of participants should be incorporated into the workshop design (Phase 6) and used in implementation (Phase 7). Counselors cannot afford to remain reflective and rely on the interest stimulated by the topic and the group process for engaging participants. Some kind of "attention getter" may be necessary early in a workshop. With some topics an introductory lecturette does not attract sufficient attention, and more dramatic steps may be needed. Possible attention getters include unexpected thought-provoking questions, information that is surprising, jokes, anecdotes, concrete examples in the form of "true stories," media "trigger" aids, role plays, and skits. For example, demonstration of an EMG biofeedback unit can serve as an attention getter in stress management workshops, in that the "electronic age" quality is appealing. With communication skills, assertiveness training, and other workshops, role plays early in the workshop to trigger discussion can stimulate participants' interest. In workshops for large groups, such as counseling skills training for residence advisers, colleagues and I have periodically introduced skits that provide comic relief and serve an organizational role by introducing different sections of the workshop. In longer workshops attention getters should be positioned strategically —at points where participants' attention and energy are likely to lag.

As mentioned previously, commitment to an outreach workshop is often tenuous. Participants are more likely to become involved if they are quickly shown how the program is relevant to them. What seems obvious to a student development professional who has studied an issue may be less obvious to students. For this reason, workshop leaders may need to be explicit in pointing out the relevance of the activities. Graphic examples can help greatly.

The mood of outreach workshop participants is often less businesslike than that of clients in individual or group counseling. They are more likely to enter discussions if the atmosphere is casual. Particularly in residence halls, outreach education workshops can best be considered "organized bull sessions." Humor can be used to attract and maintain attention in this kind of atmosphere; it can also be used to highlight important points. After reviewing research on the effects of humor on learning, colleagues and I have offered a number of suggestions to leaders of outreach education activities (Barrow, Fulkerson, and Moore, 1981):

1. Humor should *not* be used at the exclusion of careful planning of the workshop content and process. Students can be thoroughly entertained and still not learn anything of value.

2. Humorous material, as well as other attention getters, should be incorporated at needed intervals throughout a workshop and should be based on an appraisal of potential "low-energy" points.

3. Humor related to the workshop content is preferable to unrelated humor, which can be distracting. When related to important concepts, humor can provide a memorable association and enhance retention. In our workshops for residence advisers, we build humorous skits around points we want to emphasize and use them as an organizational framework for the workshop. Participants have consistently rated these skits as the most positively received aspect of the workshops. Practically speaking, it is not always possible to select jokes that are intricately related to the points of the workshop. As an alternative, topical joking related to current campus events can be helpful in establishing a bond with the audience.

4. Whether humor is used and what kind is employed should be based on consideration of the characteristics of participants, since there seem to be important individual and subgroup differences in reactions to humorous stimuli.

5. Self-deprecatory humor is probably acceptable with most audiences; however, it should not be carried to excess, because it can damage perceptions of speaker/leader credibility. Particularly since many workshops are designed to convey a certain amount of content, leaders should remain conscious of enhancing Strong's (1968) expertness perception.

6. Sexual humor should be used cautiously, since there appear to be individual, gender, and other group differences in responses to such humor. Likewise, humor directed at other individuals or groups should be used cautiously. Participants offended by humor are likely to be distracted from the actual goals of the workshop.

7. In using humor, counselors should probably capitalize on their natural strengths. Not everyone can tell a humorous story effectively or give a stand-up comedy routine. A counselor's most natural style may be to relax and think of spontaneous quips rather than to deliver planned jokes.

Providing a Clear Map of What Will Occur. As with structured groups, participants in workshops are likely to relax and commit themselves more fully to the activities if they understand what will occur. Counseling personnel need to provide clear maps of what will be involved in the workshop. The cognitive sets of some students may lead them to expect to be "shrunk" or "psychoanalyzed," and they may consequently be reluctant to take risks and self-disclose. A clear map of the agenda may enable them to surrender their cautious stances. It can also facilitate retention of important concepts by serving as a framework on which new information can be organized.

Since counselors may not have long to get participants interested, they might consider supplementing a description of the agenda with an activity that quickly provides a flavor of what the workshop will be like. Students often enter a workshop with the idea of "checking it out" for a few minutes and then heading to the library or other location if it does not "grab" them. Even if they do not leave physically, their minds may wander to the homework they plan to do afterward. If the major benefit of the workshop is some new information, the workshop leader should quickly give them a taste of what they can learn. If the main goal is to elicit thought-provoking discussion, the nature of this activity should be demonstrated early in the workshop.

Varying the Activities. In light of the comparatively low levels of motivation, counselors need to learn to vary the workshop activities. While some material can be presented didactically, more than fifteen or twenty minutes of lecturette is likely to be excessive, unless the leader is a particularly dynamic lecturer. Other activities that can be interspersed with information giving include facilitating discussion, having participants take questionnaires, conducting demonstrations, role-playing examples, and organizing participants into small buzz groups. Use of visual and media aids can also provide varied activity, as can listing ideas presented in discussion on newsprint.

Encouraging Active Participation. The "learn-by-doing" principle previously discussed can be expanded to include "learn by thinking." Many students initially attend outreach workshops with the hope of being entertained. They may not anticipate having to exert mental effort themselves. However, learning in psychoeducational workshops requires application of concepts to oneself. Workshop activities should be conducted so that participants are active—if not behaviorally, at least cognitively. Using ingenuity, workshop leaders can devise many ways of encouraging participants to be active. For instance, rather than simply lecturing on a topic, leaders can have participants take a test requiring knowledge of the concepts. The items can then serve as stimuli for discussion. Or, rather than simply asking participants to consider how a concept applies to them, counselors might give each participant a brief self-assessment questionnaire.

Pacing Workshop Activities. In designing (Phase 6) and implementing (Phase 7) workshop interventions, counselors must adapt activities to participants' resources for attending to the tasks. These will depend on factors such as the group composition, the time of the workshop, and its duration. Approximately twenty minutes of an activity can be assumed to be the maximum advisable. This guideline can then be altered in accordance with what is known about the group and what is observed as the workshop unfolds. As previously mentioned, varying activities after fifteen minutes or so can be helpful. Additional attention getters may be necessary at intervals, particularly if the workshop is planned for longer than an hour. Also, breaks should be provided every one or two hours.

The time of day of activities should be considered, especially when long workshops are planned. Effective attention getters and engaging introductory material are important at the beginning of any workshop, since participants' first impressions can influence their receptivity to other activities. Nevertheless, energy levels and enthusiasm are likely to be high in the early stages of a workshop, so that longer intervals between breaks or attention getters may be possible. Later in the day, attention spans can be expected to become shorter, and more frequent attention getters and breaks and increased variety may be required. It is easy for workshop leaders to exhaust their energizing ideas in the early part of a program.

Workshops for students are often held after classes in late afternoons or evenings. Because participants have been involved in highly focused mental work during large portions of the day, their resources of attention will probably be limited. Workshops held at such times should therefore be kept practical, brief, and active.

Adapting Group-Leading Skills. Many of the group-leading skills discussed in Chapter Seven can be applied in implementing (Phase 7) a workshop design, including summarizing, linking and pairing, contrasting, reframing, and gatekeeping. However, the pacing may be different than when these skills are used in small groups. For instance, a counselor leading a group may choose to "wait out" a lengthy period of silence and thereby encourage group responsibility. The same tactic used in a workshop might not be realistic in light of the level of group support established and might lose the attention of some participants. A workshop leader might need to move more quickly to reframe the question, elicit responses, or provide information.

Assuming an Active Role. Enhancing cognitive development in a workshop requires the counselor to take a more active role than in leading a group. In effect, the leader assumes a greater proportion of the responsibility for the direction of the activities. At times in a group, the counselor can be nondirective in order to determine the direction the group members will establish and to encourage group responsibility. This approach is less often advisable in workshops, particularly in brief ones. Leaders of workshops need to be prepared to be more directive in leading discussions—ready to redirect participants from time-wasting tangents, change the topic when the discussion becomes stalled, shift the focus of the group from a participant who appears to be feeling attacked, and so forth.

Working Toward Closure. Effectively closing a workshop is an important and difficult task. The workshop experience should end with a sense of closure—the satisfaction that some of the loose ends have been recognized, articulated, and organized. On the other hand, most topics undertaken in workshops are not fully resolvable in a brief period of time. The counselor must learn how to close workshops in a memorable way and yet avoid conveying that the issues have been resolved. In workshops lasting three or more hours, the next-step-contracting exercise described in the section on structured groups can be used. If participants have ongoing interaction with one another and/or have interacted openly in the workshop activities, this exercise may also be appropriate in briefer workshops. In many brief workshops, however, the level of group trust is not high enough for participants to risk disclosing their ideas regarding future steps. If this degree of trust is not established, participants can be asked to think about the questions without disclosing their ideas.

As an alternative to the next-step-contracting activity, the counselor can ask participants to identify potentially useful ideas they obtained during the workshop. Disclosing thoughts on useful ideas may be less threatening than revealing plans for future steps, in that participants do not have to commit themselves to future actions. Discussion of useful ideas can be combined with obtaining evaluation data (Phase 8b). Participants can be asked to complete a workshop feedback form, and their responses can serve as the basis for their contributions to the discussion.

The closure stage is a good time to convey information

about more extensive services related to the workshop theme. Participants are likely to be more receptive to this kind of information as the workshop is ending than earlier. Greater knowledge of the topic has provided them with "cognitive pegs" on which to hang the new information. Familiarity with the leaders may enhance perceptions of the significance and value of the suggestions. Individual counseling options can be described, as can structured groups and other services related to the theme. Fliers and descriptions of programs are often well received at this time. Introduction of this information reinforces the appropriate expectation of a brief workshop as an awareness-building activity that can illuminate understanding and guide future thinking but not resolve issues.

Evaluating Workshops. Written participant evaluations are frequently used in evaluating workshops at Phase 8b. Participants can be asked to rate and comment on such aspects as the helpfulness and effectiveness of the workshop, to evaluate specific activities, and to indicate ways in which they expect to behave or think differently as a result of the activities. Instead of or in addition to the evaluations of participants, it is often helpful to get written feedback from any individual who represented the group in requesting the workshop. If the workshop goals included conveying information or concepts, a brief test of participants' levels of understanding could be given in conjunction with the closure activities; however, it is unlikely that tests of personality dimensions or cognitive-behavioral skills will be suitable instruments for measuring the awareness goals realistic for brief workshops. The most informative evaluation activity might well be a follow-up procedure used after an appropriate interval, perhaps one month. Participants can be asked the degree to which they have thought about concepts or used ideas since the workshop.

Designing and Conducting Brief Workshops

All of the structured groups discussed in Part Three can be adapted to a workshop format. The sequence presented for the groups can often be used in an extended one- or two-day workshop. Unfortunately, student groups often have limited interest in workshops of this length and prefer briefer programs. With brief workshops of one or two hours in length, selection of sections and adaptation of the material are required. The goals of most brief workshops are largely cognitive and include building awareness of issues, providing guideposts that can be used in further development, and identifying available resources. While extensive cognitive development is unlikely, the beginning of a significant growth process can occur. A germ of an idea can be planted or healthy process of cognitive dissonance nurtured. As a result, these minimal cognitive gains can lead to more extensive cognitive development after the workshop. Likewise, while the learning of new behavioral skills is unlikely in one or two hours, participants may be able to form a cognitive map of a new skill and a more complete understanding of how to develop it.

For the brief workshops, the material presented in the introductory section of the structured group description (see Part Three) can often be used. A "map" of the topic can be presented, which can sharpen participants' abilities to think about the issues. Usually, there is time to discuss one coping skill or developmental theme. With many topics, it is helpful to focus on the internal dialogue concept and attempt to increase awareness of self-defeating cognitive patterns. It may be possible to illustrate coping dialogue; however, it is usually not possible to do justice to this concept in a workshop of an hour or less. There is a risk that participants will obtain a simplistic notion of this method and consequently reject it. It may therefore be better to explore self-defeating dialogue, briefly introduce but not develop the coping dialogue concept, and highlight the resources available to interested participants.

Brief one- to two-hour workshop formats are described for three topics in Part Three: self-image enhancement, male-female social expectations, and stress management. These workshops are quite popular with students and are particularly salient to the developmental tasks of the late adolescent and young adulthood periods. Readers may be interested in using and adapting these ideas in their settings. These examples illustrate use of the cognitive dimension in brief workshops, so that readers can develop their own programs on topics that are not included.

Summary and Conclusions

Structured groups and psychoeducational workshops can enable student development professionals to encourage cognitive complexity, particularly relative to developmental and preventive goals. Design of these interventions can be aided by awareness of general principles that facilitate cognitive learning. Use of the Cognitive Intervention Planning Model can help counselors plan both kinds of interventions. Stages of a structured group intervention that counselors can remember in the design and implementation phases include clarifying goals, clarifying expectations and ground rules, developing a cognitive map of the issue, testing participant commitment, developing self-awareness, developing cognitive skills, integrating new concepts and skills, change-resistance inoculation, and postintervention self-assessment and planning. Attention should also be directed to facilitating productive group processes.

Outreach education workshops represent a departure from the more private, intimate encounters counselors often enjoy in individual and group counseling, in that the interaction is with an audience rather than with an individual or a small group. While this fact can make workshops a less familiar mode of intervention, there are distinct advantages to using this approach with some issues and goals. Counselors can increase their degrees of comfort with psychoeducational workshops by using the planning model in laying the groundwork for, designing, and implementing these interventions. Considerations for counselors to remember include learning about the prospective audience, defining workshop goals, getting and keeping attention, providing a clear map of what will occur, varying the activities, encouraging active participation, pacing activities, adapting group leadership skills, assuming an active role, working toward closure, and evaluating the workshop.

Applications to Specific Developmental Needs in Groups and Workshops

The interventions described in Part Three address issues that seem particularly salient for late adolescent and young adult students. The structured group descriptions first outline the role played by cognition in the problem and then summarize stages in the intervention. In Sections A–G, structured groups are described for managing evaluative anxiety, stress management, perfectionism, assertiveness, social skills and shyness, developing self-confidence, and career planning. In Sections H–J, brief outreach workshops are described for developing self-image, clarifying male and female social expectations, and stress management.

These discussions illustrate how attention to cognitive processes can be incorporated into structured group and workshop designs. Readers should be able to use the programs discussed as models for developing interventions for difficulties that are not covered. Two excellent resources that can be consulted are the Clearinghouse for Structured Group Programs for descriptions of structured groups (Office of Counseling and Student Development, University of Rhode Island, Kingston, Rhode Island 02881) and the Clearinghouse for Innovative Programs in Mental Health for descriptions of workshops and other interventions (Counseling-Psychological Services Center, University of Texas at Austin, Austin, Texas 78712).

A. Managing Evaluative Anxiety

Students with evaluative anxiety are preoccupied with the adequacy of their performances, the judgments of others, and possible negative consequences that might arise from poor performance. Evaluative anxiety most often occurs in response to tests, speeches or other group communication tasks, social situations, and math performance. Since the cognitive elements and intervention strategies are similar in all these problems, they are discussed here as a group, with unique features mentioned where appropriate.

Crouse, Deffenbacher, and Frost (1985) found that students with different sources of test anxiety could be treated successfully in the same group. Wine (1974) has reported success in conducting coping skills training with groups composed of students whose anxiety is stimulated by different kinds of evaluative situations. However, I prefer to work with groups of individuals experiencing the same kind of anxiety problem, because group members are generally better able to contribute ideas to others with the same difficulty; also, the universalization phenomenon discussed in Chapter Seven is more powerful when group members share concerns in a specific area. Another consideration is that students seem to respond more readily to advertising directed at a specific focus than to globally defined issues.

Cognitive Features of Evaluative Activity

In that evaluative anxiety is characterized by intense pre-occupation with performance and consequences, the conscious, cognitive aspects are more pronounced than with classic phobias. Liebert and Morris (1967) identified two factors of test anxiety. The first, called *emotionality,* consists of physiological manifestations of autonomic arousal, including increased heart rate, perspiration, cold hands and feet, "butterflies," and constricted breathing. The second component, *worry,* entails cognitive preoccupation with the test, the adequacy of one's performance, and possible negative consequences of lower-than-desired performance. The cognitive worry component is more highly correlated with intellectual performance than is the emotionality component (Morris and Liebert, 1969). Deffenbacher and Hazaleus (1985) found the worry factor to be the primary source of interference in test performance. An implication of these findings is that people whose physiological indexes of anxiety are heightened may still be able to perform well if they can avoid excessive worry.

Wine (1971) extended the two-component model to other kinds of evaluative anxiety and noted that *worry* self-talk consists of direction of attention inward toward the *self* rather than outward toward immediate tasks. In her view, task-focused attention reduces anxiety and facilitates performance, whereas self-focused attention increases anxiety and interferes with performance. Carver, Peterson, Follansbee, and Scheier (1983) have provided evidence that self-focused attention may impair performance in test-anxious individuals but may improve it in those who are low in test anxiety. It may be that a realistic kind of reassurance and encouragement of oneself can be helpful rather than harmful. The evidence is clear, however, that a negative preoccupation with one's performance and catastrophic anticipations of future outcomes are self-defeating cognitive processes. Students have been successfully trained to use task-focused thinking as a coping strategy to counteract anxiety (Little and Jackson, 1974; Wine, 1974).

An "anxiety spiral" can develop as the emotionality and

worry components interact. Initially, the troublesome situation may elicit moderate levels of both emotionality and worry. Emotionality is likely to remain high only if it is restimulated periodically by the worry component. Just as the *worry* produces and maintains *emotionality* responses, the physiological anxiety responses lead to more worrying, as the anxious person becomes cognitively preoccupied with these responses: "Oh no! My heart is racing; I'm really anxious." The heightened physiological cues may be interpreted as meaning that control has been lost, a thought likely to generate even greater anxiety.

If the spiral progresses beyond a certain point, a number of negative consequences can occur. First of all, an anxious person has impulses to avoid or escape from the feared situation. A test-anxious person might put off studying for a course as a way of avoiding the aversive situation. The avoidance/escape responses can also occur cognitively. An anxious student might achieve distance from a test by daydreaming about vacation plans during study sessions. A second consequence of the spiral is inhibition of voluntary muscle movement. A person anxious in a speaking or social situation may thus appear stiff and awkward. A third consequence of an uncontrolled anxiety spiral is interference with on-task cognitive processes. Students taking tests or giving speeches can block mentally and become unable to retrieve information they have learned.

Evaluative anxiety can have significant effects on clients' constructs of themselves, their relationships with others, and their prospects for the future. Students with these concerns retain low self-efficacy expectancies of their capacities to manage their feelings and the troublesome situations. These situation-specific assumptions can reinforce their perception that they have no control over important conditions in their lives.

Some clients have struggled with evaluative anxiety since early in their lives. However, a number report no major difficulties until they enter university. Their self-critical cognitive systems may have been reasonably adaptive when the challenges could be relatively quickly mastered. With entry into university, however, the intellectual and even social demands may escalate. Without the feedback of quick mastery, the negative cognitive pattern can spiral into an increasingly self-defeating posture. Students at this stage can be helped in making the transition to increased demands by strengthening old and structuring new cognitive coping skills.

The basic cognitive patterns of the various forms of evaluative anxiety are quite similar. One difference is that appearing anxious to others is a more troubling issue for those with social or speech anxiety than for those with test or math anxiety. Also, the social and speech anxiety difficulties of some clients may be quite ingrained, in that shyness may have a genetic component (Cattell, 1973). Even so, most clients can make considerable gains in coping with these reactions. Another possible difference is that cultural attitudes may play a greater role in the formation of math anxiety than in the other kinds of evaluative difficulties. Some females may assimilate a culturally transmitted idea that women are not good at math and consequently feel intimidated by math tasks. These defeatist cognitive positions must be reexamined in learning to cope more successfully with the anxiety.

Steps in a Structured Group Intervention

A group consisting of four or five sessions of one and a half hours provides a balance between maintaining interest and preventing attrition on one hand and providing sufficient opportunities for practice of skills on the other. Training in development of anxiety management strategies can also be used as one component of a more comprehensive structured group. The methods parallel those used in individual coping skills training, as described in Chapter Five; however, the group modality both affords some advantages and requires some adjustments.

In order to foster a positive cognitive set toward the training program, discussion can be initiated with the question "What happens to you when you become anxious?" As specific points are mentioned, they are written on newsprint in three as yet unnamed columns—one for *emotionality*, the second for *worry*, and the third for *consequences*. As with the individual counseling procedures (Chapter Five), the headings are then written in as a lecturette explaining the "anxiety spiral" is given. The "face validity" of the program is thus enhanced as participants see how easily their responses are absorbed into the model, and their enthusiasm for the activities is increased. The phases of cognitive change can then be presented: (1) gaining awareness of cues of anxiety, (2) learning to "catch oneself" in the act of becoming anxious or engaging in self-defeating cognitions, (3) developing and learning to use cognitive coping strategies, and (4) eventually altering basic self-beliefs so that situations are no longer anxiety arousing. The goal of the structured group is to help participants make substantial progress in the first three of these phases; however, the fourth is more likely to occur in the future as a result of success experiences due to improved coping efforts.

In the goal-setting stage, it is important to stress that *coping* is a more realistic expectation for a time-limited group than is mastery. Several instruments have been developed—including those of Alpert and Haber (1960), Sarason (1972), Spielberger (1977), and Suinn (1969)—that facilitate self-assessment and goal setting with test anxiety difficulties. The Test Anxiety Profile by Oetting and Deffenbacher (1980) provides measures of anxiety levels stimulated by different kinds of tests. Watson and Friend's (1969) Social-Evaluative Anxiety Scale can be used with social anxiety, as can an instrument developed by Richardson and Tasto (1976). Speech anxiety can be measured with the Personal Report of Confidence as a Speaker, adapted by Paul (1966), and the Personal Report of Communication Apprehension (college form) and the Personal Report of Public Speaking Anxiety, developed by McCroskey (1970). Instruments for measuring math anxiety include the Mathematics Anxiety Rating Scale (Suinn, 1972) and the Mathematics Anxiety Scale (Fennema and Sherman, 1976). Reliability and validity data have been reported for the math scales by Dew, Galassi, and Galassi (1983).

The phase of developing "early-detection" skills is based on the individual counseling strategies discussed in Chapter Five. For test and math anxiety, participants can reflect on their thoughts, sensations, and behaviors in their most recent tests or math experiences. A guided-imagery exercise in which the event is reexperienced can bring more information to mind. For identifying early cues of social-evaluative and speech anxiety, participants can be asked to reflect on thoughts and feelings elicited by the first group session. Dyadic and group discussions can be used. In a homework assignment between the first and second sessions, group members can be asked to monitor their cognitive, behavioral, and physiological responses to evaluative situations.

In helping clients develop relaxation skills, group leaders should remember that relaxation can act as a "circuit breaker" of the worry self-talk and serve as a "cognitive modifier" in several ways (see Chapter Five). The breathing and meditation exercise adapted from Stevens (1971) is particularly well suited for use in a group. This exercise is usually introduced in the second session, with daily practice prescribed.

While relaxation training has been used successfully in groups (Goldfried and Trier, 1974), group training does present difficulties not found in individual counseling. Some members may feel self-conscious about participating in the exercise in a group and may respond with nervous laughter and other resistant behavior. The counselor may be able to avoid this problem by providing clear information prior to the exercise and suggesting that some embarrassment might be experienced at first. If participants do begin laughing, I either ignore the behavior and proceed to give instructions in a calm manner or incorporate permission to laugh into the instructions. This kind of problem rarely persists beyond the first few minutes of the exercise. Group discussion after the exercise can be fruitful, since misconceptions can be addressed; also, comments from others in the group can help participants better understand their own responses.

Group counseling is particularly well suited to helping participants recognize their patterns of self-defeating cognitive processes. Beginning with the first session, participants are asked to monitor their thoughts in difficult situations. Usually in the second session, Ellis's A-B-C system for analyzing cognitions is illustrated with an example provided by someone in the group (see Chapter Five). The group members brainstorm examples of Point-B self-talk likely to increase the degree of anxiety (Point C) experienced in the troublesome situation (Point A). Subsequent discussions in dyads or triads can help individuals hone in on their own patterns. Guided imagery or role playing can be used to help participants recapture thought processes in recent situations. Homework monitoring can also be prescribed.

When participants begin to identify self-defeating cognitive patterns, they can then evolve ways of combating, rethinking, and preventing these patterns. The various coping methods that can be fostered are discussed in detail in Chapter Five. With test anxiety, Wine's (1971, 1974) method of training participants in task-focused thinking is particularly effective. Task-focused thinking can also be emphasized with speech and social-evaluative anxiety; however, since overinvestment in how one is seen by others is almost always at the core of these difficulties, it is often fruitful to explore recognition of errors in thinking (Beck, Rush, Shaw, and Emery, 1979) and disputation of irrational beliefs (Ellis and Harper, 1975). Learning to rethink irrational assumptions can also be helpful for math-anxious students, especially women who have been enculturated into the belief that math is aversive and incomprehensible. Group brainstorming regarding coping self-statements can be very effective in helping participants evolve coping strategies. Ideas expressed by participants can sometimes have more impact than similar ideas offered by the counselor.

Unless coping strategies are so well learned that they become automatic responses to troublesome situations and anxious feelings, clients may be unable to implement the techniques when they become upset. As in individual counseling (see Chapter Five), imagery exercises can be used to give participants practice in identifying early anxiety signals and implementing coping strategies. The use of imagery in group counseling is similar to its use in individual counseling, except that the counselor must proceed slowly and allow ample discussion time so that any difficulties can be identified.

An advantage of the group modality over individual counseling is that some interesting simulation techniques can be used to enable clients to practice coping skills. In these, participants are asked to cope with anxiety and their thought processes in situations similar to ones that are difficult. Since the group meeting itself is a social experience that is anxiety arousing for many participants of social anxiety groups, members can be instructed to monitor self-talk and practice coping methods while waiting for each session to begin. Practice "parties" can also be held. Speech-anxious clients can be asked to make practice speeches to the group and to practice using coping techniques before, during, and after their presentations. Wine (1974) has used simulations of classroom tests in training test-anxious clients to initiate task-focused thinking. Role-playing methods can be used with greater variety in group than in individual counseling. The "Mind Game," discussed in Chapter Seven, is even more effective when done in a group than when used in individual work. It has an energizing effect on group members and provides a great deal of useful modeling.

Cognitive coping skills can be applied and practiced more successfully if participants leave the group with good "cognitive maps" of the anxiety process and the kinds of strategies they can use in coping. Asking them to reflect on the activities used in the group and to identify the ideas most helpful to them can enable them to clarify these maps. They can also evaluate progress on their goals by comparing their responses on postintervention instruments with their pretest responses. Goal attainment scaling procedures can also be used. Participants need to think about concrete steps they can take to solidify their work with coping skills. It is unlikely that the methods will have become fully automatic during the course of a five- or six-session group; therefore, participants need to exert continued efforts to initiate coping strategies and refine their approaches. The next-step contract is a good way to help them plan continued work on the problem.

B. Stress Management

Stress is a necessary and useful human reaction, in that it mobilizes effort to deal with threatening circumstances. The well-known "fight-or-flight" response enables us to struggle more powerfully or flee more swiftly than we would be able to do in its absence. However, the consequences of unmanaged stress can be dire. Students face stressors in such areas as academic demands, interpersonal relationships, and life planning. The impact of these stressors is often increased by students' struggles with developmental tasks, such as establishing autonomy, clarifying identity, and formulating a sense of purpose (Chickering, 1969).

When unchecked, stress can lead directly to certain health problems. Degenerative illnesses, such as ulcers and heart disease, can be an outgrowth of uncontrolled stress. These conditions are likely to become problematic well after university years; however, the unhealthy patterns probably originate during university years or earlier. Swartz and Leitch (1975) found elevated blood pressure levels in 10.5 percent of the fifteen- to nineteen-year-olds whom they studied. The attitudes and lifestyles adopted by students during their college years will almost certainly help to determine whether they become candidates for these conditions.

Several consequences of stress can affect students' lives more immediately. Depression of the immune system can make students more vulnerable to infectious diseases, such as influenza, colds, and mononucleosis. Development of avoidance and escape behavior patterns, a common response to stress, can lead

275

to procrastination and other unproductive styles. Sometimes methods chosen to reduce stress—for instance, alcohol or drug abuse, smoking, and overeating—are themselves problematic. Finally, uncontrolled stress can interfere with productive intellectual effort by producing restlessness, fatigue, and confusion. This consequence is particularly debilitating in an academic environment, where focused and sustained attention to subject matter is required (Barrow and Prosen, 1981).

Fortunately, some useful ways of coping with stress have been found. By developing stress management skills, students can control some of the more damaging immediate consequences. Even more important, the development of realistic attitudes toward stress and effective methods of coping with it can lead to a more satisfying and healthy postgraduate life.

Cognitive Features of Stress Management

An information-processing model of stress described by Schwartz (1977) is quite helpful in suggesting various means of intervention. This model can be adapted so that counselors and their clients can use it as a "cognitive map" for confronting stress problems (Barrow and Prosen, 1981). The model is presented in Figure 5.

Figure 5. Model of Stress Cycle.

Intraindividual Processes

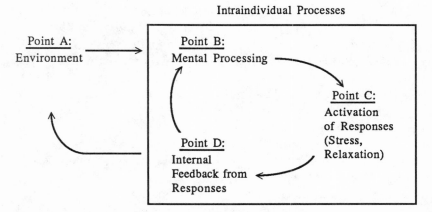

Source: Adapted from Barrow and Prosen, 1981.

It is widely recognized that environmental events contribute to stress. Holmes and Rahe (1967) found that life changes correlate with health breakdowns. Thus, events at Point A on the model contribute to stress. Yet, there is not a one-to-one relationship between environmental circumstances and the degree of stress. Our internal processing—the ways we perceive and interpret external events—determines the impact that events will have on us. Vinokur and Selzer (1975) found that the effect of an event depends partially on how positive or negative the individual thinks the event is. Point B on the model represents this mental orientation step of the stress cycle.

Point C represents the activation of physiological responses. People vary in their abilities to induce what Benson (1975) has termed "the relaxation response." Some are able to exert a great deal of control over these responses, while others have lost the ability to relax. Likewise, some individuals are unable to regulate the fight-flight response.

Point D, which is closely associated with Point C, represents the individual's reception of internal feedback regarding the physiological response. Some people can "tune into" the degree of stress in their bodies and are sensitive to the kinesthetic cues of gradations of relaxation or stress. Others have "lost touch" with the continuous feedback from within their own bodies. These individuals may build up or maintain high levels of tension without being aware of the degree of their response.

Point B of the stress cycle is the one that is most obviously cognitive, in that thoughts, expectations, interpretations, judgments, anticipations, and other cognitive processes seem at the root of stress responses. Since clients benefit from having a cognitive map of the entire stress cycle, all of the points of the cycle are relevant to a cognitive perspective. A good understanding of the factors in stress can help individuals identify stress early in the game and know how to intervene.

Using the Cognitive Dimension in Structured Groups

A self-assessment and goal-setting exercise, as previously described, can be conducted. Participants can then be directed to develop a "cognitive map" of the stress cycle. First, the topic

"What is stress?" is explored. Participants can be asked to imagine a recent stress-producing experience and then use this visualization to retrieve elements of the stress response. Better yet, a stress-inducing situation can be presented. For example, participants can be told that in later sessions they will be expected to give a talk to the group about stress. After a few minutes, they are told that they do not have to give the talk; however, their reactions to this suggestion can be listed and discussed, providing them with an experientially based understanding of the "fight-or-flight" response.

Second, participants can be asked to write down their definitions of stress. As examples are discussed, the group leaders underscore certain aspects that provide foreshadowing of concepts or strategies that will be covered. A "definition" of stress can then be offered and explained, such as "the disruption of the *internal balance* of the body as a person *adjusts* to his or her *perception* of conditions in the environment."

Third, group members (perhaps in small groups or dyads) can be asked to consider the kinds of situations that produce stress for them. When a list of situations is compiled, the leader can then summarize the list, identifying major groupings that emerge. Four environmental conditions that produce stress are likely to be represented. *Threat* is a common producer of stress and occurs when the possibility of harm, either physical or psychological, is perceived (for example, tests or oral reports). *Frustration* occurs when achievement of an important goal is blocked. For instance, a student who wants to go to medical school might feel stress if he receives low grades. Another stress-producing situation is *conflict* when a decision-making dilemma, such as choosing one's major or career, is encountered. Finally, *change* itself produces stress, in that internal adjustment is required. As these conditions are discussed, a diagram of the stress cycle shown in Figure 5 can be begun, with the stress-producing conditions inserted under the heading "Environment."

The second link in the stress cycle can then be developed. The group can be asked why some people react with more stress in a situation than others do. Most of the ideas expressed can be related to the "mental orientation" component of the cycle. The rest of the stress cycle can then be added to the diagram.

The stress cycle diagram leads to a discussion of group members' common stress management methods. They can write these down and discuss them in dyads or small groups. After some discussion, five points of intervention can be introduced and related to the examples provided by the participants. Intervention Point 1 consists of *general life-style considerations,* such as diet, sleep patterns, and exercise habits, which affect a person's overall vulnerability to stress. Intervention Point 2 is *awareness* of important factors at each of the points of the stress cycle. "Early detection" of cues signaling that one's stress cycle is being activated is particularly important. Intervention Point 3 refers to *environmental management* and can be so indicated on the diagram of the stress cycle. A number of methods of regulating environmental demands so as to reduce stress are available, including time management, assertiveness, and problem solving. Intervention Point 4 occurs in the mental orientation aspect of the stress cycle and can be called *mental management.* Finally, Intervention Point 5, *physical management,* involves learning to be sensitive to stress levels and to produce the relaxation response.

The cognitive map of stress helps to demystify stress, introduces the stress management techniques that will be presented, and provides stimulation for devising self-management approaches not covered in the group.

Attention is then directed to development of skills at some of the intervention points. In light of the limited time available in a structured group, I focus less on the first intervention point than on the others, because information on factors such as diet and exercise is readily available from other sources. Most people with problems in this area have simply failed to implement steps that they know are desirable. This difficulty can be addressed in the individualized "implementation" stage later in the group.

Intervention Point 2, awareness, is essential to early detection. Administration of the Holmes and Rahe (1967) instrument can enable participants to think about how much change they have experienced during the previous year. An instrument designed for students, the College Schedule of Recent Experiences modified by Marx, Garrity, and Bowers (1975), can be used, although it is more time consuming. Dyadic or small-group discussions can also be held concerning the time of day, day of week, and time of year that are most stressful for individuals.

Awareness of mental orientation aspects is fully developed in Intervention Point 4; however, during the awareness phase, it can be helpful to sensitize group members to global thought patterns that affect the stress response. Type A behavior can be described, with its concomitant mental orientation involving time urgency, achievement compulsivity, and hostility (Friedman and Rosenman, 1974). Also, the cognitive style of perfectionism, in which performance is equated with self-worth, can be introduced. A scale by Burns (1980b) can be used to build awareness and provoke discussion.

Awareness of one's physical stress response is begun with the previously described discussion of the imagined or actually experienced stress-producing event. Group members are encouraged to identify specific autonomic nervous system responses they experience, such as increased heart rate, perspiration, "butterflies," dry throat, and cold hands, as well as points of skeletal muscle tension. Homework assignments of monitoring such responses can be useful.

Depending on the needs of the group members, counselors can select from a number of ideas in helping group members analyze and improve their methods of managing their environments, Intervention Point 3. First, points of difficulty in their environments are analyzed, as was begun in the awareness step. Counselors can then direct participants in such strategies as problem solving, time management, and assertiveness, as well as in regulating the amount of new change sought or admitted into their systems (Barrow and Prosen, 1981).

Mental management, Intervention Point 4, is one of the intervention points to which I give most attention in a five- or six-session structured group. The steps of carrying out work in this area are actually very similar to those described in Chapter Five on cognitive coping skills training, except that the group format allows for more role playing and brainstorming. Similar handouts on the A-B-C system, stress-producing cognitive patterns, and potential coping self-statements can be used. One or more clear examples of the steps should be provided, to enable participants to understand the principles. The "Mind Game" exercise described in Chapter Seven can be played, and imagery exercises can be used to try to make the coping methods become automatic responses.

At Intervention Point 5, physical management, group members can be taught to produce the relaxation response. The term "physical management" is of course a misnomer, in that relaxation involves both physical and mental processes. I usually introduce Jacobson's (1938) progressive deep-muscle relaxation in the first or second session and the deep-breathing awareness exercise (Stevens, 1971) in the second or third session. The latter is particularly well suited to illustrating the cognitive component of relaxation, because participants can experience how awareness of one subject is decreased when the focus of attention is shifted to a new subject. This experience can highlight the potential efficacy of cognitive self-statements used in coping. Further relaxation training entails refining these methods and helping participants evolve "relaxation triggers" that can be used quickly to regulate the stress cycle in a stress-producing situation.

Imagery practice, role playing, and simulation during the group and homework assignments between sessions are used in order to help participants practice and assimilate the mental and physical management skills. In addition to reassessment of participants' goals, an individualized planning exercise is useful for winding up the group. Done individually and then discussed in the group, this exercise can help participants crystallize their cognitive maps of gains they have made and further steps they can take. An "Individual Stress Management Planning" handout is used. Participants identify aspects of stress management that are most troublesome for them and changes they could make that would help them manage stress more effectively. They are then asked to conduct a "costs-benefits analysis" of their desired changes and to attend carefully to the negative consequences, since any major change requires adjustments. Participants then consider their "sabotaging strategies"—actions and/or internal dialogue they would be likely to use to prevent themselves from making the changes. They then identify coping actions and self-talk they can use to combat these tendencies. This individualized planning exercise can help group members realistically anticipate and plan for some of the difficulties they are likely to face in implementing changes.

For a more complete discussion of stress management programming, readers may want to consult Deffenbacher and McKinley (1983).

C. The Cognitive Style of Perfectionism

Perfectionistic cognitions often underlie a number of student difficulties, including evaluative anxiety, stress, depression, guilt, procrastination, writing blocks, and study inefficiency (Barrow and Moore, 1983). Burns (1980a, 1980b) has defined perfectionism as equating self-worth with performance. Barrow and Moore (1983) have identified the following elements of perfectionistic thinking: engaging in dichotomous thinking ("all or nothing"), setting rigid goals, making unrealistic demands of self, focusing excessively on the future to the exclusion of the present, "telescoping" (magnifying unmet goals and minimizing met goals), providing little self-reward, giving selective attention to unmet goals and flaws, viewing "average" performance as shameful, and making compulsive efforts to try harder to be perfect.

Cognitive Aspects of Perfectionism

Hamachek (1978) has explored the dynamics of perfectionism as a personality trait. However, Burns (1980a, 1980b) describes it from a cognitive perspective and presents ideas for cognitive therapy. Barrow and Moore (1983) also discuss perfectionism as a cognitive pattern and prefer the concept "perfectionistic thinking" to "perfectionism," because the former suggests a pattern that people experience from time to time whereas the latter implies a trait.

A perfectionistic cognitive style may be particularly amenable to change during the college years. Students are often entering an environment that is more challenging academically and perhaps even socially than their high schools. The perfectionistic cognitive system, which may have been effective in managing earlier demands, may not work as well at college. Also, the developmental tasks undertaken in early adulthood require the individual to examine cognitive systems and to become more cognitively complex. To develop autonomy and establish identity, students must question expectations and values assimilated from parents. Thus, perfectionistic cognitive systems may be particularly permeable during this period, provided that the challenge and support factors can be appropriately balanced (Barrow and Moore, 1983).

Using the Cognitive Dimension in Structured Groups

I shall provide a summary of the steps in a structured group described at length elsewhere (Barrow and Moore, 1983). The goals of the group are to help participants become more discriminating in setting standards for themselves, develop more tolerance for times when they will inevitably fall short of goals, begin to differentiate the construct of self-worth from performance, and develop a cognitive coping process for moderating initial perfectionistic responses.

In the clarifying expectations and goals stage, the perfectionism scale developed by Burns (1980b) can be used. In order to sell the rationale and convey a cognitive map of the program, a lecturette with elicited discussion is used. Discussion of the Burns scale helps group members apply the concepts to themselves. An article by Burns (1980b) also can be assigned in the first session and discussed in the second. These activities help participants understand perfectionistic thinking and the concept of developing internal dialogue to cope with perfectionistic impulses.

In the developing self-awareness stage, use is made of posters with well-known perfectionistic slogans (for example, "Always be prepared" or "Never put off until tomorrow what you can do today"). Some are displayed in the group room in the first session. Participants are invited to add to the collection as the group progresses. These slogans illustrate the cultural reinforcement for perfectionistic thinking and stimulate participants to clarify their own perfectionistic patterns.

Ellis's A-B-C framework is used to help group members identify perfectionistic cognitions occurring at Point B. A situation is discussed and analyzed before the group. Participants then work with a handout called "Perfectionist's Worksheet" and write out the A-B-C's of situations in which their perfectionistic tendencies are activated. These are then discussed, first in pairs and then in the entire group. Homework monitoring with the worksheet is then assigned.

As in the stress management program, it is useful to have participants think about forces that work against their changing long-held cognitive patterns. Participants discuss a costs-benefits analysis sheet pertaining to changing the perfectionistic pattern. The degree of their commitment can also be explored by an exercise in which they place themselves in the room according to their positions on two dimensions: (1) the degree to which they see themselves as *free* to change and (2) how much they *want* to change.

In order to disrupt the rigid perfectionistic system, the "Do-It-Perfectly" experiment can be introduced early in the group, usually in the second session. Participants are asked to choose an activity that they will attempt to accomplish perfectly. They usually react to this paradoxical request with some confusion, since their interest in the group is to reduce the perfectionistic demands. This confusion may render their perfectionistic systems somewhat more malleable. Participants can then be asked to confront their perfectionistic self-talk patterns by working further with the perfectionist worksheets. They can consider the degree to which Ellis's irrational demands (Ellis and Harper, 1975), as well as Beck's cognitive errors (Beck, Rush, Shaw, and Emery, 1979), are represented in their perfectionistic cognitions. Burns's (1980b) method of having clients construct an experiment to test an important perfectionistic assumption is also useful (see Chapter Five). This method is particularly effective in a group, because other members can assist in framing and evaluating the experiment and thereby may vicariously challenge their own perfectionistic systems. Participants can then turn their attention to identifying coping cognitions in column D of the perfectionist worksheets. In the perfectionism groups, I refer to these cognitions as "humanizers" and "realizers." The process of developing coping dialogue is similar to that already described in Chapter Five.

In order to integrate the new concepts and skills, role playing, imagery practice, and the "Mind Game" can be used. In addition, since "the internal perfectionistic voice" can often be traced to the influence of one or more people, guided imagery, empty-chair techniques, or a simulated exchange of letters might be used to enable participants to engage the source influence in a dialogue about the perfectionistic precepts. Another method of ingraining gains is the "take a chance" experiment. Participants identify risks they can take that had been previously prevented by perfectionistic thinking. For instance, group members have chosen such activities as going jogging with a friend, being more assertive with significant others, and taking a weekend off from studying. This experiment is usually introduced in the next-to-last session, so that follow-up discussion of the results can be held in the last meeting.

In the last session, the perfectionism scale can be retaken and progress on the goal attainment scales can be rated in order to help participants become clearer about what they have achieved. An effective method of gaining closure is an appraisal of the posters with perfectionistic slogans that have been displayed throughout the group. Pairs are assigned a slogan and asked to come up with a more realistic statement of the theme. If a majority of participants find the alternative at least as credible as the original, the changes are made on the poster and it is returned to the wall. The contracting exercise can then be used to help them identify further steps they can take to continue working with perfectionistic thinking; however, they can be asked to not make these contracts "too perfect."

D. Assertiveness Training

Many clients' difficulties are related to their abilities to express themselves and negotiate the interpersonal world. The developmental tasks of late adolescence/early adulthood include becoming more independent in one's behavior and better able to relate to family, authority figures, friends, and the opposite sex (Chickering, 1969; Coons, 1970). During the 1960s and 1970s, a method called assertiveness training became popular as a treatment for social difficulties. Behavior therapists such as Wolpe and Lazarus (1966) and Salter (1949) believed that more effective interpersonal skills could be learned directly. As time passed, assertiveness training came to be influenced by therapists of other active orientations, particularly in group interventions.

Alberti and Emmons (1974) were instrumental in defining assertiveness, distinguishing it from passive and aggressive styles and outlining the concept of rights. Assertiveness concepts have been used extensively with women in helping them overcome enculturation into a passive role (Linehan and Egan, 1979). Lange and Jakubowski (1976) contributed many useful ideas to the assertiveness training field, including the use of cognitive restructuring techniques. Galassi and Galassi (1977) have produced a self-help book of discussions and exercises that is particularly useful as a workbook for an assertiveness training group. A number of studies have supported the effectiveness of assertiveness training, particularly with university students (Galassi, Galassi, and Litz, 1974; Galassi, Kostka, and Galassi, 1975;

Heimberg, Montgomery, Madsen, and Heimberg, 1977; McFall and Lillesand, 1971; McFall and Twentyman, 1973). It appears to be an effective method that is particularly applicable to the kind of development occurring in young adults.

The Cognitive Dimension in Assertiveness

Assertiveness was initially conceived as a set of behavioral skills (Salter, 1949; Wolpe and Lazarus, 1966). Lange and Jakubowski (1976) were among the first to delineate the cognitive aspects and include cognitive restructuring in the treatment. The role of cognitions in assertiveness can be explored through the distinctions offered by Linehan and Egan (1979). They have noted that assertiveness training programs are typically guided by one of three models for explaining unassertive behavior: the skills deficit, response inhibition, and faulty discrimination models. The skills deficit approach is based on the assumption that important skills of assertion have not been learned. Programs using this model have most often focused on behavioral skills; however, important cognitive skills could also be deficit, including identifying rights, discriminating types of responses, and making decisions about how to respond. In the response inhibition model, the basic responses are assumed to be within the person's capability but are inhibited by either anxiety or "maladaptive beliefs." Since anxiety includes a cognitive component, this model ascribes a sizable role to cognitive events. According to the faulty discrimination model, the unassertive person is capable of and uninhibited from behaving assertively but is unable to discriminate when assertion is appropriate. This discrimination is largely a cognitive task.

My experience in conducting assertiveness training with university students supports a combination of the response inhibition and faulty discrimination models. Students often appear to be capable of making assertive responses; however, they are inhibited by anxiety, engage in self-defeating cognitions, and/or do not have well-developed cognitive maps to guide their decisions about how to behave interpersonally.

Using the Cognitive Dimension in Structured Groups

Several assertiveness inventories have been developed, including ones by Alberti and Emmons (1974), Gambrill and Richey (1975), and Rathus (1973). The College Self-Expression Scale by Galassi, DeLo, Gallasi, and Bastien (1974) is well constructed and particularly useful with university students. One of these instruments can be given prior to screening and perhaps used in the first session to help clients reflect on and clarify their goals. The Social Avoidance and Distress and Fear of Negative Evaluation Scales (Watson and Friend, 1969) can be included in order to assess the degree to which social anxiety and self-defeating cognitions are present. The goal attainment scaling method previously described can be used; however, I think participants are better able to identify suitable goals after some demonstration role plays and discussions of assertive, aggressive, and passive responses to one or two situations.

One of the first steps is to help clients form cognitive maps that enable them to discriminate among assertive, aggressive, and passive responses. Unassertive clients often have an all-or-none concept of how they can respond to a situation. Refusing an unreasonable request may be equated with being "rude." Assertiveness is often confused with aggressiveness. The learning of this discrimination is often best begun by providing vignettes to which participants can react. The group leaders can role-play a situation, with one first adopting a passive stance. The following questions, which are used throughout the group, are then discussed: What are the rights of the people involved? How would participants feel if they were the individuals in the interaction? What consequences are likely, including short-term and long-term ones? What consequences are likely for the relationship? How will the individuals feel about themselves? Two more role plays can then be conducted and processed—one illustrating aggressive behavior and the other, assertive behavior.

An important idea to suggest while processing the role plays is that whether a response "works" in achieving the desired result is only one criterion to use in evaluating one's actions. It is just as important to consider thoughts and feelings about oneself. Even if a particular goal is not met as a result of acting assertively, an individual's self-view may be favorably influenced. A particularly important point to make in discussion of aggressive behavior is that the short-term consequences may be positive, in that aggressors often get what they want; however, the long-term consequences may be less positive, in that friendships may suffer or fail to develop. Unfortunately, short-term consequences often influence behavior more than long-term ones.

Once a demonstration vignette has been role-played and discussed, participants are better able to absorb definitions of the three styles of behavior. Assertiveness can be defined as standing up for one's rights and expressing one's thoughts and ideas in a way that demonstrates respect for others' rights, ideas, and feelings. In aggressive behavior, individuals stand up for their rights and express their thoughts and feelings; however, they are *not* respectful of the rights, thoughts, and feelings of others. A passive response occurs when one shows regard for others' rights but does *not* stand up for one's own rights or express one's thoughts and feelings (Lange and Jakubowski, 1976).

It is often helpful to have participants identify rights in their relationships with people in important roles. For instance, they can brainstorm their own rights and the rights of the other parties in interactions with teachers, friends, romantic interests, and others. After some discussion, their thoughts can be further primed with a list of general personal rights, such as those listed in Alberti and Emmons (1974) or Galassi and Galassi (1977). While it is important to help clients identify their rights in specific relationships, it is even more crucial for them to develop a general cognitive set for analyzing the rights of parties in their interactions.

A stage of addressing inhibitors of assertiveness is often useful. When the assertiveness of some participants is inhibited by social-evaluative anxiety, a module on anxiety management training, as outlined in Section A (Managing Evaluative Anxiety) can be included. Whether or not anxiety is an inhibiting force, certain cognitive patterns often inhibit the expression of assertiveness. Using methods previously discussed in Section A and in Chapter Five, counselors can help participants identify self-defeating cognitive processes, develop cognitive coping strategies, and work toward alteration of basic concepts of self and self-in-world. Galassi and Galassi (1977) encourage clients to identify counterproductive beliefs about the rights and responsibilities of individuals in difficult interpersonal situations, the perceptions others have of them, and the probable consequences of behaving assertively. As situations requiring assertiveness are role-played in the group, unproductive cognitive patterns can be pointed out and ways of disengaging from them discussed.

The situations can be introduced to the group in sequence, so that situations that are generally less difficult are undertaken first. For instance, assertiveness concepts and skills can first be applied to situations that are not highly personal, such as consumer situations. Later sessions can address personal and more complex relationships, such as ones with parents. Some of the responses developed in assertiveness training include saying "no" to unreasonable requests, setting limits, making requests, asking for clarification, giving and receiving compliments, expressing opinions, giving positive and negative feedback, and expressing anger and other emotions. Time can be reserved in each session for participants to seek ideas regarding specific situations, including ones they are anticipating or have experienced in the past.

The various situations can be discussed from the standpoint of the rights involved, the consequences of different styles of response, and the ways in which self-defeating cognitions can be overcome. Important components of assertiveness can be delineated in order to expand clients' cognitive maps of what assertive responses entail. One component is *direct expression of ideas and feelings*. Many clients are so socialized to be "polite" that they "beat around the bush" and fail to make their points clear. A second component is *assertive nonverbal behavior*. When learning to be assertive, many clients negate their verbal messages, which may be assertive, with nonverbal messages. For instance, they may avoid eye contact with the listener, speak too softly or too loudly, slouch awkwardly, orient their bodies away from the listener, and laugh nervously. Participants can become more aware of the need to keep nonverbal cues and verbalizations congruent; however, they should not become too self-conscious of these aspects. Clients who are noticeably deficient in one or more important nonverbal dimensions need to maintain a manageable focus by attempting to improve in only one area at a time. A third component is *use of "I-messages" and "feeling talk."* Clients' cognitive systems for dealing with the interpersonal world are often improved when they learn to distinguish between I- and you-messages. The latter are more likely to seem accusatory and elicit defensiveness than the former. Many students have not learned that they can offer negative feedback by expressing their own feelings instead of accusing the other person of doing something wrong.

Several specific assertive strategies can help expand participants' cognitive systems for interacting with others and for dealing with difficult situations:

1. *Empathic assertion,* described by Lange and Jakubowski (1976). Participants' rights-protecting statements can often be coupled with empathic statements that indicate an understanding of the other person's situation. This method may be particularly applicable in close, ongoing relationships. Linehan and Egan (1979) review research suggesting that an "unembellished" assertive response is effective in the short term but does not necessarily strengthen relationships. An example of an empathic assertion is "I really am sorry you're feeling so upset by this paper (empathic statement); however, I just don't believe in letting people copy my work (assertion statement)."
2. *Escalating assertion* (Lange and Jakubowski, 1976). In the initial stages of training, participants often have an all-or-none view of assertion itself and assume that there is basically one level of intensity for assertive expressions. The concept of escalating assertion helps them realize that they can start with a "minimal" level of assertion in a difficult

situation and escalate the degree of firmness if the other person does not respond in a helpful way.

3. *The "Broken Record" technique* (Smith, 1975). This technique should be presented in the context of escalating assertion, since it departs from the direct-communication philosophy of assertion and borders on being manipulative. Like Lange and Jakubowski (1976), I believe that this kind of method should be used only as a last resort. In short, the technique involves repeating a core assertion over and over in response to the arguments of an overbearing, difficult individual. For instance, a student might reply, "I don't feel comfortable letting anyone copy my paper," to whatever protestations are offered by the other person in the example previously given.

4. *The "Fogging" technique* (Smith, 1975). Another "last-resort" technique, this method entails good-naturedly agreeing with some element of a verbal attack. The attacker is usually disarmed by both the unexpected agreement and the unruffled demeanor of the person who is attacked. For instance, if a student is subjected to an unwarranted tirade about how inconsiderate she is, she can smilingly reply, "I guess I do think of myself sometimes." An element of humorous exaggeration of one's faults can be included.

Lange and Jakubowski (1976), Galassi and Galassi (1977), and Alberti and Emmons (1974) describe a number of techniques the assertiveness trainer can use in helping clients develop assertive skills: didactic presentations, modeling (provided by group leader, other participants, or media), covert modeling (participants imagine someone else dealing with a difficult situation), reinforcing emerging cognitive and behavioral skills, and coaching. One of the most frequently used methods is rehearsal of assertive responses through role playing. Colleagues and I have often used a gradual progression in involving participants in role plays. First, we ask one or two group members to play bit parts in a scene in which we take the starring roles. In subsequent role plays, we invite them to take increasingly active roles. Another rehearsal method is a "round robin," in which participants take turns executing an assertive response (Barrow and Hayashi, 1980). For instance, one member gives a compliment to the next member, who has to receive the compliment and then give a compliment to another member, and so forth. Another technique is a game in which participants draw cards with descriptions of situations requiring assertiveness. They then have to role-play an assertive response. In conjunction with rehearsal, group leaders can offer their observations as feedback on cognitive and behavioral responses. Feedback can also be provided through videotape (Galassi, Galassi, and Litz, 1974) and audiotape procedures. In addition to actual rehearsal, covert rehearsal—in which participants imagine themselves coping with difficult situations, behaving assertively, and identifying and countering assertiveness-inhibiting cognitions—can be used.

During the last two sessions of an assertiveness structured group, participants should be helped to crystallize their cognitive maps of how to decide on a response in an interpersonal situation. They can be asked to write down questions they would want to ask themselves in order to plan their response. They can then be presented with the following questions in order to refine their system: What is my goal for this relationship? What are my rights and the rights of others involved? What are alternative ways I can respond? What self-defeating cognitions might lead me to avoid assertion? How can I counter these cognitions? What are the potential consequences of the different ways of responding—long term and short term, external and internal? How do I want to respond?

Reassessment of goals with the goal attainment scaling procedure and contracting for future steps are useful closure activities. Alberti and Emmons (1974) suggest a "strength bombardment" exercise as a good way of concluding an assertiveness group. Each group member in turn receives positive feedback from the other members.

E. Social Skills and Shyness

Development of social competence is an important area of growth for late adolescents and young adults (Chickering, 1969; Coons, 1970). As they achieve more emotional autonomy from parental figures, students become more capable of high levels of intimacy. Yet, because they have not attained full autonomy or identity, individuals of this age group are still quite conscious of their social images. Not surprisingly, Martinson and Zerface (1970) found that students are more interested in learning to get along with the opposite sex than in vocational issues. Arkowitz, Hinton, Perl, and Himandi (1978) report that dating problems are often accompanied by debilitating emotions and lead students to seek counseling. They also found that 31 percent of 3,800 students surveyed admitted to being somewhat or very anxious about dating. Zimbardo, Pilkonis, and Norwood (1975) reported that 40 percent of university and high school students judged themselves to be "shy."

Cognitive Aspects of Social Skills

Cognitive factors, such as self-efficacy and outcome expectancies, are likely to determine whether one attempts social initiatives, just as they are likely to determine whether one behaves assertively. Bellack (1979, p. 98) has discussed the importance of perceptual and cognitive factors and notes that "the mere presence of such (behavioral) skills in the repertoire does not insure effective performance." In addition, one needs "social or interpersonal perception," which includes knowledge about response cues and social mores, attention to the context and other relevant aspects of the interaction, information-processing skills, and the ability to predict consequences of interpersonal encounters.

Zimbardo, Pilkonis, and Norwood (1975) discuss a number of consequences of shyness, including social problems, negative emotions, lack of assertiveness, deficiencies of thinking, confusing communications, and self-consciousness. Colleagues and I described three interrelated components that can account for much of the social difficulty experienced by students: an incompletely developed repertoire of social behaviors; negative self-evaluations regarding one's social competence; and debilitating anxiety, which contains a cognitive component (Barrow and Hayashi, 1980). Research on the role of attractiveness in male-female relationships suggests that other cognitive factors are important, including physical self-image and ways of mentally processing others' reactions to one's appearance. Galassi and Galassi (1979) report on a number of studies suggesting that more attractive people date more frequently; are rated as more likable, popular, and desirable; and are seen as having more pleasing personalities than less attractive people. An interesting aspect of this research is that attractiveness has been found to have a greater relationship with dating frequency for females than for males (Berscheid, Dion, Walster, and Walster, 1971). Also, the degree to which males like their dates seems to be more highly correlated with physical attractiveness than is the case with females (Curran, 1973).

In summary, cognitive factors are particularly important in the social area. The degree of complexity of cognitive self systems is important, in that self-image is central to social difficulties. Self-efficacy and outcome expectancies are important in whether social risks are taken. Social-evaluative anxiety, heavily influenced by negative cognitions about self and others, can inhibit social behavior and produce avoidance of and withdrawal from social situations. Glasgow and Arkowitz (1975) found low-frequency dating males to differ from high-frequency daters more often on cognitive dimensions than in behavior, although social skills seemed to account for more of the differences with females.

Using the Cognitive Dimension in Structured Groups

The importance of the cognitive factors in social behavior is underscored by the success of a cognitive self-statement intervention reported by Glass, Gottman, and Shmurak (1976), which was similar to the methods discussed in Chapter Five and Section A. Their cognitive intervention with girl-shy males produced greater generalization to new situations than did an approach consisting of teaching specific social skills. Cognitive elements were also heavily integrated into the "shyness clinic" that colleagues and I developed (Barrow and Hayashi, 1980).

In our shyness clinic, two 20-minute screening interviews were held—one to discuss clients' interests in the group and the other to discuss assessment instruments and finalize the decision regarding clients' participation. Watson and Friend's (1969) Social Avoidance and Distress and Fear of Negative Evaluation Scales can be used in assessment to provide indexes of the degree of anxiety and unproductive thinking experienced in social situations. An instrument by Richardson and Tasto (1976) also measures degrees of social anxiety. The Social Interaction Self-Statement Test (Glass and Merluzzi, 1978) indicates the extent to which clients entertain both positive and negative self-statements in social situations. In addition, it is helpful to include one of the assertiveness inventories mentioned in Section D (Assertiveness Training), such as the College Self-Expression Scale (Galassi, DeLo, Galassi, and Bastien, 1974). Measures useful in assessing social skills are reviewed by Galassi and Galassi (1979) and by Hersen and Bellack (1977).

In order to help participants better understand their social difficulties and how they can be overcome, they can be asked to write down ideas on what contributes to social success. The ideas can then be written on newsprint and organized into themes. The following areas often emerge: management of social anxiety, self-confidence, management of self-defeating cognitions, and development of social skills, including acting assertively and initiating conversations. The modules of this structured group can then be presented: social anxiety management, assertiveness training, and development of conversational skills. The cognitive dimension is focused on in all three modules.

The physical attractiveness issue is often listed by one or more of the group members. The counselor can ask what people can do about this aspect. Some ideas for improving one's appearance may be mentioned, such as exercising and grooming; however, participants generally observe that beyond a certain point there is little one can do to improve physical attractiveness. The group leader can then point out that people have control over how they think about themselves, their social roles, and their interactions, even though they have only limited control over appearance. Concern about not looking sufficiently attractive, expressed in self-defeating internal dialogue, can lead to increased social anxiety, avoidance of assertion, and inhibition of ability to converse. Group members can be alerted to the theme of "I don't look good enough" in working with the cognitive dimensions in each of the three modules.

The exercise of organizing themes from participants' views of social success can help give participants a credible cognitive map of the group activities to come. Nevertheless, a rationale-building stage must occur in each of the three modules. After this exercise and review and discussion of their preintervention instruments, participants can productively undertake the "identifying and clarifying goals" discussed in Chapter Eight.

The first module, social anxiety management, is a relatively brief version of the evaluative anxiety structured group described in Section A. It can be conducted in two or three sessions.

The second module is assertiveness training. Assertion principles are helpful in enabling clients to take the kinds of risks necessary in social relationships, including giving and receiving compliments, making requests, offering invitations, and accepting and refusing invitations. The cognitive set of identifying rights and possible consequences of alternative actions can help participants break through barriers of being excessively cautious. The assertiveness methods discussed in Section D can be adapted to be presented in three or four sessions.

The third module, conversational skills training, employs the same kind of modeling/discussion/role-playing approach described in Section D and extends the principles to interpersonal situations that are more personal and social in nature. As in the assertiveness module, a great deal of attention is directed to identifying self-defeating cognitions about self, the other, and the situation; to strengthening cognitive coping skills; and eventually to altering self-constructs.

Many students report that they are comfortable in structured conversations but "at a loss" in informal "chit-chat," particularly with people who are new, perceived to be important, or of the opposite sex. Perfectionistic demands of themselves and outcome expectancies that others will be critical fuel the belief that "If I say something, it has to be really good." Counselors can emphasize the importance of being friendly and showing interest in interactions rather than offering brilliant ideas. Giving "free information," a concept discussed by Smith (1975), is the first skill addressed. Since shy people tend to be reticent and cautious, they often give others little information about themselves and their thoughts. Through modeling and role-playing exercises, members then practice offering free information.

The next skill addressed is responding to the free information offered by another. We applied the term "branching" to the skill of identifying various lines of discussion possible in a person's disclosures. Through a stop-action role play, it can be demonstrated that at any point in a conversation the listener can "branch" the discussion in several directions. Once demonstrated, this skill is practiced through a round-robin technique in which one member starts a conversation, which is stopped at an arbitrary point. The group then discusses the different conversational directions that are possible. The second person then selects a branch and continues the conversation, until it is again stopped, the possible directions discussed, and the conversational ball handed to a third member.

Socially undeveloped individuals often speak haltingly, because they are self-conscious about what they say and engage in too much self-censorship. In order to help them disengage from this restrictive cognitive focus, we have used a variation of Lange and Jakubowski's "inane topics" exercise. Topics, such as orange pits, clouds, cement, and Kleenex, are written on pieces of paper. Group members are divided into pairs or small groups. Each person carries on a brief discourse about one of the subjects, attempting to maintain a nonstop patter. The ridiculous nature of the topics removes much of the concern with sounding competent, and participants are often surprised at how fluently they can speak when freed from worry about the impression they are making. In a variation of this exercise, pairs begin a conversation with one of the inane topics and then use the free information and branching principles to develop a discussion. Often, the conversation progresses to topics of mutual interest to both parties. This exercise helps combat the perfectionistic belief that a conversation must be initiated in "just the right way" or that an opener must be intellectually weighty or original.

Shy individuals also feel uncomfortable about ending discussions. Even in the midst of a conversation, their minds sometimes "spiral ahead" to the anticipated awkwardness of the ending, leading them to feel anxious and preoccupied. Group leaders can model several assertive, pleasant ways of withdrawing from a conversation and illustrate that a simple, unembellished statement is often sufficient. Role playing and round-robin practice can then be used. When participants have developed a mental formula for ending conversations, they can often relax more successfully during discussions.

Depending on the needs and levels of social development of the group members, other social skills and situations can be introduced for discussion, role playing, and practice. With each situation, the steps of identification of self-defeating cognitions and development of cognitive coping strategies are pursued. Some of the other skills that can be introduced include asking others for dates, accepting and refusing dates, giving and receiving feedback in a close relationship, negotiating, making romantic initiatives, accepting and refusing romantic initiatives, and dealing with sexual aspects of close relationships.

In the final session, we have held a mock social gathering, complete with refreshments. According to the preference expressed by the group, the imagined setting has taken the form of a party, a reception, or an art gallery opening. Members are reminded to use the anxiety management, assertiveness, and conversational skills learned in the group. This exercise is generally a confidence booster and helps in demonstrating how members have progressed with their goals for the group. After this activity is discussed, the goal attainment scale ratings can be made and the "next-step" contracting exercise introduced. The strength bombardment exercise is a good way to wind up the final session (Alberti and Emmons, 1974).

F. Developing Self-Confidence

Many clients report to counseling services with complaints that they "lack self-confidence." Low self-esteem ranges from common moments of self-questioning to chronically low levels characteristic of serious depression. Lack of confidence is often an integral element in a self-defeating cycle, in that it leads to avoidance and anxiety and therefore interferes with a person's performance of important tasks. In turn, the negative self-evaluations and negative feedback from others stemming from less than optimal performances provide fuel for the diminished self-esteem.

   Battles with self-confidence occur throughout the life span; however, in late adolescence and early adulthood, these struggles are particularly evident. Students leaving high schools and homes for universities and jobs are faced with new environmental demands. Their expectations of these new environments are not nearly so clearly formulated as their understanding of the environments they are leaving. These factors, together with a propensity toward dichotomous thinking and an incompletely developed ability to tolerate ambiguity, make them particularly susceptible to lowered self-confidence. Students are experimenting with greater autonomy; but they have not yet learned the mechanics of instrumental autonomy, nor are they completely free from emotional dependence on family members. Thus, developmental issues interact with the new environmental demands to leave them vulnerable to self-questioning.

   In one sense, it is desirable for university students to experience self-confidence concerns. The challenges presented by the new environments and developmental tasks probably cannot be responsibly faced without difficult self-examination. Nevertheless, without sufficient support, a lack of self-confidence can overwhelm an individual's capacity to deal with the challenges. Fortunately, questions of self-confidence are particularly well suited to a structured group intervention that is cognitively focused.

Cognitive Aspects of Self-Confidence

Low self-confidence regarding specific tasks consists of self-efficacy expectancies that one cannot perform the necessary steps. Persons with more pervasive self-confidence problems have many self-questioning cognitions in their cognitive systems of self and self-in-world and may be external in locus of control of reinforcement. Their cognitive systems for self-evaluation are likely to be insufficiently complex, leading them to make inappropriate either-or judgments rather than more refined judgments. Information-processing schemas along the lines of "I can't expect myself to accomplish very much" may lead to avoidance of situations or to selective attention to results. Some schemas may also contain perfectionistic demands, such as "Anything I do must be really top notch." Since success is hardly ever experienced when this kind of unrealistic criterion is used, self-esteem is rarely enhanced.

Self-confidence difficulties can also be conceptualized as a discrepancy between the perceived-self and the ideal-self subsystems. If a person's perceived self differs appreciably from the ideal, self-esteem is low. Overall levels of self-confidence are probably dependent on three aspects: the number of discrepancies, the perceived importance of the discrepancies, and the significance afforded the discrepancies. Self-confidence is likely to be lower as the number of perceived-ideal discrepancies increases. However, discrepancies in important areas will have more impact on self-confidence than ones in areas thought to be relatively unimportant. Finally, a rigid, dichotomous supposition, such as "I *should* be close to the way I'd like to be in all important areas or I'm a failure," will combine with an important discrepancy to substantially lower self-confidence.

Using the Cognitive Dimension in Structured Groups

The activities to be described (adapted from a program that I developed in collaboration with Ann Barrow) can be conducted in a four- or five-session structured group or a day-long workshop. Because low self-confidence is often associated with evaluative anxiety and nonassertion, inventories previously reviewed for those constructs may be useful. Rotter's (1966) internal-external locus of control of reinforcement scale may also be helpful, as might an inventory for measuring the presence of irrational beliefs, such as the Personal Beliefs Inventory developed by Munoz and Lewinsohn (1975). Global measures of self-concept, such as the Tennessee Self-Concept Scale (Fitts, 1965), may also prove useful.

In order to help clients crystallize a cognitive map of self-confidence difficulties and view the group methods as credible, the counselor can ask them to write down situations that threaten their levels of self-confidence. Initial discussion of these ideas can be conducted in pairs or small groups. Thoughts can be elicited and written on newsprint and then grouped according to the themes presented. Group members can then be asked to suggest what people can do to make their levels of self-confidence less vulnerable to such threats. The counselor can usually relate their ideas to the components of the program—increased self-awareness, combating mental distortions, communicating effectively, and behaving assertively.

The counselor can present a framework for understanding self-confidence by drawing two overlapping circles on newsprint. One is labeled the "perceived self" and is defined as "the way we see ourselves as being." The other is labeled the "ideal self," which is "the way we would like to be." The counselor explains that some aspects of our perceived selves are included in our ideal selves (in the overlapping region), while other aspects are not included. Examples are given and written into the appropriate space on the diagram. In the same way, some aspects of our ideal selves overlap with the ways we see ourselves (perceived self), while others do not. Four categories of the ways we think about ourselves are related to this framework, with examples written on the diagram. Aspects of our *physical selves,* such as our weight, hair color, or body build, may be parts of our perceived selves and may or may not overlap with our ideal selves. Likewise, physical aspects of our ideal selves may or may not be parts of our perceived selves. The other three categories of the ways we think about ourselves are *social adequacy, intellectual competence,* and *emotional functioning.* After the explanation and examples are given, participants are asked to write aspects of their physical, social, intellectual, and emotional selves that are (1) in their perceived selves but not in their ideal selves, (2) in both, and (3) in their ideal selves but not in their perceived selves.

After this exercise, participants are asked to think about what people can do to improve the congruence of their perceived selves with their ideal selves. They usually note that they can attempt to improve themselves so that their perceived selves are closer to the ideals and/or make their ideal selves less rigid and exclusive. The counselor can then present the following formula, which serves to introduce the activities to be done in the remainder of the group: Self-confidence is increased by success, which requires that people take "calculated" risks (as opposed to indiscriminate risks). The ability to take these risks is enhanced by strengthening interpersonal skills (communication and assertiveness) and combating mental distortions that could lead to avoidance of risks, inappropriate actions, and/or misinterpretation of the outcomes of risks. The counselor can then explain that the group will focus on helping them learn to combat mental distortions, improve communication skills, and improve assertiveness.

In the first module, procedures for combating mental distortions are similar to those used in the evaluative anxiety group (discussed in Section A). The concept of the "internal dialogue" is introduced, and Ellis's A-B-C system for exploring cognitive patterns is presented. One of the self-confidence-threatening situations identified in the first exercise can be diagramed on newsprint to illustrate the method. The situation can be outlined at Point A, labeled "self-confidence–threatening situation," and the consequent feelings and actions at Point C can be specified. Then the "self-confidence–lowering internal dialogue" statements at Point B can be explored. Once group members have become well acquainted with their patterns of self-defeating cognitions, attention can be directed to strengthening cognitive coping processes. The example used to introduce the A-B-C system is reexamined, with participants brainstorming coping self-statements at Point D, "perspective-regaining coping dialogue." Self-talk worksheets, pairs discussions, and other methods are used in order to help participants develop coping strategies.

Module 2, active listening skills, is then begun. While most students are aware that listening is important, they often do not realize that listening must be *communicated* to another in order for relationships to be enhanced. Rather than simply explaining the importance of active listening and discussing its properties, counselors can arrange to have participants experience interactions in which listening is key. Half of the group members are instructed to be listeners and are secretly told to avoid communicating that they are listening. The other half are told to talk about a topic of interest. Pairs are then formed, containing one speaker and one listener, and a five-minute conversation is held. The feelings and observations of the speakers are then discussed in the group. What was it like to be talking to someone who was communicating a lack of interest? What specific behaviors disrupted the communication? The feelings and observations of the listeners are also discussed, including how comfortable they felt in their roles and what reactions they noted in the speakers. The role of nonverbal communication often emerges in the discussion. Participants gain a clearer conception of the role of such nonverbal cues as eye contact, postural orientation, gestures, facial expressions, and head nods.

Once the "don't's" of active listening have been identified through discussion of the interactions, the counselor can ask participants to compile a list of "do's." These can be reinforced with a handout listing components of active listening. The pairs can then be asked to resume their discussions, except that the listeners are asked to use the active-listening principles. After several minutes of discussion, partners can be asked to reverse roles, so that both have the opportunity to use their listening skills.

An important active-listening skill is restatement, in which the listener summarizes what the other person has said. It forces the listener to listen, communicates that the listener is attentive, and provides the speaker with a reconstruction of what has been said. Again, an experiential exercise may help participants better appreciate the importance of developing this skill. First, pairs can be asked to select a topic about which they disagree, such as abortion or smoking, and to engage in a debate with one another for a few minutes. The interactions are then discussed, with such aspects as the degree of communication, emotionality, and confusion noted. The skill of restatement is then explained and modeled. Pairs are asked to continue their debates; however, participants are asked to restate the previous communications of their partners before they offer their own ideas. The nature of the discussions is again explored. Participants often comment on the calmer tone and the more complete exchange of information that occurs in the second debate.

Module 3, on assertiveness, is a condensed adaptation of the assertiveness structured group described in Section D. Particular attention is given to exploring the internal dialogue that prevents assertion.

In order to gain closure, participants can rate the attainment of the goals defined in the first session and can retake pre-post instruments. In light of the self-confidence development formula presented in the introductory phase of the group, they can be asked to identify to the group a "calculated risk" they feel ready to take as a result of the program. The next-step contracting exercise can then be used, to help them clarify what they can do after the group has ended.

G. Career Planning

Career decision making and planning are obviously important areas of concern to late adolescents and young adults. In a needs assessment survey at Duke University, career-planning items were the highest rated of all the areas sampled, including a number of interpersonal and social issues (Talley, Barrow, Fulkerson, and Moore, 1983). In Chickering's (1969) conceptualization, autonomy and identity crystallization must be mastered before purpose can be fully defined. Cognitive development is also in the process of becoming sufficiently complex to permit the kind of realistic thinking necessary for career planning (Knefelkamp and Slepitza, 1976). The developmental issues are confounded by the increasing complexity of the occupational world, which can appear baffling and overwhelming to even the most mature individual.

Counselors in universities have long been concerned with student career development. In the 1960s and 1970s, greater attention came to be directed toward group approaches. Multifaceted developmental programming was encouraged (Cochran and Rademacher, 1978). A number of career counseling experts conceived of self-awareness and self-help exercises to promote systematic career decision making (Bartsch and Sandmeyer, 1979; Bolles, 1978; Crystal and Bolles, 1974; Figler, 1975). These exercises are quite adaptable to structured group interventions.

The Cognitive Dimension in Career Planning

The cognitive dimension is well represented in the career development literature. Tiedeman's decision-making approach

(Tiedeman and O'Hara, 1963) and Super's (1957) self-concept theory are examples. Gottfredson (1981) suggests that people compare their self-concepts with their images of occupations in making career decisions. Some self-concept dimensions, such as prestige needs, operate largely on an unconscious level. These develop early in life, before more explicitly articulated dimensions, such as interests, are formed. Also, people come to categorize occupations on a male-female continuum and develop their own levels of tolerance regarding how "male" or "female" their occupations can be. According to Gottfredson, occupational choices are often founded on implicit decisions regarding the compatibility of one's self-concept with one's global images of the life-styles of people in various occupations.

Students must become more autonomous from family, peer, and other influences in order to differentiate their values, interests, and goals from the expectations held by others. Development of identity requires cognitive development, in that self-attributes must be more fully and accurately articulated. Knefelkamp and Slepitza (1976) have adapted Perry's cognitive development scheme to career development and have indicated that self-awareness, concepts of occupations, and decision-making skills can reflect different levels of cognitive complexity. Other writers have applied cognitive techniques to career counseling. For instance, Lewis and Gilhousen (1981) have identified a number of myths or irrational beliefs that can encumber the career-planning process; and Keller, Biggs, and Gysbers (1982) have offered a cognitive-behavioral conceptualization of career counseling.

In a cognitive conceptualization of career planning, the development of self-awareness is seen as a necessary first step—clients need to enrich their cognitive maps of themselves. More cognitively complex and better-integrated concepts are desirable. Self-constructs that provide accurate and precise descriptions must be differentiated from the maps that parents and others have promoted. Important aspects of the cognitive map of self are values, life-style preferences, interests, competencies, personality styles, and future goals. Greater differentiation occurs as people observe themselves in interaction with the world and make increasingly finer discriminations regarding their reactions to various situations—for example, how interested they really are in an activity. Cognitive dissonance occurs as evidence is presented that cannot be assimilated by cognitive systems. One's internal reactions to interactions with others may challenge the self-concept tenet "I like doing things with people." Feedback from the environment, such as a series of poor grades in calculus, might clash with constructs regarding ability. Attending to one's reactions to the environment and learning about oneself as a result lead to a more complex self system. Constructs that are known but unarticulated to oneself may be explicitly identified and thereby made available to the conscious decision-making process.

Cognitive maps of the "world of work" and of individual occupations are constructed, as well as the cognitive maps of self. Gottfredson (1981) reviews research suggesting that people can reliably classify occupations according to sex type and prestige level. Since people often make career decisions with very little "nuts-and-bolts" information, these global impressions of life-styles seem quite important and should be given more attention by counselors. Gottfredson suggests that specific information about job characteristics becomes important only after these more primitive preference factors have been taken into account. Counselors can encourage clients to explore these global factors, attempting to make the implicit explicit. In addition, counselors should continue to help clients become more knowledgeable about job characteristics and employment outlook. Clients also need to develop their conceptions of self-in-world. That is, they must consider how they have reacted to past and present situations in order to predict how they will react to possible future careers.

As the career-planning process continues, clients' cognitive systems for decision making are further developed. In grappling with the very important issues of career planning, clients can become more adept at systematic decision making and may be able to use their improved skills in other areas of life. While linear reasoning systems of decision making are doubtless involved, Gottfredson (1981) has emphasized the importance of variables not consciously elucidated. Intuitive impressions based on hunches and "gut feelings" may help these unquantifiable variables become included in the decision-making process. Rather than emphasizing linear methods over intuitive ones, counselors can encourage clients to compare the results obtained with both kinds of exploration.

Use of the Cognitive Dimension in Structured Groups

Several instruments can supplement interviewing in helping the counselor assess the degree to which a client's career-planning needs can be met in a group. The Career Maturity Inventory (Crites, 1978) and Super's Career Development Inventory, College and University Form (Super and others, 1981) are possibilities, although both are rather lengthy. Briefer choices include the Vocational Decision Making Checklist (Harren, 1966), Career Decision (Osipow and others, 1976), and the Vocational Decision Scale (Jones and Chenery, 1980). My Vocational Situation (Holland, Daiger, and Power, 1980) provides brief measures of career identity crystallization, need for information, and blocks to career decision making. Clients are appropriate for the group to be described when they are motivated to engage in long-range thinking (clients in career crises may need individual counseling in addition to or instead of the group), are appropriate for a group intervention (see Chapter Seven), and can benefit from extensive attention to development of self-awareness (clients who primarily need information would be better served in a program that focuses more singularly on career exploration).

Having pairs discuss what they expect to gain by participation in the group is particularly important in career planning, in that students often have unrealistic goals. This discussion can serve as a more effective get-acquainted activity if a light topic is also included, such as describing "wildest career fantasies." As participants' expectations are outlined, group leaders can reinforce realistic goals and point out the unrealistic aspects of others. Counselors can then discuss goals of the group: helping members sharpen their "maps" of themselves, progress in identifying potential occupations, improve their knowledge of exploratory steps, and clarify their overall "game plans" for planning their futures. Once clients have obtained a better idea of the group activities and have thought about how realistic their expectations are, they can be asked to write their goals.

In order to build the rationale and explore blocks to career planning, the group leader can present one or more "mind teasers" that require diverging from a standard cognitive set. Once the solutions are given and discussed, clients can be encouraged to suspend their preconceptions regarding their personal characteristics and occupational goals. Another useful activity in the early sessions of the group is to conduct a discussion of the kinds of "irrational beliefs" that inhibit career planning. Participants can be asked to react to Lewis and Gilhousen's (1981) list of "myths" of career development, including beliefs that a career decision occurs at one point in time or that directions once begun should never be altered. If participants seem unaffected by the discussion, more extensive cognitive restructuring techniques can be used, such as those presented in Chapter Five.

In the stage where the group is focusing on development of cognitive maps of self, counselors should remember that many clients are not aware of the kind of self-information that is important and may be obsessed with learning what they are "good at." This limited perspective is often reflected in the request to take "an aptitude test" to find out "what career I should go into." At this point they need to gain an appreciation of the role of life goals and values. The process of values clarification can be begun with the "hero/heroine fantasy." Participants are asked to think of someone they greatly admire and to explore the qualities that account for their admiration. The next step is to infer values contained in their reactions. As a second exercise, they can be asked to complete a "values checklist." They can imagine that they have $100 and can allocate the money according to the importance of the values on the list. Figler (1975) presents a values list derived from Super's work. Participants can also be asked to consider how their parents would complete the values checklist and to compare these parental values with their own. An optional step is to conduct a values auction. Time is unlikely to permit auctioning all the values on the list, so nominations can be taken from the group and values selected so that a number of desired values are included. Participants again imagine that they have $100 and can bid for each value according to its importance to them. Consideration of the work values in a competitive market sometimes provides new insights.

A life-style exploration exercise can help participants identify their goals. They are asked to position themselves in the room according to two axes: one representing the degree to which work is central in their self-concepts, the other representing the degree to which family or primary social group is central. Students who expect work to be central would position themselves on one side of the room, while those who see work as peripheral would move to the other side. They also position themselves on the family/social group axis, depending on the centrality of this dimension. The first position assumed is to pertain to their preferences at the present time. After discussion, they are asked to position themselves in reference to time of college graduation and discuss relevant implications, including movement from their previous positions. Subsequently, positions are taken corresponding to five and then ten years after graduation. An interesting aspect for leaders to observe is whether the males and females in the group differ in their patterns of movement.

Awareness of personality dimensions is another important aspect of the cognitive map of self. Psychological instruments can be used; however, they should be ones that are suitable for group interpretation. The Myers-Briggs Type Indicator (Briggs and Myers, 1976) can be useful in considering participants' styles of processing information. The Holland Types (Holland and Gottfredson, 1976) is another personality-style scheme that can be used. An adaptation of Bolles's (1978) party exercise can help participants think about their Holland codes. They are to imagine that they are entering a party with various sections of the room occupied by different Holland types and are asked to go to the section of the room to which they would be drawn. Their reasons for this preference are discussed. They are then invited to go to the section of the room where the people would be most like themselves. Changes in positioning can be noted and discussed. Participants also can be asked to think about and discuss where significant others, such as parents, would be positioned and thereby clarify similarities and differences with these individuals.

In order to develop their cognitive maps of competencies, clients may need to overcome dichotomous thinking about abilities. Students often believe that only exceptional levels of skill are indicative of ability and assume that they "have no ability" in an area unless they are exceptional. Students may also equate abilities with academic subject areas and may overlook social and organizational skills, likely to be manifested in nonacademic activities. These kinds of skills, which are quite important in a number of career areas, are also more difficult to assess than academically related abilities, since students have extensive histories of test performances and grades in academic subjects. An adaptation of Figler's (1975) "The Best" exercise can help students analyze both academic and nonacademic experiences in identifying skills and can broaden their understanding of the concept of ability. Participants select "the best" example of one or more activities, such as research. Working in small groups, they then specify discrete abilities that contributed to the achievement. They can then be asked to complete a skills self-rating form (Figler, 1975). The group can then brainstorm ways that members can sharpen their self-assessments of skills that are difficult to measure.

Interest tests can be helpful in developing the cognitive map of self. In work with university students, I prefer the Strong-Campbell Interest Inventory (Strong and Campbell, 1981). It has been well validated and presents clients with clear, specific information. With the addition of the Occupational Theme and Basic Interest Scales, it now offers a theoretical component that is useful in helping students expand their self-views. It is helpful for participants to think about their status on each set of scales before it is interpreted. The party exercise has already required students to categorize themselves on the Occupational Theme dimensions. They can be given a self-rating form for the Basic Scales. For the Occupational Scales, they can list five occupational groups with whom they would expect to be compatible. The test profiles are then distributed and the results interpreted, with participants asked to note discrepancies between their expectations and their actual scores. Students are not required to reveal their results to others; however, they are encouraged to ask questions to clarify the meaning of scales. They are invited to direct questions they would not wish to discuss in the group to leaders after the meeting or at a later time.

Clients need to begin constructing maps of "career destinations." Most students have several potential careers in mind when they enter the group. In order to add potentially interesting occupations to their "bags of possibilities," students are encouraged to use their Strong-Campbell results, the *Dictionary of Holland Occupational Codes* (Gottfredson, Holland, and Ogawa, 1982), and brainstorming based on their clarified maps of self. During the exploratory phase, they are encouraged to keep adding new possibilities and to delete ones found to be unsuitable.

Many students need to develop the skills of career exploration. Group and dyadic brainstorming can help them identify creative ways of getting information. Occupational and educational information resources can be introduced to them in a "tour" of career library facilities. Participants can then be given the assignment of writing down information on an occupation from several sources and reporting their findings to the group. As well as using written information, participants can be encouraged to develop word-of-mouth networks for learning about occupations. They may need to be schooled to ask specific questions and/or request examples, because interviewees often provide overgeneral or jargon-filled descriptions. Finally, participants should be encouraged to obtain information experientially by seeking internships, summer jobs, volunteer work, or apprenticeships.

In all these exploratory endeavors, participants must learn to project themselves mentally into an occupation and to identify the points of compatibility and incompatibility between their self-images and their images of the occupation. Many students hold the dichotomous belief that a job should fit perfectly. Counselors may need to provide a more realistic perspective by suggesting that any occupation is likely to have both incompatible and compatible aspects.

Students' cognitive systems for decision making may need to be made more complex. Many have simplistic ideas about the career decision-making process, such as the belief that a career decision is made at one magic point in time. Counselors can help them develop a more complex understanding of the developmental process involved and appreciate that an intricate network of many decisions constitutes a person's career choice. Participants can be exposed to systematic decision-making and problem-solving strategies, such as those outlined by Janis and Mann (1977). For instance, they can generate the positive and negative outcomes of a career direction for the following four categories: tangible gains and losses for themselves, tangible gains and losses for others, approval or disapproval from self, and approval or disapproval from others. This analysis can be completed for several of the occupations they are considering, and the results can be compared. While systematic decision-making strategies are valuable, research suggests that less explicit factors also contribute to career choices (Gottfredson, 1981). Therefore, participants should be helped to appreciate the value of "listening" to intuitive and emotional cues. Through guided-imagery techniques, participants can project themselves into each of several career alternatives for a hypothetical day. The results of the systematic decision-making strategies can be compared with the emotional and intuitive data obtained through imagery.

In light of the long-term nature of career planning, it is particularly important to help participants form cognitive maps of "next steps" they can take to further their efforts. The next-step contracting procedure is quite useful. Counselors should encourage each group member to report on the next steps they have identified, since their ideas can provide useful models for other participants.

H. Workshop: "Developing Self-Image"

One's view of self is particularly important during late adolescence and early adulthood. This workshop, which is of particular interest to women, has been requested by sororities and included in a series of programs directed at women. The workshop includes some of the material from the structured group on "Developing Self-Confidence" presented in Section F.

Goals of the Workshop

Since this workshop is designed to last an hour or so, the goals are relatively limited and primarily cognitive. They are to help participants obtain a cognitive framework for understanding and thinking about self-image issues, increase their levels of awareness of important aspects of their self-images, develop an appreciation for how internal dialogue is related to self-image, and learn about resources for improving self-image.

Attention Getting

The self-image topic is usually inherently interesting to participants; therefore, sufficient attention is generally given to a lecturette introduction, particularly if clear examples of self-image issues are provided. It can also be helpful to present several examples of advertisements and other mass media messages designed to appeal to and/or influence self-images. These are discussed at length later in the workshop.

Developing the Self-Image Framework

After introduction of the workshop leaders and the goals and agenda, a framework useful in thinking about and discussing self-image issues is presented. A lecturette format that includes ongoing participation from the audience is used. The material offered is taken from the "Developing Self-Confidence" Structured Group, presented in Section F. The concepts of the "perceived" and "ideal" selves are discussed and diagrammed on newsprint, with examples written into the diagram as the lecturette proceeds. This simple visual aid is necessary because the material can be confusing if only verbal explanations are given. The leader explains that cognitions can be held about oneself (the perceived self) that are both congruent and incongruent with the ideal self. Important incongruencies can result in anxiety, insecurity, discouragement, and depression, as well as in self-defeating behavior patterns, such as avoidance of important tasks and social withdrawal.

Cognitions about oneself can be both perceived and desired (in both perceived and ideal selves), perceived but not desired (not in ideal self), or desired but not perceived (in ideal but not in perceived self). Participants can be asked for examples in each category that would be typical of students at their university. Their responses can generally be related to the following four areas of self-image, which can then be described and illustrated: physical self, intellectual self, social self, and emotional self. It can be pointed out that these four areas are often challenged when students leave homes and high schools and enter college. The *physical self*—body image—is quite important during adolescence and early adulthood. When students leave a familiar environment for a new one, they are likely to feel less secure about how they appear physically to others. The perfectionistic concern with physical appearance, characterized by an extremely rigid and unrealistic ideal self, sometimes culminates in development of serious eating disorders, including bulimia. The *intellectual self* is also likely to be challenged by the transition, since students who have performed at higher levels than their high school counterparts may find college a "new ball game." The *social self*, too, may be tested, in that students often leave the security of social niches with family and established friends when they go to university. Concerns about their desirability to others as friends, dates, and leaders may be heightened. Finally, the *emotional self* may be tested. Since the environment may be more challenging and since university students are faced with increasingly more difficult and serious decisions, they may face failure more frequently and have to deal with more frustration and disappointment. After the lecturette, aided by the diagram, participants are invited to raise questions or offer their thoughts.

Enabling Participants to Apply the Model to Themselves

As in the structured group on self-confidence, participants can be asked to list examples of each of the four self-image areas that are in both perceived and ideal selves, in perceived but not in ideal, and in ideal but not in perceived. Since the group atmosphere of a one-session workshop is not likely to contain the trust of a structured group, some participants may not be willing to discuss personal matters. Rather than being asked to share personal examples, they can be asked, "What kinds of things do you think a lot of students at this university would list?" I have found that students are more willing to acknowledge challenge to their intellectual selves than to the other categories. Female students will often discuss physical-self issues, mostly concerning weight and comparisons with unrealistic ideals presented in the media. An all-female audience is more conducive to open discussion about body image topics than is a mixed-gender group. Social-self issues are often discussed from an environmental standpoint. For example, difficulties with the dating situation on campus are mentioned. Emotional-self issues seem to be expressed less frequently than the others, perhaps because discussion of them would require deeper levels of disclosure.

With smaller groups of students (twelve to fourteen) who are well acquainted with one another, such as might occur in a sorority, personal discussions of these questions have ensued. With larger groups, particularly when participants do not know one another well, a more abstract and/or superficial discussion is likely. Even so, this kind of discussion is useful in enabling participants to better understand and learn to apply the framework. The stimuli of the model and the discussion seem to generate productive thought that is not necessarily verbalized during the workshop.

Exploring the Development and Maintenance of Self-Image Issues

The lecturette material can help students experience universalization and become more aware that others have similar questions and have encountered similar growing pains. This effect can be enhanced if they are asked to think about how discrepancies between ideal and perceived selves occur. They are likely to mention the impact of early criticism by parents, teachers, and other "powerful" adult figures. They may also identify peer pressure as a source for creating an unrealistic ideal self. Some may mention the contributions of social stereotypes, such as those often identified with Greek organizations. Cultural influences in the form of mass media versions of the "ideal man" and "ideal woman" may also be mentioned. Female students are particularly aware of the unattainability of the images of women presented in television and magazine advertisements. At this point, the examples of advertisements that were briefly presented as an attention getter can be discussed in more depth. Slide presentations or videotaped excerpts can be used; however, it is effective simply to display and discuss several ads cut from magazines.

Developing a Map of What Can Be Done to Improve Self-Image

Participants' ideas of positive steps can be elicited by the question "What can we do in order to make the ways we perceive ourselves closer to the ways we would like to be?" As the group brainstorms about this question, the leader can summarize the two general directions that can be taken: improving aspects of oneself and making the ideal self less rigid and unrealistic. Specific ideas about each of these general possibilities can be elicited. Participants' thoughts can be listed on newsprint, so they will be more likely to be remembered.

Introducing the Concept of Internal Dialogue

Internal dialogue is the vehicle by which unrealistic ideas about the ideal self are brought into play; it can also contribute to negative shaping of the perceived self by reflecting selective attention to negative feedback. The internal dialogue concept is developed in ways similar to those used in the self-confidence group, except that more attention is given to identification of self-image–lowering internal dialogue than to altering cognitions. The steps of awareness of self-defeating patterns, catching oneself involved in these patterns, developing coping internal dialogue for regaining perspective, and eventually altering basic views of perceived and ideal self are presented; and it is explained that only the first of these can be addressed extensively in the workshop. Brief examples of coping dialogue can be given for addressing negative self-statements likely to occur in each of the four self-image areas (physical, social, intellectual, and emotional).

Gaining Closure and Building Awareness of Resources

A good way to further learning and gain closure for the workshop is to ask participants to identify the most useful outcome of the activities for them. If this discussion proceeds comfortably, the leader can ask them to indicate ways that they can implement ideas gained in the workshop. This closure exercise can be based on their written responses to a workshop evaluation form that is completed prior to the discussion. In closing, the leaders may want to summarize one or two of the most salient points that emerged in discussions. A list of readings helpful in promoting self-image can be distributed and/or examples of some of the books displayed. Finally, resources including individual and group counseling, special programming, and other related workshops can be described.

I. "Learning How the Other Half Lives and Thinks": A Workshop for Exploring Social Expectations

In order to navigate the social world, we develop cognitive maps of ourselves, the world, and self-in-world. Through these maps, we anticipate our options, predict how others will respond to our actions, and make decisions regarding how we will behave. Nowhere is this process more evident than in social interactions with the opposite sex. The "game" of getting to know people of the opposite sex and the "dating game" are generally composed of rules that are recognized implicitly rather than explicitly. Further, messages are conveyed indirectly rather than directly. One kind of smile means "I want to be friends," whereas another may mean "I find you attractive." This web of mystery has probably evolved because it provides a buffer zone for our fragile egos. The necessary "feeling-out" process allows individuals to protect themselves from the dangers of social rejection and maintain the secrecy of their actual hopes and personal feelings until they can learn more about the other person.

It provides a ritualized system in which people can take risks slowly and attempt to decipher the code of the other's cues. They can also note the other's responses to more limited risks, such as flirtatious comments, before taking greater risks, such as disclosing personal information or initiating physical intimacy.

While this web of implicit expectations and indirect messages can be helpful in providing this "limited risk buffer zone," it can often contribute to problems. Confusion can occur regarding the response that is "expected" in a situation. Indirect messages may be misread. The narrow conception that there is one set of rules for the game may develop, as well as the impression that the slightest miscue could result in rebuff and embarrassment. It is easy to retreat to an overly cautious stance and avoid meaningful risks or to react by abandoning concern for "the rules" and being boldly direct on almost every occasion. Unfortunately, neither of these approaches is likely to be very effective. Coping with this web of expectations can be especially difficult for adolescents and young adults, who may find the ambiguity of social games difficult to tolerate. Still in the process of evolving independent standards, they may worry excessively about what others would do or what approach would be "right."

In light of the great importance of social development during university years and the difficulties inherent in negotiating the social world, one would expect students to discuss these issues extensively. While some productive discussion does ensue, the amount of honest dialogue on these issues is probably less than would be ideal. The typical dormitory bull session often contains more joking and exaggerated tales of sexual exploits than open acknowledgment of questions and confusion. Their concern with making a good impression on their peers may heighten students' needs to appear in control of their social lives and unruffled by difficulties. This workshop is designed to be a "guided bull session" in which students are given permission to raise questions and issues in a manner that protects them from being perceived as "uncool."

Goals of the Workshop

The goals of this workshop are to help participants better understand the kinds of expectations and questions regarding social interactions held by individuals of the opposite sex, better articulate their own expectations and questions regarding social interactions, and receive feedback from members of the opposite sex regarding the validity of their expectations and concerns.

Attention Getting

This workshop is highly interactive, with only a brief introduction and explanation of the procedures offered before group discussion is initiated. Since students are generally quite interested in the topic of male-female interactions, no elaborate attention-getting technique is required.

Introduction: Building the Rationale and Setting the Agenda

After the leaders are introduced, the issues addressed by the workshop (as indicated in the introduction to this section) are explained. Some examples of common "guessing games" can be given: a male thinking about whether a female's friendliness reveals a romantic interest or a desire to remain "just friends"; a female wondering how her date would interpret an offer to pay part of the bill; a male trying to determine whether the way a female refused his invitation for a date means he should try again or "hang it up." In these guessing games, people can easily misinterpret cues, become excessively cautious because of confusion, and form rigid cognitive maps that fail to allow for wide individual variations. What is needed, therefore, is dialogue that enables people to learn more about the views of the other sex and to receive feedback regarding their own ideas. The goals of the workshop (described above) are then outlined.

The workshop agenda is then presented. Two or three sentence stems dealing with social expectations will be presented, and participants will be asked to write their responses to the items. These responses are then read and discussed in a way that protects the anonymity of the respondent. A final exercise, in which anonymity again is ensured, allows participants to present opposite-sex participants with their own questions. A statement regarding the kind of outcome likely from the workshop can be helpful. A few students have expressed disappointment that they did not get "definite" answers to some of their questions. Participants can be cautioned that wide preference differences might preclude their getting clear-cut answers to certain questions.

Promoting Articulation of Cognitive Maps and Validity Checking

Participants should be divided into groups of eight to fifteen, preferably with a relatively equal distribution of males and females. The group size may have to be adjusted if the number of one gender is considerably lower than the number of the other. On occasions, participants might be asked to begin the first discussion in small, same-sex groups and then join with a group of the opposite sex to continue discussion. With groups that seem particularly cautious, this strategy might be helpful; however, with most groups, beginning the discussion in mixed-sex groups seems to be the best approach. Once the groups are formed, participants are handed slips of paper with the first sentence stem ("When I first meet someone of the opposite sex, some things he or she might do to turn me off are.. " and "Some things he or she might do that I would like include . . .") and asked to write their responses. They are also asked to mark their gender on the slips. When everyone has responded, a member of each group can collect, shuffle, and redistribute the slips. Participants then read the responses and exchange ideas that are stimulated. After the first stem is discussed, the second one ("It bothers me to think that someone of the opposite sex would expect me to . . .") is used in the same way. Each stem usually elicits discussion lasting fifteen or twenty minutes. The third stem ("I find it hard to interpret what someone of the opposite sex means when he or she . . .") can be used or not, depending on the time remaining in the workshop.

In order to develop productive discussion about these themes, workshop leaders should make extensive use of the group-leading skills of summarizing and linking and pairing (discussed in Chapter Seven). These techniques can promote discussion and attune participants to important similarities and differences among the perspectives represented at the workshop. It is also important to elicit input from female participants in reference to statements or questions by males and vice versa. There are usually one or two participants who consider themselves experts on how people of the opposite sex think. Rather than letting their assertions be assumed to be accurate, the workshop leader can say something like "Let's hear ideas from some of the women (or men) on this."

Gaining Closure

The last exercise produces interesting discussions and provides an excellent closure activity for the workshop. If smaller subgroups have been used for discussion of the sentence stems, all participants can reconvene into one group. Slips of paper with the stem "Something I would like to ask members of the opposite sex is . . ." are distributed, and participants are invited to write their responses. The slips are then collected by the leader, who selects and reads interesting questions and leads discussion. In initiating discussion on a question presented by a participant, leaders should be careful to elicit answers from opposite-sex participants. When productive discussion subsides or the time to end the workshop approaches, the leader can summarize some of the main themes that arose in discussion. Finally, a workshop feedback form can be distributed and participants asked to list important ideas they gained from the workshop.

An interesting postworkshop activity is to allow participants to look at all the responses written during the workshop. The slips of paper can be taped to the wall and participants invited to read them. This addendum is particularly useful in groups that have continued interaction with one another. It is also well received if participants plan to have refreshments after the workshop. The posted items often serve as a stimulus for continued discussion of important issues. Some participants may feel more comfortable disclosing their views in this context than during the workshop.

J. Brief Workshop on "Stress Management"

A one- to two-hour workshop dealing with stress management requires an adaptation of the material presented in Section B. A major difference is that participants cannot be expected to develop new coping skills, either behavioral or cognitive.

Goals of the Workshop

The following goals are obtainable in the brief workshop: to help participants understand the stress response and ways it can be helpful as well as debilitating; to provide participants with a framework for the "stress cycle" that can guide further thought about their own stress responses and coping methods; to help participants understand the role of internal dialogue in the stress cycle; and to introduce a relaxation exercise that will enable participants to become better acquainted with ways in which tension is manifested (depending on time availability).

Attention Getting

Much of this workshop is informational and requires a didactic form of presentation; therefore, attention-getting strategies are more needed than in the two workshops previously described, which are primarily discussion based. Cartoons dealing with stress can be used to introduce the topic. Demonstrations of biofeedback equipment can stimulate interest and help participants understand components of the stress response. Inexpensive electromyograph (EMG) and skin conductance units are available, as are finger band temperature gauges. A poster illustrating the stress cycle (Figure 5 in Section B) serves as a simple but very effective visual aid.

Introducing the Stress Response

As in the structured group, participants can be asked how they react to stressful situations. In order to promote understanding and add a humorous ingredient to the introduction, their responses can be likened to the "Incredible Hulk response." With this metaphor, the components of the "fight-or-flight" response can be identified and described (this metaphor is described in Chapter Eight in the section "Building Cognitive Development on Previous Learning"). As various component responses are mentioned, biofeedback can be used to illustrate them: an EMG can demonstrate skeletal muscle tension, and a skin conductance unit can illustrate how we perspire when under stress. Finger temperature bands are useful in a workshop setting, because they can be demonstrated and then distributed so that participants can gauge their own finger temperatures.

Developing an Understanding of the Effects of Stress

Participants can be asked how the Incredible Hulk or their ancestral cavemen may have benefited from the stress response. Positive effects of the stress response can then be noted, including increased physical power and mental alertness. Participants can then be asked to specify problems that the stress response poses for people in modern times. Since fewer of our stressors are physically threatening, we cannot respond with a discharge of physical energy and may therefore maintain stress at unproductively high levels. Participants can then be asked to give examples of the debilitating effects of uncontrolled stress levels. Their responses usually include the following: development of degenerative illness (heart disease, ulcers, and others), lowered immunity and increased susceptibility to infectious ill-

nesses, avoidance of threatening tasks, mental confusion and
distractibility, and development of unhealthy methods of reducing stress, such as abuse of alcohol or drugs, compulsive eating,
and smoking.

Introducing the Stress Cycle

In order to cope with stress and regulate it so that the unproductive effects do not occur, participants can learn about
the stress cycle. A poster illustrating the cycle presented in Figure 5 in Section B can be used.

Exploring Points of Intervention

After the cycle has been discussed, workshop leaders can
lead discussion on ways of using each of the five points of intervention to regulate stress. In regard to Point 1, *general life-style,*
participants can be encouraged to try to maintain some balance
in their life-styles, recognizing that at times of high stress they
are prone to more erratic practices. For instance, around exam
time students may get less sleep, drink more coffee, and reduce
important stress-regulating activities, such as exercise programs.
They can be cautioned to try to maintain some balance, even
though a change of routine may be necessary in order for them
to get extra study time.

Point 2, *awareness of stress cycle patterns,* includes learning to understand one's stress response and "tune into" aspects
of stress at each point of the stress cycle. As discussed previously, "early detection" depends on students' learning to recognize
cues that a stress spiral is developing *before* it has progressed to
an uncontrollable level.

Point 3, *environmental management,* corresponds to the
environmental element of the stress cycle. Workshop leaders can
ask participants to brainstorm ways that they can regulate their
environments so as to manage stress better. Skills such as assertiveness and problem solving can be mentioned. Self-help materials on time management can be distributed and briefly explained; however, there is rarely time to discuss it at length. (A

follow-up workshop on time management, problem solving, assertiveness training, or other aspects of environmental management can be made available to the group.) An important environmental management skill to be noted is for students to anticipate periods of high stress and preplan how to simplify their lives during these periods. Another important strategy is to take stock of the amount of change one is experiencing and put a self-imposed moratorium on new commitments or changes.

Point 4, *mental management,* corresponds to the mental orientation element of the stress cycle and has been discussed in Section B. The concept of internal dialogue can be illustrated with a role-played demonstration. For instance, the leader can simulate a person sitting in an exam and express aloud a pattern of unproductive dialogue. This technique is particularly effective when the number of workshop participants exceeds the number common in structured groups. Handout material can be used in order to sensitize participants to their most common patterns of stress-producing internal dialogue. The leader might then ask participants how the hypothetical exam taker might redirect or "regear" internal dialogue in order to reduce stress. The four sequential steps of developing awareness, catching oneself, using coping dialogue, and eventually changing basic beliefs can be explained. However, it is difficult to help participants really develop coping dialogue skills in a brief workshop.

Point 5, *physical management,* is then introduced. Participants can brainstorm ways in which they can become more attuned to tension and better able to produce the relaxation response. If the workshop is planned for longer than an hour, there is time to have participants experience a relaxation exercise, such as Stevens's (1971) deep-breathing method. A clear explanation of the procedures prior to the exercise is even more crucial in an outreach workshop than in a structured group. Participants who experience a relaxation exercise in a one-session workshop are not likely to become proficient in relaxation skills; however, they may develop increased sensitivity to their immediate physiological responses and a heightened appreciation for the state of relaxation. These gains may influence them to continue developing relaxation skills.

Gaining Closure

The workshop leader can summarize the stress cycle and important points that have been discussed and present information on campus resources for further developing stress management skills. Workshop feedback forms can be distributed. Participants can then be asked to reflect on their responses on these forms and to identify and state changes they may implement as a result of the workshop.

Conclusion: Using Cognitive Approaches in Student Counseling Research and Practice

It is my hope that this book will lead to thoughtful applications of cognitive ideas to student development counseling and programming and to further research on the nature of cognitive functioning and cognitive change. Even more important, I hope that it stimulates further thinking about the role of cognitions in human experience, particularly that of university students.

There are, of course, limitations inherent in any conceptualization, including the ideas I have offered. All theories are cognitive systems and, as such, can help us successfully predict future events and adapt to the demands placed on us; on the other hand, they can lead us to misinterpret information and make misguided predictions. Like the "theories" that clients use for dealing with the world, the effectiveness of our student development theories depends on their *organization, complexity,* and *flexibility*. Like clients' cognitive maps of themselves and the world, our theories are *models* of reality and not reality itself. Since the "map" is not the territory, our models are always incomplete. This incomplete status is particularly evident in efforts to understand the very complex nature of human psychology. As professionals in the field of student development, we must make sure that the cognitive systems and constructs comprising our theories remain flexible and permeable. An attitude of humility regarding our ideas and a broad, flexible frame of reference can enable us to evolve models that are increasingly complex. The ideas presented in this book have undergone change during the course of the writing, as new thoughts were stimulated by the writing process, new experiences, and editorial suggestions. These ideas will continue to change as further experiences challenge tenets and provide new information. I hope that readers will find the thoughts presented helpful; however, it is just as important for them to identify weaknesses and points of disagreement—and to be stimulated to refine the ideas.

One of the "developmental tasks" of counseling and student development professionals is to formulate our individual models of human behavior in an increasingly explicit way. In my opinion, we understand more than we can articulate. In cognitive terms, encoded bits of information and expectancies that have not yet been incorporated into the cognitive systems of our explicit theories enter into our decision-making processes. Although these variables are not consciously articulated, they serve as the bases for "intuition," "hunches," and "clinical judgment." Our implicit theoretical systems will probably always extend beyond our explicit ones; but we must continually attempt to sharpen our slippery, impressionistic thoughts into more clearly defined precepts. Once these constructs are articulated, we can more consistently and reliably apply them. We can also more accurately convey the bases of our decisions and judgments to others and thereby potentially enrich their theoretical maps. Further, once these assumptions are made explicit, their validity can be better examined. Concepts that do not stand the test of more careful scrutiny and objective inquiry can be discarded and more promising principles kept and refined. Our goal should be to chart more and more of these implicit assumptions and principles into explicit cognitive maps. The ideas in this book represent my present state of progress in this ongoing endeavor. I hope they provide stimulation so that readers will further explicate their own implicit theoretical systems.

In this final chapter, I want to reflect on the ideas presented in preceding chapters. How much water do these ideas hold? Where are the leaks? What is needed to plug the holes?

Cognitive Approaches and Research

In further developing our theoretical models of human experience, we student development professionals must adhere to a flexible scientist-practitioner approach. Systematic investigation and objective study provide truer tests of the accuracy with which our theoretical models predict behavior than do subjective assessments of our own efforts. Attribution researchers have identified the attribution errors that are regularly committed—for instance, allowing preconceptions to flavor perceptions. Since student development professionals are heavily invested in viewing their efforts as effective, it is easy for them to perceive selectively and distort the data to fit the preexisting theory rather than to make necessary alterations. They must, however, take the lead in advocating a scientist-practitioner approach. In times of financial competition, some higher education administrators may short-sightedly believe that services can be provided most economically without "extraneous trappings" such as program evaluation and research.

While many of the cognitive ideas presented in this book have received research support, further research on a number of aspects is needed. Many cognitive-behavioral principles and intervention techniques have been supported (Ellis, 1977b); however, as Garfield and Bergin (1978) and others have suggested, research is needed that helps identify the potent ingredients in techniques and the kind of person with whom particular techniques are most useful. Researchers also might try to answer the question "Why do specific cognitive-behavioral techniques work?" by testing the underlying theoretical explanations. Theory can easily be ignored by proponents of technical eclecticism; however, stimulating theory can suggest new techniques, which may be found to be effective. More investigations using genuine clinical samples rather than students in psychology classes would substantiate the value of these techniques. Class samples have great value in exploring variables; however, researchers should not rely exclusively on this approach but should attempt to refine initial findings by conducting research with clinical samples. Even when the selection of class samples is based on measurement of the variable in question, such as anxiety, the sample cannot be assumed to be comparable to one composed of people who actively seek treatment.

Much of the research with cognitive techniques has focused on individual counseling and the use of structured programs in groups. Few investigations have centered on the use of cognitive techniques in less structured group counseling, psychoeducational workshops, and other outreach interventions. Further research seems warranted on the validity and applicability of some of the neurolinguistic programming concepts regarding different representational systems (visual, auditory, and kinesthetic). However, if the research results on application of these concepts to counseling continue to be questionable, counselors need to be willing to revise these ideas, no matter how intriguing they are. The concept that an individual has one "primary" representational system, which can be the focal point for counseling interventions, has not been well supported in research (Ellickson, 1983; Fromme and Daniell, 1984).

A great deal of research has supported Strong's (1968) contributions and led to further refinement of the concepts (Heppner and Dixon, 1981). The trustworthiness and expertness perceptions have been more fully supported as important factors in counseling than the attractiveness dimension. While progress has been made in identifying with whom and under what circumstances these dimensions are important and what counselor characteristics and behaviors contribute to the formation of these perceptions, it also appears that the counselor-client social interaction is even more complex than originally hypothesized. Strong and Claiborn's (1982) refinements provide an excellent framework for further research to elucidate the intricacies of the counseling process. Further study of various subtle aspects, such as counselor behaviors and the timing of an intervention in influencing client perceptions, would be valuable to the practitioner.

Many of Kelly's concepts have not received the research

attention warranted by such a divergent and well-articulated theory. In comparison with the "Rogerians" and the rational-emotive, transactional analysis, and other "brands" of counselors, there have been few "Kellians." Enough has been learned about counseling since Kelly's time to indicate that his theory probably should not be strictly applied; however, researchers could make valuable contributions to the counseling and student development fields by more carefully examining ideas emerging from this body of theory. For instance, the effectiveness of fixed role therapy could be more extensively examined.

Much of the intervention-related research has focused on cognitive events, such as the presence of irrational beliefs or anxiety-arousing self-talk. One reason for this status is the empirical emphasis of the cognitive-behavioral approach. Less is known about cognitive systems—how they are formed and changed. Self-concept theory provides some information, as does social learning theory. However, research based on a cognitive model is needed, particularly pertaining to how systems undergo change in counseling. The role of cognitive dissonance in counseling has also received little attention. Valuable questions could be addressed, such as "When should dissonance be stimulated?" "How is it resolved?" and "What factors lead to a more complex resolution?" But before such studies can be successfully undertaken, we need to know how to measure cognitive dissonance, particularly as it might occur during counseling.

The formative research on cognitive development is valuable and stimulating; however, much remains untested in this domain. The conceptual purity of Perry's constructs has been questioned. An element of thinking "mechanics" is represented, which addresses the complexity of cognitive processes; however, a morality dimension is also included, at least in the higher positions. Factor analytic research would be useful to examine the purity of the constructs. Another major difficulty with cognitive development research is that the most used measurement instruments are time consuming and cumbersome to apply and are fraught with difficulties in achieving interjudge reliability. Research would be greatly facilitated if some easily administered and scored tests of cognitive development were constructed. In this connection, Baxter-Magolda and Porterfield (1985) have presented the Measure of Epistemological Reflection in an effort to elicit written responses that can be easily rated and to clarify rating criteria, and Erwin (1983) has produced an objectively scored Scale of Intellectual Development. Possibly these and other measurement approaches will fare well in reliability and validity research and will prove to be useful. Objectively scored instruments would be particularly helpful in student service settings, where it is often difficult to expend the time and resources necessary for using rating instruments.

A major challenge has been directed toward cognitive development research by those who believe that the research methods and interpretations applied to findings have led to a misunderstanding of the quality of cognitive processes in females. Gilligan (1982) and others have raised important questions regarding the validity and applicability of the concepts offered by such researchers as Perry (1970) and Kohlberg (1971). They rightly challenge the assumptions that conclusions from research with predominantly male samples can be universalized. They assert that females' emphasis on preserving and enhancing relationships is different from, instead of less "logical" than, males' emphasis on principles and justice. Research more fully investigating the subtle complexities of male-female differences is needed to determine whether a single continuum of cognitive development can be constructed, featuring the best aspects of both reasoning styles, or whether two parallel reasoning standards are needed.

A variety of research methods can further our knowledge of cognitive processes and how they can be assessed and changed. Controlled, experimental research is valuable. On the other hand, because this kind of research is difficult to conduct in many student service offices, many professionals in these settings have abandoned research altogether. These professionals need to recognize that other kinds of research—such as case studies, exploratory correlational studies, field studies, and program evaluations—can make significant contributions. These approaches are also necessary for furthering knowledge of cognitive processes. Some of the most important cognitive variables are quite subtle and defy measurement in objective, reliable ways. Better understanding and measurement of these variables can emerge from these "less rigorous" research methods.

Cognitive Intervention Approaches

In developing cognitive intervention techniques and approaches, professionals have given more attention to individual counseling and psychotherapy than to group and outreach interventions. Cognitive techniques of self-management have been taught in groups, such as groups for test anxiety management; however, the format has been didactic and structured. Cognitive concepts, such as coping skills, have also been taught in these groups, but little attention has been given to the group process. More thinking needs to be directed to techniques of facilitating group process so that cognitive development is fostered.

Most cognitive-behavioral programs are directed at specific problems, such as stress or depression, and are largely remedial. Further discussion of the role of cognitive techniques in developmentally focused individual counseling is needed, particularly in regard to helping clients progress in important developmental tasks, such as achieving autonomy. Chapter Four contains a number of ideas; however, there are likely to be many more methods for effecting cognitive changes in this kind of counseling. More attention should also be directed at using structured groups and workshops to achieve developmental goals. In order to evaluate cognitive interventions that are development focused, a way of measuring developmental gains must be devised. Until recently most measures have been developed for clinical and remedial problems. Finally, we must improve our capacities to tailor interventions to the particular needs of individuals or groups. This advance would require improved precision in assessing the recipient of services and in identifying the components of interventions, followed by research designed to illuminate the interactions of these variables.

As well as more thoroughly researching the role of cognitive dissonance in counseling and other interventions, student development professionals might give more consideration to how intervention techniques can be fashioned around this concept. Counseling often entails working with clients who have not "accepted" important external events or internal experiences or who recognize an issue "intellectually but not emotionally." Cognitive dissonance is a useful way of conceptualizing these kinds of difficulties. Attention given to devising counseling and programming techniques for helping students experience needed dissonance and achieve resolution would enrich the repertoire of intervention methods available.

Sensitive application of the Cognitive Intervention Planning Model will require awareness of the interactional nature of counseling. Martin (1984) has presented a cognitive mediation model that illustrates how counselor cognitions influence counselor behaviors, which influence client cognitions, which influence client behaviors, which in turn influence counselor cognitions. As Kelly noted, each individual—client or counselor —constructs and tests hypotheses regarding interactions with others. While the counselor is using the Cognitive Intervention Planning Model in assessing and intervening with the client, the client is using a model in attempting to predict interactions with the counselor. Although perhaps less explicit and systematic than the counselor's model, clients' models contain similar constructs; for instance, they make their own formulations of the counselor and set their own stated or unstated goals for the interactions. Counselors need to remember, then, that they are important stimuli of a client's cognitive activity and occupy sections of the client's world and self-in-world cognitive systems.

Further development of cognitive intervention techniques will occur as research with the cognitive dimension continues. I hope that the Cognitive Intervention Planning Model provides enough flexibility to serve as a framework for student development professionals as they integrate new research and practice concepts into their counseling and programming activities.

Applications of the Model to Other Professional Activities

Several important areas of counseling and student development have not been addressed in this book. However, the

Cognitive Intervention Planning Model can be useful in these areas as well.

Media-Based Outreach Education. Morrill, Oetting, and Hurst (1974) include media as a mode of intervention in their cube model of dimensions of counselor functioning. A number of successful uses of media have been reported, including stress management education over closed-circuit campus radio (Lowenstein, 1978), articles on various developmental topics produced by counseling center professionals and published in student newspapers (Wheaton, 1984), use of tape-slide materials in career planning (O'Neil and Van Loon, 1979), and dispersal of career information with films (Miller, 1979).

Media interventions seem well suited for enhancing cognitive development. Cognitive systems of self, world, and self-in-world can be expanded through the presentation of new information. Awareness of issues, ways of coping, and resources for further development can be sharpened. Carefully prepared media can stimulate low to moderate levels of cognitive dissonance. When interacting with ongoing support structures, this dissonance may lead to further thought and perhaps to accommodation of excessively narrow cognitive systems. While a great deal of professional time is required for the development of media programs, interventions can be offered quite efficiently once the materials are available. They can be used alone or in the context of workshops or other activities conducted by peer counselors.

Unfortunately, most student development professionals know little about developing and using media in outreach education. As professionals trained in counseling or student services administration, we are well schooled in counseling students one to one or in groups. While workshops represent a departure from more intimate counseling interactions, group-leading and teaching techniques can be adapted to this format. But media? Unfortunately, the kind of writing we learned in completing term papers, theses, and dissertations does not equip us to write catchy self-help pamphlets or to prepare engaging newspaper articles. Even so, we probably know a great deal more about writing than about designing other media, such as radio, videotape, tape-slide, and television programs. It may be advisable for student affairs divisions to work out arrangements whereby professionals interested in developing media interventions can obtain help and support from people skilled in this field.

The Cognitive Intervention Planning Model can help student development professionals systematically plan media interventions that favorably affect cognitive development. The three key considerations mentioned in regard to designing workshops also apply to media outreach education. A program is more likely to be effective in fostering cognitive development if members of the target population perceive it to be *understandable, relevant,* and *significant.* Several kinds of media seem particularly well suited to student development programming, including tape-slide shows, videotape, and print. Also, campus media facilities—newspapers and radio and television stations—can often be used inexpensively. The formulation of the problem or issue of interest (Phase 4a), the nature of the target group (Phase 4b), and the goals identified for the project (Phase 5) are likely to determine the choice of the media form used and the design of the intervention.

A number of counselors have developed tape-slide shows for use in counseling programs, including O'Neil and Van Loon (1979) and Wiley and Richardson (1983). The visual cues of this medium are helpful in getting and holding the attention of students, particularly those in the *"Sesame Street* generation" who are used to rapidly presented images. The visual mode can increase the speed and degree of completeness with which certain concepts can be learned. An advantage of tape-slide programs is that the slides can depict local situations likely to be of high interest to the audience. Also, the visual material can be easily changed as it becomes outdated.

Videotape can also be used effectively in outreach education. It is especially useful as a way of presenting vignettes to stimulate discussion or model skills. For instance, a series of male-female interactions can be used to trigger discussion of relationship issues, or contrasting counseling styles can be shown to demonstrate attentive listening skills. Cognitive skills can be modeled by overdubbing the self-talk that enters a person's mind in a difficult situation. This method can be used in illustrating coping self-talk, systematic decision making, and other cognitive skills. The videotape medium is particularly well suited to showing the subtleties of interpersonal situations and to demonstrating ongoing cognitive processes.

In considering various media for programming, counselors should not overlook printed material. As old fashioned as the written word is in the electronic age, it is still one of the most economical methods of conveying certain kinds of information. An advantage of print over some of the other media forms is that the reader has a great deal of control over its use. Students can pick up pamphlets and read them at times of their own choosing. Further, material can be perused at one's own pace. If desired, the reader can return to an article or a pamphlet again and again. The ongoing thought stimulated by well-prepared written materials can extend beyond the content actually presented. Printed items can be set aside during hectic periods and retrieved at times when careful thought is possible.

A danger of print is that students may become so inundated with required academic reading that they avoid material that appears too imposing. For this reason, written media should be kept relatively brief, uncluttered, attractively spaced, and relevant. Also, writers should avoid professional jargon and make the material as "visualizable" as possible, perhaps with graphic examples and/or accompanying cartoons or illustrations.

At Duke University a four-page pamphlet entitled *Surviving Exam Stress,* which incorporates a number of cognitive suggestions regarding stress, has been used in workshops led by peer counselors and as a stand-alone self-help aid distributed at various points on campus during the "exam crunch." An alternative that is less expensive for student services offices and perhaps less imposing for student readers than the pamphlet is to include one or two ideas on managing exam stress on a bookmark. Bookmarks are relatively restricted in the amount of information conveyed; on the other hand, they are particularly transportable, so that students can keep them in their books and glance at the ideas from time to time.

Student-run media facilities can be inexpensive and excellent resources for student development programs. Almost all universities have at least one student-run newspaper. Many have other periodicals produced by schools, departments, or offices. Student newspapers tend to be widely read by those in the university community and are therefore excellent vehicles for outreach education efforts. A series of articles on developmental themes was produced at the University of Florida (Wheaton, 1984), and articles on stress written by counseling center staff have appeared in Duke University's paper prior to exams. As another option, student services staff members might ask the editorial staff to assign a student reporter to interview knowledgeable professionals and write a feature story about a psychoeducational topic.

Many universities also have student-run radio and television stations. These units are often interested in including material directly relevant to students and may be eager for programming ideas. Since psychological topics are popular in national network magazine-format shows, topics related to students' psychological development are often of interest. The FM radio station at Duke was willing to air a four-minute segment on "Surviving Exam Stress" during exams. In addition, a feature dealing with stress was included on a magazine-format show. While radio listeners may do something else as they listen to a music program in the background, television viewers are likely to give undivided attention to a show for twenty or thirty minutes. Perhaps because television requires both visual and auditory pathways, there is less opportunity to have these senses focused on different subjects. Thus, outreach education efforts presented on television can be lengthier and perhaps more thought provoking than those presented on radio.

Counselor Training and Supervision. Educators, trainers, and supervisors are interested in cultivating certain attitudes, value structures, and thought systems in counselors-in-training; therefore, cognitive development is a goal in the training and supervision of counselors. Several thought-provoking articles have been written on the use of cognitive techniques in supervision. Wessler and Ellis (1980, 1983) describe supervisory methods used in rational-emotive psychotherapy; however, they devote little space to how RET principles can be used to help supervisees counteract irrational beliefs about themselves, their clients, their roles, and other aspects of counseling. Schmidt (1979) offers a cognitive-behavioral perspective of supervision and suggests that supervisors use cognitive restructuring in helping supervisees manage anxiety and combat self-defeating beliefs. He notes that beginning therapists often have irrational beliefs about needing to appear perfect for supervisors, fearing that terrible consequences will result if the "right" decision is not made, and thinking that they should always love doing therapy. He also advocates rational restructuring methods with cognitions that underlie supervisees' emotions of anger, boredom, guilt, and anxiety. Blocher (1983) has discussed a "cognitive development" approach to supervision. The focus of his method is on helping supervisees acquire "more complex and more comprehensive schemas for understanding human interaction." Aspects of the learning environment likely to promote this kind of cognitive development are presented, including challenge, involvement, support, and structure; however, specific aspects of desirable cognitive development are not explored. The model of supervision proposed by Loganbill, Hardy, and Delworth (1982) is compatible with a flexible cognitive approach. Issues encountered by supervisees—such as confidence in one's competence, emotional awareness, and autonomy—are identified. Levels of sophistication on these issues are viewed as ranging along a developmental continuum of stages from "stagnation" to "confusion" to "integration." This stage conceptualization is based on the cognitive development concepts of Perry (1970) and Harvey, Hunt, and Schroeder (1961). Supervisees' attitudes toward the world, themselves, and the supervisor are described for each of these stages.

While the writings cited have provided useful ideas, further thought and development of models relating the cognitive dimension to supervision would be welcomed. The Cognitive Intervention Planning Model may have promise for directing the activities of the supervisor as well as those of the counselor. The cognitive events (Phase 1) and systems (Phase 2) assessed are likely to be more theoretical than ones identified for clients. How organized, complex, and flexible is the supervisee's cognitive map of the client? The developmental level of the supervisee's maps (Phase 3) can also be assessed. For instance, are simplistic, dualistic constructs used? Are these developmental levels manifested generally in conceptualization, or in more restricted domains of certain problems or kinds of clients? At Phase 4a the supervisor constructs formulations of the supervisory problem, which usually entails how to help supervisees learn what is necessary in order to help clients with their difficulties. Supervisors and supervisees together attempt to construct a workable problem formulation by expanding their cognitive maps of the client, the client's problem, and the counselor-client interaction. In effect, the supervisor and supervisee may assess the aspects of the Cognitive Intervention Planning Model that the counselor is having difficulty implementing with the client. At Phase 4b the supervisor constructs a formulation of the supervisee's personal characteristics that might positively or negatively affect the supervisee's work with the client. For instance, it might be relevant to note whether the counselor and the client have divergent cognitive styles or whether the supervisee has constrictive or irrational beliefs, such as perfectionistic demands regarding a counselor's performance, unrealistic "should's" pertaining to client behavior, or restricted concepts of professional role. Formulations of the supervisor-supervisee interaction process are constructed at Phase 4c. Supervisors need to be aware of unproductive supervisee responses to supervisory efforts, including oppositional, resistant, or dependent behavior. At the same time, supervisors should recognize their roles in interaction patterns.

At Phase 5 outcome (5a) and process (5b) goals are identified for the supervisory interactions. Outcome goals might include increasing the complexity, organization, or flexibility of cognitive systems used in conceptualizing clients and their problems. Another possibility is adding complexity to the self and self-in-world cognitive systems and perhaps rethinking irrational beliefs associated with the counselor role. In formulating process goals, the supervisor might consider such questions as how supportive or confrontational to be with a particular supervisee. At Phase 6 the supervisory intervention is planned, taking into account the Phase-4 formulations and Phase-5 goals and using any of the methods previously reviewed for enhancing the complexity of relevant cognitive maps. Supervisors should remember the value of modeling as a method of conveying concepts and skills. The supervisory process itself may serve as a model for the supervisee of how to conduct sensitive discussions. Other ways of presenting models include role playing during the supervisory session, co-counseling, and inviting supervisees to observe audio- and videotapes of the supervisor's counseling work. At Phase 7 the intervention is implemented. At Phase 8a the supervisee's progress and reactions to supervisory methods are monitored, with feedback information returned to earlier phases in the model, particularly Phase 4. A final evaluation (Phase 8b) of the supervision should also be conducted, focusing on how much supervisees have progressed with outcome goals. As with other uses of the model, supervisor and supervisee may repeatedly recycle through a number of the phases as new client information is obtained and different stages of the supervision are entered.

Cognitive concepts can also be self-applied by the supervisor. The same kinds of irrational beliefs that beset the beginning counselor can occur with the novice supervisor—or, for that matter, with more experienced ones. Supervisors may be able to apply the Cognitive Intervention Planning Model to themselves and effectively deal with cognitions that could potentially hamper the supervisory process.

Paraprofessional Training. Many of the workshop and some of the structured group interventions that have been discussed are amenable to being conducted by trained peer counselors; however, I have not discussed cognitive applications to the training of paraprofessionals. A cognitive perspective appears to have much to offer, in light of the need for expanding narrow perspectives and teaching cognitive skills. Delworth and Moore (1974), Delworth, Sherwood, and Casaburri (1974), W. F. Brown (1977), and others have noted the potential advantages of paraprofessional programs and have provided excellent suggestions for selecting, training, and supervising paraprofessionals and administratively initiating and conducting programs.

Further consideration of the role of cognitive variables would be valuable, particularly regarding two aspects. First, cognitive concepts and the Cognitive Intervention Planning Model might help counselors decide how to influence the attitudes of paraprofessionals-in-training. The attitudes manifested by such individuals toward their roles, other students, the agency with which they are working, and the training and supervision formats are crucial to the success of the paraprofessional program. Cultivation of favorable attitudes entails development of cognitive systems that are organized, complex, and flexible. Second, rather than simply focusing on training paraprofessionals in behavioral skills, trainers can be aware of the importance of developing cognitive skills, such as assessing, planning, decision making, and conveying "cognitive maps" related to behavioral skills. The planning model provides a useful framework for this kind of skills teaching.

Consultation. Hamilton and Meade (1979) and Meade and Hamilton (1979) emphasize that consultants must take into account the systems and subsystems related to a consultation problem. Since interpersonal systems interact with individual's cognitive systems, systems-focused consultation can be enhanced by awareness of the role played by cognitive systems in influencing change. The cognitive dimension appears to be important in a number of facets of consultation identified by Kurpius and Brubaker (1976), Parsons and Meyers (1984), and other experts in the field, including gaining entry, establishing rapport and trust, teaching, and persuading. Parsons and Meyers (1984) recommend that consultants use cognitive methods for defusing "dysfunctional beliefs" stimulated by consultees or events in the consultation process.

Consultation based on a campus ecology model, which emphasizes understanding the person-environment interaction, appears to be a particularly promising way of promoting cognitive development, which is affected by the balance of challenge and support factors in the environment. Banning (1980) has described the campus ecology philosophy, and effective environmental assessment and redesign methods have been developed (Conyne, 1975; Corazzini, 1980). More careful attention to the effects of environmental factors on cognitive development and change could extend the effectiveness of ecological consultation. Blocher's (1974) discussion of the role of the environment in nurturing development provides a good start toward a more complete understanding of the influence of the university environment on cognitive development.

Cross-Cultural Counseling. Ellis (1977b) has asserted that irrational beliefs exist and influence behavior in all cultures; however, more research on this aspect is needed. It does appear that some important cognitive differences may exist across cultures. For instance, several differences found between Asian Americans and Caucasian Americans suggest divergence in important cognitive systems. Asian Americans seem to have different attitudes toward mental health and are guided by a more externally focused locus of control of reinforcement than are Caucasians (Sue and Morishima, 1982; Sue and Kirk, 1972). Different attitudes and behaviors regarding counseling and mental health services have been noted in other minority groups. Black clients evidently are more likely to terminate counseling prematurely when seen by white than by black counselors (Terrell and Terrell, 1984). Similarly, Native American college students are more likely to use a counseling center if they can be seen by a counselor of their own race (Haviland, Horswill, O'Connell, and Dynneson, 1983). Among Mexican-American students, those who are strongly committed to Mexican-American culture, rather than the Anglo-American culture, tend to express the greatest preference for a same-race counselor and are the least willing to self-disclose (Sanchez and Atkinson, 1983). Ruiz and Padilla (1977) and Szapocznik, Kurtines, and Fernandez (1980) have noted that the attitudes of Hispanics may affect their use of counseling. These attitudinal and behavioral differences imply that culturally transmitted schemas may influence the processing of information about counseling and programming services and about counseling itself.

Cross-cultural counseling can be aided if researchers can discover the problematic cognitive mediational patterns that are unique to a culture and the specific cognitive approaches that are most effective with specific cultural groups. Fukuyama and

Greenfield (1983) found that their samples of Asian-American and Caucasian students differed in degree of inventory-measured assertiveness and suggest that cultural values might influence factors on the inventory. On the other hand, Sue, Ino, and Sue (1983) did not find Asian Americans to be less assertive than Caucasian Americans. They hypothesize that nonassertiveness may be situation specific and suggest that cognitive techniques be incorporated into assertiveness training in order to facilitate the making of appropriate discriminations regarding when to be assertive.

Two recent thought-provoking articles have offered cognitive-based models for conducting cross-cultural counseling. Helms (1984) proposes an interactive model that recognizes the variability of counselor and client attitudes regarding racial issues and is based on developmental levels of racial consciousness. She acknowledges the "cognitive development" orientation of this model. Carney and Kahn (1984) have offered a cognitive-stage model for training counselors in cross-cultural counseling. Their approach, based on the cognitive development concepts of Hunt (1971) and Widick, Knefelkamp, and Parker (1975), emphasizes the construction of learning environments to foster the cognitive development necessary for effectively counseling members of other cultural groups. They propose five stages, ranging from a position in which the trainee is "ethnocentric" and has "limited knowledge of other cultural groups" to a position characterized by promotion of "cultural pluralism." They then describe the differing roles and strategies that can be used by supervisors/trainers to address needed development at each of the stages. The Cognitive Intervention Planning Model might provide both counselor and trainer/supervisor with a vehicle for understanding the organization, complexity, and flexibility of the counselor's world and self-in-world cognitive systems as they apply to cultural perspectives and for examining the roles of these systems in ongoing counseling.

Administration. Many counselors and student development professionals fulfill some administrative duties. In light of the current period of financial contraction in higher education, it is particularly important that student development departments and programs be well administered. A better understanding of the application of cognitive concepts to an administrative role is potentially quite useful. Administrators might hope to expand the cognitive development of certain thought systems of employees whom they supervise and might also want to improve employees' cognitive skills in areas such as decision making and planning. Helping employees recognize and counteract self-defeating cognitions that limit their productivity and satisfaction on the job would be an appropriate direction in "administrative counseling." Administrators might also be conscious of encouraging a work environment that contributes to the development of complex and flexible cognitive systems and fosters a healthy, self-enhancing internal dialogue. Finally, the Cognitive Intervention Planning Model might help administrators design their own interventions for overcoming their self-defeating cognitive responses to the frustrations that they will inevitably face.

Conclusion

My "concluding cognitions" are now almost exhausted. If I continued offering ideas, I am afraid that the crucial cognitive systems would prove to be lacking in development. While they might be sufficiently flexible, they would be insufficiently organized and complex to allow me to offer a lucid discussion. In closing, I hope that this book has provided some useful insights and stimulated the reader's thinking about cognition and its role in student development counseling and programming. Our cognitive processes help shape the world we envision and mold the kind of life we create for ourselves. As the glasses through which we perceive and interpret the world, they guide our groping efforts to navigate the complex demands of our life stages and circumstances. Cognition may well be our most human resource. As counselors and student development professionals, we have accepted the responsibility of attempting to improve the personal and emotional lives of others. In light of this commitment, we must do our best to understand and use this central aspect of human experience.

References

Alberti, R. E., and Emmons, M. L. *Your Perfect Right: A Guide to Assertive Living.* (2nd ed.) San Luis Obispo, Calif.: Impact, 1974.

Alpert, R., and Haber, R. N. "Anxiety in Academic Achievement Situations." *Journal of Abnormal and Social Psychology,* 1960, *61,* 207–215.

Arkowitz, H., Hinton, R., Perl, J., and Himandi, W. "Treatment Strategies for Dating Anxiety in College Men Based on Real-Life Practice." *Counseling Psychologist,* 1978, *7,* 41–46.

Aronson, E. *The Social Animal.* New York: W. H. Freeman, 1972.

Bandler, R., and Grinder, J. *The Structure of Magic: A Book About Language and Therapy.* Vol. 1. Palo Alto, Calif.: Science and Behavior Books, 1975.

Bandura, A. "Influence of Models' Reinforcement Contingencies on the Acquisition of Imitative Responses." *Journal of Personality and Social Psychology,* 1965, *1,* 589–595.

Bandura, A. *Principles of Behavior Modification.* New York: Holt, Rinehart & Winston, 1969a.

Bandura, A. "Social Learning Theory of Identification Processes." In D. A. Goslin (ed.), *Handbook of Socialization Theory and Research*. Skokie, Ill.: Rand McNally, 1969b.

Bandura, A. "Self-Efficacy: Toward a Unifying Theory of Behavior Change." *Psychological Review,* 1977a, *84,* 191–215.

Bandura, A. *Social Learning Theory.* Englewood Cliffs, N.J.: Prentice-Hall, 1977b.

Bandura, A., and Adams, N. E. "Analysis of Self-Efficacy Theory of Behavior Change." *Cognitive Therapy and Research,* 1977, *1,* 287–308.

Bandura, A., Ross, D., and Ross, S. A. "Imitation of Film-Mediated Aggressive Models." *Journal of Abnormal and Social Psychology,* 1963, *66,* 3–11.

Bandura, A., and Walters, R. H. *Social Learning and Personality Development.* New York: Holt, Rinehart & Winston, 1963.

Banning, J. H. "The Campus Ecology Manager Role." In U. Delworth, G. R. Hanson, and Associates, *Student Services: A Handbook for the Profession.* San Francisco: Jossey-Bass, 1980.

Barrow, J. C. "A Five Year Evolution of Structured Group Interventions for Shy Adolescents." *Journal of Psychiatric Treatment and Evaluation,* 1983, *5,* 209–214.

Barrow, J. C., Fulkerson, K. F., and Moore, C. "The Use of Humor as a Teaching Tool in Outreach Educational Interventions." Paper presented at annual convention of the American College Personnel Association, Cincinnati, March 1981.

Barrow, J. C., and Hayashi, J. "Shyness Clinic: A Social Development Program for Adolescents and Young Adults." *Personnel and Guidance Journal,* 1980, *59,* 58–61.

Barrow, J. C., and Hetherington, C. "Training Paraprofessionals to Lead Social-Anxiety Management Groups." *Journal of College Student Personnel,* 1981, *22,* 269–273.

Barrow, J. C., and Moore, C. A. "Group Interventions with Perfectionistic Thinking." *Personnel and Guidance Journal,* 1983, *61,* 612–615.

Barrow, J. C., and Prosen, S. S. "A Model of Stress and Counseling Interventions." *Personnel and Guidance Journal,* 1981, *60,* 5–10.

Bartsch, K., and Sandmeyer, L. *Skills in Life/Career Planning.* Monterey, Calif.: Brooks/Cole, 1979.

Baxter-Magolda, M., and Porterfield, W. D. "A New Approach to Assess Intellectual Development on the Perry Scheme." *Journal of College Student Personnel,* 1985, *26,* 343–351.

Beck, A. T. *Cognitive Therapy and the Emotional Disorders.* New York: International Universities Press, 1976.

Beck, A. T. *Depression Inventory.* Philadelphia: Center for Cognitive Therapy, 1978.

Beck, A. T., Rush, A. J., Shaw, B. F., and Emery, G. *Cognitive Therapy of Depression.* New York: Guilford Press, 1979.

Beck, A. T., and Shaw, B. F. "Cognitive Approaches to Depression." In A. Ellis and R. Grieger (eds.), *Handbook of Rational-Emotive Therapy.* New York: Springer, 1977.

Bellack, A. S. "Behavioral Assessment of Social Skills." In A. S. Bellack and M. Hersen (eds.), *Research and Practice in Social Skills Training.* New York: Plenum, 1979.

Bem, D. J. "Self-Perception Theory." In L. Berkowitz (ed.), *Advances in Experimental Social Psychology.* Vol. 6. Orlando, Fla.: Academic Press, 1972.

Benson, H. *The Relaxation Response.* New York: Morrow, 1975.

Bergin, A. E. "The Effects of Psychotherapy: Negative Results Revisited." *Journal of Counseling Psychology,* 1963, *10,* 244–255.

Berne, E. *Transactional Analysis in Psychotherapy.* New York: Grove Press, 1961.

Berscheid, E., Dion, K., Walster, E., and Walster, G. W. "Physical Attractiveness and Dating Choice: A Test of the Matching Hypothesis." *Journal of Experimental Social Psychology,* 1971, *7,* 173–189.

Blackwell, R. T., Galassi, J. P., Galassi, M. D., and Watson, T. E. "Are Cognitive Assessment Methods Equal? A Comparison of Think Aloud and Thought Listing." *Cognitive Therapy and Research,* 1985, *9,* 399–413.

Blanck, G., and Blanck, R. "Toward a Psychoanalytic Developmental Psychology." *Journal of the American Psychoanalytic Association,* 1972, *20,* 668–710.

Blocher, D. H. "Toward an Ecology of Student Development." *Personnel and Guidance Journal,* 1974, *52,* 360–365.

Blocher, D. H. "Toward a Cognitive Development Approach to Counseling Supervision." *Counseling Psychologist,* 1983, *11,* 27–34.

Bolles, R. N. *The Three Boxes of Life, and How to Get Out of Them.* Berkeley, Calif.: Ten Speed Press, 1978.

Briggs, K. C., and Myers, I. B. *Myers-Briggs Type Indicator.* Form F. Palo Alto, Calif.: Consulting Psychologists Press, 1976.

Brown, A. L. "Knowing When, Where and How to Remember: A Problem of Metacognition." In R. Glaser (ed.), *Advances in Instructional Psychology.* Hillsdale, N.J.: Erlbaum, 1977.

Brown, W. F. *Student-to-Student Counseling: An Approach to Motivating Academic Achievement.* Austin: University of Texas Press, 1977.

Burns, D. D. *Feeling Good: The New Mood Therapy.* New York: Morrow, 1980a.

Burns, D. D. "The Perfectionist's Script for Self-Defeat." *Psychology Today,* Nov. 1980b, pp. 34–52.

Butler, L., and Meichenbaum, D. "The Assessment of Interpersonal Problem-Solving Skills." In P. C. Kendall and S. D. Hollon (eds.), *Assessment Strategies for Cognitive-Behavioral Interventions.* Orlando, Fla.: Academic Press, 1981.

Carkhuff, R. R. *Helping and Human Relations: A Primer for Lay and Professional Helpers.* Vol. 1. New York: Holt, Rinehart & Winston, 1969.

Carney, C. G., and Kahn, K. B. "Building Competencies for Effective Cross-Cultural Counseling: A Developmental View." *Counseling Psychologist,* 1984, *12,* 111–119.

Carver, C. S., Peterson, L. M., Follansbee, D. J., and Scheier, M. F. "Effects of Self-Directed Attention on Performance and Persistence Among Persons High and Low in Test Anxiety." *Cognitive Therapy and Research,* 1983, *7,* 333–353.

Cattell, R. B. *Personality and Mood by Questionnaire: A Handbook of Interpretive Theory, Psychometrics, and Practical Procedures.* San Francisco: Jossey-Bass, 1973.

Cattell, R. B., Eber, W. H., and Tatsuoka, M. M. *Sixteen Person-*

ality Factor Questionnaire. Form A. Champaign, Ill.: Institute for Personality and Ability Testing, 1967.

Cautela, J. R. "Covert Negative Reinforcement." *Behavior Therapy and Experimental Psychiatry,* 1970a, *1,* 273-278.

Cautela, J. R. "Covert Reinforcement." *Behavior Therapy,* 1970b, *1,* 33-50.

Cautela, J. R. "Covert Extinction." *Behavior Therapy,* 1971, *2,* 192-200.

Chapman, L. J., and Chapman, J. P. "Genesis of Popular but Erroneous Psychodiagnostic Observations." *Journal of Abnormal Psychology,* 1967, *72,* 193-204.

Chickering, A. W. *Education and Identity.* San Francisco: Jossey-Bass, 1969.

Cochran, D. J., and Rademacher, B. G. "University Career Development Programming." *Journal of College Student Personnel,* 1978, *19,* 275-281.

Conyne, R. K. "Environmental Assessment: Mapping for Counselor Action." *Personnel and Guidance Journal,* 1975, *54,* 151-154.

Coons, F. W. "The Resolution of Adolescence in College." *Personnel and Guidance Journal,* 1970, *48,* 533-541.

Corazzini, J. G. "Environmental Redesign." In U. Delworth, G. R. Hanson, and Associates, *Student Services: A Handbook for the Profession.* San Francisco: Jossey-Bass, 1980.

Corsini, R. J. "A Medley of Current Personality Theories." In R. J. Corsini (ed.), *Current Personality Theories.* Itasca, Ill.: Peacock, 1977.

Crites, J. O. *Career Maturity Inventory.* Attitude Scale, Counseling Form B-1. Monterey, Calif.: CTB/McGraw-Hill, 1978.

Crouse, R. H., Deffenbacher, J. L., and Frost, G. A. "Desensitization for Students with Different Sources and Experiences of Test Anxiety." *Journal of College Student Personnel,* 1985, *26,* 315-318.

Crystal, J. C., and Bolles, R. N. *Where Do I Go from Here with My Life?* New York: Seabury Press, 1974.

Curran, J. P. "Correlates of Physical Attractiveness and Interpersonal Attraction in the Dating Situation." *Social Behavior and Personality,* 1973, *1,* 153-157.

Deffenbacher, J. L., and Hazaleus, S. L. "Cognitive, Emotional, and Physiological Components of Test Anxiety." *Cognitive Therapy and Research,* 1985, *9,* 169–180.

Deffenbacher, J. L., and McKinley, D. L. "Stress Management: Issues in Intervention Design." In E. M. Altmaier (ed.), *Helping Students Manage Stress.* New Directions for Student Services, no. 21. San Francisco: Jossey-Bass, 1983.

Delworth, U., and Moore, M. "Helper plus Trainer: A Two-Phase Program for the Counselor." *Personnel and Guidance Journal,* 1974, *52,* 428–433.

Delworth, U., Sherwood, G., and Casaburri, N. *Student Paraprofessionals: A Working Model for Higher Education.* Washington, D.C.: American Personnel and Guidance Association, 1974.

Denny, D. R., and Rupert, P. A. "Desensitization and Self-Control in the Treatment of Test Anxiety." *Journal of Counseling Psychology,* 1977, *24,* 272–280.

Dew, K. M. H., Galassi, J. P., and Galassi, M. D. "Mathematics Anxiety: Some Basic Issues." *Journal of Counseling Psychology,* 1983, *30,* 443–446.

Dinkmeyer, D. C., and Muro, J. J. *Group Counseling: Theory and Practice.* Itasca, Ill.: Peacock, 1979.

Dowd, E. T., and Pety, J. "The Effect of Counselor Predicate Matching on Perceived Social Influence and Client Satisfaction." *Journal of Counseling Psychology,* 1982, *29,* 206–209.

Drum, D. J. "Implementing Theme-Focused Prevention: Challenge for the 1980s." *Personnel and Guidance Journal,* 1984, *62,* 509–514.

Drum, D. J., and Figler, H. *Outreach in Counseling: Applying the Growth and Prevention Model in Schools and Colleges.* Cranston, R.I.: Carroll Press, 1973.

Drum, D. J., and Knott, J. E. *Structured Groups for Facilitating Development: Acquiring Life Skills, Resolving Life Themes, and Making Life Transitions.* New York: Human Sciences Press, 1977.

Dusay, J. M., and Dusay, K. M. "Transactional Analysis." In R. J. Corsini (ed.), *Current Psychotherapies.* (2nd ed.) Itasca, Ill.: Peacock, 1979.

D'Zurilla, T., and Goldfried, M. "Problem Solving and Behavior Modification." *Journal of Abnormal Psychology,* 1971, *78,* 107–126.

Ellickson, J. L. "Representational Systems and Eye Movements in an Interview." *Journal of Counseling Psychology,* 1983, *30,* 339–345.

Ellis, A. *Reason and Emotion in Psychotherapy.* Secaucus, N.J.: Lyle Stuart, 1962.

Ellis, A. "The Basic Clinical Theory of Rational-Emotive Therapy." In A. Ellis and R. Grieger (eds.), *Handbook of Rational-Emotive Therapy.* New York: Springer, 1977a.

Ellis, A. "Research Data Supporting the Clinical and Personality Hypotheses of RET and Other Cognitive-Behavior Therapies." In A. Ellis and R. Grieger (eds.), *Handbook of Rational-Emotive Therapy.* New York: Springer, 1977b.

Ellis, A. "Rational-Emotive Therapy." In R. J. Corsini (ed.), *Current Psychotherapies.* (2nd ed.) Itasca, Ill.: Peacock, 1979.

Ellis, A. "New Developments in Rational-Emotive Therapy." Paper presented at annual convention of the American Personnel and Guidance Association, Detroit, March 1982.

Ellis, A., and Harper, R. A. *A New Guide to Rational Living.* North Hollywood, Calif.: Wilshire, 1975.

Erikson, E. H. *Identity and the Life Cycle: Psychological Issues.* New York: International Universities Press, 1959.

Erikson, E. H. *Identity, Youth and Crisis.* New York: Norton, 1968.

Erwin, T. D. "The Scale of Intellectual Development: Measuring Perry's Scheme." *Journal of College Student Personnel,* 1983, *24,* 6–12.

Fennema, E., and Sherman, J. "Fennema-Sherman Mathematics Attitudes Scales." *Journal Supplement Abstract Service Catalog of Selected Documents in Psychology,* 1976, *6,* 31 (Ms. no. 1225).

Festinger, L. *A Theory of Cognitive Dissonance.* Stanford, Calif.: Stanford University Press, 1957.

Figler, H. E. *A Career Workbook for Liberal Arts Students.* Cranston, R.I.: Carroll Press, 1975.

Fisch, R., Weakland, J. H., and Segal, L. *The Tactics of Change: Doing Therapy Briefly.* San Francisco: Jossey-Bass, 1982.

Fitts, W. H. *Tennessee Self-Concept Scale.* Los Angeles: Western Psychological Services, 1965.

Frank, J. *Persuasion and Healing.* Baltimore: Johns Hopkins University Press, 1961.

Friedman, M., and Rosenman, R. *Type A Behavior and Your Heart.* New York: Knopf, 1974.

Fromme, D. K., and Daniell, J. "Neurolinguistic Programming Examined: Imagery, Sensory Mode, and Communication." *Journal of Counseling Psychology,* 1984, *31,* 387–390.

Fukuyama, M. A., and Greenfield, T. K. "Dimensions of Assertiveness in an Asian-American Student Population." *Journal of Counseling Psychology,* 1983, *30,* 429–432.

Galassi, J. P., DeLo, J. S., Galassi, M. D., and Bastien, S. "The College Self-Expression Scale: A Measure of Assertiveness." *Behavior Therapy,* 1974, *5,* 165–171.

Galassi, J. P., and Galassi, M. D. "Modification of Heterosocial Skills Deficits." In A. S. Bellack and M. Hersen (eds.), *Research and Practice in Social Skills Training.* New York: Plenum, 1979.

Galassi, J. P., Galassi, M. D., and Litz, M. C. "Assertive Training in Groups Using Video Feedback." *Journal of Counseling Psychology,* 1974, *21,* 390–394.

Galassi, J. P., Kostka, M. P., and Galassi, M. D. "Assertive Training: A One Year Follow-Up." *Journal of Counseling Psychology,* 1975, *22,* 451–452.

Galassi, M. D., and Galassi, J. P. *Assert Yourself: How to Be Your Own Person.* New York: Human Sciences Press, 1977.

Gambrill, E. D., and Richey, C. A. "An Assertion Inventory for Use in Assessment and Research." *Behavior Therapy,* 1975, *6,* 550–561.

Garfield, S. L., and Bergin, A. E. (eds.). *Handbook of Psychotherapy and Behavior Change.* (2nd ed.) New York: Wiley, 1978.

Gilligan, C. *In a Different Voice: Psychological Theory and Women's Development.* Cambridge, Mass.: Harvard University Press, 1982.

Glasgow, R. E., and Arkowitz, H. "The Behavioral Assessment of Male and Female Social Competence in Dyadic Heterosexual Interactions." *Behavior Therapy,* 1975, *6,* 488–498.

Glass, C. R., Gottman, J. M., and Shmurak, S. H. "Response Acquisition and Cognitive Self-Statement Modification Approaches to Dating Skills Training." *Journal of Counseling Psychology,* 1976, *23,* 520–526.

Glass, C. R., and Merluzzi, T. V. "Approaches to the Cognitive Assessment of Social Anxiety." Paper presented at annual meeting of the Association for the Advancement of Behavior Therapy, Chicago, Nov. 1978.

Goldfried, M. "Systematic Desensitization as Training in Self-Control." *Journal of Consulting and Clinical Psychology,* 1971, *37,* 228–234.

Goldfried, M., and Davison, G. *Clinical Behavior Therapy.* New York: Holt, Rinehart & Winston, 1976.

Goldfried, M., Decenteceo, E., and Weinberg, L. "Systematic Rational Restructuring as a Self-Control Technique." *Behavior Therapy,* 1974, *5,* 247–254.

Goldfried, M., and Goldfried, A. "Cognitive Change Methods." In F. Kanfer and A. Goldstein (eds.), *Helping People Change.* Elmsford, N.Y.: Pergamon Press, 1975.

Goldfried, M., and Goldfried, A. "Importance of Hierarchy Content in the Self-Control of Anxiety." *Journal of Consulting and Clinical Psychology,* 1977, *45,* 124–134.

Goldfried, M., and Robins, C. "On the Facilitation of Self-Efficacy." *Cognitive Therapy and Research,* 1982, *6,* 361–379.

Goldfried, M., and Trier, C. "Effectiveness of Relaxation as an Active Coping Skill." *Journal of Abnormal Psychology,* 1974, *83,* 348–355.

Goodyear, R. K., and Shaw, M. C. "Introduction to the Second Special Issue on Primary Prevention." *Personnel and Guidance Journal,* 1984, *62,* 507–508.

Gottfredson, G. D., Holland, J. L., and Ogawa, D. K. *Dictionary of Holland Occupational Codes.* Palo Alto, Calif.: Consulting Psychologists Press, 1982.

Gottfredson, L. S. "Circumscription and Compromise: A Developmental Theory of Occupational Aspirations." *Journal of Counseling Psychology*, 1981, *28*, 545–579.

Gough, H. G. *California Psychological Inventory*. Palo Alto, Calif.: Consulting Psychologists Press, 1956.

Grinder, J., and Bandler, R. *The Structure of Magic*. Vol. 2. Palo Alto, Calif.: Science and Behavior Books, 1976.

Haley, J. *Strategies of Psychotherapy*. New York: Grune & Stratton, 1963.

Haley, J. *Uncommon Therapy: The Psychiatric Techniques of Milton H. Erikson, M.D.* New York: Norton, 1973.

Haley, J. *Problem-Solving Therapy: New Strategies for Effective Family Therapy*. San Francisco: Jossey-Bass, 1976.

Hamachek, D. D. "Psychodynamics of Normal and Neurotic Perfectionism." *Psychology: A Journal of Human Behavior*, 1978, *15*, 27–33.

Hamachek, D. E. "The Self's Development and Ego Growth: Conceptual Analysis and Implications for Counselors." *Journal of Counseling and Development*, 1985, *64*, 136–142.

Hamilton, M. K., and Meade, C. J. "Mediated Services: Making the Whole More Than the Sum of Its Parts." In M. K. Hamilton and C. J. Meade (eds.), *Consulting on Campus*. New Directions for Student Services, no. 5. San Francisco: Jossey-Bass, 1979.

Hammer, A. L. "Matching Perceptual Predicates: Effect on Perceived Empathy in a Counseling Analogue." *Journal of Counseling Psychology*, 1983, *30*, 172–179.

Hansen, J. C., Warner, R. W., and Smith, E. M. *Group Counseling: Theory and Process*. Skokie, Ill.: Rand McNally, 1976.

Harren, V. A. "The Vocational Decision Making Process Among College Males." *Journal of Counseling Psychology*, 1966, *13*, 271–277.

Harvey, O. J., Hunt, D. E., and Schroeder, H. M. *Conceptual Systems and Personality Organization*. New York: Wiley, 1961.

Haviland, M. G., Horswill, R. K., O'Connell, J. J., and Dynneson, V. V. "Native American College Students' Preference for Counselor Race and Sex and the Likelihood of Their Use of a Counseling Center." *Journal of Counseling Psychology*, 1983, *30*, 267–270.

Heimberg, R. G., Montgomery, D., Madsen, C. H., and Heimberg, J. S. "Assertion Training: A Review of the Literature." *Behavior Therapy*, 1977, *8*, 953–971.

Helms, J. E. "Toward a Theoretical Explanation of the Effects of Race on Counseling: A Black and White Model." *Counseling Psychologist*, 1984, *12*, 153–165.

Heppner, P. P., and Anderson, W. P. "The Relationship Between Problem-Solving Self-Appraisal and Psychological Adjustment." *Cognitive Therapy and Research*, 1985, *9*, 415–427.

Heppner, P. P., and Dixon, D. N. "Effects of Client Perceived Need and Counselor Role on Clients' Behaviors." *Journal of Counseling Psychology*, 1978, *25*, 514–519.

Heppner, P. P., and Dixon, D. N. "A Review of the Interpersonal Influence Process in Counseling." *Personnel and Guidance Journal*, 1981, *59*, 542–550.

Heppner, P. P., Neal, G. W., and Larson, L. L. "Problem-Solving Training as Prevention with College Students." *Personnel and Guidance Journal*, 1984, *62*, 514–519.

Heppner, P. P., Reeder, B. L., and Larson, L. L. "Cognitive Variables Associated with Personal Problem Solving Appraisal: Implications for Counselors." *Journal of Counseling Psychology*, 1983, *30*, 537–545.

Hersen, M., and Bellack, A. S. "Assessment of Social Skills." In A. R. Ciminero, K. S. Calhoun, and H. E. Adams (eds.), *Handbook for Behavioral Assessment*. New York: Wiley, 1977.

Holland, J. L., Daiger, D. C., and Power, P. G. *My Vocational Situation*. Palo Alto, Calif.: Consulting Psychologists Press, 1980.

Holland, J. L., and Gottfredson, G. D. "Using a Typology of Persons and Environments to Explain Careers: Some Extensions and Clarifications." *The Counseling Psychologist*, 1976, *6*, 20–29.

Holmes, T. H., and Rahe, R. H. "The Social Readjustment Rating Scale." *Journal of Psychosomatic Research*, 1967, *11*, 213–218.

Holroyd, K. A. "Cognition and Desensitization in the Group Treatment of Test Anxiety." *Journal of Consulting and Clinical Psychology*, 1976, *44*, 991–1001.

Horney, K. *New Ways in Psychoanalysis.* New York: Norton, 1939.

Hunt, D. E. "A Conceptual Systems Change Model and Its Application to Education." In O. J. Harvey (ed.), *Experience, Structure and Adaptability.* New York: Springer, 1966.

Hunt, D. E. *Matching Models in Education: The Coordination of Teaching Methods with Student Characteristics.* Toronto: Institute for Studies in Education, 1971.

Ivey, A. *Microcounseling.* Springfield, Ill.: Thomas, 1971.

Jacobson, E. *Progressive Relaxation.* Chicago: University of Chicago Press, 1938.

Janis, I. L. (ed.). *Counseling on Personal Decisions: Theory and Research on Short-Term Helping Relationships.* New Haven, Conn.: Yale University Press, 1982.

Janis, I. L., and Mann, L. *Decision Making: A Psychological Analysis of Conflict, Choice and Commitment.* New York: Free Press, 1977.

Johnson, D. W., and Johnson, F. P. *Joining Together: Group Theory and Group Skills.* Englewood Cliffs, N.J.: Prentice-Hall, 1975.

Jones, E. E., and Davis, K. E. "From Acts to Dispositions: The Attribution Process in Person Perception." In L. Berkowitz (ed.), *Advances in Experimental Social Psychology.* Vol. 2. Orlando, Fla.: Academic Press, 1965.

Jones, E. E., and Nisbett, R. E. "The Actor and the Observer: Divergent Perceptions of the Causes of Behavior." In E. E. Jones and others (eds.), *Attribution: Perceiving the Causes of Behavior.* Morristown, N.J.: Silver Burdett, 1972.

Jones, L. K., and Chenery, M. F. "Multiple Subtypes Among Vocationally Undecided College Students: A Model and Assessment Instrument." *Journal of Counseling Psychology,* 1980, *27,* 469–477.

Kaul, T. J., and Schmidt, L. D. "Dimensions of Interviewer Trustworthiness." *Journal of Counseling Psychology,* 1971, *18,* 542–548.

Kazdin, A. "Covert Modeling, Model Similarity, and Reduction of Avoidance Behavior." *Behavior Therapy,* 1974, *5,* 325–340.

Keller, K. E., Biggs, D. A., and Gysbers, N. C. "Career Counseling from a Cognitive Perspective." *Personnel and Guidance Journal,* 1982, *60,* 367-371.

Kelley, H. H. "The Processes of Causal Attribution." *American Psychologist,* 1973, *28,* 107-128.

Kelly, G. A. *The Psychology of Personal Constructs.* (2 vols.) New York: Norton, 1955.

Kernberg, O. F. *Object-Relations Theory and Clinical Psychoanalysis.* New York: Jason Aronson, 1976.

Kerr, B. A., and others. "Overcoming Opposition and Resistance: Differential Functions of Expertness and Attractiveness in Career Counseling." *Journal of Counseling Psychology,* 1983, *30,* 323-331.

King, P. M. "William Perry's Theory of Intellectual and Ethical Development." In L. Knefelkamp, C. Widick, and C. A. Parker (eds.), *Applying New Developmental Findings.* New Directions for Student Services, no. 4. San Francisco: Jossey-Bass, 1978.

Kirsch, I., and Henry, D. "Extinction Versus Credibility in the Desensitization of Speech Anxiety." *Journal of Consulting and Clinical Psychology,* 1977, *45,* 1052-1059.

Kitchener, K., and King, P. "Reflective Judgment: Concepts of Justification and Their Relationship to Age and Education." *Journal of Applied Developmental Psychology,* 1981, *2,* 89-116.

Knefelkamp, L. L., and Slepitza, R. A. "A Cognitive Developmental Model of Career Development and Adaptation of the Perry Scheme." *Counseling Psychologist,* 1976, *6,* 53-58.

Kohlberg, L. "Stages of Moral Development." In C. M. Beck, B. S. Crittenden, and E. V. Sullivan (eds.), *Moral Education.* Toronto: University of Toronto Press, 1971.

Kornhaber, R., and Schroeder, H. "Importance of Model Similarity on Extinction of Avoidance Behavior in Children." *Journal of Consulting and Clinical Psychology,* 1975, *43,* 601-607.

Kurpius, D. J., and Brubaker, J. C. *Psychoeducational Consultation: Definition, Functions, Preparation.* Bloomington: H. L. Smith Center for Research in Education, Indiana University, 1976.

Lakin, M. "Some Ethical Issues in Sensitivity Training." *American Psychologist,* 1969, *24,* 923-928.

Lakin, M. "Group Sensitivity Training and Encounter: Uses and Abuses of a Method." *Counseling Psychologist,* 1970, *2,* 66-70.

Lakin, M. *Interpersonal Encounter: Theory and Practice in Sensitivity Training.* New York: McGraw-Hill, 1972.

Lange, A. J., and Jakubowski, P. *Responsible Assertive Behavior: Cognitive/Behavioral Procedures for Trainers.* Champaign, Ill.: Research Press, 1976.

Lazarus, A. A. *Behavior Therapy and Beyond.* New York: McGraw-Hill, 1971.

Lazarus, A. A. *Multi-Modal Behavior Therapy.* New York: Springer, 1976.

Lazarus, A. A. "Distorting the Point: A Reply to Wolpe." *American Psychologist,* 1983, *38,* 1028.

Lazarus, R. S. "Thoughts on the Relations Between Emotion and Cognition." *American Psychologist,* 1982, *37,* 1019-1024.

Lazarus, R. S. "On the Primacy of Cognition." *American Psychologist,* 1984, *39,* 124-129.

Lee, D. Y., Uhlemann, M. R., and Haase, R. F. "Counselor Verbal and Nonverbal Responses and Perceived Expertness, Trustworthiness, and Attractiveness." *Journal of Counseling Psychology,* 1985, *32,* 181-187.

Lerner, M. J. "Evaluation of Performance as a Function of Performer's Reward and Attractiveness." *Journal of Personality and Social Psychology,* 1965, *1,* 355-360.

Lewis, R. A., and Gilhousen, M. R. "Myths of Career Development: A Cognitive Approach to Vocational Counseling." *Personnel and Guidance Journal,* 1981, *59,* 296-299.

Lieberman, M. A., Yalom, I. D., and Miles, M. B. *Encounter Groups: First Facts.* New York: Basic Books, 1973.

Liebert, R. M., and Fernandez, L. E. "Effects of Vicarious Consequences on Imitative Performance." *Child Development,* 1970, *41,* 847-852.

Liebert, R. M., and Morris, L. W. "Cognitive and Emotional Components of Test Anxiety: A Distinction and Some Initial Data." *Psychological Reports,* 1967, *20,* 975-978.

Liebert, R. M., and Spiegler, M. D. *Personality: Strategies and Issues.* (3rd ed.) Homewood, Ill.: Dorsey Press, 1978.

Linehan, M. M., and Egan, K. J. "Assertion Training for Women." In A. S. Bellack and M. Hersen (eds.), *Research and Practice in Social Skills Training.* New York: Plenum, 1979.

Little, S., and Jackson, B. "The Treatment of Test Anxiety Through Attentional and Relaxation Training." *Psychotherapy: Theory, Research and Practice,* 1974, *11,* 175-178.

Loganbill, C., Hardy, E., and Delworth, U. "Supervision: A Conceptual Model." *Counseling Psychologist,* 1982, *10,* 3-42.

Lowenstein, T. J. "Biofeedback Relaxation Training via Radio." *Journal of College Student Personnel,* 1978, *19,* 373.

Luria, A. *The Role of Speech in the Regulation of Normal and Abnormal Behaviors.* New York: Liveright, 1961.

Luria, A. "Speech and Formation of Mental Processes." In M. Cole and I. Maltzman (eds.), *A Handbook of Contemporary Soviet Psychology.* New York: Basic Books, 1969.

McArthur, L. A. "The How and What of Why: Some Determinants and Consequences of Causal Attribution." *Journal of Personality and Social Psychology,* 1972, *22,* 171-193.

McCroskey, J. C. "Measures of Communication-Bound Anxiety." *Speech Monographs,* 1970, *37,* 269-277.

McFall, R. M., and Lillesand, D. B. "Behavior Rehearsal with Modeling and Coaching in Assertion Training." *Journal of Abnormal Psychology,* 1971, *77,* 313-323.

McFall, R. M., and Twentyman, C. T. "Four Experiments on the Relative Contributions of Rehearsal, Modeling, and Coaching on Assertion Training." *Journal of Abnormal Psychology,* 1973, *81,* 199-218.

Mager, R. F. *Preparing Instructional Objectives.* Belmont, Calif.: Fearon-Pitman, 1962.

Mahoney, M. J. *Cognition and Behavior Modification.* Cambridge, Mass.: Ballinger, 1974.

Mahoney, M. J. "Personal Science: A Cognitive Learning Therapy." In A. Ellis and R. Grieger (eds.), *Handbook of Rational-Emotive Therapy.* New York: Springer, 1977.

Martin, J. "The Cognitive Mediational Paradigm for Research on Counseling." *Journal of Counseling Psychology,* 1984, *31,* 558-571.

Martinson, W. D., and Zerface, J. P. "Comparison of Individual Counseling and a Social Program with Nondaters." *Journal of Counseling Psychology,* 1970, *17,* 36–40.

Marx, M. B., Garrity, T. F., and Bowers, F. R. "The Influence of Recent Life Experience on the Health of College Freshmen." *Journal of Psychosomatic Research,* 1975, *19,* 87-98.

Maultsby, M. C. "Rational-Emotive Imagery." In A. Ellis and R. Grieger (eds.), *Handbook of Rational-Emotive Therapy.* New York: Springer, 1977.

Meade, C. J., and Hamilton, M. K. "Campus Consultation: Toward a Coherent Conceptualization." In M. K. Hamilton and C. J. Meade (eds.), *Consulting on Campus.* New Directions for Student Services, no. 5. San Francisco: Jossey-Bass, 1979.

Meador, B. D., and Rogers, C. R. "Person-Centered Therapy." In R. J. Corsini (ed.), *Current Psychotherapies.* (2nd ed.) Itasca, Ill.: Peacock, 1979.

Meichenbaum, D. "Examination of Model Characteristics in Reducing Avoidance Behavior." *Journal of Personality and Social Psychology,* 1971, *17,* 298–307.

Meichenbaum, D. "Cognitive Modification of Test Anxious College Students." *Journal of Consulting and Clinical Psychology,* 1972, *39,* 370–380.

Meichenbaum, D. "A Self-Instructional Approach to Stress Management: A Proposal for Stress Inoculation Training." In C. D. Spielberger and I. G. Sarason (eds.), *Stress and Anxiety.* Vol. 1. New York: Halsted, 1975.

Meichenbaum, D. "Toward a Cognitive Theory of Self-Control." In G. Schwartz and D. Shapiro (eds.), *Consciousness and Self-Regulation.* Vol. 1. New York: Plenum, 1976.

Meichenbaum, D. *Cognitive-Behavior Modification: An Integrative Approach.* New York: Plenum, 1977.

Meichenbaum, D., and Asarnow, J. "Cognitive-Behavioral Modification and Metacognitive Development: Implications for the Classroom." In P. C. Kendall and S. D. Hollon (eds.), *Cognitive-Behavioral Interventions: Theory, Research, and Procedures.* Orlando, Fla.: Academic Press, 1979.

Meichenbaum, D., and Cameron, R. "Training Schizophrenics to Talk to Themselves: A Means of Developing Attentional Controls." *Behavior Therapy,* 1973, *4,* 515–534.

Meichenbaum, D., and Cameron, R. "The Clinical Potential of Modifying What Clients Say to Themselves." *Psychotherapy: Theory, Research and Practice,* 1974, *11,* 103–117.

Meichenbaum, D., Gilmore, B., and Fedoravicius, A. "Group Insight vs. Group Desensitization in Treating Speech Anxiety." *Journal of Consulting and Clinical Psychology,* 1971, *36,* 410–421.

Meichenbaum, D., and Goodman, J. "Training Impulsive Children to Talk to Themselves: A Means of Developing Self-Control." *Journal of Abnormal Psychology,* 1971, *77,* 115–126.

Meichenbaum, D., and Turk, D. "The Cognitive-Behavioral Management of Anxiety, Anger and Pain." In P. Davidson (ed.), *The Behavioral Management of Anxiety, Depression and Pain.* New York: Brunner/Mazel, 1976.

Miller, E. K. "The Use of Media in Career Information Dispersal." *Journal of College Student Personnel,* 1979, *20,* 273.

Mischel, W. *Personality and Assessment.* New York: Wiley, 1968.

Morrill, W. H., and Hurst, J. C. "A Preventive and Developmental Role for the College Counselor." *Counseling Psychologist,* 1971, *2,* 90–95.

Morrill, W. H., Oetting, E. R., and Hurst, J. C. "Dimensions of Counselor Functioning." *Personnel and Guidance Journal,* 1974, *54,* 354–359.

Morris, L. W., and Liebert, R. M. "Effects of Anxiety on Timed and Untimed Intelligence Tests: Another Look." *Journal of Consulting and Clinical Psychology,* 1969, *33,* 240–244.

Mosak, H. H. "Adlerian Psychotherapy." In R. J. Corsini (ed.), *Current Psychotherapies.* (2nd ed.) Itasca, Ill.: Peacock, 1979.

Munoz, R. F., and Lewinsohn, P. M. *The Personal Beliefs Inventory.* Form M-1. Technical Memorandum. Eugene: University of Oregon, 1975.

Oetting, E. R., and Deffenbacher, J. L. *The Test Anxiety Profile (TAP) Manual.* Fort Collins, Colo.: Rocky Mountain Behavioral Sciences Institute, 1980.

Ohlsen, M. M. *Group Counseling.* New York: Holt, Rinehart & Winston, 1970.

O'Neil, J. M., and Van Loon, K. C. "Career Planning Sensitization: Slide Tape Show During Freshman Orientation." *Journal of College Student Personnel,* 1979, *20,* 85–86.

Oppenheimer, B. T. "Short-Term Small Group Intervention for College Freshmen." *Journal of Counseling Psychology,* 1984, *31,* 45–53.

Osborn, A. F. *Applied Imagination: Principles and Procedures of Creative Problem-Solving.* (3rd ed.) New York: Scribner's, 1963.

Osipow, S. H., and others. *Career Decision.* Columbus, Ohio: Marathon Consulting and Press, 1976.

Paritzky, R. S., and Magoon, T. M. "Goal Attainment Scaling Models for Assessing Group Counseling." *Personnel and Guidance Journal,* 1982, *60,* 381–384.

Parnes, S. J. *Creative Behavior Guidebook.* New York: Scribner's, 1967.

Parsons, R. D., and Meyers, J. *Developing Consultation Skills: A Guide to Training, Development, and Assessment for Human Services Professionals.* San Francisco: Jossey-Bass, 1984.

Paul, G. *Insight vs. Desensitization in Psychotherapy.* Stanford, Calif.: Stanford University Press, 1966.

Perls, F. S. *Gestalt Therapy Verbatim.* Moab, Utah: Real People Press, 1969.

Perry, W., Jr. *Forms of Intellectual and Ethical Development in the College Years: A Scheme.* New York: Holt, Rinehart & Winston, 1970.

Pfeiffer, J. W., and Jones, J. E. *A Handbook of Structured Experiences for Human Relations Training.* (7 vols.) San Diego: University Associates, 1974–1979.

Piaget, J. *The Language and Thought of the Child.* New York: New American Library, 1955.

Piaget, J. "Cognitive Development in Children." In R. Ripple and V. Rockcastle (eds.), *Piaget Rediscovered: A Report on Cognitive Studies in Curriculum Development.* Ithaca, N.Y.: School of Education, Cornell University, 1964.

Prince, J. S., Miller, T. K., and Winston, R. *Student Develop-*

mental Task Inventory. Athens, Ga.: Student Development Associates, 1974.

Rachman, S. "Systematic Desensitization." *Psychological Bulletin,* 1967, *67,* 93–103.

Rathus, S. A. "A 30 Item Schedule for Assessing Assertive Behavior." *Behavior Therapy,* 1973, *4,* 398–406.

Richardson, F. C., and Tasto, D. L. "Development and Factor Analysis of a Social Anxiety Inventory." *Behavior Therapy,* 1976, *7,* 453–462.

Rogers, C. R. *Client-Centered Therapy.* Boston: Houghton Mifflin, 1951.

Rogers, C. R. "The Necessary and Sufficient Conditions of Therapeutic Personality Change." *Journal of Consulting Psychology,* 1957, *21,* 95–103.

Rogers, C. R. "A Theory of Therapy, Personality, and Interpersonal Relationships, as Developed in the Client-Centered Framework." In S. Koch (ed.), *Psychology: A Study of a Science.* Vol. 3: *Formulations of the Person and the Social Context.* New York: McGraw-Hill, 1959.

Rosen, S. (ed.). *My Voice Will Go with You: The Teaching Tales of Milton H. Erickson, M.D.* New York: Norton, 1982.

Rosenbaum, M. E., and Tucker, I. F. "Competence of the Model and the Learning of Imitation and Nonimitation." *Journal of Experimental Psychology,* 1962, *63,* 183–190.

Rotter, J. B. *Social Learning and Clinical Psychology.* Englewood Cliffs, N.J.: Prentice-Hall, 1954.

Rotter, J. B. "Generalized Expectancies for Internal Versus External Control of Reinforcement." *Psychological Monographs,* 1966, *80* (Whole no. 609).

Ruiz, R. H., and Padilla, A. M. "Counseling Latinos." *Personnel and Guidance Journal,* 1977, *55,* 401–408.

Rush, A. J., Beck, A. T., Kovacs, M., and Hollon, S. "Comparative Efficacy of Cognitive Therapy and Imipramine in the Treatment of Depressed Outpatients." *Cognitive Therapy and Research,* 1977, *1,* 17–37.

Salter, A. *Conditioned Reflex Therapy.* Toms River, N.J.: Capricorn Books, 1949.

Sanchez, A. R., and Atkinson, D. R. "Mexican-American Cultural Commitment, Preference for Counselor Ethnicity, and Willingness to Use Counseling." *Journal of Counseling Psychology,* 1983, *30,* 215-220.

Sanford, N. *The American College.* New York: Wiley, 1962.

Sanford, N. *Self and Society: Social Change and Individual Development.* New York: Lieber-Atherton, 1966.

Sarason, I. G. "Experimental Approaches to Test Anxiety: Attention and the Uses of Information." In C. D. Spielberger (ed.), *Anxiety: Current Trends in Theory and Research.* Vol. 2. Orlando, Fla.: Academic Press, 1972.

Satir, V. *Peoplemaking.* Palo Alto, Calif.: Science and Behavior Books, 1972.

Schachter, S. "The Interaction of Cognitive and Physiological Determinants of Emotional State." In C. D. Spielberger (ed.), *Anxiety and Behavior.* Orlando, Fla.: Academic Press, 1966.

Schachter, S., and Singer, J. "Cognitive, Social and Physiological Determinants of Emotional State." *Psychological Review,* 1962, *65,* 379-399.

Schmidt, J. P. "Psychotherapy Supervision: A Cognitive-Behavioral Model." *Professional Psychology,* 1979, *10,* 278-284.

Schwartz, G. E. "Biofeedback and the Self-Management of Disregulation Disorders." In R. Stuart (ed.), *Behavioral Self-Management: Strategies, Techniques and Outcomes.* New York: Brunner/Mazel, 1977.

Sechrest, L. "Personal Constructs Theory." In R. J. Corsini (ed.), *Current Personality Theories.* Itasca, Ill.: Peacock, 1977.

Shaw, B. F., and Beck, A. T. "The Treatment of Depression with Cognitive Therapy." In A. Ellis and R. Grieger (eds.), *Handbook of Rational-Emotive Therapy.* New York: Springer, 1977.

Simkin, J. S. "Gestalt Therapy." In R. J. Corsini (ed.), *Current Psychotherapies.* (2nd ed.) Itasca, Ill.: Peacock, 1979.

Skinner, B. F. *Science and Human Behavior.* New York: Macmillan, 1953.

Smith, D. "Trends in Counseling and Psychotherapy." *American Psychologist,* 1982, *37,* 802-809.

Smith, M. J. *When I Say No, I Feel Guilty.* New York: Bantam Books, 1975.

Smith, R. E., Keating, J. P., Hester, R. K., and Mitchell, H. E. "Role and Justice Considerations in the Attribution of Responsibility to a Rape Victim." *Journal of Research in Personality*, 1976, *10*, 346–357.

Spielberger, C. D. *The Test Anxiety Inventory*. Palo Alto, Calif.: Consulting Psychologists Press, 1977.

Spielberger, C. D., Gorsuch, R. L., and Lushene, R. E. *The State-Trait Anxiety Inventory (STAI) Test Manual for Form X*. Palo Alto, Calif.: Consulting Psychologists Press, 1970.

Stevens, J. O. *Awareness: Exploring, Experimenting, Experiencing*. Moab, Utah: Real People Press, 1971.

Stone, G. L. "Effects of Experience on Supervisor Planning." *Journal of Counseling Psychology*, 1980, *27*, 84–88.

Storms, M. D. "Videotape and the Attribution Process: Reversing Actors' and Observers' Points of View." *Journal of Personality and Social Psychology*, 1973, *27*, 165–175.

Strong, E. K., and Campbell, D. P. *Strong-Campbell Interest Inventory*. Form T325. Stanford, Calif.: Stanford University Press, 1981.

Strong, S. "Counseling: An Interpersonal Influence Process." *Journal of Counseling Psychology*, 1968, *15*, 215–224.

Strong, S., and Claiborn, C. *Change Through Interaction: Social Psychological Approach to Counseling and Psychotherapy*. New York: Wiley-Interscience, 1982.

Strong, S., and Matross, R. N. "Change Processes in Counseling and Psychotherapy." *Journal of Counseling Psychology*, 1973, *20*, 25–37.

Strupp, H. H., and Bergin, A. E. "Some Empirical and Conceptual Bases for Coordinated Research in Psychotherapy." *International Journal of Psychiatry*, 1969, *7*, 18–90.

Sue, D., Ino, S., and Sue, D. M. "Nonassertiveness of Asian Americans: An Inaccurate Assumption?" *Journal of Counseling Psychology*, 1983, *30*, 581–588.

Sue, D. W., and Kirk, B. A. "Psychological Characteristics of Chinese-American College Students." *Journal of Counseling Psychology*, 1972, *19*, 471–478.

Sue, S., and Morishima, J. K. *The Mental Health of Asian Americans: Contemporary Issues in Identifying and Treating Mental Problems*. San Francisco: Jossey-Bass, 1982.

Suinn, R. M. "The STABS, a Measure of Test Anxiety for Behavior Therapy: Normative Data." *Behaviour Research and Therapy,* 1969, *7,* 335–339.

Suinn, R. M. *Mathematics Anxiety Rating Scale.* Fort Collins, Colo.: Rocky Mountain Behavioral Science Institute, 1972.

Super, D. E. *The Psychology of Careers: An Introduction to Vocational Development.* New York: Harper & Row, 1957.

Super, D. E., and others. *Career Development Inventory.* College and University Form. Palo Alto, Calif.: Consulting Psychologists Press, 1981.

Swartz, H., and Leitch, C. J. "Differences in Mean Blood Pressure by Age, Sex, Ethnic Origin, Obesity, and Family Tendency." *Journal of School Health,* 1975, *45,* 76–82.

Szapocznik, J., Kurtines, W. M., and Fernandez, T. "Bicultural Involvement and Adjustment in Hispanic-American Youths." *International Journal of Intercultural Relations,* 1980, *4,* 353–365.

Talley, J. E., Barrow, J. C., Fulkerson, K. F., and Moore, C. A. "Conducting a Needs Assessment of University Psychological Services: A Comparison of Telephone and Mail Strategies." *Journal of American College Health,* 1983, *32,* 101–103.

Terrell, F., and Terrell, S. "Race of Counselor, Client Sex, Cultural Mistrust Level, and Premature Termination from Counseling Among Black Clients." *Journal of Counseling Psychology,* 1984, *31,* 371–375.

Tiedeman, D. V., and O'Hara, R. P. *Career Development: Choice and Adjustment.* New York: College Entrance Examination Board, 1963.

Truax, C. B. "The Process of Group Psychotherapy: Relationships Between Hypothesized Therapeutic Conditions and Intrapersonal Exploration." *Psychological Monographs,* 1961, *75* (7) (Whole no. 511).

Truax, C. B. "Reinforcement and Non-Reinforcement in Rogerian Psychotherapy." *Journal of Abnormal and Social Psychology,* 1966, *71,* 1–9.

Truax, C. B., and Carkhuff, R. R. *Toward Effective Counseling and Psychotherapy: Training and Practice.* Hawthorne, N.Y.: Aldine, 1967.

Valins, S. "Cognitive Effects of False Heart-Rate Feedback." *Journal of Personality and Social Psychology,* 1966, *4,* 400–408.

Valins, S., and Ray, A. A. "Effects of Cognitive Desensitization of Avoidance Behavior." *Journal of Personality and Social Psychology,* 1967, *7,* 345–350.

Vinokur, A., and Selzer, M. "Desirable vs. Undesirable Life Events: Their Relationship to Stress and Mental Distress." *Journal of Personality and Social Psychology,* 1975, *32,* 329–337.

Watson, D., and Friend, R. "Measurement of Social-Evaluative Anxiety." *Journal of Consulting and Clinical Psychology,* 1969, *33,* 448–457.

Weissberg, M. "A Comparison of Direct and Vicarious Treatments of Speech Anxiety: Desensitization, Desensitization with Coping Imagery, and Cognitive Modification." *Behavior Therapy,* 1977, *8,* 606–620.

Weissberg, M., and Lamb, D. "Comparative Effects of Cognitive Modification, Systematic Desensitization, and Speech Preparation in the Reduction of Speech and General Anxiety." *Communication Monographs,* 1977, *44,* 27–36.

Wessler, R. L., and Ellis, A. "Supervision in Rational-Emotive Therapy." In A. K. Hess (ed.), *Psychotherapy Supervision: Theory, Research and Practice.* New York: Wiley, 1980.

Wessler, R. L., and Ellis, A. "Supervision in Counseling: Rational-Emotive Therapy." *Counseling Psychologist,* 1983, *11,* 43–49.

Wheaton, J. "Mental Health and the Campus Newspaper: Creating a Coping Column." Paper presented at thirtieth annual convention of the Southeastern Psychological Association, New Orleans, March 1984.

Widick, C., Knefelkamp, L., and Parker, C. A. "The Counselor as a Developmental Instructor." *Journal of Counselor Education and Supervision,* 1975, *14,* 286–296.

Widick, C., Knefelkamp, L., and Parker, C. A. "Student Development." In U. Delworth, G. R. Hanson, and Associates, *Student Services: A Handbook for the Profession.* San Francisco: Jossey-Bass, 1980.

Wiley, M. O., and Richardson, T. "Two Brief Audio-Visual Counseling Center Public Relations Demonstrations: How Do We Tell People What We Do Using Media." Paper presented at annual convention of the American College Personnel Association, Houston, Texas, March 1983.

Wine, J. "Test Anxiety and Direction of Attention." *Psychological Bulletin,* 1971, *76,* 92–104.

Wine, J. "Counselor's Manual for Attentional Strategies in Evaluation Anxiety Management." Paper presented at Atlantic Regional Conference of the Canadian Universities Counselling Association, Halifax, Nova Scotia, April 1974.

Wolpe, J. "Behavior Therapy According to Lazarus." *American Psychologist,* 1984, *39,* 1326–1327.

Wolpe, J., and Lazarus, A. *Behavior Therapy Techniques: A Guide to the Treatment of Neuroses.* Elmsford, N.Y.: Pergamon Press, 1966.

Wylie, R. C. "The Present Status of Self Theory." In E. F. Borgatta and W. W. Lambert (eds.), *Handbook of Personality Theory and Research.* Skokie, Ill.: Rand McNally, 1968.

Yalom, I. D. *The Theory and Practice of Group Psychotherapy.* (2nd ed.) New York: Basic Books, 1975.

Zajonc, R. B. "On the Primacy of Affect." *American Psychologist,* 1984, *39,* 117–123.

Zimbardo, P. G., Pilkonis, P. A., and Norwood, R. M. "The Social Disease Called Shyness." *Psychology Today,* May 1975, pp. 69–72.

Zung, W. W. K. "A Self-Rating Depression Scale." *Archives of General Psychiatry,* 1965, *12,* 63–70.

Name Index

Munoz, R. F., 304, 369
Muro, J. J., 225, 227, 229, 233, 358
Myers, I. B., 67, 89, 313, 356, 369

N

Neal, G. W., 47, 363
Nisbett, R. E., 13, 364
Norwood, R. M., 295, 296, 376

O

O'Connell, J. J., 349, 362
Oetting, E. R., 31, 236, 249, 271, 341, 369
Ogawa, D. K., 315, 361
O'Hara, R. P., 308-309, 374
Ohlsen, M. M., 224, 229, 370
O'Neil, J. M., 341, 342, 370
Oppenheimer, B. T., 208, 370
Osborn, A. F., 26, 197, 210, 370
Osipow, S. H., 311, 370

P

Padilla, A. M., 349, 371
Paritzky, R. S., 148, 244, 370
Parker, C. A., 21, 62, 69, 77, 136, 350, 375
Parnes, S. J., 26, 197, 210, 370
Parsons, R. D., 348, 370
Paul, G., 271, 370
Perl, J., 295, 353
Perls, F. S., 104, 201, 370
Perry, W., Jr., 6, 21, 22, 35, 49, 53, 57, 59, 60-61, 69, 76, 77, 88, 137-138, 218, 309, 337, 338, 345, 370
Peterson, L. M., 268, 356
Pety, J., 25, 358
Pfeiffer, J. W., 232, 233, 248, 370
Piaget, J., 20, 76, 370
Pilkonis, P. A., 295, 296, 376
Porterfield, W. D., 338, 355
Power, P. G., 311, 363
Prince, J. S., 68, 89, 370-371
Prosen, S. S., 276, 280, 354

R

Rachman, S., 166, 371
Rademacher, B. G., 308, 357

Rahe, R. H., 277, 279, 363
Rathus, S. A., 289, 371
Ray, A. A., 375
Reeder, B. L., 27, 363
Richardson, F. C., 271, 297, 371
Richardson, T., 342, 376
Richey, C. A., 289, 360
Robins, C., 29, 361
Rogers, C. R., 4, 51-52, 112-113, 114, 337, 368, 371
Rosen, S., 193, 371
Rosenbaum, M. E., 74, 213, 371
Rosenman, R., 56, 280, 360
Ross, D., 74, 213, 354
Ross, S. A., 74, 213, 354
Rotter, J. B., 28-29, 55, 87, 88, 304, 371
Ruiz, R. H., 349, 371
Rupert, P. A., 6, 141, 358
Rush, A. J., 18, 41, 47, 59, 65, 66, 80, 85, 121, 141, 146, 159, 162-163, 165-166, 192, 204, 273, 285, 355, 371

S

Salter, A., 287, 288, 371
Sanchez, A. R., 349, 371-372
Sandmeyer, L., 308, 355
Sanford, N., 22, 136, 213, 372
Sarason, I. G., 271, 372
Satir, V., 188, 198, 372
Schachter, S., 372
Scheier, M. F., 268, 356
Schmidt, J. P., 345, 372
Schmidt, L. D., 111, 364
Schroeder, H., 75, 365
Schroeder, H. M., 21, 69, 345, 362
Schwartz, G. E., 276, 372
Sechrest, L., 28, 372
Segal, L., 182, 194, 360
Selzer, M., 277, 375
Shaw, B. F., 18, 41, 47, 59, 65, 66, 80, 85, 121, 141, 146, 159, 162-163, 165-166, 192, 204, 273, 285, 355, 372
Shaw, M. C., 249, 361
Sherman, J., 271, 359
Sherwood, G., 347, 358
Shmurak, S. H., 6, 141, 297, 361

Subject Index

Commitment: to coping skills training, 146-148; in groups, 245, 255-256

Commitment in relativism stage, of cognitive development, 60

Communication: in developmental counseling, 112-120; facilitative conditions for, 112-115; in groups, 222-223; nonverbal, 39-40, 65-66, 111, 134; reflections in, 115-118; and self-confidence, 306-307; and social skills, 298-300; summary and integration in, 118-120

Complexity. *See* Cognitive complexity

Confrontation, cognitive-focused, 135-316

Constructive alternativism: and cognitive inferences, 43; in role constructs, 7, 10

Consultation, planning model for, 348-349

Contracts: behavioral, 204; next-step, 274, 301, 307, 316

Coping skills, in cognitive system, 57

Coping skills training: analysis of, 140-175; background on, 140-143; client ownership of, 167-172; cognitive analysis in, 152-167; commitment to, 146-148; concept and uses of, 141; conclusion on, 174-175; for early detection, 150-152; for evaluative anxiety, 271, 273, 274; formulation of problem in, 143-146; goal setting for, 148-150; in groups, 246; humor in, 165-166; relaxation training in, 166-167; for speech anxiety, 81-83, 85-89; termination of, 172-174

Counseling: applications of planning model in, 340-351; background on, 333-335; and cognitive development, 333-351; cross-cultural, 349-350; experiential category of, 103-104, 176-206; facilitative category of, 102-103,

109-139; in groups, 207-235, 267-316; implicit theories in, 334; practice of, 339-340; rapport and self-exploration in, 109-139; research on, 335-339; training and supervision for, 344-347; training category of, 103, 140-175; in workshops, 249-263, 317-332

Cuing techniques, in coping skills training, 169-170

D

Decision making: and career planning, 310-311, 316; theories of, 26-28

Deep structures: awareness of, 48; in representational theory, 23-25

Defenses, of clients, 91-92

Depression Inventory, 69

Development: approach of, 20-22; and experience, 22; theory of, 20-21

Development level: analysis of assessing, 34, 35, 58-63; assessment of, 64; of clients, 88-89; and cognitive change, 75-78; in domains of experience, 61-62; and outcome goals, 98-99; and psychosocial development, 62-63; stages of, 59-61

Developmental counseling: analysis of, 109-139; background on, 109-112; challenge and support in, 136-138; communication and self-exploration in, 112-120; interviewing in, 120-128; perspective-challenging responses in, 128-136; summary and conclusions on, 138-139

Dissonance. *See* Cognitive dissonance

Drama triangle game, 184-187

Dreams, and information processing, 197-198

Dualistic thinking: challenge and support for, 77-78, 220; in cognitive system, 49-50, 53, 59; and self-talk, 88